"This book is a compass, polarized in the superlative subtropiques of the Gulf Coast, orienting cardinal points in the landscapes of the Zapatistas, the Black Panther Party, the Kurdish freedom movement, and West Papua. The diamantine dialectics of freedom breathing through the pages of this book will be a decisive factor in the final battles between earth and empire, between evolution and extinction. Which side are you on?"
—Quincy Saul, cofounder of Ecosocialist
Horizons and editor of *Maroon Comix*

"John Clark's book is a measured manifesto. It is a must read for any activist or scholar concerned with the alternatives to capitalism's ongoing war on nature."
—Andrej Grubačić, coauthor of *Living at the Edges of Capitalism*

"Whether in Rojava, where women are fighting for their people's survival, or in the loss and terror of New Orleans after the Katrina flood, Clark finds models of communality, care, and hope. Finely reasoned and integrative, tracing the dialectical play of institution and ethos, ideology and imaginary, this book will speak to philosophers and activists alike."
—Ariel Salleh, author of *Ecofeminism as Politics*

"Clark presents very sophisticated philosophical concepts in a style that is quite comprehensible to the general public. Each page sheds new light on our age of planetary turbulence and demolishes all pseudo-truths about it."
—Ronald Creagh, author of *American Utopias*

"John Clark's *Between Earth and Empire* is a guide to that which is obvious yet confoundingly obscure—namely, that models of social organization based in care and cooperation are infinitely more constructive and mutually beneficial than those based in competition and conquest."
—Alyce Santoro, conceptual/sound artist and activist

D0913838

# Between Earth and Empire

## From the Necrocene to the Beloved Community

John P. Clark

*John P. Clark*

*Between Earth and Empire: From the Necrocene to the Beloved Community*
John P. Clark
© 2019 PM Press.

ISBN: 978–1–62963–648–1
Library of Congress Control Number: 2018949077

Cover by John Yates / www.stealworks.com
Interior design by briandesign

10 9 8 7 6 5 4 3 2 1

PM Press
PO Box 23912
Oakland, CA 94623
www.pmpress.org

Printed in the USA.

# À LA TERRE

# Contents

# Foreword

## by Peter Marshall

This is a timely and relevant collection of essays and articles first published elsewhere, but it also contains new work, forming a coherent whole. The author John Clark is a sincere and authentic man, widely read and traveled, putting theory into practice, who offers in this compelling book his acute powers of analysis as well as the condensation of his life's experiences, all written in a lively and accessible style.

It finds a source in the joy and the suffering of the author, in particular the catastrophe and devastation left by Hurricane Katrina in 2005 in New Orleans, where he dwells and where his family has lived for twelve generations. Not only was his daughter's house destroyed, but also his son went missing. Since leaving university teaching, he has helped set up La Terre Institute for Community and Ecology, which works for social and ecological regeneration. Under different noms de plume, particularly that of Max Cafard, he has also been a Surrealist who has entertained and awakened the minds of his readers and changed their lives.

While being a bioregionalist who cares greatly for the city of New Orleans and Louisiana, he does not advocate a narrow localism and patriotic regionalism but would like society and the state to be turned into a community of communities, founded in a strong sense of place yet caring for the Earth as a whole. Indeed, human beings are embedded nature, not separate but an integral part of the Earth. Like most Americans, he has grown up and lived for most of his life in a society of advanced capitalism that is obsessed with mass consumption, self-image, egoistic individualism, and the immediate gratification of inflamed desires. It has a widespread belief that possession will bring happiness. Most of its population, searching endlessly for personal wealth and power, are ready to be led by charismatic or authoritarian leaders and to succumb to the technological megamachine.

He is rightly aghast at the disappearance of natural biodiversity and the coming of the sixth mass extinction. It would appear that we are entering not only the Anthropocene, a geological period during which human activity is the dominant influence on climate and environment, but the Necrocene, the Age of Death, in which Empire works inevitably against the Earth. There is clear evidence of a global ecological crisis, but political leaders and corporate managers fail to recognize it, let alone do anything. They blindfold themselves as they move toward the abyss of extinction, if not for themselves personally then for future generations.

Most already know the real dangers of climate change, ocean acidification, ozone depletion, the diminution of drinkable water, chemical pollution, and the destruction of ecosystems but do not wish to change their lifestyle radically. They are in a state of disavowal, if not of serious denial. The best that the global political class, for instance, could do at Paris was to make a voluntary agreement to try to limit climate change, demonstrating the optimism of shallow environmentalism, when a radical and immediate break with former habits is required in order to save the biosphere and life on this planet.

But Clark is not pessimistic. He argues for a "reversal of the suicidal course of history." There is therefore a deep need to increase an awareness of biodiversity integrity and to overcome climate change, to address what humans are doing to the planet that supports them and other life. The walls of the school and university should give way to a liberating form of education involving the community and grassroots social movements. Only in this way can learning become a transformative experience to take off the shackles of illusion and cleanse, as William Blake said, "the doors of perception." Certainly, this book contributes to that process.

Out of the present crisis there arises an alternative. Clark is heartened by the increasing awakening of consciousness and awareness. "Another Sun is possible." Another world can be created, here and now, beneath our feet. Out of the disaster, both personal and social, he finds salvation in the "Beloved Community" based on an economy of the gift, mutual aid, and solidarity.

As a professor of philosophy and author, he is capable of abstract thinking and standing back and observing, well aware of past history and present dilemmas. At the same time, he is a deeply engaged thinker who participates in social and ecological experiments. He is deeply concerned about the condition of the *oikos*, our home, and uses both the *logos*, rational thought, and *poesis*, poetic thinking, to make his convincing case.

He lives on the edge in New Orleans, between land and sea, between North America and Latin America, Apocalypse and Survival, Heaven and Earth. He lives in a liminal city, on the threshold of the American Dream and the Corporate State. It is a city where the collective consciousness can erupt through the everyday reality of advanced capitalism, where grass can push up through concrete pavements, and the surrounding jungle can absorb the temporary buildings erected by humanity in the face of the unknown and mysterious. As the Mardi Gras shows, it rejects the Protestant ethic with its emphasis on hard work, sexual repression, and stiff upper lip, in favor of pleasure, play, sensuality, music, and dance. Where one stands like stone, the other flows like water. But the city shouldn't really be there, surrounded by swamps and marshes, built on sandy loam, in the delta of the mighty Mississippi River on the Gulf of Mexico.

Clark describes himself somewhat ironically as a "slow learner," but now he appears as a truly radical thinker and activist, a communitarian anarchist and ecologist. He has gone beyond the social ecology of Murray Bookchin to forge a deep critique of modern corporate capitalism and the authoritarian and dominating state (Empire). He shows a joyous alternative vision and practice involving participatory democracy based on consensus and mutual aid, federating with other communities, caring for the planet and all sentient beings (the Earth) in their bioregions. He is less certain of an immediate and fundamental transformation of society than he was in his youth, but he still believes that it is possible to work in cooperative affinity groups and communities so organized to create a genuinely democratic new society to replace the old one.

He would like to see the existing authoritarian state replaced by a community of self-organizing communities in harmony with the land and sea. It will not involve the union of Empire and Earth but the end of Empire to save the Earth. Paraphrasing William Blake, it will be a marriage of Heaven and Earth.

He understands that the ecological whole is a dynamic unity in diversity, the equivalent of what Hegel called the "concrete universal." As a result, he feels the need to understand how we as humans fit in the "planetary dialectic of developing parts and wholes" and can develop our thought and practice in accord with an ecological perspective.[1]

With Spinoza and Coleridge, he recognizes that nature can be *Natura naturata*, "nature natured," referring to nature considered as a passive product, as well as *Natura naturans*, "nature naturing," or more loosely, "nature doing what nature does." Nature therefore not only "is" but is also "becoming," revealing the "wonders of creation and creativity"[2]

He is also a dialectical thinker, delighting in apparent paradox. He understands like the Daoists, Buddhists, Heraclitus, Hegel, and Nietzsche that a thing or being "is" and "is not." He quotes Nagarjuna's tetralemma (A, not-A, both A and not-A, neither A nor not-A) to overcome the dualistic thinking that has bedeviled the West since Aristotle.

In these pages, Clark also appears deeply spiritual. He does not dismiss religion in a loose sense, pointing out that after Marx's famous description of it as "the opiate of the masses" he went on to say that it is also "the sigh of the oppressed creature, the heart of a heartless world."[3] He draws therefore on the traditions of Daoism, Buddhism, and Sufism (particularly in the work of the poet Rumi) and of indigenous people.

He agrees with ancient Chinese Daoism, that one should lead (if at all) by following, in a decentralized society of local communities living close to the land. He argues rightly that one the greatest books ever written about nature is *The Book of the Way and Its Power*, or the *Daodejing*, attributed to Laozi. It contrasts the "Way of Heaven" or Wild Nature, which combines unity in diversity, to the Way of modern humans, which has been the march of so-called Civilization based on profit, progress, patriarchy, and the degradation of the Earth. Opposed to this, Daoism is a form of what Clark calls "dialectical maternalism"[4]:

> To give birth and to nourish,
> to give birth without taking possession,
> to act without obligation
> to lead without dominating.[5]

Clark also quotes the beautiful passage from Laozi concerning the Way of Nature: "Heaven and Earth combine to drip sweet dew. Without the command of man, it drips evenly over all."[6]

In Buddhism, Clark is impressed by the ideas of "mindfulness" and "care" that recognize the indivisibility of moral rationality, moral sensibility, and moral imagination. He agrees with its emphasis on the impermanence of all things and the Four Noble Truths, which recognize that this world is based on suffering, that suffering is a result of craving, but we can find a way out by ending the craving that gives rise to suffering in the first place. He finds in Buddhism a radical critique as well as revolutionary practice. The "Three Jewels" of Buddhism are the Buddha, Dharma, and Sangha, representing the awakened mind, the teachings (the Way of Truth), and the compassionate community. The first is to leave behind a life of disavowal and denial and unlock all the chains of illusion, the second is to recognize that craving is the source of suffering (expressed in the Four Noble Truths), and the third speaks for itself. He particularly recommends the "Heart Sutra," which says "form does not differ from emptiness; emptiness does not differ from form,"[7] and he suggests that it could be called the "Anarchy Sutra,"[8] since its message is a negation of every principle or *arché*.

He is no less impressed by the combination of Buddhism and Daoism in Ch'an or Zen Buddhism. He recognizes the need to "kill the Buddha" (reliance on abstract principles) and even one's parents (personal attachments): only by "not clinging to anything, you will be free wherever you go."[9] And rather than being obsessed with the cravings of the ego, as many of us are in advanced capitalism, it is better to recognize that ultimately we have "no self." As Dōgen said:

> To study the buddha way is to study the self.
> To study the self is to forget the self.
> To forget the self is to be actualized by myriad things.[10]

Zen is also deeply ecological, as is implied in the Buddhist affirmation that all sentient beings have a Buddha nature. It follows for me at least that we should not eat the dead flesh of animals. It also holds that the world is a sacred place. "To be" is more important than "to crave" or "to possess" or to have power over others and dominate the world. Indeed, "Property is not only theft," as the nineteenth-century anarchist thinker Proudhon thought, but as Clark argues, it is the very "theft of being."[11] Buddhism, particularly in its Zen form, seeks to create a benevolent and compassionate community and practice mindful care for Planet Earth.

Within the Islamic tradition of Sufism, he discusses the thirteenth-century poet and thinker Rumi, particularly his story "Muhammad and the Huge Eater." It demonstrates how obsessive desires, in this case for food, inflamed by our commodity economy, can devastate the soul and rob us of things of true value. The "Huge Eater" is in many ways the ideal consumer in the Age of Mass Consumption. He is the reigning monster called Empire that sucks up all he can get. He is the all-consuming ego. Yet a true person, as Rumi suggests, is more calm, moderate and deliberate in his or her life.

Having already edited a collection of his writings, Clark is inspired by the French nineteenth-century geographer Elisée Reclus, whom he claims as an anarchist "discovered the Earth" and opposed, as Clark does, all forms of social and ecological domination.[12] He recognizes that humanity is an integral part of nature; indeed, in his words "nature becoming self-conscious" ("*L'Homme est la Nature prenant conscience d'elle-même*").[13] In other words, the Earth is in ourselves and we are the Earth. He conceived *anarché* as a critique of class, patriarchal, racial, technological, and state domination while recognizing past and present human domination of other species and nature itself. His form of "anarchography," which Clark approves, is at once the writing of the universal and of the particular, of the ecosystem and of the stream. He was prophetic in seeing the possibility of an egalitarian, libertarian, and communitarian society based on mutual aid as well as a process of globalization from below in which nature and humanity become one.

He analyses the radical "social imaginary" of Cornelius Castoriadis, who opposed an autonomous society against the authoritarian state and tried to create a form of democratic eco-politics. Every society, he claimed, "institutes itself" according to the idea of its "social imaginary." It interacts dialectically with the material substratum and is not merely a product of the economic base. While the prevailing imaginary involves the domination of women, the split between humanity and nature, and mass consumption, we need a new radical one that works for social and individual autonomy. Clark also considers Charles Taylor's "social imaginary," which the latter defines as "the ways people imagine their social existence." Although somewhat idealistic by conflating ideology with the imaginary, it does at least stress what Marx called the "fetishism of commodities." Clark, however, defines the social imaginary as "the sphere of the community's collective fantasy life."[14] It includes the dominant myths of the society, moving from a fantasy of hard work, self-control, and obedience to a consumerist ethic of immediate gratification and personal power and wealth.

He also looks back to Guy Debord's *The Society of the Spectacle*, the foremost work of the Situationist movement half a century ago. He certainly brought out the power of the commodity and the imaginary of consumption. But while Debord called for workers and neighborhood councils, he and the Situationists were unable to transform their revolutionary ideas into practice. Situationism often degenerated into *détournement*—that is, culture jamming and cultural subversion. It turned into a form of benign aestheticism or, by contrast, insurrectionism run by invisible committees. The notion of the *dérive* has also become a harmless form of psychogeography in which one appreciates and explores where one lives.

At the same time, Clark perhaps underestimates the power of surveillance as well as the spectacle in modern advanced capitalism and the authoritarian state. He sees in the revolutionary Situationist slogan "Be realistic, demand the impossible" an infantile fantasy or simply a "naive liberationism."[15] Instead, I would argue that it is a paradoxical and dramatic appeal to the imagination to break with the chains of illusion as well as existing bonds in society and culture. The Situationists may have helped usher in the so-called permissive society and entrenched the consumerist capitalism and existing state, but at least Debord, by emphasizing the "spectacle," brought out the importance of the social imaginary in culture and the role it has played in nationalism, racism, patriarchy, and religious fundamentalism. The Situationists may have thus enabled many to shake off the paralysis of the everyday life, even though they may not have called for social and ecological regeneration and communal solidarity.

In addition to old traditions and modern individual thinkers, Clark examines the lessons of social movements and experiments from around the world that have tried to realize, often in difficult circumstance and fraught with contradictions, a form of a participatory democracy close to the land, to bring about social and ecological liberation. In the case of the Zapatistas, we can learn much from the wisdom of indigenous people. They oppose hierarchy and domination and the dualistic outlook of the mainstream culture in the West. They do not look to the seizure of state power and the leading role of a vanguard party but rather local autonomy and self-determination for the people themselves. The notions of the "heart" and the "spirit" are very important to them—they try to give expression to democracy as the "big collective heart."[16] For them, the so-called leader Marcos/Galeano, for instance, is more of a spokesperson or "servant" to his community than an authoritarian commander. The Zapatistas wish to overcome patriarchy, hierarchy, and domination in favor of a community based on free association and voluntary agreements or consensus. The assembly is all-important, and its members practice mutual aid and caring work. They have tried to restore the commons as a benevolent common good and work through the gift economy; as such, their ideal is communitarian and libertarian. The center is therefore everywhere in the "sacred community and the sacred Earth."[17]

Clark draws further lessons from the Rojavan Revolution and the democratic autonomy movement in North Syria. The revolutionaries there are concerned with the destiny of the person, community, and nature. They are against the state and neoliberal globalism and modern capitalism. In particular they have made great strides in becoming libertarian, communitarian, and feminist—in other words, they are anti-hierarchy, anti-authority, and anti-patriarchy. They have made a concerted effort to create participatory democracy through their popular assemblies, even in a time of war. In their People's Defense Units, for instance, they do not have traditional "officers" who order their inferiors about but "Team" or "Company" leaders who are chosen either by consensus or, when that cannot be achieved, by majority vote. Like the Zapatistas, leaders are considered servants of the community. They have been partly inspired by Abdullah Öcalan, who is held in a Turkish jail and whose revision of Marxism was influenced by the social ecology and social anarchism of Murray Bookchin. Their popular militias have also been inspired by the example on the Republican side in the Spanish Civil War. There are even women fighters who reject meat-eating as part of their growing ecological awareness and sensibility, rejecting the Empire of authoritarian and patriarchal power.

Clark has also been involved in, and offers a vivid case study of, the indigenous struggle in West Papua against international corporations and state domination, especially in the form of the Freeport-McMoRan Corporation long allied with the Suharto dictatorship in Indonesia. It proved to be a genocidal partnership, lasting from 1965 to 1997, for the Amungme people. It was a case of "Cowboy Capitalism" confronting indigenous ethics and spirituality. In the name of Progress and Profit, Freeport undertook mining operations on a mountain which the local people saw as the "sacred mother." Their struggle was part of a wider movement against the dominant world system and the struggle for peace, justice, and ecology.

Further back home in the United States, there is the example of the Black Panthers' attempt to bring "power to the people." Many were committed to neighborhood assemblies and localism. Clark brings out well the radical decentralist, communitarian, and anarchistic dimensions of the movement. Despite forming a political party, the Black Panthers in their Platform and the Program, declared: "We want freedom. We want power to determine the destiny of our Black Community."[18] They wanted self-management and community power, building from the bottom up a commune of communes.

Similarly he also looks at the movement of occupation in the aftermath of Hurricane Katrina in his home city of New Orleans. It was based on participatory direct democracy and consensus and tried to create what Martin Luther King called the "Beloved Community." Members of the Common Ground Collective, for instance, which appeared spontaneously one week after Hurricane Katrina hit, decided to take direct action to save what was left of the community. In its early months of existence it attracted over eight thousand volunteers, and its aid programs helped at least eighty thousand people. It mounted projects in a number of neighborhoods, including establishing a large center at St. Mary of the Angels School. It was a wonderful and inspiring example of anarchy in action, of mutual aid and participatory democracy, of caring in a compassionate way for the Beloved Community.

★

The third part of the book is called "The Awakening of Consciousness." In a meditation on the Summer Solstice, Clark acknowledges, as ancient people did all over the world, the power of the Sun, a major source of life on Earth. Its light falls equally on all. It is not a form of dominating "power over" but rather a kind of "power to" or "power through" in the sense of unleashing the creative energies of all beings. He concludes that "another Sun is possible."[19] Another society can emerge by practicing an economy of sharing in a decentralized and federated society without government, in other words, communal anarchism in which the state would become a community of communities in a regenerated Earth.

At the moment, there is world poverty in the midst of untold wealth. Yet the Necrocene, the epoch of death and destruction, and the suffering of all sentient beings and their ecosystems, is not inevitable but is the result of the choices of those humans in power and authority who devastate the natural world in which we dwell. If we tread more carefully and act more wisely, humans can have another future, another Sun can rise. These clichés have a profound meaning. If enough people think and act accordingly an alternative future is still possible. We can locate and found Utopia. Clark would like to substitute for the Necrocene a new era which he calls the "Eleutherocene" in which all life flourishes on Earth and Empire is no more.

All this may sound distinctly "utopian," but Clark defends utopian writing as a way of undermining the dominant "social imaginary." But the ultimate "utopian" fantasy was called the "American Dream" lived out in suburbia, on the one hand, or Stalin's vision of a "Workers' State" on the other. And now we have the "capitalist sublime" of the corporate-state.[20] Nevertheless, there have been many other smaller "utopias" of intentional communities or communes which show, however briefly, that life could be lived based on new relationships and on voluntary and libertarian principles. I know because I have lived in one. We therefore realize "utopia" by becoming citizens of utopia, a utopia which is not as in its original Greek meaning, first used by Thomas More, "nowhere," but is somewhere or "topian." Utopia can be here and now, that is to say, where people live out the "dream" of a free, equal, just, and ecological society. *Ou-topos*, "nowhere," can therefore become *eu-topos*, a "good place."

★

*Between Empire and Earth* may seem mystical in parts, but it is also down-to-earth. It is against social domination and hierarchy, recognizing that we should care for each other, other species, and the Earth as a whole. It deserves to be read, widely discussed, and acted upon before it is too late. Already it is late, as the Necrocene advances, but not too late. The last part of this book is inspired by the 1968 slogan "power to the imagination." We need imagination to perceive a new way of living on the sacred Earth of land and sea that make up this planet.

This very readable account offers great insight. It is a very important, relevant and urgent book. Anarchist society, a community governing itself without the need for central, coercive government, is always present, like seeds in a desert that can blossom again with life-giving rain. The natural order of society is below the artificial disorder of the modern government and the state.

Clark celebrates an "interstitial" that can lead to the "antistitial." He welcomes the cracks (interstices or what lies between) in the façade of consumerist society and the corporate state. Through the interstitial, the interstices of modern society, culture and the state, one can get glimpses of what is to be done and what is required to become a fully awakened being in a society of free and equal beings, based on federation, mutual aid, cooperation, participatory democracy, and consensus. The interstitial can thus become the "antistitial," against the government and state, rejecting all forms of *arché*, or rule. As Nietzsche observed and Clark reminds us, the state is "the coldest of cold monsters."

Every mystic and awakened person knows that out of the "dark night of the soul" comes light, redemption and hope. Out of the Apocalypse can emerge at the grassroots level a movement that opposes hierarchy, domination, patriarchy, capital, and the state. A beautiful transformation is possible, a world of personal and social liberation to herald a decentralized and federated society in harmony with the Earth. It now becomes possible to demand and realize what was long thought "impossible."

In his postscript, Clark hopes that the "Poeticene" can also arise. Rather than the Necrocene, the death of the planet, a new epoch may emerge in which the creative powers of both the Earth and the creatures of the Earth are allowed to flourish. It is a battle of *anarché* versus *arché*, of anarchy against rule, of a free society in harmony with the Earth, against the megamachine, capital, the state, and patriarchy. "In wildness is the preservation of the world," as Thoreau claimed, but this includes the wildness of the poetic mind, as Gary Snyder understood. Nature and artistic creativity both work best through what the ancient Daoists called *wu-wei*, doing without doing, effortless ease. If they are not interfered with, if they are left to their own devices, nature and sentient beings will create of themselves. *Poesis* can therefore help save *oikos*, our home, our Earth, the wild within and the wild without.

★

After Hurricane Katrina hit New Orleans in 2005, I went to stay with John Clark in order to give a paper at Loyola University on my own version of liberation ecology as expressed in my book *Riding the Wind*. It was a work greatly inspired by Daoism with anarchistic conclusions, which followed on from my exploration of ecological thought in *Nature's Web* and my history of anarchist ideas and movements in *Demanding the Impossible*.

Clark was severely shocked by the aftermath of Hurricane Katrina, and there are several chapters in his book dealing with this period. He finds the official view, which celebrates the so-called resilience of the New Orleans community, condescending and demeaning. The disaster was not so much the storm but the criminal governmental and corporate negligence that followed. Randolph Bourne famously said that "war is the health of the state," but even worse is the war of a state against its own people. Over one hundred thousand people have not returned to the city.

While staying in New Orleans, I was taken to a spontaneous rave at the top of a disused power station. We had to enter it through a small entrance and climb up some rickety metal stairs lit by candles. It proved to be very much like Hakim Bay's TAZ—temporary autonomous zone—an oasis of peace, happiness, creativity, and freedom in which young people listened and danced to their own music.

At the same time, I saw from the top of the tall building corporate America far below as barges and ships chugged up and down the mighty Mississippi, one of the world's greatest rivers. The goods they contained were the symbols of hard labor of exploited workers, products of "free trade" that left a few Americans with gold in their pockets but iron in their souls. So high up in the air, it reminded me that the city was built within a bend in the river, extending out into the swamp, constantly under threat from the sea on one side and fresh water and jungle on the other. It was a possible impossibility, a place on the edge, which could disappear forever at any time.

I left after midnight, but apparently in the early hours police came and, with their weapons drawn, forced the people who had been enjoying themselves in a peaceful way to lie spread-eagled on the rough floor. They said they were looking for "terrorists" and took some innocent individuals away, claiming that they had drugs on them. It was the ugly face of the police and military and the state that sustains them.

I was taken also to see the amazing work of the Common Ground Collective, the center of which was housed in an old school once run by nuns. At its height, thousands of people from around the city and from outside volunteered to work at the grassroots level, helping neglected citizens to rebuild their lives and dwellings, since there was no help coming from above. It was a great example of a community organizing itself through public meetings based on mutual aid and consensus as much as possible. The experience of the volunteers and of those they helped to help themselves was truly transformative and impressive. They served their own beloved community in their beloved city.

I also participated with John Clark in the carnival of Halloween, followed by All Saints' Day and All Souls' Day. It was a minor Mardi Gras, with joyous processions and dancing to street brands, at a time when the Dead can erupt into the Living. I went dressed as an alchemist and/or astrologer, deliberately ambiguous, at such a liminal time betwixt life and death, with golden stars on my black cape, reflecting the magic and transformation, the mystery and creativity, the enchantment and wisdom, which summed up for me the old culture of New Orleans. It was a mysterious rainbow formed over the centuries by indigenous Indians, imported Africans, and Spanish and French colonialists before the coming of white Anglo-Saxons. I walked and danced on "the wild side of the spirit."[21] The wild carnival at Halloween and Mardi Gras, not the controlled and official one, continues to be opposed to the corporate world of consumerism and of the authoritarian state with its laws, prisons, police, and soldiers. Everything is not what it is and is what it is not. It is the opposite of the Protestant ethic and the American Dream, of hard work and endless consumption, and instead celebrates play, enjoyment, sensuality, creativity, and wildness.

All this offered me a glimpse into the interstices, a chink in the reality, and a new way of being which has had such an enormous influence on Clark and partly inspired his book. He says to live mindfully in New Orleans is "to dwell dialectically on the edge, to border borders ambiguously, and to inhabit interstices precariously."[22] It puts him a privileged position to understand what is happening in his own city, bioregion, and country of birth as well as what is happening elsewhere in the world. I share his wish to end Empire and save the Earth before it is too late for all beings and their shared ecosystems on land and sea. Take this book seriously, act on it, and it will go far in making that wish a reality.

## NOTES

1    John P. Clark, *Between Earth and Empire: From the Necrocene to the Beloved Community* (Oakland: PM Press, 2019), 18.

2    Clark, 26.

3    Karl Marx, "A Contribution to the Critique of Hegel's Philosophy of Right: Introduction," http://www.mlwerke.de/me/me01/me01_378.htm.

4    Clark, 204.

5    Sanderson Beck's translation of the *Daodejing*, 10:7, http://www.wayist.org/lindauer-daodejing-english-translation/94-scriptures/tao-teh-ching.

6    Wing-Tsit Chan's translation of *Daodejing* 32:3, https://terebess.hu/english/tao/chan.html#Kap32.

7    *The Heart Sutra*, http://www.heartspace.org/writings/traditional/HeartSutra.html.

8    Clark, 195–96.

9    Lin-Chi, "Lin-Ch Record," in Stephen Addiss, ed., *Zen Sourcebook: Traditional Documents from China, Korea, and Japan* (Indianapolis: Hackett, 2008), 49.

10   Dōgen, *Actualizing the Fundamental Point (Genjō Kōan)* in Addiss, 152.
11   Clark, 204.
12   Clark, 30–31, 36.
13   Elisée Reclus, *L'Homme et la Terre* (Paris: Librairie Universelle, 1905–8), 1:i.
14   Clark, 22.
15   Clark, 260.
16   Dylan Fitzwater, *Autonomy Is in Our Hearts: Zapatista Autonomous Government through the Lens of the Tsotsil Language* (Oakland: PM Press, 2019), 44.
17   Clark, 122.
18   "Black Panther Party Platform and Program: What We Want/What We Believe," in Philip S. Foner ed., *The Black Panthers Speak* (Philadelphia: J.B. Lippincott, 1970), 2.
19   Clark, 175–80.
20   Clark, 283.
21   Clark, 298.
22   Clark, 295.

# Some Basic Concepts

## De Profundis

Since antiquity, mining has for very good reason been associated with the oppression of human beings and the plunder and desecration of the Earth. Ecofeminist Carolyn Merchant in her classic work *The Death of Nature* outlines this history. She quotes the Roman author Pliny, who, in the first century, laments that "we penetrate into [Nature's] entrails, and seek for treasures that only "urge us to our ruin" and "send us to the very depths of hell.""[1] He looks back to a primordial state of abundance in which "Earth, untroubled, unharried by hoe or plowshare, brought forth all that men had need for, and those men were happy."[2] He concludes that "precious metal" is "the root of evil" in which humans first "found the guilt of iron" and later discovered "gold, more guilty still," so that, in the end, "War came forth."[3] It has been a long war, and we are only now beginning to see its ultimate outcome.

The image on the cover of this book shows the U.S.-based Freeport-McMoRan corporation's Grasberg mine in West Papua. It is the largest gold mine and the second-largest copper mine in the world. It produces over a million ounces of gold and a billion pounds of copper per year. The *Super Structures of the World* TV series begins its episode on Grasberg with these words: "On a stone-age island at the ends of the earth [sound of explosion] is an astonishing superstructure whose very existence defies imagination."[4] This superstructure in the hands of superpower does indeed dazzle the imagination. It is a superb example of the Technological Sublime at the service of power and wealth.

My interest in Freeport-McMoRan began in the late 1980s, when the company proposed dumping twelve million tons of gypsum waste into the Mississippi River. This waste, which contained low-level radioactive uranium and radium, would have further damaged an already highly polluted river ecosystem and threatened the water supply for a large population. I soon learned about the company's even more shocking ecocidal and genocidal activities in support of its massive mining operations in Indonesian-occupied West Papua and made this a major focus of my activism, research, writing, and everyday life for the next decade. I organized a group called Freeport Watch and edited and wrote for a small publication by that name for several years. I am deeply grateful for what I learned from the Papuans over those years.

## On Being between Earth and Empire

The concept of being situated "between Earth and Empire" emerged in the 1990s from my study of indigenous Papuan cultures and communities and their place in the late modern capitalist world system. When Tom Beanal, head of the Amungme Tribal Council, spoke at Loyola University in 1996, he recounted the traditional story of the origins of various geographical features of the island of Papua, imagined as parts of the body of the primordial Mother. He explained that "the sacred mountain grew out of the head of the Mother. The mountain we see as our Mother is sacred. It is where the souls of men go when they die. We keep this place holy and worship it in our traditional ceremonies."[5]

Beanal recounted the long history of state and corporate oppression and destruction imposed on the land and people. He remarked: "Gold and copper have been taken by Freeport for the past thirty years, but what have we gotten in return? Only insults, torture, arrests, killings, forced evictions from our land, impoverishment, and alienation from our own culture. We have become strangers in our own land." Beanal's eloquent words contrast poignantly with Freeport CEO Jim Bob Moffett's brutal assertion that the corporation was "thrusting a spearhead of development into the heartland" of West Papua.[6] Inadvertently, Moffett was admitting that the corporate-state agenda was to kill the heart, kill the land, kill the Earth itself, for the sake of profit and power.

Moffett's terrifying words recall the ringing indictments of the corrupting effect of the lust for gold of the great anarcho-syndicalist and anti-imperialist writer B. Traven in *The Treasure of the Sierra Madre*. In that work, the veteran prospector Howard explains that "gold is a very devilish sort of a thing," and that "it is the power which gold gives to man that changes the soul of man." He then adds that this power "is only imaginary."[7] The word "only" does not imply that this power is in any way diminished by its imaginary character, but rather that the force of the imaginary is so great that it can perform wonders—even move mountains—on its own.

Working with the Papuans, I heard accounts of this ongoing war for the imagination that is also a war against the land and the Earth. As I listened to the story of the Papuans, it began to reveal in a very striking manner the nature of their precarious position "between Earth and Empire." The state, capital, and megamachine—collectively, the forces of Empire—conspire to destroy their connection to the Earth and their culture of nature that has developed over vast periods of social evolution. It gradually became evident to me that the predicament of the Papuans was a particularly striking version of the common predicament of humanity. The struggle of the Papuans is especially prophetic because it confronts our collective destiny in a far more brutal and far less mystified form than the versions experienced closer to the centers of imperial power and ideology.

## A Message to the Terrestrials

The concept of the Necrocene, "the new era of death," is central to the analysis here. Years ago, I began telling my students on the first day of class that there is certain information that they urgently need to know. I told them that if an extraterrestrial were sent here to bring back the big news from Planet Earth, there's no doubt what this intergalactic investigator would report to the home planet. It's that Earth is going through the sixth period of mass extinction in hundreds of millions of years of highly developed life on the planet. E.T. would phone home the following message: "It's the Necrocene!" It seemed to me that Earthlings should also be in on this news. Shockingly, however, I found that the vast majority of my students had never heard this fact mentioned *in any class* during twelve years of primary and secondary education, and often several years of college.

I have always been critical of the term "Anthropocene," the popular concept for our new geological era. I found it to be, rather obviously, an anthropocentric concept—the "anthropo" part is a hint—focusing on the species that has caused the degradation of the biosphere, rather than on the condition of the biosphere itself that will be reflected in the fossil record. I was also motivated by the need to respond to reactive varieties of anti-catastrophism that lapse into forms of disavowal in which the severity of the global ecological crisis is simultaneously affirmed and denied. (Admittedly, we are facing catastrophe ... but any forthright recognition of this fact is reactionary, confused, disabling, nihilistic, etc., and must fail.)[8]

Consequently, a few years ago I began using the term "Thanatocene" for the present era.[9] This term is synonymous with "Necrocene" but has the advantage of evoking the world-historical battle between the forces of Eros and those of Thanatos. It thus carries on the radical Freudo-Marxian critique of civilization associated with theorists such as Herbert Marcuse and Norman O. Brown.[10] The present work, in counterposing to this reign of death and destruction an emerging community of life, love, rebirth, and creativity, seeks to preserve the centrality of this historical dialectic.

Despite the merits of this term, I soon concluded that "Necrocene" was perhaps an even better one for our new era. It ties in with "Necropolitics," a concept popularized by Achille Mbembe in his well-known article,[11] and which I see as an apt term for the politics of Empire. In addition, it has a certain visceral quality that the term "Thanatocene" lacks, though it fails to evoke so immediately the dialectic between Eros and Thanatos. Above all, it conveys very starkly the idea of a "new era of death" that is the successor to the "Cenozoic," the "new era of life."[12]

The other concept that captures powerfully the reality of our present moment in Earth history is the "Capitalocene."[13] This term is a vast improvement over "Anthropocene," since it identifies specifically the economic system that causes biospheric devastation through its inherent logic of destruction, rather than treating the harm as a consequence of some generic human activity. The position defended here is strongly in accord concerning the central role of capital in driving the development of the Necrocene.

However, the present analysis also emphasizes heavily the roots of the crisis of the Earth in the history of patriarchy, the state, and the technological megamachine, in addition to that of capital. It defends the need for a thoroughly dialectical analysis of the interaction between historical forms of domination and of the ways in which they are embodied in the deep structures of the institutional, ideological, imaginary, and ethotic spheres of social determination. "Necrocene" goes one step beyond "Capitalocene" and names the era based on what the Earth itself is now undergoing, as the result of the normal everyday operations of capital, in addition to those of the other major dialectically interacting elements of the system of domination.

The term "Necrocene," as used here, is a biopolitical, geopolitical, and even geo-ontological concept.[14] The term is *biopolitical* because it critically engages the relationship between power and the conditions of life. It is *geopolitical* because its concern is the condition of all of life on Earth, that is, the condition of the living Earth itself. And it is *geo-ontological* because it leads us to question the mode of being that is responsible for that condition. Here, it converges with the concept of the Capitalocene. When the dominant mode of being-human becomes a mode of consumption, that mode of being becomes a mode of "being-toward-death" in the most ominous sense of that term.

We might reinterpret Guy Debord's favorite Latin palindrome and puzzle, "In girum imus nocte et consumimur igni,"[15] in the light of this geo-ontology. We have entered into the vicious circle of disbeing or misbeing, in which to be is to consume and be consumed. This is our Dark Night of the Soul. And the Earth's. Will we together emerge from it?

## A Note on the Beloved Community

The idea of the Beloved Community has roots two and a half millennia ago in the Buddhist idea of the *sangha* based on wisdom and compassion, and two millennia ago in the Christian idea of the community of *agape*. In American history, it had more explicit roots in the thought of the communitarian idealist philosopher Josiah Royce, and came to fruition and concrete actualization, as is well known, in the communitarian liberation theology of Martin Luther King. But long before any of this history began, it was already implicit in the ways of life of indigenous peoples everywhere.

As used more specifically here, the term is synonymous with two other ones, "the community of liberation and solidarity" and "the community of awakening and care." In each case, the term refers to the form of primary community that will be most basic to the process of social and ecological regeneration. However, it should also be understood as pointing, as in Martin Luther King's original formulation, to the universal human community as a community of love and solidarity. And finally, it should be thought of as encompassing the entire Earth community, of which the human community is an integral part.[16]

Dr. King explains that the Beloved Community is a mode of living together in which division and separation are overcome, ushering in a new era of reconciliation. He contends that such a community will arise as the result of creative and redemptive love. He observes, moreover, that its attainment appears miraculous—it is the realization of what had seemed impossible according to the world's disordered ways of thinking and imagining. For Dr. King, humanity is lost and in need of salvation, which is another word for liberation.

All of these ideas are central to the analysis presented here. We are in the thralls of deep forms of alienation that are the result of the long history of social domination. Consequently, there must be a turning around, a process of conversion, which is to say revolution. This turning will lead to a reconciliation between humans and humans, between humans and other living beings, and between humans and the Earth itself, of which they are all an integral part.

## Gifts of Impossibility

One may ask how realistic it is to imagine that when there are a multitude of "living examples of the new way of life embodied in thriving communities of liberation" that masses of people will be inspired to "flock to the new communities in which human and natural potentialities freely flourish?"[17] Stated differently, it is the question of how realistic it is to "demand the impossible," and even more, to expect vast numbers of people to join together in demanding it, here and now.

I would suggest that it may not be realistic to *expect* the impossible, as if it or anything were certain in the future (except, as Heraclitus long ago pointed out, the unexpected). However, it is realistic to demand, that is, to "ask for,"[18] the impossible if we know that the impossible sometimes occurs. It is realistic to ask for the impossible, just as it is realistic to ask for a gift—with hope but not expectation—if we know that such gifts are sometimes given.

Thus, the best answer that I can find is the fact that in my own lifetime I have seen many examples of the power of charismatic social movements that have made such demands and seen them in some ways fulfilled (for better or worse). I mean by charismatic power a power (or inspiration) that motivates millions of people to change their lives significantly and impels many of them to risk persecution, imprisonment, and even death for what they see as the deeper truths, greater realities, and better way of life that they have discovered through such movements. It is not at all unusual for masses of people to get swept up in this manner in movements based on nationalism, race and ethnicity, or religious identity. It is perhaps most obvious today in the Islamic fundamentalist movements that have been sweeping across parts of the world.

Fortunately, charismatic power is not limited to right-wing and reactionary movements. It was evident in the U.S. civil rights movement of the early 1960s and the black power movement of the late 1960s. It was also manifested in a spectrum of radical and revolutionary movements that came out of the May–June 1968 events in France and the much larger global revolt of which it was a part. In the subsequent period, we have seen such power in Maoist movements, in national liberation movements, and, more recently, in indigenous movements that have increasingly asserted the rights and defended the lands of native peoples.

It was also evident in what was generically called "the Movement" in the late 1960s in the United States. While this movement was in many ways amorphous and difficult to define, it synthesized elements of the peace movement, the radical student movement, and the countercultural movement, based on a rejection of the society of mass consumption and the expression of vague communitarianism and ecological yearnings. While it was inadequately critical in overlooking its own many internal contradictions and the depth of the recuperative or co-optative powers of the dominant system, it expressed implicitly a profound critique of domination and an inspiring vision of a liberated world. Charles Reich's popular work of that period, *The Greening of America*, while extremely naive overall, revealed the way in which the Movement tapped into certain transformative possibilities and depicted the kind of conversion process that could take place rapidly among masses of people who are under the influence of, or are deeply inspired by, a charismatic social movement.

One of the conclusions that one must draw from the collapse of that movement (beyond the large lesson of the limits of reactivity as a basis for supposed liberation) is the corrosive role of the mass media in creating radical stars and leaders and transforming forms of self-organization into modes of performance for the sake of the spectacle. The nature of the ego and ego-gratification in the society of mass consumption, including the consumption of images, was never confronted entirely seriously by activists of that era or those who have come since then. In short, the problem of the diversion of charisma (generally, back into the spectacle, and specifically, into the images of charismatic leaders) was largely overlooked. Even among those who have been nominally anticapitalist, the nature of social capital has not been understood. This is the eternal problem for the creation of "utopias," including even those that are most topian and down-to-earth. How can charismatic power be invested in the charismatic community itself, rather than in charismatic leader and elites? That is the real question.

The problem is not that charismatic power is a mere illusion, or that it once existed and has now disappeared. The problem is that although it has always existed and still exists today, it has seldom been retained and exercised collectively by communities of liberation and solidarity and has instead been co-opted by authoritarian leaders and vanguardist elites. The problem is not how to achieve "l'imagination au pouvoir," (the "power to the imagination" of May '68), since the imagination, as expressed through the dominant social imaginary, is always in power. The problem is to determine which imaginary it is that prevails and what kind of power it serves.

Then we must ask how it could possibly serve anything other than what it has served throughout the history of civilization. How much deep reflection has there been on the question of how communities can create nonhierarchical, nondominating charismatic power? How much thoughtful and dedicated experimentation has been devoted to the communal creation of such power?

When our universities have become centers for study of the Universe and Earth Stories and of diverse forms of universal particularity as forms of liberation, we will have courses in which we study historical examples of charismatic community, such as the Yellow Turbans, the Movement of the Free Spirit, and the Canudos community, for exactly this purpose.

## Land and Liberty

Five years ago, I decided to leave the university after many years of teaching philosophy and environmental studies, to work on developing a project called La Terre Institute for Community and Ecology, a continuation of almost twenty-five years of preparatory work on the land. The name derives from the geographical site on which the project is located, a small sandy creek called Bayou La Terre, which, in turn, is located on a planet called La Terre. Since the first piece of land was acquired almost thirty years ago, those of us who have spent time there have always called this place "the Land." Many also call it La Terre. We say that we are "going to the Land" or "going to La Terre."

"La Terre" means both the Earth as a whole and also the land, the particular place on Earth that is our home and dwelling place. Even in English, the corresponding term has both of these meanings. "Earth" refers not only to our most universal geographical reality, the planet itself, but also to the most particular geographical reality, the earth beneath our feet, our place on Earth. This expresses geographically what radically dialectical thinking and practice require, an awakened awareness of the priority of both the most universal and the most particular. This is the meaning of "the universal particular" that is mentioned often in these pages. It follows that the beloved saying "Think Globally, Act Locally" has to be thrown into the recycling bin or compost pile so that something else can grow out of it. We need to think both locally and globally, and act both locally and globally, and beyond this, see how the local is implicit in the global and the global is implicit in the local.

In 1910, the anarchist Magonist movement adopted the slogan "Tierra y Libertad" as it instigated the outbreak of the Mexican Revolution. This same call for "land and liberty" expresses our most urgent need and the Earth's most urgent need. Landauer, the great communitarian anarchist theorist, entitled one of his most important works "Call to Socialism."[19] We should read the term "call" as referring not only to an appeal to the people to revolt but also to the fundamental spiritual and political vocation or "calling" (*Berufung*) of each human being. We are "called" to help create a way of life—a libertarian, communitarian, and ecological ethos—that allows the Earth and its inhabitants to grow and flourish. We might say that "the free development *of each person is the condition* of the free development of the community, and the free development *of each community is the condition* of the free development of the entire Earth community." Conversely, we are "called" to destroy an ecocidal and genocidal system of domination that stands in the way of such free development and which decrees the inevitability of mass extinction and ecological devastation.

The means toward fulfilling this need is the community of liberation and solidarity, awakening and care. Such a community must also be a land or Earth community, which means that it is a community of place. It must have a communal institutional structure, a communal system of values, a communal imaginary, and a communal ethos. In addition, it must exist at a human and geographical scale that allows it to act, freely, democratically, and compassionately for the good of each person, for its own good as a human community, for the good of the larger ecological community, and for the good of the Earth as a planetary community. Another way of expressing all this is that it must strive to act in all ways as a community of care. Landauer's call is the call of the Earth to the Earth, expressed through human beings who have accepted their calling to act as nature (Earth) becoming self-conscious. The liberation of the Earth means its positive freedom, along with ours as part of it, to grow and develop, to continue the path of discovery and realization of its, and our own, greatest good.[20]

## Eros, Thanatos, Communitas

The struggle for social and ecological freedom in the Necrocene is a struggle of life against death. This struggle carries on the legacy of Herbert Marcuse, who depicted revolutionary politics as part of the world-historical battle between Eros and Thanatos, that is, between the forces of life, growth, love, and reconciliation and the forces of separation, division, death, and domination.[21] This is also the legacy of Joel Kovel, who even more profoundly proclaimed a politics of Spirit based on Eros, on the desire for Being, a politics that seeks to overcome separation and domination by overcoming an Egoic Civilization that is based on the fear and denial of death and that creates a culture of death.[22] This legacy culminates in an ecosocialism that is an erosocialism, and most fully in a communitarian anarchism that is both an ecopolitics and an eropolitics.

To the extent that we adopt this eco/eropolitics we are engaged in a struggle against the drive toward social atomization and universal alienation (the World-Historical Death Drive) that began with the rise of the state and its assault on kinship-based, deeply relational, tribal communities. It has culminated in a society that combines growing economic, political, bureaucratic, and technological totalization with social, cultural, psychological, and spiritual fragmentation and disintegration. When Margaret Thatcher famously said that "society does not exist," many concluded that she was absurdly denying an obvious reality. In fact, she was outlining the system of domination's practical program for the future.

The alternative to the society of separation is not a vague "oneness," or "togetherness." Such ideals always remain abstract and ideological. The comforting sentiment that "We are the World," leads to political praxis of the "I'd like to buy the world a Coke" variety. The real alternative is, rather, the achievement of the concrete universality that results from a highly differentiated and articulated unity in diversity and unity in difference. This means becoming an integral part of a real community of real communities. This is what we mean by the free ecological society, a becoming-communal, an "always-coming-home." This is what we mean by the Beloved Community.

# NOTES

1    Carolyn Merchant, *The Death of Nature: Women, Ecology, and the Scientific Revolution* (San Francisco: Harper & Row, 1980), 30. Merchant quotes similar passages from the Roman poet Ovid.

2    Merchant, *Death of Nature*, 31. This period was mythologically expressed in the Garden of Eden, the Golden Age, and other primal utopias but is based on real historical or "prehistorical" evidence, as Marshall Sahlins shows in his crucially important work *Stone Age Economics*. See the recently reprinted edition (Abingdon, UK: Routledge, 2017).

3    Merchant, 32.

4    *Superstructures of the World* episode, "Grasberg Mine: Gold Mine in the Clouds," produced by Steven R. Talley, January 1998, online at https://www.youtube.com/watch?v=zjg_SVHdrWQ.

5    Quotes from *Freeport Watch Bulletin*, Summer 1996, 1.

6    IWGA (International Work Group for Indigenous Affairs) *Newsletter*, April–June 1992.

7    The text can be found at https://libcom.org/library/treasure-sierra-madre-b-traven.

8    Dissatisfaction with such disavowal is expressed in the 2014 Max Cafard satirical piece, "Welcome to the Idiocene," which proposed eighty-one alternatives to the term "Anthropocene," many of which (Collapsocene, Extinctocene, etc.) focus on the fact that we have entered a new age of planetary death. It was published in the *Fifth Estate* and *Exquisite Corpse* and is online at https://www.academia.edu/7784643/_Welcome_to_the_Idiocene_by_Max_Cafard_.

9    See John Clark, "Oikos and Poesis: Art and Our Planetary Future," *Brooklyn Rail*, November 2015, https://brooklynrail.org/2015/11/criticspage/oikos-and-poesis-art-and-our-planetary-future (revised slightly and retitled as the postscript to this volume, 316–17). This term is also used in Christophe Bonneuil and Jean-Baptiste Fressioz, *The Shock of the Anthropocene: The Earth, History and Us* (London: Verso, 2016).

10   See Herbert Marcuse, *Eros and Civilization: A Philosophical Inquiry into Freud* (Boston: Beacon Press, 1955) and Norman O. Brown, *Life against Death: The Psychoanalytic Meaning of History* (Middletown, CT: Wesleyan University, 1959).

11   Achille Mbembe, "Necropolitics," *Public Culture* 15, no. 1 (2003): 11–40.

12   More literally, of "animals."

13   See Jason Moore's extensive work on the Capitalocene, especially *Capitalism in the Web of Life: Ecology and the Accumulation of Capital* (London: Verso, 2015), which has quickly become a classic of political ecology.

14   Justin McBrien develops the concept of the Necrocene extensively in his insightful article "Accumulating Extinction: Planetary Catastrophism in the Necrocene," in Jason Moore, ed. *Anthropocene or Capitalocene? Nature, History, and the Crisis of Capitalism* (Oakland: PM Press, 2016), 116–37.

15   The beginning is translated variously as "we go round and round," "we spin around," or "we enter the circle," while the rest is usually translated as "in the night and are consumed by fire."

16   I am grateful to Peter Marshall for reminding me of the importance of always emphasizing explicitly this third signification, which is so often forgotten or neglected.

17    See below, 210. In this, I follow the tradition of communitarian anarchist phi-
      losopher Gustav Landauer, along with Gandhi and the Sarvodaya Movement,
      among others. I am grateful to Laurence Davis for encouraging me to give more
      thought to this question.

18    To ask for, *demander*, as in the famous French slogan.

19    *Aufruf zum Sozialismus* (1911). See Gustav Landauer, *For Socialism* (St. Louis:
      Telos Press, 1978).

20    For a discussion of the three major dimensions of a developed communitarian
      anarchist conception of freedom, see "The Third Concept of Liberty," in my
      book *The Impossible Community: Realizing Communitarian Anarchism* (New York:
      Bloomberg Academic, 2013), 53–91.

21    See Javier Sethness Castro, *Eros and Revolution: The Critical Philosophy of Herbert
      Marcuse* (Chicago: Haymarket Books, 2017).

22    Joel Kovel, *History and Spirit: An Inquiry into the Philosophy of Liberation* (Boston:
      Beacon Press, 1991), 236.

# Lessons from the School
# of Radical Change
# (Notes of a Slow Learner)

In the late 1960s and early 1970s I participated in what was rather vaguely called "the Movement," and which seemed to offer hope for fundamentally transforming the world through community-based democratic and cooperative projects. During that time, I gradually learned certain lessons about both the possibilities and also the limitations of grassroots organization as the result of participation in child care co-ops, food co-ops, alternative schools, the free university, the worker co-op movement, the IWW, the antinuclear and antiwar movements, various ecological, feminist, and post-Situationist anarchist groups, and an anarchist affinity group, in addition to many other experiences.

Out of this milieu came a vision of a new society based on values such as mutual aid and solidarity, equality, dignity and freedom, peace, love, compassion, and care. In the new world that we envisioned, not only production and consumption but also personal relationships and family life, education and child care, care of the body and soul, arts, music and recreation, and all other spheres of existence would be transformed in accord with these values.

Though the movement of the period did not ultimately fulfill the hopes many of us had for the imminent fundamental transformation of society, it made many breakthroughs and revealed much about the processes of radical social transformation. I learned that there exists at certain points in history the possibility for creating a vast movement in which large numbers of people quickly become open to change. I learned that a proliferation of small-scale transformative communities and projects can become the basis for a large-scale movement for social transformation. I learned about the power of the radical social imaginary and the power of a transformative ethos or way of living everyday life.

1

For example, in 1974, I visited the Adams Morgan neighborhood in Washington, DC. I discovered there that it is possible that in one specific locality, at one particular moment, there can be a convergence of initiatives in community technology, local self-reliance, neighborhood self-government, community co-ops, and communal living, in the context of an emerging liberatory culture with its own forms of art, music, and communication. From seeing the reality of such a convergence, there and in many other places, I learned that we have the ability to collectively create a new culture and new forms of organization based on freedom and solidarity.

I also learned difficult lessons from seeing, by the mid to late 1970s, the disappearance or co-optation of most of the constructive social projects that I had found so inspiring. I learned, on the one hand, that there are powerful and usually underestimated or ignored obstacles to the creation of a free, just society, but that, on the other hand, these obstacles are not material or technical ones. I learned that to sustain the kind of breakthroughs that we achieved, we would have to address more seriously and, in effect, much more radically, issues concerning the self and character-structure, human relationships and interactions, forms of social organization, the nature of ideology and social control, and (as I learned from the Situationists in particular) the battle for the imagination.

By the 1980s I had become heavily involved in a theoretical and political tendency called social ecology. Through it, I learned more about the history of and possibilities for decentralized, direct democracy and community control of all major aspects of social life. I learned that we need to have a vision of social transformation that recognizes the problem of the transition. I developed a deeper understanding of the rather obvious truth that we cannot merely do good and hope for the best, but rather we must consider, carefully and realistically what kind of organizational forms could create the new society and replace the old one. I began to think more seriously about the question of preconditions. I also learned about the pitfalls of political sectarianism and the ease with which one can fall into it when surrounded by those with similar views and commitments. I realized more clearly the need for radical openness to many sources of truth and enlightenment, and, above all, openness to the experience of real communities of people struggling for personal and collective liberation.

At this time, I also became active in Central America solidarity movements. From these movements, I learned about the intimate connection between the domination around me and the more intensified and brutal forms of domination elsewhere in the world. I learned that the struggle for liberation and solidarity must be at once local, regional, and global. This process of learning continued during the 1990s, as my political ideas were transformed deeply by day-to-day involvement in support for the West Papuan and East Timorese peoples, and especially by engagement in the struggle against the global mining industry in West Papua.[1] I learned from the tragic betrayal of East Timor by the world community that we should never forget the genocides going on at this very moment and that it is very easy for the vast majority of us to do so. I learned from the Papuans about how extractive industry can transform places with the greatest concentrations of natural wealth into sites of sickness, death, oppression, poverty, and devastation. I learned, especially from the Papuans, that there are many fundamental forgotten truths to relearn from indigenous and traditional communities. I learned that we have to break with the Eurocentric models of political organization and revolution that had been integral to my own political formation.

I also became increasingly involved at this time with the green movement. I worked on grassroots issues such local control and municipalization of utilities, decentralization of political power, community garden projects, and, above all, the fight against ecocidal and genocidal transnational corporations and their powerful influence over local political systems and communities across the globe. I learned that our local struggles in the semiperiphery are in a great many ways one with the struggles at the center and in the periphery.

A crucial turning point at this time was the decision to take the opportunity to begin acquiring land on Bayou La Terre in the forest of the Mississippi Gulf Coast. I had begun to study bioregionalism and to think about the process of reinhabitation, that is, learning to create a culture and way of life rooted in a sense of place and a knowledge of the land and the life forms that are part of it. This was the beginning of almost three decades at Bayou La Terre, in which I slowly learned about the power and beauty of the way of nature and about what Gary Snyder calls the goodness, wildness, and sacredness of the land. This place, whose name means both "the Earth" and "the Land," was to become one of my greatest educators.

At this time, I also became very active in the movement against the several strong political campaigns of former neo-Nazi and Klansman politician David Duke and, more fundamentally, against the resurgence of neofascism. I learned about the depth and the insidious nature of long-neglected and long-denied authoritarian and racist tendencies within contemporary society. I also undertook extensive study of and writing about the resurgent religious fundamentalism and the growing power and influence of televangelists and their media empires. I learned that, in addition to becoming adept at the use of mass media, the religious Right was doing in practice the kind of grassroots organization that the Left, with a few notable exceptions, has primarily merely talked about since the civil rights, black power, student, antiwar, and community control movements of the 1960s and early 1970s.

In the early 2000s I began spending time in India and working with Tibetan refugees fleeing their tragic history of conquest, genocide, and ongoing oppression and colonization. I learned additional lessons about the power of community and of traditions of dedicated practice of compassion and non-egocentrism. I also began studying Buddhist philosophy, especially Zen, more seriously. I discovered the relationship to radical critique and revolutionary social transformation of what are called the Three Jewels. I learned, first, about the importance of the fully awakened mind, and what some Boddhisattva once called "the ruthless critique of all things existing." I learned, second, about the importance of complete dedication to following the truth along whatever path it takes and of being completely open to experience of the world and the way of nature. I learned, third, about the importance of the small awakened community of love, compassion, and care. At the same time, I was studying the great anarchist geographer Elisée Reclus, and learned that he had also discovered the crucial importance of these "small loving associations" to the process of social transformation.

I learned many lessons from direct participation in, or contact with, communities of this kind. For a number of years, I attended the local Friends meeting and learned much about consensus decision-making, respect for the person and the individual conscience, dedication to peace and justice, and the value of having a long tradition of communal practice to draw upon. I learned from friends who worked in or were inspired by the Catholic Worker Movement about the great power of a small community living a life together based on the everyday practice of peacemaking, pursuing justice, and expressing love, especially for those in greatest need. I also learned from increasing participation in several Zen meditation groups and sanghas about the deeper meaning of the awakened mind, and the challenges of overcoming egocentrism and the debilitating distractions of a world of obsessive consumption and accumulation. I learned that a good criterion for assessing the value of a group is whether, when one is with its members, one immediately becomes a better and more joyful person.

Perhaps the most decisive turning point in the transformation of my perspective on radical change occurred in 2005, when I experienced the trauma of Hurricane Katrina, the devastation of much of New Orleans in the flooding, and the corporate capitalist and structurally racist reengineering of the city in the post-Katrina period. I learned the most important lessons from participation in post-Katrina grassroots recovery communities. I learned to appreciate more deeply the meaning of crisis and collapse. I learned about the role of trauma in personal and group transformation. I learned that another good criterion for assessing groups is the extent to which at crucial moments they put aside everything that is merely habitual and inessential and respond wholeheartedly to the greatest and most vital needs. I learned that extraordinary disasters can help wake us up to the truth that the decisive moment is always now.

I was affected powerfully by working with a small recovery community in the Upper Ninth Ward of New Orleans. I learned that living and working together full-time with a small community devoted to serving the most real and urgent needs of the community is the most fulfilling life possible. I later learned from working closely with the legendary community leader Mama D and the Seventh Ward Soul Patrol of the miraculous powers of a grassroots, matricentric, Rastafarian-influenced neighborhood group that followed only one principle, "Neighbors Helping Neighbors." Contact with many volunteers from the anarchist-inspired Common Ground Relief, some of whom stayed with me in my home, taught me about the vast underappreciated reservoir of compassion that exists in our world, and how engagement in grassroots recovery can bring out the cooperative and communitarian impulses in people. I learned from Common Ground about the enormous good that comes from practicing "Solidarity Not Charity" and about the invaluable human quality that my friend scott crow calls "emergency heart."[2]

I learned above all about the awe-inspiring power of small communities of care. I learned that such communities can help people appreciate more deeply what is of greatest intrinsic value, that which we must recognize as sacred and beyond all price. At the same time, the experience of disaster, mourning, and regeneration gave me an increasing sense of urgency about the need to change the entire present tragic course of world history. I learned to have a much deeper awareness of and concern about the degree of suffering and loss that is taking place at this moment as well as the vastly greater level that is to come should we continue the suicidal and ecocidal course of capitalist, statist, patriarchal civilization. As the 2010s began, these same lessons and feelings were intensified through the additional trauma of the BP oil spill, with its horrifying spectacle of devastation, despoliation, and ecocide.

Over many of the post-Katrina years, I learned much (as much as from anything else in my life) from the unanticipated experience of again taking on the challenging vocation of single parenting and dealing on a day-to-day basis with addiction, alcoholism, mental and spiritual sickness, and suffering within our family and among many others close to us. Seeing so many young people lost to a society of nihilism, I have learned crucial lessons about the need to reassess priorities and the craving for and obsessive consumption of objects and substances, ideas and fantasies. I have learned equally important lessons from seeing others, including those close to me, saved by the power of the compassionate community. All these experiences and lessons led me to begin studying nonhierarchical, nonmedicalized therapeutic communities.

I was invited to visit one of the largest and most studied therapeutic communities in the UK. I had the opportunity to spend time with people engaged in extraordinary processes of mutual aid and self-transformation, based on unconditional love and complete acceptance of each unique person. I learned much from seeing the processes of healing and regeneration at work, there and elsewhere. I learned that miracles are possible through good practice, through care, and through openness to possibilities. I learned that given the ways that the system of domination generates the voracious, insatiable, self-destructive ego, the communities of liberation and solidarity that will be capable of transforming and liberating the world must also be therapeutic—that is, healing—communities.

It was as the result of all these slow processes of learning that I decided five years ago that it was necessary to leave the university where I taught for decades, and to start working more directly, full-time, for the process of social and ecological regeneration. To help in this work, I organized the small project called La Terre Institute for Community and Ecology, situated on what has now grown to eighty-seven acres at Bayou La Terre, in addition to its programs in New Orleans. I have learned from the early stages of this project that it is urgently necessary to find a small community of similarly motivated people who can work together, in order to make any such undertaking a success.

I have become preoccupied with the question of how, given the actual conditions in the world, we can break with, and then overcome, the capitalist, statist, patriarchal system of domination and prevent global collapse, while at the same time creating a free, just, and caring society. I have learned that it is necessary to focus carefully on the question: "What is the decisive step?" or perhaps more accurately, "What is the decisive process?" A few years ago, in a book called *The Impossible Community*, a work that was very much a product of the post-Katrina experience, I argued for the need to address at once all the primary spheres of social determination. These include the social institutional structure, the social ideology, the social imaginary, and the social ethos. I concluded that to achieve this goal the most urgent necessity is the creation of small communities of liberation and solidarity, of awakening and care. It is what is also called here the Beloved Community.

I have learned from many years of study of social movements that emerging communities of this kind can find inspiration in a rich history of microcommunities, including (to mention just a few examples) anarchist affinity groups, Latin American base communities rooted in Liberation Theology, and the "ashrams" of the Sarvodaya Movement in India, which meant small prefigurative and transformative ecovillages to be created in every village and neighborhood of India. Further inspiration now comes from what is being created at this very moment by the Zapatistas in Chiapas, by the Democratic Autonomy Movement in Rojava, and by our neighbors at Cooperation Jackson, just a couple of hours away from Bayou La Terre.

I learned, as is recounted in a chapter below, that the values and practices of indigenous people in Chiapas offer much richer and more radical concepts of mutual aid and solidarity, and much deeper images of communal personhood, than even the most radical political theory that the dominant society has to offer. I also learned, as is discussed in another chapter, that the revolutionary movement in Rojava has not only challenged the centralized state, capitalism, and authoritarian religion but has also gone further than any other popular social movement in working to destroy patriarchy and the dominating, appropriating, hypermasculinist ego built on it.

I am continually led back to certain core questions that are implied by everything I have learned and experienced. What would a movement be like that included each person in prefigurative and indeed *transfigurative* affinity groups and base communities—that is, in primary communities of liberation and solidarity, awakening and care? Could such a socially regenerative movement increasingly move on to create participatory democratic block, street, neighborhood, town, and city assemblies, councils, and committees? Could such a movement ultimately replace the capitalist, statist, patriarchal system of domination? Could it create a free, just, and compassionate human community, living in dynamic harmony with the whole of life on Earth? These questions have only one answer. It is our lives.

## NOTES
1  Discussed in chapter 8 in this volume, 140–53,
2  See the appendix, "Emergency Heart Sutra," below, 318–19.

**PART I**

# EMPIRE VERSUS EARTH IN THE NECROCENE

1

# Ecological Thinking and the Crisis of the Earth

"The earth died screaming while I lay dreaming." —Tom Waits

## Facing the Crisis

As was mentioned above, any competent extraterrestrial reporter sent to cover the news from Earth would certainly report that our planet is going through one of the six periods of mass extinction in its entire four-and-a-half-billion-year history and that other major disruptions in the biosphere are interacting to cause a major crisis for terrestrial life. In short, the big story from Planet Earth is that we have entered a period of massive planetary death. Thus, among the various competing terms that have been suggested for the emerging geological era, the most precisely appropriate is the *Necrocene*, the "new era of death."[1] Strangely, this rather shocking news is met with either denial or disavowal among the members of our own species, who are living in the very midst of this crisis. The deniers among us simply reject the clear evidence of global ecological crisis. The disavowers, on the other hand, accept the truth of the evidence but fail to undertake actions that are even vaguely proportional to the gravity of our predicament.

Information on the severity of the ecological crisis has hardly been a well-kept secret. For example, researchers at the Stockholm Resilience Centre and their colleagues have in recent years formulated a conception of "planetary boundaries," seeking to define the limits in various areas beyond which there is likelihood of ecological disaster. They summarize their findings in three concise articles that are readily available to the public.[2] The authors conclude that "transgressing one or more planetary boundaries may be deleterious or even catastrophic due to the risk of crossing thresholds that will trigger non-linear, abrupt environmental change within

11

continental- to planetary-scale systems."[3] The boundaries are identified as lying in the areas of climate change, ocean acidification, stratospheric ozone depletion, biogeochemical nitrogen and phosphorus cycles, global fresh-water use, rate of biodiversity loss, land-system change, chemical pollution, and atmospheric aerosol loading. They find that at least three boundaries had already been passed and that most others are in danger of being trans-gressed soon. In the most recent article, the authors conclude that "two core boundaries—climate change and biosphere integrity—have been identified, each of which has the potential on its own to drive the Earth system into a new state should they be substantially and persistently transgressed."[4]

The dire implications of the term "a new state" should not be underes-timated. Science writer Peter Forbes notes that the November 2017 COP23 Climate Summit in Bonn acknowledged the likelihood that by 2100 global warming will reach a disastrous three degrees centigrade, since there will be a doubling of preindustrial $CO_2$ levels from 280 to 560 parts per million by 2050, and another doubling by 2100. Such conditions will not only be unprecedented in the history of our species, they will mean a return of the planet to the climate of the Cretaceous period of 145–65.95 million years ago. Forbes observes that "in a Cretaceous rerun, there would very likely be no ice at the poles once again, and sea levels would be about 216 feet (66 meters) above current levels."[5]

While ecologists and eco-activists usually stress the biological basis of global crisis it is important not to neglect the physics of extinction and collapse, which conveys a powerful message. Schramskia, Gattiea, and Brow in "Human Domination of the Biosphere: Rapid Discharge of the Earth-Space Battery Foretells the Future of Humankind," show that it is illuminating to conceive of the biosphere as a massive chemical battery that has been charged over the history of life on the planet.[6]

Over the course of three and a half billion years of evolution, "billions of tons of living biomass were stored in forests and other ecosystems and in vast reserves of fossil fuels." This process has been reversed in the brief and rapidly concluding chapter of human history that we call "civiliza-tion." The authors point out that the "rapid discharge of the earth's store of organic energy fuels the human domination of the biosphere" and that because of "the rapid depletion of this chemical energy, the earth is shifting back toward the inhospitable equilibrium of outer space."

The evidence is staggering to anyone capable of taking a geological or Earth-historical perspective. At the beginning of the current era, the

Earth "contained ~1,000 billion tons of carbon in living biomass," which existed primarily "in the form of trees in forests." Over the past two millennia "humans have reduced this by about 45 percent to ~550 billion tons of carbon in biomass." This news seems dire enough, but the authors find another even more striking way of representing our planetary predicament.

They introduce "a new sustainability metric $\Omega$," which represents (on extremely conservative assumptions) "the number of years at current rates of consumption that the global phytomass storage could feed the human race." They note that in the past 2000 years humanity has reduced this metric $\Omega$ by 98.5 percent. Furthermore, the rate of depletion has been rapidly accelerating since industrialization. Their graph of this process shows the level of "sustainability," and thus human survivability, rapidly plummeting toward zero.

In considering the fateful implications of their analysis, the authors describe the biosphere's tendency toward catastrophe with a degree of understatement befitting their technical and scientific audience. "There is," they say, "considerable uncertainty in how the biosphere will function as $\Omega$ decreases from the present $\Omega = $ ~1,029 y[ears] into an uncharted thermodynamic operating region." Yet the message is clear. What the authors correctly call the project of "domination of the biosphere" is threatening us with imminent planetary death, that "inhospitable equilibrium of outer space." This is the threat, the ultimate threat of the Necrocene, that we must face.

## The Insistent Question of Technique

Our era is a new era of death in more senses than one. While we are faced with the threat of the death of the *biosphere* as the result of ecological crisis, we are also faced with the death of the *humanisphere*[7] as we have known it over the course of human history. This is in large part the result of growth of the megamachine and the forces of technological domination, in dialectical interaction with other forms of domination. The decisive role of technics in the unfolding of the Necrocene must not be underestimated, as it is in many accounts of the Anthropocene and Capitalocene. Crucial in understanding the history of domination and the possibilities for an escape from that history is the question of technique.[8]

The radical critique of technological rationality and technological domination has been highly developed for at least three quarters of a century.[9] Nevertheless, this critique hardly occupies the central place in contemporary philosophy and social theory that it deserves, despite a few notable exceptions.[10] It is important to return to the groundbreaking critiques of Jacques Ellul, the Frankfurt School, Lewis Mumford, and others and develop them further in relation to the emergence of deeply transformative new information technologies and biotechnologies.[11] These recent developments reflect a postmodern logic of technological domination that demands the most urgent attention and action.[12]

The reconsideration of the history of critique of technology will not be undertaken here.[13] However, it will be useful to reflect briefly on the currently unfolding course of technological domination as presented strikingly in the analysis of visionary megahistorian Yuval Noah Harari.[14] Harari argues that developing information technologies and biotechnologies will "create unprecedented upheavals in human society, eroding human agency and, possibly, subverting human desires." It will, he says, produce a world in which the dominant social institutions, including "liberal democracy and free-market economics might become obsolete." These technologies will triumph while at the same time marginalizing a large segment of the global population and creating a new class of the "useless." Harari's speculations (or rather, extrapolations) seem well grounded in a world in which we already see the emergence of whole marginalized regions and countries in which a large percentage of the population has been rendered "useless" according to the demands of the global capitalist economy and the technological megamachine.

Harari observes that the prevailing liberal order based its hegemony on "promising everybody a larger slice of the pie" but that this legitimation process no longer works. In the future, the economic growth that underwrote the promise of material abundance will no longer depend on the functioning of so-called liberal democracy and so-called free markets, but will rely instead on "the invention of more and more disruptive technologies." Harari predicts that technology will for a certain period continue to create jobs that require "high levels of expertise and ingenuity" while at the same time generating a growing class of "unemployed unskilled laborers, or workers employable only at extremely low wages." However, the silver lining that this disaster offers to the erstwhile elite is seriously at risk. As AI continues to improve, "even jobs that demand high intelligence and creativity might gradually disappear."

Harari takes the story of the recent triumph of technology and the technical intelligentsia in the field of chess as a paradigm for future developments. He speculates that the definitive proof of the superiority in chess of "human-AI teams" may well be replicated in "policing, medicine, banking, and many other fields." The crucial qualities that give AI its clear superiority over human beings are "connectivity and updatability." Harari observes that AI "might make centralized systems far more efficient than diffuse systems" since the system operates more effectively the greater the pool of data available for analysis. The technical advantages of centralized data for studies in genetics and for medical research are obvious. This is also true in the case of the projected system of autonomous or self-driving vehicles, which "will know all the traffic regulations," will "never disobey them on purpose," and "could all be connected to one another." Thus, individual cars will not function as "separate entities," but rather as "part of a single algorithm." In short, the technological system will become a "system" in a much stronger sense than ever before.

One implication of this systemization is that the same technologies that increasingly relegate much of the population to a condition of uselessness will also make the population "easier to monitor and control." Such a neo-Panopticonist system will take the Baconian precept that "knowledge is power" to a new totalitarian level. In fact, the corporate state is already well advanced in this project of technological domination. Harari notes that "Israel is a leader in the field of surveillance technology and has created in the occupied West Bank a working prototype for a total-surveillance regime." He suggests that the anonymity of the technical system will give it an unprecedented power to control dissent, since it is more difficult for the "useless" to organize against mysterious marginalizing forces than for the oppressed to organize against the exploitation and injustices of an identifiable ruling class.

Walter Benjamin stated famously that "the sight of immediate reality has become an orchid in the land of technology."[15] In reality, very little of reality is "immediate"; however, there are many forms and levels of mediation.[16] So in place of Benjamin's "immediate" we might substitute "reality free from certain forms of mediation," specifically those associated with forms of social domination. These include mediation by technical rationality and the technological imaginary, mediation by statist and bureaucratic rationality and the statist imaginary, mediation by patriarchal instrumental rationality and the patriarchal imaginary, and mediation by economic rationality and the economistic imaginary (in both their productionist and their consumptionist forms).

What has become in the land of technology an "orchid," with all its connotations of rarity and fragility, is not "immediate reality," but rather *singularity*. It is the singular that possesses something like what Benjamin described as the "aura" of the thing, and what has also been called the "sacred" within the thing, and the "spirit" of the thing, or within the thing. Ironically, just as this rare and fragile singularity is threatened, so is its converse, universality. Just as there is no orchid without its rainforest (or other suitable ecosystem—perhaps a swamp) there is no gap between the singular and the universal, and both are subject to the same forms of predation.

In the land of technology, the singular is the orchid, and the universal is the rainforest in which the orchid flourishes. In the Necrocene, both are threatened with death. Technical rationality and the technological imaginary are destroying the metaphorical orchids and rainforests at the same time as they are destroying the literal orchids and rainforests. And they are doing so, ultimately, for the same reasons. Thus, reflection on the question of technique helps us understand the ways in which the murder of the biosphere and the withering away of humanity, the Necrocene and the Age of Nihilism, are inseparably interconnected.

In a sense, technical rationality is the most "environmental" form of thinking that is possible. Under the reign of technique everything becomes "environment." As technical reason invades all aspects of reality, even the being that supposedly *had an environment* becomes *part of the environment*. At the nihilistic end of civilization, even the absurd illusion of a sovereign ego at the center of reality dissolves. What remains at the "center" is only a sovereign lack, an imperious death drive, a destructive nothingness, surrounded by a field of objects of consumption and domination. We finally discover the true horror of "nihil unbound."

## The Limits of Environmental Thinking

It is not only scientists and science writers who have sounded the alarm about ecological crisis in rather clear and not uncertain terms. Recently, the *Guardian*, a major British newspaper, announced the gravity of the biodiversity crisis in almost alarmist language, saying that the "'biological annihilation' of wildlife in recent decades means a sixth mass extinction in Earth's history is under way" and that "it threatens the survival of human civilization, with just a short window of time in which to act."[17] Yet this seemingly inflammatory article was not at the top of the stories for the day, and if one reads the numerous readers' replies to it, one finds very little sense of direction about how to respond to this developing global catastrophe. Furthermore, such news somehow quickly fades from the popular consciousness. We might therefore conclude that there is simply not enough good "environmental thinking" going on in today's world. It may seem that the public is just not prepared to understand adequately the meaning of global ecological crisis and that it is therefore incapable of facing it with full seriousness. Thus, there are injunctions that we need to work harder on creating good environmental education, so that the public can engage in more effective environmental thinking.

Granted, this would be a very good thing. However, one of the problems with conventional ideas of "environmental thinking" or even "ecological thinking" is that they assume that correct thinking will in itself have a significant transformative effect or, more to the point, the kind of effect that will be necessary in order to avoid disaster. For example, it is thought to be crucial that climate deniers be convinced that anthropogenic climate change really exists. This is not at all a bad idea, but it almost inevitably ignores the fact that the vast majority of *nondeniers* are in a state of *disavowal* and that reformed deniers are highly likely to join the ranks of these disavowers. The disavowers are willing to admit that a problem exists, and they may get certain satisfactions out of being on the right side of history, and perhaps even from engaging in various beneficial activities that reduce greenhouse gasses. Yet they are not willing to consider, and then actually work diligently for, the kind of deep, fundamental changes in society that will be necessary to change the ecocidal course of history. A basic problem for the problematic of "better environmental thinking" is that the needed transformation cannot result from abstract thought and the understanding of concepts. It can only come from engaged thinking that is an integral part of an engaged participation in transformative social ecological processes. We need therefore to consider how such engagement might begin to take place. But first, we might consider further the implications of our conventional language, concepts, and modes of thinking.

Part of the problem with the appeal to "environmental thinking" is the very idea of the "environment." The dominant conception of "environment" assumes a certain practical ontology. According to this ontology, there is a world that consists of individual egos surrounded by "environments," and societies that consist of collections of separate egos, surrounded in turn by larger "environments." This prevailing conception of the environment is an expression of the binary subject-object thinking that is built into to the dominant social ideology and subject-object feelings and perceptions that are built into the dominant social ethos. Meanings are social, not merely individual. Thus, even when this ontology is not consciously intended, or when it is even abstractly rejected, such a problematic reinforces the pervasive hierarchical dualism that is the deep ideology and sensibility of civilization. Given such problems, explicitly *ecological* thinking is a great advance over *environmental* thinking and a step toward ecological *imagining* and *feeling*.

The term "ecology" derives from the Greek terms *oikos* and *logos*. It is concerned with the *logos*, or underlying meaning, truth, and way of the *oikos*, the local, regional, or planetary household. In its emphasis on the *oikos*, ecological thinking replaces both the egocentric and the anthropocentric perspective with the perspective of the larger ecological whole. This is a whole that is never a completed or closed totality but rather is always in a process of becoming whole. The ecological whole is an ever-becoming-one that is also an ever-becoming-many, a dynamic unity in diversity. Ecological thinking is inspired by the quest for the social-ecological equivalent of Hegel's "concrete universal," the universal that must always be expressed through the particular and the singular, the regional and the local, the communal and the personal.[18] This implies that we need to contemplate how we fit into the planetary dialectic of developing parts and wholes. Our question here is how we might begin to develop a thought and practice that is in accord with such a truly social-ecological perspective and that will open a clear pathway out of our planetary crisis.

**Finding the Way**

Though it cannot be developed in any detail in this introductory discussion, the answer that seems most promising is that we must begin to create a well-grounded and multidimensional social and political base for the regeneration of human community and the community of life on Earth. This means reorganizing our social world into networks of awakened and caring transformational communities that are dedicated to undertaking whatever actions are necessary to put an end to the Necrocene and initiate a new era characterized by the flourishing of life on Earth. We might call such a new era the *Eleutherocene*, meaning the era of a liberated humanity and a liberated Earth. In this endeavor, we can find inspiration in the ancient Buddhist concept of appamāda. "Appamāda" is a Pali word ("apramada" in Sanskrit) that conveys the ideas of both "mindfulness" and "care." The practice of appamāda implies that we must be awakened to the world and all the beings around us and that in such an awakened state we become capable of responding to and caring for them effectively. In this, it has much in common with concepts in contemporary feminist, and especially ecofeminist, care ethics, which rejects the patriarchal model of an abstract ethics of principles in favor of an approach that nondualistically recognizes the inseparability of moral rationality, moral sensibility, and moral imagination.[19] It affirms that what we need more than anything is neither environmental thinking, which takes us in the wrong direction, nor even ecological thinking, which takes us only part of the way, but an *ethos* of appamāda that pervades and shapes both our everyday practice and our social institutions. The practice of care involves attention to the truth of all beings, acceptance of the way of all beings, and responsiveness to the needs of all beings. It also implies engagement in the personal, social, and political practice that is necessary to establish mindful care for all beings in our purview, and for the Earth itself as our overriding priority.

Such an outlook of attentiveness, acceptance and responsiveness helps us discover what we might call the Four Noble Truths about the Earth.[20] These truths are that the Earth is suffering, that there is a cause of this suffering, that there is a cure to this suffering, and that there is a way to carry out this cure.[21] As in the case of the ancient Noble Truths, we find that obsessive craving is the cause of this suffering. Such craving has a transhistorical element, it is rooted in our natural being as needing and wanting creatures, but it develops to differing degrees and takes on different qualities in different historical contexts. So, in order to cure our own suffering and that of the Earth, we must come to an understanding of the very particular, historically conditioned nature of the craving that causes it.

We all have knowledge of its nature at some level. If we cannot express it consciously, we do so through our symptoms and our defense mechanisms. However, to confront our predicament authentically, we must develop a clear, fully conscious awareness of its nature, and the specific ways that it causes the suffering of the Earth, the suffering of a myriad of other living beings on Earth, the suffering of billions of other human beings, and our own personal suffering. We must understand, for example, how the craving that causes the suffering of the billion human beings who live in a deprived and dispossessed world of absolute poverty also causes the suffering of another billion who live in a privileged and affluent world of nihilistic egoism.

We must, moreover, understand that the craving that causes so much suffering has, in turn, a cause of its own. This cause is the world in which most of us live, which is best described as the late capitalist, statist, technocratic, patriarchal society of mass consumption. It is this society, as a powerfully functioning yet self-contradictory social whole, that generates a certain form of selfhood that is inclined to obsessive desires, powerful addictions, and sick attachments. As Jason Moore has aptly stated it, the crisis we are facing is above all "capitalogenic,"[22] though this should not lead us to neglect the degree to which it is simultaneously "statogenic," "technogenic," and "patriarchogenic." There is an entire system of production that depends on the generation of such craving to operate successfully (at least in the precatastrophic short term). There is an entire system of consumption that feeds such craving. There is an entire culture of consumption that socializes us into believing that a world of obsessive craving is the only one possible, or, if we do not believe that this is true, that socializes us into resigning ourselves in practice to the inevitability of that world, and to living our lives as if we believed that it is true.

As in the case of the ancient Noble Truths, the cure to suffering is not merely knowing the cause of the disease or even knowing that the cause must be removed. The teaching is that the cure can only be carried out through following the Way, which was called the Noble Eightfold Path. There was no onefold, twofold, or threefold path. The cure was not effected by choosing one or more forms of practice that appealed most to one personally, or that seemed to be leading generally in the right direction, or that might "hopefully" have some kind of mysterious "snowball effect." This would be succumbing to mere whim or superstition. The path consisted of all the forms of practice that were necessary conditions for the radical transformation that was needed. The promise was that if the path is followed "another world is possible."

## How Is This World Possible?

So we are in need of another world. It is another world that we find in many ways by returning in a more awakened and compassionate way to this one. However, the means by which this other world that is our world might be fully actualized (the Way) has not been given the kind of diligent thought that is essential to effective social practice. "Another world is possible" becomes mere abstract, escapist ideology unless it is expressed through transformative action that is not only prophetically "prefigurative" but also immediately "figurative." Such action not only announces the arrival of another world; it also shows us the very "face" of that other world, here and now. It is in an important sense "world-making," for no world ever exists, including the present one, except by unceasing, moment-to-moment efforts on the part of all its inhabitants to bring it into being. It is also in a very important sense less a *making* than an *openness* to the world and to its common *logos*, its mode of revealing itself, in opposition to the privatized or "idiotic"[23] *logoi* that are egoically generated artifacts. "Another world" is "possible" in part because that other world is a creative possibility. But another world is also possible because that other world has existed and still endures in the midst of the present one. We must therefore ponder the questions of *how the present social world is possible* and *how it can be made impossible.* This means that we need to undertake a thorough inquiry into the major spheres of social determination that are the grounds of possibility of any world, either actually existing or imagined.

There are four spheres of determination that are essential to the analysis of how social reality is generated, how it is maintained, and how it might be transformed. These spheres are the social institutional structure, the social ideology, the social imaginary, and the social ethos.[24] Since there is a dialectical relationship between these spheres, they should not be thought of as discrete realms. For example, no social institutional structure is conceivable without reference to the social ethos, since these structures embody, in part, structures of social practice. Thus, mass media as an institutional structure is inseparable from forms of concrete social practice that make use of and are in turn deeply conditioned by mass media technologies. Similarly, no social imaginary signification is conceivable apart from its relation to social ideology, since images in many ways reflect and interact with concepts. For example, the imaginary signification "rugged individualist" reflects and interacts with moral injunctions about the virtues of "hard work" and "self-reliance" that form part of the social ideology. Very significantly, the megastructures of the society of advanced consumer capitalism, the technobureaucratic militaristic state, and the technological megamachine all immediately generate awe-inspiring images of power and wealth. In short, the spheres of determination are theoretical constructs or systemic abstractions that are useful in analyzing a social whole that consists of constellations of phenomena that interact dialectically and are internally related.

It will perhaps be helpful to summarize the content of these four interrelated spheres of social determination. The social institutional sphere consists of the objective and external structures of social determination (when abstracted from the simultaneously internal-external and objective-subjective social whole). It includes, notably, the structure of capital and its various sectors, the structure of the state apparatus, and the structure of the technological and bureaucratic systems. It includes the external, formal structure of social practices, and the material infrastructure, since institutions consist not merely of structural principles but also of the actual structuration of material resources in accord with such principles. The other three spheres are the internal and subjective realms of social determination (given all the qualifications just mentioned). It is important that we not look upon the relation between the "objective" institutional sphere and the three "subjective" spheres as a "base-superstructure" relationship, but rather one of mutual determination and internal relation. Thus, perhaps paradoxically, the "external" is *internally* related to the "internal."

The second sphere of social determination consists of the social ethos. "Ethos" is used in the sense of the constellation of social practices, feelings, and sensibilities that constitute a way of life.[25] Ethos is the sphere of social psychological reality and of the tone and mood that pervade everyday life. It is at once the most physiological and the most metaphysical sphere,[26] since it is the realm of feelings, perceptions, and sensations, but also the realm of the sense of being. It can only be understood through a very specific analysis of everyday life and all the habits, practices, gestures, and rituals that it entails. Ethos consists of the way that we live within and enact the social and cultural world in which we live, and which lives in and through us. The weakness and ineffectiveness of the counterideologies to which many give lip service, and which some believe in very deeply, results from the fact that while they abstractly theorize that "another world is possible," their adherents at the same time proclaim and legislate through their everyday lives, through their immersion in the dominant social ethos, that "this world is inevitable."

The third sphere of social determination is the realm of the social imaginary. This is the sphere of the community's collective fantasy life. It is the realm of the "fundamental fantasy," a self-image that is much more highly invested with psychical energy than any mere "self-concept" and is a central determinant in the life of each person. The social imaginary includes socially conditioned images of self, other, society, and nature. It encompasses the images of power, success, heroism, and personal gratification expressed in the prevailing myths and paradigmatic narratives of the community and culture. The study of the social imaginary explores the social dimensions of desire and demand. Because social imaginary significations are so intimately related to our quest for meaning and, in the contemporary world, for self-justification, they are invested with intense levels of psychical energy. Much as in the case of the social ethos, this sphere has been generally neglected not only in mainstream social theory but also in most leftist and radical social thought.

Finally, the fourth sphere of social determination is the realm of social ideology. A social ideology can mean simply a system of ideas that is socially significant and contains a greater or lesser degree of truth and value to the society. However, in the critical sense, an ideology is a system of ideas that purports to be an objective depiction of reality but, in fact, constitutes a systematic distortion of reality on behalf of some particularistic interest or some system of differential power. Though we might be tempted to say that we aspire to replace the dominant institutional structure, social imaginary, social ethos, and social ideology with new liberatory ones, in the case of ideology it would be better to say that we aim to replace all social ideology with a form of ecological and communitarian reason. In this way, we will restore the common *logos*, the logic of the commons.

What is important for liberatory social transformation is an understanding of the ways in which the spheres of social determination interact dialectically to create a social world. Among the major goals of the project of a dialectical social ecology are the following: to theorize adequately, and in a historically and empirically grounded manner, the spheres of social determination as spheres of dialectical mutual determination; to explore the ways in which the interaction between these spheres of social determination shapes the nature of the social whole; to explain the ways in which many elements of these spheres also contradict and subvert one another, and thus to point the way toward possibilities beyond the existing social world; and to demonstrate the relation between the modes of functioning and the dynamic movement and transformation of these spheres and the social ecological crisis of humanity and the Earth.

## Is This the End?

Let us conclude by going back to the beginning. This means "the beginning" in the sense of origins. But it also means the process of "beginning" by returning to the most elementary, simplest, most obvious, and most essential truths. These are the kind of truths that can often be recognized only by those with "beginner's mind." If only we could all become, in the deepest sense, "masters of the obvious"!

If we hope to engage in authentic ecological thinking, which implies that we engage at the same time in transformative ecological practice, it is essential that we ask the question: What are the deep, fundamental causes of ecological degradation and impending ecological collapse (the causes of suffering, and the systemic causes of these causes)? We often have much less difficulty focusing on the obvious when we examine distant historical epochs. If we look back at the social and ecological destruction at the beginning of civilization, the role of Empire is quite obvious. The imperial system, given both its ultimate ends (the amassing of imperial power and the imposition of a hierarchical system of values glorifying this power) and its adoption of means that were eminently suitable for those ends, was both a human and an ecological catastrophe. The ancient empires initiated massive wars of conquest, enslavement of populations, and rituals of large-scale human sacrifice, while at the same time devastating the natural world, causing the first anthropogenic ecological collapses and widespread desertification.[27] However, it is more difficult for people today to recognize the role of Empire in global social and ecological crisis, even as the cost of denial and disavowal become so much greater. As we now approach the death of Empire, we are confronted with the question of what it will take with it, as it finally succumbs to its fatal condition. We now know the etiology of the disease and have a good idea of the prognosis. We have certainly been given enough hints concerning the nature of the cure. Yet, even if we can follow the diagnosis this far, we usually remain at an impasse in one area: the initiation of treatment.

So we need to return to the question of the determinants of our crisis today. If "four spheres" is too abstract, we might look at the more specific content of these spheres: concentrated economic power that becomes socially and ideologically dominant; a system of values based not on intrinsic and systemic good but on the constraints of profit maximization and capital accumulation; the continuing power of an even more primordial system of patriarchal values rooted in aggressiveness, conquest, and domination; a system of mass marketing and manipulation of conscious-ness that gains increasing power to shape selfhood and character-struc-ture; a centralized nation-state that negates any authentic, participatory democracy; state and corporate bureaucracies that impose an instrumen-tal, manipulative rationality; a culture of commodity-worship that traps people in an alienated world of privatized consumption; forms of nature-denying anti-spirituality in the form of fundamentalist religion; a system of technology that becomes a de facto self-moving and autonomous mega-machine; a voraciously appropriating egoic self that is the condensation of all these social realities.

We need to admit to ourselves that the ecological crisis will not be resolved, and global ecological catastrophe will not be avoided, without imminent, far-reaching, and fundamental changes in the dominant insti-tutions, ethos, ideology and imaginary. Ecological destructiveness is built into the hegemonic structures, operating procedures, and decision-making processes. We need to allow the realization of this fact to penetrate deeply into our being, particularly as we open ourselves up to the deep experi-ence of the tragedies and losses that the system of domination inflicts on humanity and nature. This is called learning solidarity with humanity and nature. We need to allow ourselves to go through the trauma of disillu-sionment with the dominant system and the dominant reality, so that this can lead to a radical break with that reality. As sages in the great wisdom traditions and guides in traditional vision quests have rightly taught, we need to go through the agony of the Dark Night of the Soul, so that so that we can emerge from its depths as another kind of being. We can emerge as a fully awakened and caring kind of being.

In practical terms, the reversal of the disastrous, ecocidal course of history will require a radical devolution of power through the democ-ratizing of political, economic, and informational systems. It will also require a radical transformation of values (a deep, world-historical cultural revolution) that encompasses a rejection of economistic values, consumer culture, patriarchal values, and the egocentric self. In short, it will require a radical break with the political institutions, the economic institutions, the technological system, the means of communication, the ideology, the imaginary and symbolic expressions, the cultural values, and the forms of selfhood that are now dominant.[28]

To put it differently, it will require the creation of a material, spiritual and practical basis for the liberatory, transformative vision presented by the axial philosophies and religions that emerged two and a half millennia ago and that, in turn, looked back to the sane, humane and ecologically sound aspects of the indigenous communities that existed over the vast majority of human history.[29] We need to seek the rational core of what ancient societies expressed poetically in such concepts as the Garden of Eden, the Golden Age, and the Dynasty of the Yellow Emperor, that is, the image of a free, cooperative, and ecologically attuned world that existed before the rise of systems of social domination. We need to be able to express this idea of reason and attunement in nature (called the Logos, the Dharma, or the Dao) in a way that is meaningful for our own age.

We will then be able to face the difficult and demanding truth that we are nearing the end of that world-historical Fall we call civilization. The question is whether we can emerge from an age of nihilism and resignation and give birth to a new era of creative and regenerative action. We must ask whether there is still hope that the historic Fall and all the suffering that it has entailed can be redeemed, a hope expressed classically in the Latin exclamation *"felix culpa!"* or *"blessed fall!"* The question is whether it is an ultimate Fall into the abyss of planetary death and devastation, or a provisional Fall that culminates in a rebirth, in a "true resurrection of humanity-in-nature." Through such a rebirth, we would learn again to celebrate ourselves, our communities, the Earth, and the entire cosmos as *Natura naturata* and *Natura naturans*, as wonders of creation and creativity.

## NOTES

1    This would focus quite logically on the fact that the current "new era of death" follows an era called the "Cenozoic," meaning the "new era of life" (literally, of "animals"). The current era is a radical break with the Cenozoic but is continuous with developments in the brief epoch called the "Holocene" (its meaning is the rather noncontroversial concept of "entirely recent").

2    Johan Rockström et al., "A Safe Operating Space for Humanity," *Nature* 461 (September 2009): 472–75; Johan Rockström et al., "Planetary Boundaries: Exploring the Safe Operating Space for Humanity," *Ecology and Society* 14, no. 2 (2009), https://www.ecologyandsociety.org/vol14/iss2/art32/; and a recent update, Will Steffen et al., "Planetary Boundaries: Guiding Human Development on a Changing Planet," *Science* 347, no. 6223 (February 13, 2015): 736–47; http://science.sciencemag.org/content/347/6223/1259855, in which there is a new focus on five planetary boundaries that have "strong regional operating scales." The delineation of areas in which boundaries are located was also revised slightly.

3    Rockström et al., "Exploring the Safe Operating Space."

4    Steffen et al., "Guiding Human Development."

5    Peter Forbes, "We Are Heading for a New Cretaceous, Not for a New Normal," *Aeon*, October 29, 2018, https://aeon.co/ideas/we-are-heading-for-a-new-cretaceous-not-for-a-new-normal?utm_source=Aeon+Newsletter&utm_campaign=3d7448ad70-EMAIL_CAMPAIGN_2018_10_29_12_28&utm_medium=email&utm_term=0_411a82e59d-3d7448ad70-68704457

6    John R. Schramskia, David K. Gattiea, and James H. Brow, "Human Domination of the Biosphere: Rapid Discharge of the Earth-Space Battery Foretells the Future of Humankind," *Proceedings of the National Academy of Sciences* 112, no. 31 (August 4, 2015): 9,511–17, https://www.pnas.org/content/112/31/9511.

7    To adapt Joseph Déjacques's anarcho-utopian term for the purposes of this discussion.

8    This is a classic question in modern philosophy and social theory. As used here, "technique" includes not only technologies, tools, and machines but also technological systems and institutions, the technological imaginary, techno-logical ideology, technological rationality, and techniques as elements of ethos or habitus, that is, as personal and collective practice.

9    There were important predecessors in the nineteenth and early twentieth cen-turies, but there was a qualitative leap with Lewis Mumford's publication of *Technics and Civilization* (New York: Harcourt, Brace & World, 1934). This was followed by a proliferation of radical critique of technology at the end of World War II and in the postwar period, in large part in reaction to that war, to the totalitarian systems that emerged in the period, and to the dawning of the Nuclear Age and the specter of global annihilation.

10   For example, the profound and extensive work of Bernard Stiegler, whose cri-tique is unusual in addressing diverse dimensions of the institutional, ideo-logical, imaginary and ethotic spheres of social determination. See his series of works *Technics and Time* (3 vols.), *Symbolic Misery* (2 vols.), and *Disbelief and Discredit* (3 vols.).

11   See Jacques Ellul, *The Technological Society* (New York: Vintage Books, 1964); Herbert Marcuse, *One-Dimensional Man* (Boston: Beacon Press, 1964); and Lewis Mumford, *The Myth of the Machine*, vol. 1, *Technics and Human Development* (New York: Harcourt, Brace, Jovanovich, 1967), and vol. 2, *The Pentagon of Power* (New York: Harcourt, Brace, Jovanovich, 1970). See also David Watson, *Against the Megamachine* (Brooklyn: Autonomedia, 1998).

12   I use "postmodern" in a very specific sense. I would argue that our historical period (at least until very recently) is best labeled "late modernity," rather than "postmodernity," since most of the phenomena that are usually associated with the postmodern were always at the core of modernity and were in a process of working themselves out within modernity. We can with a certain justice claim either that as moderns "we have always been postmodern" or that "we have never been postmodern," depending on how we look at the relationship between contending tendencies within modernity. The later formulation (which I adopt) is, however, the more dialectical one, if one considers the broad sweep of modernity and its degree of unity-in-difference. However, there is evidence that the recent development of information technologies and biotechnologies has opened up the possibilities for a truly radical break with modernity as a whole, including the traditional countercurrents within the modern. Granted, the system of domination still faces serious problems of global "underdevelopment"

and resistance (fetters on technological "progress") that will for some time remain intractable and perhaps even be aggravated by global crisis tendencies. The most probable response, in the absence of the needed revolutionary turn in world history, will be the further proliferation of technocratic fascist regimes, with growing hegemony of the most technologically rational of these regimes. This is the irony of history. In the absence of revolution, China will bury us.

13  I hope to accomplish some of this work in a forthcoming book that will focus on the development of a comprehensive dialectical social ecology.

14  Yuval Noah Harari, "Why Technology Favors Tyranny" *The Atlantic*, October 2018, https://www.theatlantic.com/magazine/archive/2018/10/yuval-noah-harari-technology-tyranny/568330/. This brief article usefully summarizes material from Harari's *21 Lessons for the 21st Century* (New York: Spiegel and Grau, 2018).

15  In "The Work of Art in the Age of Mechanical Reproduction" (1936) in Walter Benjamin, *Illuminations* (New York: Schocken Books, 1969), 233. In fact, orchids are a very diverse and widespread plant family, but they are also the plant family most threatened with species extinction.

16  It can be argued that the closest approximation of "immediacy" in human experience is found in what has been called the "pure consciousness" of thusness, *tathata*, and of non-dual wholeness, *sunyata*. To the extent that this demediating consciousness exists, it is also extinguished by the spread of technical rationality.

17  Damian Carrington, "Earth's Sixth Mass Extinction Event Under Way, Scientists Warn," *Guardian*, July 10, 2017, https://www.theguardian.com/environment/2017/jul/10/earths-sixth-mass-extinction-event-already-underway-scientists-warn.

18  Ecofeminist theorist Vandana Shiva, who has contributed much to this quest, states at the beginning of her analysis of "Earth Democracy" that it "connects the particular to the universal, the diverse to the common, and the local to the global." Shiva, *Earth Democracy: Justice, Sustainability, and Peace* (Cambridge, MA: South End Press, 2005), 1.

19  The most advanced form is materialist ecofeminism, which situates the ethical most explicitly in real-world practice and everyday life. It shows that the most significant sphere of ethical practice today, and our model in many ways for social-ecological transformation, remains the caring labor of women and indigenous people around the world. See Ariel Salleh, *Ecofeminism as Politics: Nature, Marx, and the Postmodern* (London: Zed Books, 2017).

20  "Truth" should not be taken in the sense of "object of belief," but rather in the sense of a "truth-process" that encompasses both understanding and engagement.

21  By "suffering" is meant damage to the good of a being and interference with the flourishing of that being. Suffering is manifested in all dimensions of a being's existence. The ancient teaching pointed out that the subjective manifestation of suffering is a feeling of pervasive dissatisfaction with the world. Accordingly, the Earth's objective suffering is manifested subjectively (within the Earth's self-conscious dimensions or "organs of consciousness") through an ethos of anxiety and depression and through a nihilistic sensibility and ideology.

22  See, for example, Jason W. Moore, "The Myth of the 'Human Enterprise': The Anthropos and Capitalogenic Change," *World-Ecological Imaginations: Power and*

     *Production in the Web of Life*, October 30, 2016, https://jasonwmoore.wordpress.com/2016/10/30/the-myth-of-the-human-enterprise-the-anthropos-and-capitalogenic-change/.

23    From the Greek *idiōtēs*, a private person.

24    See John P. Clark, *The Impossible Community: Realizing Communitarian Anarchism* (New York: Bloomberg Academic, 2013). The conceptualization of "four spheres" of social determination seems the most useful theoretically. Yet there are, of course, valid alternative conceptualizations of a social topology of such spheres. The social imaginary as discussed here encompasses the Lacanian imaginary and symbolic orders (or "registers"). Some theoretical advantages would be gained and some lost by dividing the sphere of the social imaginary into two spheres in a Lacanian manner. Furthermore, there are, of course, other useful social topologies, such as a topology of fields, that are not discussed here, but which may further deepen and enrich the analysis.

25    The social ethos is the realm of "culture" and "habitus," but the question of social ethos should also lead us to think about the education of the feelings and the paideia of sensibilities.

26    In the sense that the ontological is thought of as a sphere of the metaphysical.

27    This story is summarized concisely in Clive Ponting, "Destruction and Survival," in *A New Green History of the World: The Environment and the Collapse of Great Civilizations* (New York: Penguin Books, 2007), 67–86, though perhaps no one has summarized it more succinctly than the anarchist Romantic poet Percy Bysshe Shelley in his poem "Ozymandias."

28    As subsequent chapters will show, we find powerful evidence of progress in this direction in the Zapatista communities in Chiapas, in the Democratic Autonomy movement in Rojava, and in indigenous movements in Bolivia and elsewhere.

29    Even if we trace "human history" back only to the advanced artwork of the Chauvet-Pont-d'Arc Cave, dated to as early as about 35,000 years ago.

2

# How an Anarchist Discovered the Earth

## Reclus Discovers the Earth

The Earth was discovered by a French anarchist geographer, philosopher, and revolutionary named Elisée Reclus. Unfortunately, it is impossible to assign a precise time and place to this discovery, though we know that it took place in the nineteenth century and that it occurred on the very planet in question.

Admittedly, it must seem like a rather extreme case of hyperbole to say that Reclus "discovered the Earth." But it is, in fact, merely the literal truth. Most human beings throughout the history of civilization have, to the degree that they have been integrated into the dominant ethos, lived on the Earth without having an everyday, moment-to-moment consciousness of its reality or of the depth of their relationship to it. We are conditioned, as civilized people, as political subjects, and as mass consumers, to allow the Earth to remain largely undiscovered. It is hardly by coincidence that the founding philosophy of Western Civilization, Platonism, was based on an explicit denial of the reality of the Earth. Yet Platonism only expressed in ideal form what emerging Empire was decreeing in the sphere of material reality. The civilized mind is always occupied, and it is occupied with things other than the Earth. For a long time, the civilized thought that they were *discovering* things like New Worlds, spices, and slaves. In reality, they were only *covering* more and more of the Earth.

Reclus discovered the Earth in the strong sense of having both an ongoing, participatory Earth-consciousness and a deep and expansive geohistorical knowledge of the Earth. He discovered the way in which our place on it and within it conditions all our experience. He discovered that *our* way is on the deepest level *its* way. Reclus's life work as a geological

and ecological educator and revolutionary was to bring others to an awareness of the *logos* of Gaea and the *logos* of the *oikos*. The goal of geological
and ecological education, and, coincidentally, the goal of authentic social
revolution, is to create a world in which each person goes through a similar
process of discovering the Earth, and in which each lives life in the light
of this discovery process.[1]

Such discovery is less the experience of encountering what is distant
than the experience of uncovering what is present. Or, more accurately, it
is the process of allowing what is present to reveal itself. It is the hard work
of letting-be. To begin with, discovery of the Earth requires the arduous
task of removing deep layers of ideology. But even more dauntingly, it
requires the demolition of thick layers of the imaginary that obscure the
thing in itself, which is ultimately also the thing in ourselves. The history
of civilization has been a "covery" process: the depositing of the ideological, imaginary, and ethotic layers that, along with their material corelates,
cover over the Earth. The discovery process reveals, beneath these layers,
the Earth awakening to the Earth, becoming aware of its own processes of
unfolding and emergence. Reclus's social geography merely formulated
on a scientific and theoretical level what was unfolding on the social level,
though it was doing so only very gradually, according to human standards
of temporality.

Reclus's discovery of the Earth is inseparable from his simultaneous
discovery of anarchism. Again, it seems strange to claim that Reclus "discovered" anarchism, since it had already been around in an explicit form
for some time before he adopted the term. However, the claim here is not
that he "invented" anarchism but that he "discovered" it. He brought to
light what in anarchism had been left implicit and hidden. It is hardly
a coincidence that it was a geographer who was the first to formulate a
vision of anarchism that was *global*, in more than one sense. The first sense
of this globality is that of a comprehensive global critique, as opposed to
a fragmentary one. Reclus was the first thinker to theorize *anarché* as a
many-sided critique of class domination, patriarchal domination, state
domination, bureaucratic domination, technological domination, racial
and ethnic domination, domination of nonhuman species, and domination of nature.

The second sense of globality refers to the fact that Reclus was the
first thinker to incorporate such a critique into a comprehensive, global
account of the Earth Story as a struggle between freedom and domination.

In this account, "freedom" signifies the quest for self-realization not only by humanity but by all terrestrial beings and by the living Earth itself. Reclus's project is to disclose the underlying logic of geohistory as the development and fuller realization of planetary unity in diversity, and as a process in which humanity progressively assumes its role as an aspect of the self-consciousness of the Earth. His work is aimed at helping make explicit humanity's role as (in the words with which Reclus begins page one of volume one of *L'Homme et la Terre*) "nature becoming self-conscious."[2]

## The Law According to Reclus

One of the most widely cited concepts in Reclus's social geography is his idea that there are "Three Laws" whose operation spans the course of geohistory. In the preface to *L'Homme et la Terre* (*Humanity and the Earth*), he discusses "three orders of facts that are revealed to us through the study of social geography, and which remain so constant amidst the chaos of things that one might well label them 'laws.'"[3] He identifies these lawlike phenomena as "the class struggle, the quest for equilibrium and the sovereign decision of the individual."[4]

Though these "laws" are almost inevitably mentioned by commentators, their precise meaning and significance are not often analyzed. However, they denote tendencies that are quite central to Reclus version of geohistory. They are, of course, laws that are not laws. Calling them "laws" is a challenge to the dominant conception of "law," as meaning either a body of dictates imposed by the state through force and coercion or a system of observed regularities in nature that have no normative implications. Reclus's "laws," on the other hand, relate to the sources of meaning and value both in human society and in the encompassing natural world in which humanity is included.

The first law, that of "class struggle" focuses on the human struggle for freedom as the quest for universal flourishing and the realization of our highest potentialities, and the concomitant struggle against all forms of domination as constraints on that flourishing and realization.[5] If we abandon any false human/nature dualism, we see that this social struggle is continuous with processes found throughout the natural world. It is part of the vast evolutionary processes of the unfolding of life and consciousness on Earth. "Natural" barriers to biological evolution are succeeded by social barriers to both natural and social evolution that are created by the system of domination. As we follow the story of freedom and domination through the six volumes of *L'Homme et la Terre*, we discover that although the struggle between the economic classes of property owners and exploited workers has a certain priority, "class struggle" also encompasses other historical conflicts, such as the struggle between those with hierarchical political power and those who are subject to it, and the struggle between those with patriarchal power and those who are oppressed by it. The class struggle includes all struggle between those dominant groups who act on behalf of the system of domination and those subordinate groups who are dominated by it.

The "quest for equilibrium" must be looked upon as the dialectical correlate of the impulse toward change and development expressed in the idea of struggle. The system of domination constantly produces disequilibrium through the imposition of constraints on the satisfaction of needs, and barriers to the optimal self-development and self-realization of beings subjected to its rule. Yet it also constantly seeks, with various degrees of temporary success, to contain such contradictions and bring an inherently unstable and self-destructive system into balance through certain steering mechanisms. At the same time, the forces of evolutionary and revolutionary progress seek to bring the larger system of human and ecological community into greater dynamic balance. They do this by working to end the destructive disequilibrium caused by domination, through the satisfaction of needs and the facilitation of healthy growth and development of all life forms and the biosphere as a whole. This goal can only be achieved through the creation of a new liberated society based on a culture of mutual aid and solidarity that will succeed the present one founded on competition and conquest.

The dialectic between these first two laws aims at an ideal envisioned since the time of ancient thinkers such as Heraclitus and Laozi: the realization of an ordered anarchy, a dynamic equilibrium, a discordant harmony, a precarious and productive balance of cosmos and chaos. It should also be noted that social evolution requires not only a dynamic equilibrium but also a kind of "punctuated equilibrium." There are moments in which cumulative social evolution can only continue through a qualitative advance in which major barriers to progressive change are quickly surmounted and more gradual social evolution can then continue. Such moments are called "revolutions."

We come then to the third "law." It might seem contradictory for a communitarian, indeed, a *communist* anarchist thinker, to stress so heavily the "sovereign decision" of each person. Yet this focus follows logically from Reclus's espousal of what has been called "communal individuality," which might better be described as the attainment of universal particularity and universal singularity. It is, Reclus says, "the human person, the primary element of society" that is the source of "the creative will that constructs and reconstructs the world."[6] It is out of this creative will (the negation of the will to dominate) that all forms of voluntary association and free cooperation arise. Reclus's idea of the human person is the conception of a thoroughly social and communal being. However, this communal person is also a free and, to borrow Kantian terminology, a "self-legislating" being who is capable, in concert with others, of challenging and then destroying an alienated and mechanized social order.

Reclus's concept of the free person in community with others parallels the idea in Buddhist philosophy that although there is "no separate selfhood," nevertheless one must "work out one's own salvation with mindful care."[7] In both visions of communal personhood or individuality, we cannot achieve this goal as mere individuals, without the help of the community. For Buddhism this collectivity is called the "sangha," the compassionate community. For Reclus, it includes what he calls "*small, loving, and intelligent associations*,"[8] or affinity groups, that initiate change, and also the primary communities and mutualistic, cooperative federations of these communities in which social being ultimately comes to fruition.

The message of Reclus is that there is a great world-historical struggle between planetary domination and the freedom of humanity and the Earth to flourish and realize themselves. Furthermore, in the midst of this struggle, we as "human persons," and as agents of humanity and the Earth, have the ability to determine the outcome of that struggle. We can choose to succumb to the machinery of domination, or we can decide, joining together in solidarity with others, to act as nature becoming self-conscious and self-creative. This is the Reclusian vision of liberty, equality, and community.

## Writing the Earth Story

According to Reclus, "Geography is nothing other than History in Space, just as History is nothing but Geography in Time."[9] In this dialectical formulation, Reclus affirms the nonduality of moving, developing, spatiotemporal reality. What he called "Universal Geography" and "World History" are for him dimensions of one geohistory, a single Earth Story. Through the project of writing this story, he became the unfounding founder of anarchist geography. He shows that all geography, like writing in general, must always reflect either an anarchic or an archic perspective. It will always be either an expression of the quest for freedom, an apology for the system of domination, or a self-contradictory mixture of these two standpoints. It is true, as Lévi-Strauss proclaimed, that "the primary function of *writing*, as a means of communication, is to facilitate the enslavement of other human beings,"[10] and geography has suffered from being one dimension of this larger archography of domination. Fortunately, writing has had other, nonprimary, functions. Graphism is never innocent, but it can make amends.

Thus, the idea of the so-called grand narrative or *grand récit* (alias "metanarrative," with its undertones of "metaphysics") has been widely questioned and widely rejected because of its very grandiosity, and its seemingly irredeemable implication in the system of domination. Typically, the grand narrators have deceptively and ideologically projected their own and their own cultures' particularistic biases into a purportedly universal story. The demolition of such pretensions is well deserved. When we are dealing with structures of domination, it is certainly wise to move in a destructuralizing direction. Yet there are also distinctive, albeit dynamic and self-transforming, *structures* and *forms* of liberation. These also always need to be questioned ruthlessly, but they will not dissolve entirely under even the most caustic critique. Thus, the idea of grand narrative need not be rejected reactively, but should rather be negated, preserved, and transcended (*aufgehoben*). This is precisely what Reclus undertakes in his major works.

Reclus recounts the Earth Story implicitly throughout his 17,000-page *Nouvelle Géographie Universelle* (*New Universal Geography*) and other works, and quite explicitly in his 3,500-page *L'Homme et la Terre*. He challenges the dominant ideological myth of the grand narrative of domination, of transcendent "Man's" conquest of nature, and civilized "Man's" conquest of the world. Yet he does not reject the idea of grand narrative entirely, but rather incorporates and surpasses it dialectically in another kind of narrative that is at once great and small. He certainly engages in what we might call "Big Geohistory" through his creation of an anarchistic and anti-ideological narrative. This great and small narrative shows that to be true to the phenomena, the facts of geohistory, analysis and critique must be at once macro, meso, and micro. It must address the universal, the particular, and the singular at the same time. Reclus's Earth Story is founded not on a unitary or identitarian discourse, but rather on a discourse of unity in diversity; not on a universalistic discourse, but rather on a discourse of universal particularity and universal singularity.

Such an anarchistic and dialectical narrative performs an indispensable function in this postist age, as a reminder that we must not ignore or dismiss the moment of universality in geohistory. Our place in geohistory is hardly "post," or beyond, the global struggle between freedom and domination, and the moments of both universality of struggle and also universality of liberation are very much alive. Yet the moments of particularity and singularity (of struggle, of liberation, and of ways of knowing) are no less alive. The Earth is, in one sense, the universalistic whole, but it is in another sense the very ground beneath our feet, in this place, here and now.

If our geography is to be a form of anarchography, it must be at once the writing of the universal, the writing of the particular, and the writing of the singular. They all must write and be written together. We will never find the universal anywhere other than in the particular and the singular. This is the message of Zen poetry, which is anarchographic in its insistence on the numinous qualities of singularity, thusness, *tathata*. For Zen (the paying-attention school), the Universe Story is the story of a frog jumping into a pond. The Earth Story is the story of grass growing, all by itself. This message is also conveyed powerfully, if less concisely, by Reclus's works, ranging from the enormous *Universal Geography* to the small *History of a Stream*. This is the radical dialectic in which extremes are never reconciled in some sort of pacified, harmonious "synthesis," but in which, rather, the extremes retain all their extremity. Unity is achieved precisely through an affirmation of extreme diversity. Universality is achieved precisely through an affirmation of extreme singularity.

## The Birth of Geo-ontology[11]

Reclus explored not only the geographical but also the epistemological, historical, political, moral, phenomenological, and, on the deepest level, ontological, dimensions of the process of discovery of the Earth, in addition to the interaction between these various dimensions. We find that if we participate in this process at all of these levels, we not only discover the Earth *in itself*, but we also discover the Earth *in ourselves*, and we increasingly become the Earth *for itself*.

Western philosophy has always, if only implicitly, taken knowledge and reflection to be at their core an expression of what Aristotle defined as the Divine: *Thought Thinking Thought*. Reclus's epistemological and onto-logical break brings knowledge and reflection down to Earth. Knowing and reflecting are, above all, forms of "Earth Thinking Earth." The French geog-rapher Yves Lacoste, at the beginning of the Reclus revival of a few decades ago, concluded that Reclus's work is "a crucial epistemological moment" and indeed "an epistemological turning point," not only in "social and political geography" but in "geography in general."[12] In fact, Reclus's work constitutes not only an "epistemological turning point" but also an onto-logical one.

Reclus made crucial advances in social ontology by challenging con-ventional ideas about the kind of social beings that we humans are. To reveal human beings as the self-consciousness of nature and the self-consciousness of the Earth—we might even say, as a mode of self-disclo-sure of the Earth—implies the need for modes of knowing and acting that are in accord with this mode of being. Reclus's phrase, "L'Homme est la Nature prenant conscience d'elle-même," means literally that "Humanity is Nature taking consciousness of itself." In this statement, the emphasis is on the larger whole of which we humans are a part. It is "Nature," and more specifically the Earth, that "gains" or "takes" ("*prend*") consciousness of itself (in French, "herself"), through us.

Humans thus become planetary or terrestrial beings in a much deeper sense than they are in conventional ideas of globalization. This becoming-planetary implies a kind of "peace with the planet" through an ecological solidarity that is, on the deepest level, an ontological solidarity. Geohistorically, it implies an end to Empire, which has waged a millen-nia-long war with the planet. The ontological rejection of the human-nature dualism implies an ethical/ethotic (that is, relating to both morality and practice) rejection of the idea that human activity is fundamentally a process of appropriation. Reclus's conception of Humanity (*l'Homme*) rejects the conventional wisdom of civilization in which the drive for "dominion" over the Earth, and over those supposedly backward peoples who still remain rooted in Earth-oriented cultures, is inherent in our being-human, or in the delusive being-fully-human of being-civilized.

In Reclus's beautiful work of nature writing, *Histoire d'un Ruisseau* (*History of a Stream*), he observes that "the history of a stream, even the smallest one that emerges from the mossy earth and disappears again into it, is the history of infinity."[13] For Reclus, we are all such streams. To say this is to recognize the dialectical relationship between the singular, the particular, and the universal. The singular, in its very singularity, and the particular, in its very particularity, lead us into the universal (which was always already present within them). In order to understand the singular terrestrial phenomenon in the most concrete and specific manner, it is necessary to understand its origins and history, to understand that which it was, to understand its mode of determination, to understand its relations to that with which it coexists, and which codetermines its nature, to understand that which it is not, and to understand its course of unfolding, or evolution, its tendency toward that which it will become. Understanding each, and all, of these dimensions leads us into the concrete universality of the complex geographical and geohistorical whole, a whole that is an open, evolving, and always-becoming-whole.

This non-reifying, dialectical, process view of reality is exemplified in Reclus's analysis of social and geographical phenomena. For example, he describes the all-pervasive and unceasing water cycle that streams through the entire biosphere in the form of rivers, water vapor, clouds, rain, snow, sleet, hail, seas, oceans, lakes, ponds, moisture in the soil and in rock fissures, and which flows through underground caverns, accumulates in aquifers, and bursts forth in springs. He says that this "great circuit" is "the image of all life" and "the symbol of true immortality."[14] Similarly, he describes the physiology of the human body and concludes that, despite our skeletal structure, we are above all "nothing other than a liquid mass, a river in which innumerable molecules flow . . . coming from every region of the earth and space, and resuming their infinite voyage after a short passage within our organism."[15]

Reclus expresses here the radical view, rooted in modern science yet harking back to ancient wisdom traditions, that we are fundamentally geological and cosmological beings. We are *a way* in which Gaea and Cosmos act, *an expressive flow*. We are in our very mode of being a form of geographism and cosmographism, a form of cursivity. Cursivity is, linguistically, "imperfective." It describes a flow that is never completed, that continues to flow, that always flows beyond itself. As this was anciently expressed, "Dao in the world may be compared to rivers and streams running into the sea."[16]

As part of his radically dialectical and anti-essentializing project, Reclus challenges the fundamental ontological delusion of the self-identity of beings, in which the mind turns a useful fiction into a metaphysical dogma. "Much like a stream that rushes off, we change in each instant, our life is renewed from minute to minute, and though we may believe that we remain the same, this is only an illusion created by the mind."[17] In reality, things do not possess a self-contained, atomistic identity. Rather their very being is a process of becoming. As Reclus, echoing Heraclitus, remarks, "Not only a person considered in isolation, but society as whole can be compared to flowing water."[18] This image expresses the idea that the unity of any particular being is only a relative unity, a unity in difference, not a discrete identity.

This does not conflict with the fact that there is within nature a tendency toward the realization of a larger unity, a becoming-one of the many that always still remain many. Reclus describes the evolution of humanity as such a kind of directional flow, in fact, a flow of flows, since each being is a flow, in which "peoples merge together like rivers merge with other rivers," so that "sooner or later they all constitute one single nation, just as all the waters within the same basin end up combining into a single river."[19] More literally expressed, this means that our destiny is to become global, planetary, and thus geological beings. We are the logicians of Gaea. We express the *logos* of Gaea, both through our being, and through our graphism.

## Nature Becomes Self-Conscious

One of the most important and widely quoted concepts in Reclus's social philosophy and geography is the idea that there is a process of growing globalization or planetization in which humanity progressively realizes its (non-)identity as "Nature becoming self-conscious." If this conception of planetization were limited to the emergence of a common consciousness, it would constitute an abstractly idealist position. At best, Reclus might deserve the dubious distinction of being a founding figure in New Age thought. But, in fact, he describes it as much more than this. He notes that while "for a long time we were nothing more than [the Earth's] unconscious products, we have become increasingly active agents in its history."[20] The important point is that at the same time that we become conscious of our role as the consciousness of the Earth (or, perhaps we should say, a very important aspect of the Earth's consciousness), we also become an increasingly powerful expression of the agency of the Earth. The Earth not only *thinks* through us but also *acts* through us, at times in a revolutionary manner.

Planetization has for Reclus both material and moral implications. He states that "the essence of human progress consists of the discovery of the totality of interests and wills common to all peoples; it is identical to solidarity."[21] As the majority of human beings globally become aware of their common interests and develop the common will to act on behalf of those interests, the possibility for global social revolution emerges. To state this differently, "Nature becoming self-conscious" assumes the role of the Revolutionary Subject. However, Reclus extends this concept far beyond humanity when he recognizes that we must "become fully conscious of our human solidarity, forming one body with the planet itself," and "promote each individual plant, animal, and human life."[22] Ultimately, from Reclus's geocentric perspective we come to recognize that the quest for freedom encompasses not only the flourishing of humanity but the flourishing of the Earth as a whole. It is the flourishing not merely of *humanity and nature* but of *humanity-in-nature*. The culmination of nature becoming self-conscious is social-ecological transformation, global revolution on behalf of planetary evolution.

There are numerous passages in Reclus in which he addresses various aspects of this developing globalization or planetization of humanity. He contends that advances in transportation and communication make the global unity of humanity a more conscious reality. He notes that "industrial appliances, that by a single electric impulse make the same thought vibrate through far continents, have distanced by far our social morals," and that the movement of travelers between all countries has made us "citizens of the planet."[23] He speculates that communications systems are creating (as later thinkers such as Teilhard de Chardin were to echo) a planetary nervous system: "Thanks to a continuous network of postal and telegraphic services, [the planet] has been enriched by a nervous system for the interchange of thought."[24] He concludes that "despite the rancors fostered by war, despite hereditary hatreds, all [humanity] is becoming one."[25]

Ultimately, for Reclus, the process of globalization is much more than a social (or even a social, political, and economic) phenomenon. On the deepest level, it is a planetary evolutionary phenomenon that has biological, psychological, social, political, and ecological dimensions. Using an organic metaphor for the evolution of life on Earth, Reclus holds that there is "a general tendency of things to merge themselves into one living body in which all the parts are in reciprocal interdependence."[26] He contends that the direction of evolution is toward a realization of unity in diversity in which there is an interdependent flourishing of both the whole and of the parts that constitute it. Freed from the constraints of domination and exploitation, the whole "would constitute a harmonious cosmos in which each cell retains its individuality, corresponding to the free labor of each individual, and in which all would mesh together with one another, each one being necessary to the work of all."[27] It is within this general context that Reclus develops his conception of *l'entraide*, or mutual aid and social cooperation.[28]

Reclus was prophetic in seeing the possibility for a libertarian, egalitarian, and communitarian process of globalization from below. He offers us an alternative to the prevailing corporate and statist forms of globalized domination and exploitation. Rather than a globalization imposed from above by systems of centralized power, it is a globalization that is deeply rooted in the evolutionary processes of nature, including human nature, and has its basis in the integrity and flourishing of all beings. In place of a world divided into a powerful, wealthy, and hegemonic core or center, and a weak, poor, and dominated periphery, he envisions a world that will have "its center everywhere, its periphery nowhere."[29]

### The History of Freedom and Domination

Reclus's Earth Story depicts evolving human society as being in dialectical interaction with the rest of the natural world and as itself being an integral part of that world. The progress of human society is measured by the degree to which it can overcome the contradictions between humanity and the rest of nature created by the system of domination, and permit human self-realization to be incorporated within the larger flourishing of the whole of life on Earth. Reclus's Earth Story is a version of the perennial narrative of primordial unity, fall into alienation and separation, and a final reconciliation that is not a mere return or repetition, but rather a progression in which the fall itself becomes the condition for a greater realization.

According to Reclus, we begin as "the children of the 'beneficent mother,' like the trees of the forest and the reeds of the rivers. She it is from whom we derive our substance; she nourishes us with her mother's milk, she furnishes air to our lungs, and, in fact, supplies us with that wherein we live and move and have our being."[30] This primordial harmony is broken as forms of domination such as patriarchy, the state, and, later, capitalism arise. In his early essay "The Feeling for Nature," Reclus writes of a "secret harmony" that exists between the Earth and humanity, warning that when "reckless societies allow themselves to meddle with that which creates the beauty of their domain, they always end up regretting it."[31] He concludes that when humanity degrades and devastates the natural world, it necessarily degrades and devastates itself. He observes that "where the land has been defaced, where all poetry has disappeared from the countryside, the imagination is extinguished, the mind becomes impoverished, and routine and servility seize the soul, inclining it toward torpor and death."[32] Significantly, Reclus here connects the destruction of the poesis of nature, the creative powers of the Earth, with the loss of the poesis of humanity.[33]

This account is reminiscent of "geologian" Thomas Berry's view of the geography of the imagination. Berry contends that the human imagination is so rich and wonderful because it reflects the richness and wonders of the Earth that has given birth to and nurtured it. "If we lived on the moon, our minds would be as empty as the moon, our imagination would be as limited as the lunar landscape."[34] The corollary of this proposition is that the more we turn the terrestrial landscape into a kind of moonscape, the more we will degrade our imagination. The consequences of this degradation are also quite material. As Reclus states it, "the brutal violence with which most nations have treated the nourishing earth" has been "foremost among the causes that have vanquished so many successive civilizations."[35] Taken together with his thesis of the planetization of humanity, this is an implicit prediction of our present global ecological crisis and of the impending "vanquishing," or collapse, of global society. Such a result would signal the end of Empire, the society of global domination that initiated the process, but it would also constitute the reversal, for a long period in Earth history, of planetary processes of evolutionary development.

The other side of the Earth Story is the long and expansive history of the struggle for the liberation of the human and Earth community. This struggle is grounded, first, in the evolutionary achievements through which life itself is liberated through the realization of its capacity to develop and flourish. Within the larger creative planetary milieu, the specifically human form of life emerges and develops in large part through the community's ability to generate forms of mutual aid and solidarity that foster the simultaneous flourishing of the person and the group. Reclus emphasizes the central role of women in this process, beginning in so-called prehistory, for example, in the early horticultural societies of the Neolithic. He credits the matricentric and matrilineal practices that prevailed in this period and before, for producing "the first impulse to the future civilization" by uniting and socializing early humanity around the maternal hearth.[36]

In early horticultural societies, women's labor was the major source of food for the group, and the culture was focused heavily on cooperative, mutualistic, and nurturing maternal values. In such societies, Reclus contends, "the general prosperity depends absolutely on capable management by the mothers, and on the spirit of order, peace, and harmony that they introduce into the household."[37] He depicts the subsequent history of civilization as a story of both progress and regression, as material, moral, intellectual, and spiritual advances are accompanied by the dissolution of the ancient forms of mutual aid and solidarity, and the growing hegemony of ever more complex and powerful forms of social domination.

For Reclus, the problematic of social revolution and social regeneration is in many ways the task of regaining the moment of solidarity and communal being that existed in many early human societies and of finding a future path of development in which the technical and intellectual achievements of humanity are placed at the disposal of personal, communal, and planetary well-being.[38] Reclus's ideas on mutual aid and solidarity contributed significantly to a tradition, carried on today by ecofeminism, in which the most revolutionary politics is a politics of care based on a recognition of the needs of all sentient beings, in addition to those of all biotic communities. This tradition also extends to the field of geography. Thus, Simon Springer in *The Anarchist Roots of Geography* notes the recent "affective turn" toward a "caring geography" and points out the roots of the emergent geography of care in Reclus's works of a century and a half ago.[39]

### From the Commune to the Universal Republic

Reclus's history of the quest for freedom is an expansive one that takes him thousands of pages to outline. However, he singles out one chapter in this history that he sees as being of particular significance. He judges the establishment of the International Working Men's Association—the First International—to be one of the most crucial points in all of world history, because of its significance in the struggle between freedom and domination. This historical juncture can be looked upon as the founding moment of globalization from below, a globalization of freedom that was finally beginning to challenge the globalization of domination (the entire history of Empire). In *Evolution, Revolution, and the Anarchist Ideal*, Reclus calls it "the major event" in "that totality of both peaceful and violent transformations" called "social revolution."[40] He observes that this breakthrough had as its precondition the long history of human solidarity that existed "ever since people of different nations began practicing mutual aid, in complete friendship and for their common interests."[41]

This liberatory history generated a sphere of ethical substantiality, or grounded historical practice, that made the emergence of the International possible. Reclus says that the growing solidarity of human beings across the globe "acquired a theoretical existence when the philosophers of the eighteenth century inspired the French Revolution's proclamation of the 'rights of man.'"[42] However, the "future normative unity" that was then envisioned on the theoretical level began to be realized materially only "when the English, French, and German workers, forgetting their different origins and understanding one another despite their diversity of languages, joined together to form a single nation, in defiance of all their respective governments."[43] This step opened up the possibility for the real material and historical development of a form of anarchic, non-dominating solidarity that had institutional, ideological, imaginary, and ethotic dimensions.

We might, in fact, identify this historical step not only as the founding of the International but also as the almost simultaneous emergence of the International and the Commune,[44] for the constructive work of the International achieved its most concrete social embodiment in the Paris Commune. Reclus lauds the Commune for "establishing, not through its rulers, but through its defenders, an ideal for the future that was far superior to that of all the revolutions that preceded it."[45] Both in France and throughout the world, it enlisted in the struggle all those who would continue to carry it out, "fighting for a new society in which none would be masters thanks to their birth, title, or wealth, and none would be servants because of their origin, caste, or income."[46] Reclus contends that the term "Commune" was understood by these "defenders" in the expansive sense of "a new humanity made up of free and equal companions who know nothing of ancient borders and who peacefully practice mutual aid from one end of the world to the other."[47] It is this idea of the Commune that still lives on in Rojava, in Chiapas, in El Alto, and in other politically advanced regions of the world.

The International was, in fact, for Reclus a kind of "vanishing mediator" between the Commune and something else. In a kind of dialectical movement, it will disappear when it is realized, becoming Nothing at the point at which it becomes All. And the communards had a term for this "All." According to the *Official Journal of the Paris Commune*, "the flag of the Commune is that of the Universal Republic,"[48] and letters in the *Journal* sometimes concluded with the exclamation, "Vive la République Universelle! Vive la Commune!" These phrases, taken together, indicate that the Commune was the negation of the state in two senses. It was, on the level of particularity, through its practice of direct local power, the antithesis of all state domination. And it was, on the level of universality, through its participation in the global human community, the antithesis of all exclusive nationalism.

We might ask, almost a century and a half later, to what degree the world-historical promise of the Commune and the International, the Universal Republic, the Commune of Communes, has been realized. Where is global organization today? Centralized bureaucratic nation-states are organized into a United Nations Organization that represents the interests of these hierarchical entities, and it is dominated by the largest and most powerful of these states. In addition, there are powerful regional state organizations such as NATO and ASEAN. Correspondingly, the global corporate capitalist system, in alliance with the nation-state system, is organized globally through the World Bank, the International Monetary Fund, and the World Trade Organization, in addition to regional trade organizations in alliance with nation-states.

Yet, contrary to the hopeful vision of Reclus, the Universal Republic remains primarily a social ideological and social imaginary vision, with limited realization in the spheres of social institutional structure and social ethos. There are some significant global organizations outside the nation-state and corporate capitalist system, for example Via Campesina, which has several hundred million members. However, there is today no broad revolutionary organization equivalent to the First International that has carried on its work continuously and expanded the level of organization and participation over the past century and a half. If Reclus is right in looking upon the founding of the International as the major event in the history of freedom, the successful repression and co-optation of the historic tendency expressed in the International has been one of the major achievements in the history of domination.

## The Dialectical Geographer

I have often used the term "dialectical" to describe Reclus's thought. Furthermore, I argue at some length in *Anarchy, Geography, Modernity* that Reclus is a dialectical social geographer.[49] I do all of this even though he did not make use of the term "dialectic" or the technical language of dialectical philosophy and made no effort to place himself consciously within that tradition. His thought (perhaps fortunately) does not correspond to conventional ideas of dialectic. This should not, however, be surprising. Reclus did not learn dialectic from Hegel. He learned it from the Earth. So it might be useful to recapitulate briefly (and therefore inadequately) some of the ways in which his thought does, in fact, express a dialectical perspective.

*It is what it isn't.* Federico Ferretti notes that in 1882, Albert Delpit attributed Reclus's radically iconoclastic ideas and practice to the geographer's extensive traveling and his immersion in diverse geographical studies, which "had thrown him in a sort of psychopathological condition" that Delpit labeled "l'ivresse de la géographie."[50] Thus, according to this critic, Reclus was a product of "geography inebriation."[51] This unintentionally brilliant concept of Delpit ties in with the crucial theme of how disorientation and even traumatization are so often instrumental to the process of awakening—to other humans, to other living beings, to the Earth itself. Through such states, we sometimes discover that reality is quite different from, or even directly contrary to, our commonsense ideas of a stable, clearly defined world of self-contained things. At times, it is the process of culture shock that performs this function, but it is most effectively achieved through a combination of culture shock and nature shock. It is only through a kind of dialectical disorientation that one can reach the truth of relation, the truth of nonidentity, the truth of the negative, the truth of the ever-becoming whole that is the Earth. If the philosopher Spinoza has been called a "God-intoxicated man," Reclus can rightly be labeled an "Earth-intoxicated man."

*It is what it was.* Reclus adheres to the dialectical precept that a being contains within itself the entire history of that being and its interactions with other beings. Reclus states, for example, that "the history of the development of mankind has been written beforehand in sublime lettering on the plains, valleys, and coasts of our continents" and that "present-day society

46

contains within itself all past societies."[52] This concept is the "preservation" moment of the dialectical process of *Aufhebung* (or "sublation"), which is not mere "synthesis," but rather a simultaneous process of negation-preservation-transcendence. Reclus applies this concept to human nature and evolution, expressing a variation on the idea that ontogeny recapitulates phylogeny. In his formulation, "Man recollects in his structure everything that his ancestors lived through during the vast expanse of ages. He indeed epitomizes in himself all that preceded him in existence, just as, in his embryonic life, he presents successively various forms of organization that are simpler than his own."[53]

*The universal is concrete.* As has been mentioned in the discussion of Reclus's view of geohistory and of his great and small narrative, he made a concerted effort to defend universality. However, this is never an abstract universality of principles, but rather a differentiated universality that is always expressed through the particular and the singular. For Reclus, as for all truly dialectical thinkers, the universal is a concrete one that is rooted in history, and which is in a constant process of development and transformation. According to his an-archic or anti-archic ontology, there is no principle (*archê*) that has higher ontological status than that of the phenomenon (that which appears) in the world. Reclusian anarchist geography is a discourse of unity in plurality, in which not only the human community and the person but also geographical phenomena, are seen as forms of universal particularity and universal singularity.

*The truth is the whole that is not whole.* There is a strong holistic dimension to Reclus's analysis of terrestrial phenomena. For example, he says that the Earth "ought to be cared for like a great body, in which the breathing carried out by means of the forests regulates itself according to a scientific method; it has its lungs which ought to be respected by humans, since their own hygiene depends on them."[54] This is a typical example of the kind of use of organicist metaphors that has pervaded ecological discourse since Reclus. Yet a truly dialectical holism is always an anti-holistic holism. It avoids the lapses into varieties of reification, essentialism, and substantialism that plague uncritical forms of holistic and organicist thought. And Reclus's analysis goes precisely in this dialectical direction. For Reclus, all social and geographical phenomena are what they are not, and they are not what they are. As he states this dialectical verity, "it is only through an act of pure abstraction that one can contrive to present a particular aspect of the environment as if it had a distinct existence, and strive to isolate it from all the others, in order to study its essential influence."[55] This insight is also at the core of Reclus's idea that all social phenomena contain both progressive and regressive dimensions and that every phenomenon is "at once a phenomenon of death and a phenomenon of revival" and "the result of evolution toward decay and also toward progress."[56] Thus, anarchist geography rejects all attempts to impose abstract, objectifying conceptual schemes on a dynamic, self-contradictory, and interdependently determined reality—in short, a *living* reality. We do not "murder to dissect," and neither do we dissect in order to dominate.

## NOTES

1    Edgar Morin's important investigation of the deeper meaning of living on Earth culminates in a kind of neo-Reclusianism that echoes some of the themes that will be discussed here. Morin says that even into the second half of the twentieth century we were still "living on a misapprehended Earth, on an abstract Earth. We were living on the Earth as object. By the end of this century, we discovered Earth as system, as Gaia, as biosphere, a cosmic speck—Homeland Earth." See Edgar Morin, *Homeland Earth: A Manifesto for the New Millennium* (Cresskill, NJ: Hampton Press, 1999), 143. Morin adds that part of this discovery process is "Learning to 'be there' (*dasein*) on the planet," that is, learning "to live, to share, to communicate and commune with one another" (145). If Morin is right, in the last several decades important dimensions of Reclus's discovery have finally begun to spread through global society.

2    Elisée Reclus, *L'Homme et la Terre* (Paris: Librairie Universelle, 1905–8), 6 vols. In fact, Reclus goes so far as to judge that, in a meaningful sense, human consciousness becomes the consciousness not only of the Earth but of the Universe. As early as the 1860s, he says that "since civilization has connected all the nations of the earth in one common humanity—since history has linked century to century—since astronomy and geology have enabled science to cast her retrospective glance on epochs thousands and thousands of years back, man has ceased to be an isolated being, and, if we may so speak, is no longer merely mortal: he has become the consciousness of the imperishable universe." See Elisée Reclus, *The Earth: A Descriptive History of the Phenomena of the Life of the Globe*, trans. B.B. Woodward (New York: Harper and Brothers, 1871), 567.

3    John Clark and Camille Martin, eds. *Anarchy, Geography, Modernity: Selected Writings of Elisée Reclus* (Oakland: PM Press, 2013), 5.

4    Clark and Martin, *Anarchy, Geography, Modernity.*

5    The Spanish edition of *Anarchy, Geography, Modernity* is entitled *Libertad, Igualidad, Geografía* (Madrid: Enclave de Libros, 2015)—*Liberty, Equality, Geography*. It uses a title that was originally proposed for the first English edition, and which stresses the central place of revolutionary freedom in Reclus's thought.

6    Clark and Martin, *Anarchy, Geography, Modernity*, 6.
7    On the radical implications of certain basic concepts in Buddhist philosophy, see chapter 13 in this volume and Max Cafard, "Zen Anarchy," https://www.academia.edu/2542500/_Zen_Anarchy_by_Max_Cafard_.
8    Clark and Martin, *Anarchy, Geography, Modernity*, 70 (emphasis added).
9    "La Géographie n'est autre chose que l'Histoire dans l'Espace, de même que l'Histoire est la Géographie dans le Temps." This is stated on the title page of each volume of *L'Homme et la Terre*.
10   Claude Lévi-Strauss, *Tristes Tropiques* (New York: Criterion, 1961), 292.
11   In the sense of the investigation of the nature and modes of being and being-human in relation to the Earth, as distinguished from "geo-ontology" as a subset of the field of ontology in information science.
12   *Herodote* 22, no. 3 (1981): 157.
13   Elisée Reclus, *Histoire d'un Ruisseau* (Arles: Actes Sud, 1995), 1.
14   Reclus, *Histoire d'un Ruisseau*, 204.
15   Reclus, 204.
16   *Daodejing* 32:5, trans. Wing-Tsit Chan.
17   Reclus, *Histoire d'un Ruisseau*, 204.
18   Reclus, 205.
19   Reclus, 205–6.
20   Clark and Martin, *Anarchy, Geography, Modernity*, 47.
21   Clark and Martin, 225
22   Clark and Martin, 233.
23   Clark and Martin, 48
24   Clark and Martin, 48.
25   Clark and Martin, 48–49.
26   Clark and Martin, 49.
27   Clark and Martin, 49.
28   Especially in the English-speaking world, Kropotkin is given almost exclusive credit for the development of the anarchist view of mutual aid, though Reclus began writing extensively about this topic earlier than Kropotkin, and it was quite central to all of Reclus's work.
29   Reclus, *The Earth and Its Inhabitants: The Universal Geography* (London: H. Virtue, 1876–94), 1:3.
30   Clark and Martin, 17.
31   Clark and Martin, 25.
32   Clark and Martin, 25.
33   Joël Cornuault notes that Reclus commented that Herodotus "knew how to make geography more appealing than poetry" and points out the poetic quality of Reclus's own work. See the "préface" to Reclus's *Histoire d'un Montagne* (Arles: Actes Sud, 1998), 13, and Cornuault's excellent small book on Reclus, *Elisée Reclus: Géographe et Poète* (Église-Neuve-d'Issac: Fédérop, 1995).
34   Thomas Berry, preface to *The Earth Charter: A Study Book of Reflection for Action*, by Elisabeth M. Ferrero and Joe Holland (Miami: Redwoods Press, 2005), 18.
35   Clark and Martin, 110.
36   Clark and Martin, 92.
37   Clark and Martin, 93.

38  He docs not, however, assume that any technical or intellectual achievement is a pure "advance" that can unproblematically be used for beneficent purposes. In fact, he asserts the precise opposite. In his concluding chapter of *L'Homme et la Terre* on "Progress," he asserts that "all modification, no matter how important, is accomplished through a combination of progress and a corresponding regression." See *Anarchy, Geography, Modernity*, 17. He thus rejects any idea of either the neutrality of technology or the purity of political ideology.

39  Simon Springer, *The Anarchist Roots of Geography* (Minneapolis: University of Minnesota Press, 2016), 137, 31.

40  Clark and Martin, 149.

41  Clark and Martin, 150.

42  Clark and Martin, 150.

43  Clark and Martin, 150. Reclus's analysis parallels Hegel's discussion of the importance of moving from the realm of abstract morality (*Moralität*) to the historically, practically, and institutionally grounded ethical realm (*Sittlichkeit*). Though there is no evidence of any direct influence of Hegel on Reclus, he may have encountered Hegel's concepts indirectly through his early study in Berlin with geographer Karl Ritter, whose ideas of historical development were influenced by Hegel, albeit in a conservative direction.

44  1864 and 1871.

45  From Reclus's response to the "Enquête sur la Commune," *La Revue Blanche*, Tome XII (Geneva: Slatkine Reprints, 1968; orig. Paris, 1891), 298.

46  Reclus's response to the "Enquête sur la Commune."

47  Reclus's response to the "Enquête sur la Commune."

48  From the *Journal officiel de la république française sous la Commune*, https://babel. hathitrust.org/cgi/pt?id=msu.31293107630539;view=1up;seq=99, 103.

49  See "The Dialectic of Nature and Culture," in Clark and Martin, *Anarchy, Geography, Modernity*, 16–34.

50  Federico Ferretti, "Commentary by Federico Ferretti," in "Rediscovering the 'Inebriation of Geography,' Book Review Forum on Simon Springer's *The Anarchist Roots of Geography* (Minneapolis, 2016)," *AAG Review of Books* 5, no. 4 (2017): 284.

51  Ferretti, "Commentary."

52  Clark and Martin, *Anarchy, Geography, Modernity*, 23, 18.

53  Clark and Martin, 18.

54  Clark and Martin, 20.

55  Reclus, *L'Homme et la Terre*, 1:114–15.

56  Reclus, *Evolution, Revolution, and the Anarchist Ideal* in Clark and Martin, *Anarchy, Geography, Modernity*, 140.

3

# Education for the Earth or
# Education for Empire?

The following reflections undertake an exploration of the question of the nature of geopedagogy. In posing this question, we ask what meaning education should have at the present moment in geohistory. This question presupposes numerous other questions. For example, "What is the authentic goal of education in general?" "What is the de facto function of education under the prevailing social, political, and economic system?" and "What is the larger geohistorical context in which we ask any of these questions?" Let's start with the last one and then see if from there we can make a little progress in answering some of the others, especially in the light of the anarchist social geography of Elisée Reclus, which is in large part the inspiration for these reflections. Using this Reclusian framework, which is founded on the critique of all forms of domination and the quest for freedom as the realization of personal and planetary flourishing, our question can be reformulated in a much more specific manner: "Given that we are conditioned to become egocentric, anthropocentric, ethnocentric, acquisitive, competitive, defensive, distracted, hierarchical, patriarchal, statist, power-seeking beings, how can we come to see ourselves, and to recreate ourselves, as communal, compassionate, caring, creative, spontaneous, awakened, loving, empathetic, mutualistic, cooperative, solidaristic, geological, cosmological beings?"

## The State of Extinction

The Earth is going through one of the six periods of mass extinction and biodiversity loss in its four and half-billion-year history. This and other major disruptions in the biosphere are interacting to cause a major crisis for life on Earth. Although the term "Anthropocene" has become the popular label for the emerging era of life on Earth, and the alternative suggestion of "Capitalocene" has certain definite merits, it is argued here that the most precisely appropriate term for it is the *Necrocene*, the "new era of death." This follows from the fact that the current era of mass extinction succeeds immediately an era called the "Cenozoic," meaning a "new era of life."[1] Achille Mbembe deserves recognition for his insight that we must move beyond the concept of biopolitics to that of necropolitics and recognize that "the ultimate expression of sovereignty resides, to a large degree, in the power and the capacity to dictate who may live and who may die."[2] However, we need to go even further and move beyond this important insight. A recognition of the truth of the Necrocene discloses that the ultimate expression of the absolute sovereignty of Empire resides in its capacity to destroy most of life on Earth and, as we now see, if our vision does not fail us, in the actual exercise of that power. The supreme manifestation of sovereign power lies in its ability to enact a *state of extinction*.

However, we are in an age of the failure of vision. The severity of the global ecological crisis is met overwhelmingly with either denial or disavowal. The deniers simply reject the clear evidence of crisis, while the disavowers accept the truth of the evidence but fail to undertake actions that are even vaguely proportional to the gravity of the predicament. They know but act as if they do not know.[3] Institutions in American society often follow this denial/disavowal split. Why is there a two-party system in the United States? It is because we need one party for the deniers and another for the disavowers.[4] Education also follows this pattern, though, despite fundamentalist universities, textbooks that suppress information on climate change, and other aberrations, self-satisfied disavowal is generally the rule, especially at the level of higher education.

Yet today, even the driest scientific analyses of the state of the planet are no less than delicately worded declarations of catastrophism. As stated earlier, researchers at the Stockholm Resilience Centre developed the pedagogically useful concept of "planetary boundaries," beyond which there is a high probability of ecological disaster, and published their findings in three concise articles that are among the most effective summaries of the current state of the planet.[5] To reiterate briefly, the researchers identified boundaries in the areas of climate change, ocean acidification, stratospheric ozone depletion, biogeochemical nitrogen and phosphorus cycles, global freshwater use, rate of biodiversity loss, land-system change, chemical pollution, and atmospheric aerosol loading and concluded that transgressing any of the boundaries could have catastrophic effects on a continental or planetary level.[6] They also concluded that at least three boundaries have been crossed, that most others are in imminent danger of being transgressed, and that especially serious danger of biospheric catastrophe lies in the areas of climate change and biosphere integrity.[7]

Analyses such as these have been widely disseminated; nevertheless, awareness of their import remains at best peripheral to the collective consciousness. Few are even aware of the existence of planetary boundary conditions other than climate change, and fewer yet are mobilized to demand a reversal of the ecocidal course of history. It is true that the mass media have at times picked up the theme of global ecological crisis, especially in the area of climate; however, reports concerning this problem, even highly alarmist ones, do not get top billing in the media, and they inevitable fade quickly into the realm of background noise.

## Living the Questions

Rilke suggested famously that we should "live the questions" that arise in our hearts.[8] His great insight was that rather than rushing toward superficial answers to deep, existential questions, we need to open ourselves up to them, live with them patiently, and allow the answers to appear in time. The poet offers excellent guidance concerning how to become a sensitive and awakened person. But there are other crucial questions that are not only about our own destiny as a person and our own hearts but about the destiny of the world, and the heart of the world. We need to open ourselves up to these questions fully and live them intensely, with a certain kind of patience but at the same time with the greatest degree of immediacy and urgency.

What must we do when we discover, with Thoreau, that the sacred itself "culminates in the present moment," but we also discover that it is, at this same moment, in danger of being destroyed? This is our common question. If we live deeply with such a question, this sheds intense light on the moment and at the same time casts a heavy shadow over it. How can we live such a question? How we can opt for Eros and against Thanatos, for the Earth and against Empire? How can we choose the one "living option"—the option for life on Earth? How, given the actual conditions in the world, can we break with and then overcome Empire, that is, the entire capitalist, statist, technocratic, patriarchal system of domination, and prevent global collapse, while at the same time creating a free, just, and caring community as well as a free, just, and caring world, or community of communities?

To relate this to our topic of education: Can any truly liberatory form of education possibly exist, except in the context of a movement to create such a world?

## Desperately Seeking Alternatives

My official pedagogical experience consists of forty-five years in higher education, working through that entire period in philosophy programs, and twenty-seven years of it in an environmental studies program. From the beginning, however, I believed that truly transformative possibilities for education do not lie within the established educational system. I became heavily involved in the alternative education movement in the early 1970s, as a parent, teacher, program organizer, and writer. I was convinced at that time that education (along with other transformed spheres such as personal life, popular culture, and the alternative media) could be a revolutionary force that offered real hope of radically transforming American, and perhaps even global society, over the subsequent decades. The strategy envisioned to achieve this goal included fundamental reform of the existing system, but it focused especially on more radical and revolutionary alternatives such as free schools and what was at the time called "deschooling" (decentralized educational networks) as the source of real hope. I am now highly critical of some of our assumptions and illusions in that period; yet I believe that we had certain insights that were valuable and that were inspired by a kind of coherent and hopeful transformative vision that is much needed today.

During the 1970s, I participated as a parent-teacher in two cooperative preschools and worked with, and had children in, an open classroom school, a Montessori school, and a free school. I taught for many years in the New Orleans Free University, worked on organizing a free high school, and was the co-organizer of two major alternative education conferences. One of my main commitments was as a board member for a citywide alternative education coalition, and I wrote extensively for its newsletter. Starting in the early 1980s, and continuing into the early '90s, I lectured at the eco-anarchist Institute for Social Ecology Summer program in Vermont. Later, I taught in the New Orleans Lyceum community education program, coordinated philo cafés, was an advisory board member for a land-based arts education project, worked with the New Orleans

Free School community education project, helped organize its successor, Common Knowledge, and have taught in a monthlong foreign study program working with Tibetan refugees in India for over a decade.

As has been mentioned, these efforts in education have culminated in a project called La Terre Institute for Community and Ecology, located on an eighty-seven-acre site on Bayou La Terre near the Mississippi Gulf Coast. The project sponsors programs there and in New Orleans that focus on education for social and ecological regeneration, with the ultimate aim of creating, in alliance with similar projects elsewhere and with grassroots movements across the globe, diverse communities of liberation and solidarity as well as federations of these communities that might become the basis for fundamental social-ecological transformation.

## Reclus and Integral Education

One of my major inspirations over the past twenty-five years has been the life and work of the social geographer-philosopher-revolutionary Elisée Reclus. Beginning over a century and a half ago, Reclus delineated some the basic qualities of the kind of transformative, liberatory education that might play a key role in confronting the crisis of humanity and the Earth. These ideas were part of his comprehensive social, political, and intellectual project.

On the theoretical level, Reclus's project encompasses a sweeping geohistorical synthesis in which he interprets the Earth Story and the human story as one epochal struggle between freedom and domination. This synthesis encompasses a groundbreaking critique of all forms of domination, including not only capitalism, the state, and authoritarian religion but also patriarchy, racism, technological domination, and the domination of nature. He presents crucial insights concerning the interrelation between personal and small-group transformation, broader cultural change, and large-scale social organization. His critique of domination shows him to be a pioneer in what is now labeled an "intersectional" analysis of its various forms. In addition to being an anticapitalist and antistatist, he was a radical feminist, an antiracist, a radical ecologist, an animal rights activist, a cultural radical, a naturist, and a vegetarian.

Reclus was a model of the many-sided, awakened human being and was not only a major intellectual figure but also an engaged activist and dedicated revolutionary. He was an important figure in the Paris Commune and suffered confinement in numerous prisons and many years of exile as a result of his revolutionary activities. He also played a significant role in the First International and in the development of the anarcho-syndicalist and anarcho-communist movements. He was an active crusader against racism, for the rights of women, and for the humane treatment of nonhuman animals, to mention a few of his many activist causes. The radical transformation of educational systems and of pedagogical methodologies was for Reclus a central concern that was inseparable from all these other struggles. Consequently, he developed a theory of "integral education," a form of pedagogy that was ecological and Earth-centered but at the same time focused on human self-realization and the project of social revolution. It can be argued that his educational theory was part of the most comprehensive social-ecological vision ever formulated.

Reclus is known for proposing several Earth-oriented pedagogical projects. The most famous was his Great Globe Project.[9] He proposed that an enormous globe at the scale of 1:100,000 (about 420 feet or 128 meters in diameter) with a network of surrounding walkways should be constructed at the center of Paris, so that the citizens could pass at various levels, examining the details of the Earth and thereby begin both understanding it in its regional particularities and also visualizing it as a vast interconnected, universalistic whole. He also proposed a new geohistorical calendar that would have no cultural, religious, or political biases.[10] The calendar would take as its starting point an event with both a planetary and a cosmic significance, rather than a particularistic, culturally specific one. He suggests for this point of reference the first recorded solar eclipse, a momentous event in human history, but also part of the larger history of the interrelationship between humanity, the Earth, the Sun, and the Moon. Such a calendar would illustrate and affirm our nature as social, natural, and cosmological beings. Furthermore, by beginning with a notable event in the history of astronomy, it would celebrate the growth of scientific knowledge of natural phenomena and of the entire universe.

However, Reclus's vision of Earth- and nature-centered integral education goes far beyond such specific projects. His very expansive and far-ranging ideas on education and pedagogy are dispersed through his tens of thousands of pages of writings but are concentrated in his sixty-six-page chapter on education in his six-volume magnum opus of social geography, *L'Homme et la Terre*, which will be cited a number of times here.[11] The following constitutes only a brief summary of a few of the major concepts in his educational vision that are not only still relevant but are even more crucial today, given the gravity of our growing social and ecological crisis.

## 1. The Community as Educator

The first such concept is that society, and more particularly the community, is a more important educator than any single person or group of people who are formally given that label. Reclus states that the goal of education is "to make society itself into a great body for mutual instruction, where all will be at once pupils and professors, where each child, after having received 'the basics' in primary education will learn how to develop him or herself integrally, according to his or her own intellectual capacities, in the existence that he or she has chosen for him or herself."[12] Since it is impossible for the dominant society to perform such a function, the implication is that communities must be created in which this kind of all-encompassing educational atmosphere can exist. Or, if such communities already exist to a rudimentary degree, they must be nurtured and helped to grow. In this way, forms of liberatory education—whether primary and secondary schools, people's universities, or other forms popular education—can be situated within locally based communities that can creatively and democratically shape these forms to serve their own needs, in addition to those of the larger human and ecological communities of which they are a part.

It follows from this emphasis on the need for primary communities of liberation and solidarity that the school, and especially the small learning group or class, must itself be such a community. Reclus says that "a good [primary] education requires that the group of children be large enough for them to become fully engaged in collective work that will be undertaken and carried out joyfully and enthusiastically" (440). He adds that it is also important that the class not become a large, amorphous crowd in which it is impossible for every child to receive the special attention of the teacher. The goal is that the class should be "in the joys of both work and play, a true family" (440). Accordingly, the teacher must be able to play the roles of both parent and sibling, "placing his or her mind in close contact with the minds of the students, grasping clearly the content of both their conscious and their unconscious thinking processes, evoking in these young minds a capacity for thought that is equal to his or her own, and leading them to an understanding of truth and a joy in their activities" (440).

Furthermore, in Reclus's system of communitarian education, "community service" will not be a supplemental activity for students, but will, rather, define the core of the curriculum. The goal of the educational process should not be the awarding of credentials that are useful for advancement in a corrupt and unjust system, but rather for "success in carrying out valuable work" (457). He explains that if "studies are directed toward useful work," then "graduation" will mean that students will be able to "show what they have already done to contribute to the common tasks of humanity" (457). Their education will reach its culmination when they will be able to "give evidence of their participation in serious projects on behalf of the public good, and, above all, projects that require a spirit of devotion and sacrifice" (457).

## 2. Education Rooted in Grassroots Social Movements

For Reclus, a system of integral education can only be fully realized when it is the expression of the good community and of the good society. However, on the way to that society, it must be an expression of that community and society in a process of development. Thus, effective liberatory education must be rooted in grassroots social movements in which the end is realized in the means. Such movements are not only "prefigurative" but also "figurative" and "transfigurative." The goal of revolution is also a condition for revolution. As the IWW has said since its founding in 1905, we must "build the new society within the shell of the old." The strategy of waiting until after the revolution is untenable. The strategy of waiting until the shell crumbles in the wake of global ecological collapse is even less promising.

The historical anarchist movement (along with other tendencies within the classical workers' movement) made movement-based and community-based local educational institutions an important part of their project of social transformation. An institution that was of major significance for the movement in a number of countries was the popular community-based school (called the *Athenée* in French, the *Ateneo* in Spanish, and the *Ateneu* in Catalan), in addition to workers' schools and people's universities. Reclus and his works played an important role in the proliferation of these institutions, which spread widely and thrived in many parts of the Mediterranean and Latin American world. For example, by the 1930s "virtually every neighborhood" in Barcelona "had its own ateneu," and a similar situation prevailed in much of Catalonia.[13]

Today, there are still a few places, such as Chiapas and Rojava, where popular education of this kind is highly advanced. Significantly, these are places where a transformative political movement has taken power. This tradition of libertarian and communitarian education also has connections with U.S. political and educational history. Many years ago, Jonathan Kozol pointed out in his book *Free Schools* that the most advanced free schools were the Freedom Schools of the civil rights movement in Mississippi. One should add that they were so advanced because they were rooted in a living, vibrant, charismatic freedom movement, a movement that has never died and is in fact being revitalized in Mississippi today.

Reclus thought that the educational role of "the press" (we would expand this today to "the media") is even more important than that of formal alternative educational institutions (462). He states that, despite all the "vulgarity, banality, obsession with scandal, and hypocritical patriotism" of much of the press, it has, on the whole, "enlarged the intellectual space of its readers" (464). Reclus participated actively in the radical press, writing for movement newspapers and periodicals, and authoring a number of widely reprinted political pamphlets. His books were also an important dimension of his efforts in public education and had a wide readership. His liberatory version of the Earth Story is recounted throughout his works, ranging from vast scholarly ones such as *The Earth*, the *New Universal Geography*, and *Humanity and the Earth* to eloquent popular ones aimed especially at young people, such as his *History of a Mountain* and *History of a Stream*. *Humanity and the Earth* was published in weekly installments that sold to a popular readership for fifty centimes each.

Reclus lived in a period in which in many countries it was common to find daily newspapers from the perspective of radical labor unions and revolutionary political movements. In addition, reading the daily radical press was part of a larger ethos that included speeches, lectures, study groups, training programs, and celebrations in addition to union, party, and movement schools. There is nothing to compare to this today in countries like the United States and nations in Europe that consider themselves to be the most advanced political cultures of the world.

## 3. The Earth as the Great Educator

A third important Reclusian pedagogical concept is the idea that nature and the Earth must be at the center of all education. The renowned "geologian" Thomas Berry has said that the most extraordinary and distinctive quality of our human species is that we have the ability to contemplate and celebrate the entire universe.[14] We are capable of having such a contemplative and celebratory relationship not only to the universe as a whole but, more specifically, to the Earth and to the places on Earth that we cherish most. Berry claims that "the natural world is the great educator" because of its great power to inspire awe, curiosity, and joy. Ecological education, from this point of view, must consist of both reasoned inquiry into the nature of the Earth, and the nurturing of our ability to appreciate the Earth deeply and celebrate it joyfully.

Expressing a similar pedagogical vision, Reclus holds that "the true school should be free nature, including not only the beautiful landscapes that one contemplates, and the laws that one studies in the field, but also all the obstacles that one must learn to overcome."[15] It follows from this precept that the vast majority of schools are "false schools." They have as their primary function the adaptation of the students to the system of social domination and the domination of nature. For this reason, the first task of a true school must be to create a sphere in which the student can begin to step outside of that system. For Reclus, this meant that it must in a certain sense also "step back into nature."

Reclus contends that "a school that is truly liberated from ancient forms of servitude cannot develop freely except in nature" (444). In such a school, activities that are usually considered special events, such as "hikes and races through the fields, forests, and countryside, on riverbanks and at beaches, will become the rule," since "it is only in the open air that one becomes familiar with plants and animals, and with workers, that one learns to observe them and to develop a precise and coherent idea of the nature of the external world" (444–46). Reclus points to the example of schools in his day that promoted both physical and moral well-being through "joyful outdoor work," for example, Coupvray, which created a student ornithological society that in one year protected 570 bird nests from damage, and Cinquétral, whose students worked on reforesting eroded slopes, planting fifteen thousand trees (446).

Reclus also delves into the question of how nature can be an educator in a larger sense. He begins *The History of a Mountain* with an apparently autobiographical depiction of the state of disillusionment and despair into which a human being can descend when personal relationships and projects for the future all seem to fail. He describes a process of immersing himself in wild or free nature (in this case the mountains) and going through an educational process in which he learned not only about mountains but about "the vast earth" and "all those infinitely small creatures" within it.[16] He describes this learning process as leading not just to abstract knowledge but to a renewal of one's life, an appreciation of the intrinsic value of living things, and a deep feeling of joy.[17]

In a passage in *The History of a Stream*, Reclus remarks that the immersion in wild nature allows us to "return temporarily to the lives of the ancestors," to become freer physically to cast off temporarily the trappings and constraints of civilization and to be "free of all convention."[18] This touches on the question of the nature of civilized selfhood and what has been lost through the dissolution of communal relations, interpersonal ties, and connections with the place, the region, and the Earth, over the history of civilization.

## 4. Education as Self-Transformation

This leads to a final Reclusian pedagogical concept: that true education is a process of radical self-transformation. Liberatory education is, we might say, a collective practice of overcoming enslavement to the civilized ego. It is a process of reversing the effects of the dominant form of (mis)education, which is education for domination, that is, as a means of inculcating in the students the values of hierarchical dualism, dominance and subordination, alienation, and separation. As a result of the long history of such "compulsory miseducation," true education must become a therapeutic process that aims at treating the sickness called civilization and the disease called ego.[19] Reclus complains that prevailing forms of education promote conflict rather than cooperation. The students soon learn, he says, that they are "rivals and combatants" (492). In this, formal education merely plays its assigned role in the system of domination. It works to reinforce the structure of the ego, and helps it evolve as a response to the evolution of that system (for example, from the classical capitalist culture of production to the late capitalist culture of mass consumption or from a classical colonial system to a neocolonial one). It creates either a highly structured ego or a more complex and flexible one, according to whether one or the other is optimal for purposes of organizing class domination and capital accumulation, while it imposes either a rigid and hierarchical social structure or a minimally structured and less complex one, depending on what is required to evoke obedience and compliance most effectively.

In his chapter on education, Reclus discusses the nature of the authoritarian educational system of his time and outlines the underlying values
and the pedagogical methods of an alternative system of integral education that might replace it. He states, for example, that it is necessary "to recognize the freedom of the child from birth and reject despotic patriarchal
authority" (438). He holds that the teacher should never exercise arbitrary
authority but should rather only make use of the natural, noncoercive
authority that comes from having "greater size and power, age, intelligence,
scientific knowledge, moral dignity, and life experience" (439), qualities
that will be voluntarily recognized and accepted by the child. Thus, the
educational process will not impose external authority but will rather
"assist the child in developing according to the 'logic of his or her nature,'"
so that it will "have no other goal than the blossoming in the child's intelligence of what was already present unconsciously" (439).

According to Reclus, education as such an integral process of self-
realization will consist largely of free, creative play. He maintains that
"free amusement is one of the great educators of humanity,"[20] and that
the child's studies must be "supported by passion" (439). He presents an
inspiring image of a system of education (or perhaps of the *anti-system*
of a *community of education*) as an expression of the intelligence, ability,
creativity, and curiosity of each student. Reclus develops in considerable
detail these general ideas concerning libertarian, communitarian, person-
centered education and the corresponding evils of authoritarian, capitalist,
statist, patriarchal education, especially in regard to primary education. It
would be useful to explore the many aspects of his very rich elaboration
of these topics, but that must be undertaken elsewhere. However, there is
one crucial dimension of his analysis that should be mentioned briefly,
in conclusion.

Reclus looks back to classical Greek philosophy and notes that one
finds there, in the dialogues of Plato for example, "a permanent conver-
sation between the student and his [or her] own self (*moi*), a constant
examination of thought by thought," that "concerns above all the issue
of 'knowing yourself'" (452, 454). He asks, "How much more does this
[conversation] now become necessary, since it concerns 'knowing nature,'
of which each is but a mere cell?" (454). He contends that "the young
person who lives his or her education should interrogate him or herself
and respond unceasingly, with complete probity and sincerity" (454).
He judges that "compared to this personal self-examination, the usual

formalities of acceptance into the world of 'the qualified' are insignificant trifles" (454).

I would suggest that we should follow to its ultimate conclusion Reclus's idea of the centrality to education of this process of self-discovery. Education, to fulfill its pedagogical destiny, must provoke a crisis of selfhood. We might think about the origin of the word "pedagogy" in *agōgos*, "leading," and *agein*, "to lead." Its destiny is to be a guide, and to take us where we need most to go. It is for this reason that education must involve trauma. We might recall the "steep and rugged ascent" of Plato's cave allegory, though in this case, the journey is just as much a descent, moving from the heights of empty abstraction and ideological illusion to the solid (yet empty and ever-changing) ground of the Earth and to the groundless ground of being. It is the journey from Anti-Nature to that "Nature that is No-Nature." This journey is not an easy one, though it can be a deeply fulfilling voyage of discovery. To realize its traumatic destiny, pedagogy must help lead the learner, the seeker of the deepest truths, through that Dark Night of the Soul in which radical self-transformation becomes possible and there can emerge a new form of being-human that has overcome the will to dominate, with its attendant alienation from others, from our own species, from other life forms, and from the Earth.

Without this transfigurative experience, without this passionate opening of the doors of perception to the sublime wonders of the person, of humanity, of the multitude of beings, and of the Earth itself, without opening them to the excruciating tragedy of the crushing and ruthless destruction of these wonders, *nothing* will be possible.

## NOTES

1    Literally, of "animals," though the Greek term *zoon* has primordial roots in the verb "to live."

2    Achille Mbembe, "Necropolitics," *Public Culture* 15, no. 1 (2003): 11. Mbembe begins his analysis with this statement.

3    Because disavowal involves a form of splitting, it can also be said that they both know and do not know.

4    Since the disavowers are those who know (without knowing), while the deniers are those who do not know, this generates contempt for the deniers on the part of the disavowers, and resentment of the disavowers on the part of the deniers.

5    Johan Rockström et al., "A Safe Operating Space for Humanity," *Nature* 461 (September 2009): 472–75. Johan Rockström et al., "Planetary Boundaries: Exploring the Safe Operating Space for Humanity," *Ecology and Society* 14, no. 2 (2009): 32–64, https://www.ecologyandsociety.org/vol14/iss2/art32/; and Will Steffen et al., "Planetary Boundaries: Guiding Human Development on

a Changing Planet," *Science* 347, no. 6223 (February 13, 2015): 736–47, http://science.sciencemag.org/content/347/6223/12 59855.full.

6   Rockström et al., "A Safe Operating Space for Humanity" and "Exploring the Safe Operating Space for Humanity."

7   Steffen et al., "Guiding Human Development on a Changing Planet."

8   Rainer Maria Rilke, *Letters to a Young Poet* (Malden, MA: Burning Man Books, 2001), 14.

9   A project that has been revived in recent years. See "The Great Globe Project" website, http://thegreatglobe.com/.

10  Few have, like Reclus, engaged in this kind of long-term thinking on a practical-symbolic level. Another exceptional thinker, Gary Snyder, ends *Earth House Hold: Technical Notes and Queries to Fellow Dharma Revolutionaries* with the date "Eighth Moon, 40067 (reckoning roughly from the earliest cave paintings)" (New York: New Directions, 1969), 143.

11  Numbers in parentheses below refer to pages in that chapter, which is found in vol. 6 of *Homme et la Terre* (Paris: Librairie Universelle, 1905–1908).

12  *Anarchy, Geography, Modernity: Selected Writings of Elisée Reclus* (Oakland: PM Press, 2013), 73.

13  Rachel Hadfield, "Politics and protest in the Spanish Anarchist Movement: Libertarian Women in Early Twentieth-Century Barcelona," *University of Sussex Journal of Contemporary History*, no. 3 (2001), https://www.sussex.ac.uk/webteam/gateway/file.php?name=3-hadfield-politics-and-protest&site=15.

14  He often states it this way in his lectures. In *The Dream of the Earth*, he expresses the idea in a very Reclusian manner, defining "the human" as "that being in whom the universe comes to itself in a special mode of conscious reflection." (San Francisco: Sierra Club Books, 1990), 16.

15  Elisée Reclus, *The History of a Mountain* (New York: Harper and Brothers, 1881), 192.

16  Reclus, *History of a Mountain*, 15.

17  Reclus, 11–12.

18  Elisée Reclus, *Histoire d'un ruisseau* (Arles: Actes Sud, 1995), 138.

19  The term "compulsory miseducation" is taken from anarchist social theorist and writer Paul Goodman, in *Compulsory Mis-education and The Community of Scholars* (New York: Vintage Books, 1964). His book *Gestalt Therapy* is one of the best sources on how education and culture in general can develop this therapeutic process. See Frederick Perls, Ralph Hefferline, and Paul Goodman, *Gestalt Therapy: Excitement and Growth in the Human Personality* (New York: Dell, 1951). The two volumes of the work were published together. Vol. 2, 225–466, is by Goodman.

20  Reclus, *L'Homme et la Terre*, 1:134.

# 4

## The Summit of Ambition:
## The Paris Climate Spectacle and
## the Politics of the Gesture

We now know what kind of summit the 2015 Paris Climate Summit really was. COP21 was the Summit of Ambition. During the negotiations, a source reported tantalizingly that there was a "huge, secret coalition that could deliver a climate win in Paris."[1] But by the middle of the proceedings, the secret was, to say the least, out. The "parties" that were "conferring" at this "Conference of the Parties" were quite vocally proclaiming themselves the "High Ambition Coalition." "Ambition" had become the new climate buzzword.

The Paris Agreement also taught us that "ratcheting" was the de rigueur method of manifesting this ambition. In one interview, a climate pundit managed to mention "ratcheting up ambition" three times in three minutes. If there was anything more concrete than ambition that was to be ratcheted, this was a well-kept secret. However, Fred Krupp, president of the Environmental Defense Fund, enlightened us a bit. He said that "the agreement provides a framework to ratchet up ambition over time: a transparent system for reporting and review, regular assessments of progress, and strengthening of commitments every five years beginning in 2020."[2]

So we discover that in the end the much-heralded "ratcheting" process includes reporting and review, reporting and review in slightly different words, and "strengthening of commitments." I think that we can with complete confidence believe that as a result of this agreement a lot of reports will be written. On the other hand, there are no mechanisms to enforce the commitments.

In the end, the Paris Agreement is an agreement to strengthen commitments if, *par hazard*, a country decides to strengthen them. Countries then have the right to do something about these strong commitments, or to do little other than congratulate themselves on how committed they are. Countries have the right to agree with themselves—or to change their mind and disagree with themselves. I would hate to try to tighten a bolt with this kind of ratchet.

## It's, Like, *Immense*

Yet much of the media seemed convinced of the world-historical nature of the Agreement. Though the *Guardian* is usually somewhat more percep-tive than most of the mainstream press, its article "How US Negotiators Ensured Landmark Paris Climate Deal Was Republican-Proof" echoes the vacuous claims made for the "pact" and the sort of breathless media boosterism that accompanied its announcement.[3]

We are told rather dramatically that White House officials aspired to "craft a deal congressional Republicans would not be able to stop," that this deal had to be "bullet-proof," and that such an achievement "required major political capital." Even more breathtakingly, we find that "the US needed a very particular kind of deal—and it required immense politi-cal capital to achieve it." Exactly how immense this capital was, why this particular degree of immensity was needed, and how precisely all this immensity was employed are not explained, though we *are* told that the whole effort was "an immensely complicated challenge."

In spite of all these theatrics, the article quickly bursts its own bubble of puffery by giving away the big secret. The tactic that the Obama admin-istration planned to use to "outsmart" the Republicans was simply to give up on anything that the Republicans would object to very strongly. In short, if the Paris Agreement contained nothing that was of real consequence or was binding, there would be nothing for the Republican Congress to veto. One could almost say that it was a strategy of being immensely underambitious.

This brilliantly defeatist strategy for success is exactly what was finally deployed. As the article recounts, "under U.S. insistence" the Paris Agreement "was explicitly crafted" to *exclude*: 1) any binding agreement to emissions reductions; 2) any binding agreement to financing of emissions reductions; 3) any binding agreement to fines or penalties of any kind for failure to reduce emissions. Only one thing was agreed to legally: written reports every five years. So Paris has given us our stirring slogan for the climate revolution: *Vive la paperasse!*[4]

## Faux Pas

Despite this underwhelming outcome, even the normally sober Global Footprint Network exuded fervent optimism in articles unironically enti-tled "World Leaders Unanimously Agree to End the Fossil Fuel Age within a Few Decades" and "Paris: The Mother of All COPs."[5] The first of these articles proclaimed that the Paris Agreement "represents a huge historic step in re-imagining a fossil-free future for our planet," musing that it was "nothing short of amazing that 195 countries around the world—including oil-exporting nations—agreed to keep global temperature rise well below 2 degrees Celsius *and*, to the surprise of many, went even further by agreeing to pursue efforts to limit the increase to 1.5 degrees above pre-industrial levels."

Contrary to initial appearances, the GFN had not, in fact, gone entirely insane, since a few paragraphs down it admits that "science tells us that the pledges submitted by each nation are projected to result in a tempera-ture rise of between 3 and 7 degrees Celsius, exceeding the 2-degree limit or 'global handrail' acknowledged by the agreement." It adds that "the final agreement requires countries to return every five years with new emission reduction targets" and notes that "whether this essential requirement will be sufficient to catalyze more action remains to be seen."

In other words, the GFN recognizes that the nations had *not* in reality made any real, binding agreement to do what was celebrated just a few sentences earlier. What is true is that these nations had made a big step in *reimagining* a carbon-emissions-free future, even as they remained practically committed to a future that is disastrously dependent on such emissions. This gap between pleasant fantasy and brutal reality provides an excellent example of bad faith in action. It also presents a textbook example of the process of disavowal: *I know very well* that even the com-pletely nonbinding targets agreed on would result in climate catastrophe, *but nevertheless* I assert that the Paris Agreement was "a huge historic step" and "nothing short of amazing."

## The Turning Point

Fortunately, *Democracy Now!* offered its usual challenge to the conven-tional wisdom by presenting a very illuminating debate between Michael Brune, executive director of the Sierra Club, and journalist and writer George Monbiot.[6] Though Monbiot is far from radical, he has the virtues of being highly intelligent, perceptive, and honest, so he had no trouble politely demolishing the naive and uncritical optimism of mainstream environmentalism.

Brune joined the rest of the environmental establishment in proclaiming COP21 to be a momentous "turning point." He said that "what we saw in the last two weeks was that every country around the world agreed that we have to do much, much more to fight climate change effectively, and to begin to set up a dialogue and a mechanism for rich countries to aid the poor countries," adding that we have to "make room for continuous ambition moving forward."

But the very wording of his claim belies the existence of any real "turning point." To believe that there was such a change implies a belief that these countries previously didn't agree that we "have to do more," "set up dialogues," or create "mechanisms to aid poor countries." But this is absurd. Such assertions are all commonplaces of global environmental discourse. However, we can grant Brune one thing: his point was that the countries agreed that we "have to" do these things, in the sense that "we ought to," not that we "will" do them, in the sense that they have entered into a binding commitment. So the big (non-)deal seems to be that a lot of countries agreed that such things are really, really important. And, of course, that they will be sure to develop a great deal more ambition. One can only hope that peak ambition doesn't coincide with the collapse of the biosphere.

Monbiot deserves recognition for maintaining a positively shocking level of clear-sightedness in the midst of the post-COP orgy of self-congratulation by the global political class and mainstream environmentalists. He remarks that "what I see is an agreement with no timetables, no targets, with vague, wild aspirations. I mean, it's almost as if it's now safe to adopt 1.5 degrees centigrade as their aspirational target now that it is pretty well impossible to reach." Which is exactly the point. Aspiration and ambition are cheap, and these are the goods that have been bought and sold at COP21.

### Feet, Don't Fail Me
COP21 perpetuates the tendency—rampant among environmentalists and the politicians who want to appease them—to substitute spectacle for substantive action. They continue to put far too much effort into the politics of the gesture and far too little into massive direct action on behalf of a rapid end to carbon emissions.

The much-heralded People's Climate March of 2014 exemplifies the same kind of spectacularism that the Paris Summit does. The march was planned to be "so large and diverse that it cannot be ignored" and since then has been continually hailed as "the largest climate march in history." But that's exactly the problem. It was a very pleasant and upbeat way to spend the day, but with its three to four hundred thousand well-behaved attendees, it wasn't nearly monstrous enough or scary enough to convince anyone that there are seething masses of righteously indignant citizens who are ready to say no to ecocide in a very decisive way.

The march had absolutely no traumatic, transformational effect. On the way to the march, I heard people on the subway ask where everybody was going. Ordinary New Yorkers going about their daily routine seemed to be unaware of the existence of the event. And the attendance was equivalent to only 1.5 to 2 percent of the metro New York City population, so this isn't really all that surprising. Several months later, the pope's turnout of six million at just one of a series of events in the Philippines was *forty-eight times greater* per capita nationally than the widely trumpeted U.S. event. The size of the pope's event was noted in the media, but there was no particular gloating about it being one of "the biggest" anything in history. It was a pope-level event, not a mere planetary-survival-level event, which is in a different (minor) league.

Illusions about the Climate March mentality are reminiscent of the grandiose claims about the Woodstock Festival during the heyday of the American counterculture. The word on the street, and certainly the word out in the fields of Max Yasgur's farm, was that the festival was the largest gathering in the history of humanity. As Yasgur himself proclaimed to the crowd, "This is the largest group of people ever assembled in one place,"[7] but there had already been many assemblies vastly greater than its attendance of four or five hundred thousand. The largest convergence of human beings on the planet has for a very long time been the periodical Kumbh Mela in India, which has attracted as many as 120 million people, including 30 million on a single day.

So, if the climate movement wants to experiment seriously with the tactic of marches and mass gatherings, it should get to work on convening thirty million people on single day in Paris, New York, New Delhi, or other centers of power and pollution, capital and contamination. The crowd wouldn't even have to do much marching, since it would already be everywhere. Its very presence would begin to shake the foundations of the system of domination. But to do this would require that thirty million people would have to think that saving the planet from climate catastrophe is as important as what thirty million people go to the Kumbh Mela for.

## All Aboard the Train, All Aboard the Train

Three years after the Paris Agreement, we are already seeing the awesome power of ambition in action. A recent article points out that "the world's governments are 'nowhere near on track' to meet their commitment to avoid global warming of more than 1.5C above the pre-industrial period." In fact, last year's "global greenhouse gas emissions rose slightly again after a short period of stasis."[8] Maybe it's time to conclude that whatever stuff climate ambition is made out of, it's clearly not all that stern.

Let's return briefly to the climate spectacle of Paris for a parting thought. It seems to me that a fitting *au revoir* to the Summit of Ambition would have brought all the Chief Negotiators, or Negatiators, on stage to belt out the following Anthem of Ambition:

> We are the World
> We are the Parties
> Our ambition will make a cooler day
> So let's have ambition
> That's the choice we're making
> We're saving our own lives
> It's true we'll make a cooler day
> Ambitious you and me

## NOTES

1    Ben Jervey, "The Huge, Secret Coalition That Could Deliver a Climate Win in Paris," *GOOD: A Magazine for the Global Citizen*, http://magazine.good.is/articles/secret-climate-coaltion-high-ambition-paris-cop21.

2    "Statement on Paris Final Text from Environmental Defense Fund President Fred Krupp," Environmental Defense Fund website, https://www.edf.org/media/statement-paris-final-text-environmental-defense-fund-president-fred-krupp.

3    Suzanne Goldenberg, "How US Negotiators Ensured Landmark Paris Climate Deal Was Republican-Proof," *Guardian*, December 13, 2015, http://www.theguardian.com/us-news/2015/dec/13/climate-change-paris-deal-cop21-obama-administration-congress-republicans-environment.

4    "Long live the Paperwork!" Which it will.

5    Matthis Wackernagel, "World Leaders Unanimously Agree to End the Fossil Fuel Age within a Few Decades" at http://www.footprintnetwork.org/en/index.php/GFN/blog/world_leaders_unanimously_agreed_to_end_the_fossil_

fuel_age_within_a_few_de, and Sebastian Winkler, "Paris: The Mother of All COPs" at http://www.footprintnetwork.org/en/index.php/GFN/blog/mother_of_all_cops.

6    "A Turning Point for the Climate or a Disaster? Michael Brune vs. George Monbiot on the Paris Accord," http://www.democracynow.org/2015/12/14/a_turning_point_for_the_climate

7    Pete Fornatale, *Back to the Garden: The Story of Woodstock* (New York: Touchstone, 2009), 224.

8    Oliver Milman, "World 'Nowhere Near on Track' to Avoid Warming beyond 1.5C Target," *Guardian*, September 26, 2018, https://www.theguardian.com/environment/2018/sep/26/global-warming-climate-change-targets-un-report. The results cannot be attributed primarily to the Trump administration's climate denialism, and the failure of the unambitious United States to sign the Agreement. The U.S. produces less than 15 percent of greenhouse emissions while the ambitious countries signing the Agreement produce over 80 percent of the emissions. There is a global solidarity of climate disavowal that works together with denial to produce failure.

# 5

# Against Resilence: Hurricane Katrina and the Politics of Disavowal

## Forgetting Commemoration

When I began writing these words, New Orleans had just gone through the ten-year commemoration of the Hurricane Katrina disaster. I should say the "commemorations," since there were several quite divergent and sometimes conflicting modes of commemoration. At one end of the spectrum, there was the "Tenth Annual Katrina March and Second Line," the most serious political event of the day, which included speeches and performances at the site of the levee break in the devastated and still depopulated Lower Ninth Ward. The event had a significant turnout. Nevertheless, there were less than a thousand participants.

At the other extreme was the Krewe of OAK, which practiced a kind of "commemorating by not commemorating" in its annual "Midsummer Mardi Gras" parade and celebration. OAK stands for "Outrageous and Kinky," in addition to "Oak St.," the procession's starting point at the Maple Leaf Bar. The parade is noted for its wild costumes and zany ambience. It was estimated that this year about ten thousand people were attracted to this Carrollton neighborhood event. According to the *Times-Picayune*, the Krewe chose the theme "Tie Dye Me Up," to evoke the famous "Summer of Love" and "bring good vibes to this annual parade." It added: "No mention of the 'K' word, please."

Most of what were officially called the "Katrina10" activities fell somewhere between these two extremes. However, they tended more in the direction of the Krewe of OAK, in that they were overwhelmingly in a *celebratory mode*. This was certainly true of the official commemoration sponsored by the city administration and local businesses. It focused on recovery, economic and educational successes, and, above all, the remarkable "resilience" of the local community. It presented an upbeat official narrative that erased many of the ongoing problems and tragedies of the city. It also effaced many of the most significant struggles and achievements of the community when these did not fit into the official story. The major focus here will be on this official narrative, which pictures the city's post-Katrina history through the distorting lens of a politics of disavowal, and on the many realities that this narrative disavows.

As has been mentioned, disavowal is a phenomenon that is quite common in everyday experience, and which we have all experienced many times. There are two very common psychological processes in which the truth is negated. One of these, "denial," is a defense mechanism in which the truth is rejected. In denial, one cannot speak the truth. Denial seeks to *silence* the truth. The other process, "disavowal," is a defense mechanism in which the truth is recognized and even spoken, but it is nevertheless systematically forgotten or silenced at every decisive moment, when it really counts. Disavowal is *resilencing* the truth. It is a mode of silencing through speaking the truth, while at the same time negating through ones actions the implications of the truth that one speaks. The Hurricane Katrina Ten-Year Anniversary has been a celebration of disavowal and resilencing.

## Resilience Kills

Much of this resilencing has paraded under the banner of "resilience." While this concept has been ubiquitous throughout the post-Katrina period, it has become a kind of watchword and rallying cry for the official commemoration and the politics of disavowal that it expresses. It is important to uncover the key ideological functions that the term performs under a regime of disaster capitalism and a neoliberal model of "recovery." This will be done shortly. However, it should first be pointed out that the term "resilience" is, on the face of it, a strange one to use to describe post-Katrina New Orleans.

Resilience is defined as "the capability of a strained body to recover its size and shape" and "an ability to recover from or adjust easily to misfortune or change."[1] Neither of these definitions describes post-Katrina New Orleans terribly well. As for the "strained body" part, consider this. If someone had a serious accident or disease and after ten years is alive and doing tolerably well—except at only three-fourths of his or her original size—we wouldn't think of that as the most admirable of recoveries.

There are also problems with the "easily" part. Comedian and social critic Harry Shearer deserves recognition for defying the forces of complacency and boldly popularizing the term "the Big Uneasy," while vigorously exposing many of the perpetrators of the uneasiness.[2] Whatever the degree to which New Orleans has really recovered, it is indisputable that the decade after the flood was not particularly "easy" for most New Orleanians. Maybe those long years weren't so hard for the ones who had the good fortune to be extremely wealthy, delusional, comatose, or dead. But for the rest, they were difficult and even excruciating.

These absurdities aside, the major problem with the term "resilience" is its ideological use. In post-Katrina New Orleans, the term is associated with tendencies toward regression and mindless compliance. The voice of resilience says, "Congratulations, you're still here! (Those of you who are still here)," and asks, "How about doing a second line or cooking up some gumbo for the tourists?" It asks, a bit more delicately, "How about making their beds, cleaning their toilets, serving their food and drinks, maybe even selling them some drugs, and doing a special dance for them at the club?" It urges, above all, "Be resilient. Be exactly what you are expected to be."

The ideology of resilience ignores the extraordinary creative achievements and visionary aspirations of New Orleanians in the post-Katrina period. Instead, it celebrates survival, bare life. It focuses on the community's continued existence as a site for imposition of the corporate-state apparatus's hierarchically formulated and externally imposed redevelopment plans. All the compliments to the people of New Orleans for being resilient are a bit condescending and demeaning. After all, it's not the greatest tribute to people to compliment them on their ability to survive. "Thank you for not just giving up and dying en masse." After all, if they had done that, it would have been somewhat of an embarrassment to the greatest country in the world.

The real post-Katrina story is not a story of resilience. If you want to see the real post-Katrina story, check out the powerful documentary film *Big Charity*.[3] It's an account of heroic courage and dedication to saving lives and caring for the community. It's a story of crimes against humanity that are systematically repressed and forgotten. If you want to see the real post-Katrina story, which encompassed a large coastal region far beyond New Orleans, check out the film *My Louisiana Love*.[4] It's the story of passionate struggle for the Beloved Community and the Beloved Land. It's another story of the many crimes against humanity and nature that are systematically repressed and forgotten. Both sides of this story, the nobility of struggle and dedication on the one hand, and the criminality and betrayal on the other, are lost in the fog of resilience. They are lost in the resilencing process. They are lost in the Official Story. It is versions of this Official Story that were presented by President Bush, President Obama, and New Orleans Mayor Landrieu as part of the official Katrina commemoration.

## The Official Story: The Bush Version

According to President George W. Bush's typically blunt and unnuanced judgment, "New Orleans is back, and better than ever." In fact, he says that he is *amazed* by what has happened in New Orleans. This is not so astounding, since he specializes in being amazed. He was amazed by the atrocities of September 11, 2001, claiming that "nobody could have predicted" that there would be an attack on the World Trade Center—though about ten years before there had already been an attack on the World Trade Center. (Hint!) He was amazed by the post-Katrina flood in 2005, exclaiming that no one could have "anticipated the breach of the levees"—though several experts actually did, and it had already happened in recent memory during Hurricane Betsy.[5] (Hint!)

So we should not be surprised, much less amazed, by Bush's reaction to post-Katrina New Orleans in 2015: "Isn't it amazing?" What amazes him is that "the storm nearly destroyed New Orleans and yet, now, New Orleans is the beacon for school reform."[6] But what alternative universe does he inhabit? On Planet W, "the storm nearly destroyed New Orleans." But what storm? Hurricane Katrina didn't hit New Orleans and even while missing New Orleans had lost much of its force by the time its winds came our way. The *real* disaster was not a *storm*, but rather flooding caused by criminal governmental and corporate negligence. Furthermore, over a quarter of New Orleans was not damaged at all by the storm and flooding, and most of the rest could have recovered relatively easily, as it always had through almost three hundred years of disasters, given a reasonable level of response and support.[7] What should be truly astounding is that the victimizers of the city made the recovery so difficult for the victims. Bush should also not be amazed by the quasi-privatization of the school system, since his own administration was responsible for promoting exactly the kind of predatory opportunism and disaster capitalism that led to that privatization.

One begins to wonder whether Bush remembers what actually happened in Hurricane Katrina. It gradually becomes clear that he does in fact have no idea of the realities of the disaster and that he's counting on everyone else to forget, if they ever knew. As he twice implores his listeners, "*I hope you remember what I remember.*" This recalls the delusional wife-killer Fred Madison in *Lost Highway*, David Lynch's classic story of monumental forgetfulness. As Fred announces, unconsciously diagnosing his own delusional rewriting of history, "I like to remember things my own way." Similarly, Bush's voice is the voice of denial. Never even reaching the level of *resilence*, it is deceptive and self-deceptive silence about everything that counts.

## The Official Story: The Obama Version

Curiously, the same day that President Barack Obama visited New Orleans I got an email from him saying, "Let me be perfectly frank—I'm emailing to ask you for $5 . . ."[8] My first thought was, "Why don't you pass by, so I can give you the $5 in person? That would give me a chance to be perfectly frank too, and to explain how things in post-Katrina New Orleans are not quite as rosy as you've been painting them to be." It then occurred to me that Obama's problem was probably not a lack of information, as his Katrina speech in fact confirmed.

Admittedly, Obama's speech was infinitely better than the ramblings of Bush, whose unfortunate native tongue is English as a Second Language. Obama usually manages to combine a certain amount of intelligent and lucid analysis (even if it is often intelligently and lucidly deceptive) with a calculated folksiness that is aimed at mitigating any sins of excessive sophistication and erudition.

Folksiness certainly prevailed in his Katrina anniversary address, which gets the award for more clichés per sentence than any speech ever given here, and perhaps anywhere else on Planet Earth. In just the first paragraph, Obama managed to cover every obligatory local references and a number of optional ones, including "Where y'at," "the Big Easy," "the weather in August," "shrimp po' boy," "Parkway Bakery and Tavern," "Rebirth," "the Maple Leaf," "Mardi Gras," and "what's Carnival for."[9] Fortunately, somebody caught him before he told the crowd "jockamo fee nané."[10]

But the agenda was basically about resilencing. Obama enthusiastically promoted the neoliberal corporate capitalist project, including the quasi-privatization and de-democratization of the local schools. He actually citied some damning statistics about child poverty and economic inequality in New Orleans, and he noted that the city "had been for too long been plagued by structural inequalities." "Had been" before Hurricane Katrina, it seems.

However, this brief moment of quasi-recognition was lost in the deluge of upbeat generalization. He told the citizens that "the progress that you have made is remarkable" in achieving, among other things, a "more just New Orleans." In case we didn't get his point, he added, "The progress you've made is remarkable." So we are told that post-Katrina New Orleans is not only a model of opportunity for entrepreneurs and developers, as the Chamber of Commerce will enthusiastically inform us, but also a model for *progress in justice.*

Obama's voice is clearly the voice of disavowal. He is intelligent and perceptive. He knows the truth, and he can even tell you that he knows it. But this truth is consigned to footnotes and asides to a larger ideological pseudo-truth that must become the focus of our attention. The truth is there, only to be strategically forgotten. The dominant discourse remains the verbose but empty speech of resilencing.

So much for *les Menteurs en Chef.*[11]

## The Official Story: The Landrieu Version

Next, the local political and corporate establishment, led by Mayor Mitch Landrieu, joined in the celebration. For the anniversary, Mayor Landrieu and Walmart, along with other corporate entities, cosponsored a "Citywide Day of Service." It's unfortunate that the community couldn't organize a large-scale volunteer effort itself, as it did after Katrina, when our state and corporate masters largely abandoned the city, except to the extent that they took advantage of opportunities for mass incarceration and then economic exploitation. The mayor's version of a "Day of Service" was four hours of service projects in the morning, followed by four hours of speeches and celebration.

From Mayor Landrieu's perspective, there was much to celebrate. On his "Katrina 10: Resilient New Orleans" website he claimed that the Katrina disaster turned out to be a positive opportunity. As a result "New Orleans has turned itself around and has built the city that we should've built the first time."[12] Presumably the city had to wait 287 years for the current experiment in neoliberal social engineering to arrive before it could realize its true potential. Mayor Landrieu's boosterish assessment of post-Katrina

New Orleans can be summed up in his depiction of it as "America's best comeback story." In a blatant attempt to mislead readers, he boasted that "the New Orleans region has now returned to approximately 95 percent of its pre-Katrina population."[13] In fact, at that moment New Orleans had about 78 percent of its pre-Katrina population, and the recent growth rate has been 1.4 percent.[14] Aggregating the population with surrounding parishes was a transparent ploy to confuse the public concerning the state of the recovery.

Many have not come back to New Orleans because of lack of opportunities locally and because the dominant model of redevelopment has created obstacles to their return. To make them disappear through fake statistics is an outrage. Mayor Landrieu obviously didn't grasp the ludicrous but painful irony of calling the post-Katrina era, in which almost a quarter of the city's population did not return, "the best *comeback story*" in U.S. history!

Mayor Landrieu's voice is the voice of denial, deception and delusion. Let's be explicit about what is denied, silenced, and resilenced.

## Resilencing: Social Injustice

New Orleans—a city that has, according to Obama, made "remarkable" strides in becoming "more just"—is second on the list of U.S. cities with the most extreme economic inequality, and the gap between rich and poor has been increasing.[15] The level of economic inequality is comparable to the rate in Zambia.[16] It has very high levels of poverty, and child poverty in particular. Recent studies show that 39 percent of the city's children live in poverty, which is 17 percent above the national average. Childhood poverty has been increasing since 2007. The 27 percent poverty rate for families is also very high, both compared to other U.S. cities and by historic standards for New Orleans itself. The Jesuit Social Research Institute issued a report showing the shockingly high cost of living compared to income levels in Louisiana, especially in the New Orleans area, which has seen skyrocketing property values in the post-Katrina period.[17] In addition, despite heroic efforts by local groups, homelessness has remained a severe problem.

We must not forget that over one hundred thousand citizens of New Orleans have never returned home, many because of lack of recovery support and the vast proportional increases in cost of living for poor and working-class people. The replacement of public housing by mixed-income housing that displaces many or even most former residents has also contributed to a process that should be recognized as a form of ethnic and economic cleansing. There was also a 55 percent decrease in public transportation service as of 2015, and in 2013 the budget of the Regional Transit Authority was still almost 40 percent below its pre-Katrina level.[18] New Orleans was once appreciated by locals and newcomers for its combination of *joie de vivre*, rich culture, and modest cost of living, especially for housing. But this financial accessibility disappeared in the post-Katrina housing crisis and the drastic cutback in affordable public services.

The struggle over housing was a crucial one (and one in which I participated actively for a long time, including on behalf of public housing). However, the movement unfortunately fell under the influence of narrow leftist sectarians who suffer from fetishism of the state.[19] The result was a one-sided obsession with the less than 5 percent of pre-Katrina units that were in public housing and an almost complete neglect for the half of all housing consisting of commercial rental units, not to mention a lack of concern for the less privileged home owners who were struggling desperately for just and adequate compensation for damages. Almost fifty-two thousand of about seventy-nine thousand seriously damaged housing units were rental properties.[20] The vocal activist focus on public housing divided the citizenry and played into the hands of developers and their bureaucratic allies, who quickly concocted schemes to reengineer both public housing and the housing market overall for purposes of profitable ethnic cleansing and gentrification. The possibility for a broad-based movement for housing justice was lost, and the result has been over ten years of continuing injustice to renters in particular.

Another area of acute injustice in post-Katrina New Orleans has been health care. Medical services collapsed after the disaster, have continued to lag in some areas, and have remained in a state of crisis in others. Mental health care and addiction treatment have suffered the worst. Emergencies related to mental health, alcoholism and drug addiction are all commonly treated in the same manner, by consignment to Orleans Parish Prison. Furthermore, one of the great tragedies of the neoliberal reengineering of New Orleans was the fraudulent condemning and closing of Charity Hospital and the deliberate destruction of a historic Mid-City neighborhood for the sake of lucrative opportunities in developing its replacement. Charity Hospital could have been returned to service immediately after the disaster, when it was most desperately needed. The story of its permanent closing is rife with lies by the Jindal administration and involved literal sabotage of the closed facility in an effort to secure FEMA funds for a new medical center. The public was duped out of $283 million by deception and disinformation that disguised the fact that the old hospital could have been successfully adapted to fulfill current needs.[21] In addition, it is likely that many lives were lost, and a great many people suffered needlessly, as a result of this criminal injustice.

Such abuses have been part of the neoliberal engineering process that has gone under the rubric of "New Orleans as a Boutique City." This concept was met with considerable contempt in the early days after Katrina, but it has returned with a vengeance. Sean Cummings, a prominent real estate developer and CEO of New Orleans Building Corporation, boasted that "the city is a magnet again for new talent and new ideas, co-creating a new New Orleans." Cummings disingenuously explained, "A boutique city stands for something. It's original. It's authentic. It's one-of-a-kind."[22] In fact, this isn't what it means at all. New Orleans already stood for something, was original, was authentic, and was one-of-a-kind. Creating a "new" New Orleans is based on a quite different agenda. To make it into a "boutique city" means that it will be marketed to more affluent tourists, to new residents from the entrepreneurial and technical ("Silicon Bayou") sectors, and to wealthy buyers looking for a second or third home in a town with extraordinary entertainment and tourism opportunities. More recently, it has become evident that it will mean above all large-scale displacement of locals by massive purchasing of housing units by absentee owners for Airbnb rental.

## Resilencing: The Education Disaster

Post-Katrina New Orleans has gained considerable notoriety as the site of one of the nation's most far-reaching experiments in the destruction of a public school system and its replacement with a network of charter schools. Andrea Gabor, in a brief analysis in the *New York Times*, discusses many of the problems that have arisen for charter schools in New Orleans and that critics have long found to plague such schools everywhere.[23] The general case against these schools has been argued convincingly, and indeed devastatingly, by Diane Ravitch in a series of articles in the *New York Review of Books* starting with "The Myth of Charter Schools" and in her book *The Reign of Error*.[24]

In her article, Gabor applies many of these same arguments to the New Orleans case. She notes the discriminatory (a euphemism for "racist") nature of school reform. She cites "growing evidence that the reforms have come at the expense of the city's most disadvantaged children, who often disappear from school entirely and, thus, are no longer included in the data." Even establishment education figure Andre Perry, onetime CEO of the Capital One–University of New Orleans Charter Network, admits (as cited by Gabor) that "there were some pretty nefarious things done in the pursuit of academic gain," including "suspensions, pushouts, skimming, counseling out, and not handling special needs kids well." In other words, the case for charter schools depended significantly on injustices to the less privileged students: those who, in reality, have the greatest needs and who, from the standpoint of justice, deserve the most attention.

Gabor points out the questionable nature of claims for high performance by charter schools. She observes that studies ignore the fact that many disadvantaged students have been excluded from high-performing schools, or from schools entirely, and do not appear in statistics. She cites a recent study that concluded that "over 26,000 people in the metropolitan area between the ages of 16 and 24 are counted as 'disconnected,' because they are neither working nor in school." The Cowen Institute for Public Education Initiatives was forced to retract, due to flawed methodology, a study that concluded that the reengineered New Orleans school system had "higher graduation rates and better test scores than could be expected, given the socio-economic disadvantages of their students."[25] The biggest innovation introduced by charter schools may be that cheating on tests and reports, a practice once restricted to naughty students, has now become official policy.

However, the biggest flaw in defenses of charter schools in New Orleans is that they are based on comparison with the neglected and underfunded pre-Katrina school system. They do not consider what would have been possible if the same kind of support and resources that have been lavished on some charter schools had been devoted to creating a just, democratic, community-controlled school system that is dedicated to the welfare of every student and every neighborhood in the city.

## Resilencing: The Migration Disaster

In the midst of global turmoil over issues of migration, not a single politician was able to even speak the word "migrant" in relation to our city's recent history. As is often the case, *the truth is too conspicuous to be noticed.*

I grew up hearing New Orleans called the "Gateway to the Americas,"[26] a term that was popular during the long tenure of Mayor deLesseps "Chep"

Morrison, who became the ambassador to the Organization of American States. It was only much later that I heard the story of the United Fruit Company and the history of plunder of Latin America that was directed in part from boardrooms in New Orleans. I discovered that New Orleans was a gateway to the exploitation of those *Other Americas* that are excluded from the official definition of "America."[27] This aspect of history is, however, systematically forgotten.

Another forgotten reality is that in many ways, New Orleans, "the Queen City of the South," is a *northern city*. This is true geographically. Our city lies at the northern edge of one of our great bioregional points of reference, the Western Mediterranean Sea, consisting of the Gulf of Mexico and the Caribbean.[28] This is also true culturally. We are a northern city because of our position at the northern edge of Latin America. We have in fact *been* the northern part of Latin America. Louisiana was for its first 121 years part of the French and Spanish empires, and New Orleans in particular has never entirely lost its Latin character. It is becoming more Latin once again.[29]

Thus, we might have thought that the city would celebrate the renewed ties with Latin America that were created when Latino and Latina workers came to rebuild the city after the Katrina disaster. We have always relied on the kindness of *extraños*, but government and business gave at best an ambiguous welcome to these workers, even when they were most desperately needed. When they became less urgently needed, the authorities then either abandoned them or redirected their attention to disposing of them. The local administration still gives lip service to the efforts of these workers in rebuilding the city, at least on ceremonial occasions. However, it does little to address their problems, while creating additional ones, and at the same time facilitating attempts to expel them from the city.

The treatment to which migrant workers have been subjected has been outrageously unjust and intolerable. For over a decade, they and their families have been subject to wage theft, dangerous health and safety conditions, housing discrimination, police harassment, arbitrary arrests, ethnic profiling, predation by criminals, terrorization by authorities, and subjection to demeaning tracking with ankle bracelets. In the early years after Hurricane Katrina, while migrants were hard at work rebuilding the city, they were commonly called "walking ATMs," since they were regularly preyed upon by thieves and had no recourse to a legal system that was only interested in criminalizing the victims. When one looks carefully at the history of perseverance and determination of these migrants in the face of harsh struggles and extreme hardships, they make many of the locals look somewhat less "resilient" by comparison.[30]

We need to rethink that history and begin to celebrate New Orleans again as the Gateway to the Americas. We just have to remember one more thing this time: *A gateway opens in both directions.*[31]

## Resilencing: The Incarceration Disaster

Randolph Bourne famously proclaimed, paraphrasing Hegel, that "war is the health of the state." What is usually forgotten is that war on its own citizens is the highest expression of that health. After Katrina, we in New Orleans got to see what the state is like when all its mitigating qualities collapse and it is reduced to its essential repressive nature. This is the "minimal"—in the sense of maximally brutal—state. It is the state revealed as a state of war against the people.[32]

It is important that we remember the terroristic conditions that prevailed when New Orleans became a city *with* a penal system (the state's essential moment) and *without* a legal system (the state's inessential moment). This is what existed during the post-Katrina "state of exception."[33] This period was a state of "exception," not in the sense that it varied in principle from the normal and unexceptional. It was "exceptional" in the sense that normal brutality reached an unusual level of intensity and at certain moments even realized its full potential. Consequently, its nature could not, for a certain period of time, be ignored, denied, or disavowed very easily. It became the object of horror and public outrage.

But resilencing and forgetting has followed. For this reason, we have a solemn obligation to remember. We must not forget the prisoners who were trapped in Orleans Parish Prison in the rising floodwaters or herded away to spend countless hours stranded on overpasses in the hot sun. We must not forget the horrors of the makeshift Greyhound Station Prison, "Guantánamo on the Bayou," where prisoners were put in outdoor wire cages, made to sleep on concrete floors reeking of oil and diesel fuel, where they were harassed, intimidated, and controlled by being hosed and shot with beanbag rounds.

We need to remember the subhuman conditions at Hunt Correctional Center, where inmates from OPP, and victims of often-arbitrary mass post-Katrina arrests were herded together indiscriminately. Where they were for a time thrown naked in bare cells, kept in solitary confinement, and then moved to cells with hardened criminals or schizophrenics (imprisoned for their illness) as cellmates. Where they were then given nothing to wear but jumpsuits, and nothing to read for over a month. Where they were often kept in cells for twenty-four hours a day. Where mattresses were taken away every day so prisoners could only sit or lie on concrete or metal. Where loud bells were rung every fifteen minutes, every day, all day, in disciplinary tiers. We must remember the coercion of innocent citizens and volunteers into forced labor with the threat of being sent to Hunt. We need to remember the period in which there was widespread police repression, while at the same time racist vigilantes were allowed to terrorize some neighborhoods with impunity. We must remember the period in which power as domination was allowed to reveal its true face. The period in which *archy reigned supreme.*

Finally, we must remember one of the most horrifying of the stories that have been silenced, not only in Katrina commemorations but in the everyday world of Big Easyist business as usual. This is the brute fact that New Orleans has for many years been the world capital of "incarceration," which is merely a sanitized, Latinized term for the caging and torture of human beings. We must not forget that the United States leads the world in incarceration, that Louisiana leads the United States in incarceration, and that New Orleans leads Louisiana in incarceration. We must remember that in some ways incarceration in Louisiana has been the continuation of slavery by other means. We must never forget the murderous nature of a carceral system that destroys generations and destroys communities. This is a stark post-Katrina reality that no politician dares mention or commemorate.

### Resilencing: The Ecological Catastrophe

Beyond all these forms of resilencing lies the most extreme form of Katrina-disavowal, and disavowal regarding the fate of New Orleans itself. This concerns the fate of the city in relation to entrenched and accelerating global social ecological trends. No meaningful discussion of the future of New Orleans can afford to ignore the continuing loss of coastal wetlands, the implications of the accelerating rise in sea level, and the very real possibility (and long-term inevitability) of a much more powerful hurricane than Katrina hitting New Orleans directly. The specter of doom, indeed, highly likely doom, hangs over the city and cannot be exorcised by denial, by disavowal, or by any amount of happy talk by politicians and corporate executives.

The depth of ecological disavowal was highlighted in a Katrina anniversary segment of the public radio program *On Point*. Never during the hour-long program was the severity of the global ecological crisis and its implications for New Orleans really explored. However, an exchange with Dr. Paul Kemp, a coastal oceanographer and geologist at Louisiana State University, was particularly striking.[34] Kemp is one of the major advocates of Mississippi River diversion to create coastal wetlands. He is certainly a good guy, standing up for the region and, in particular, for the need to restore the coastal wetlands. But this is what makes his comments in some ways so troubling, since they also reflect the larger dominant ideology of disavowal.

Kemp didn't take on directly the details of how we are to cope with something between the three-foot rise in sea level commonly accepted, and the ten foot rise recently suggested by a team headed by James Hansen and sixteen colleagues.[35] Furthermore, we must face the fact that a rapid melting and collapse of large segments of the Greenland or Antarctic ice sheets would produce a much more rapid rise that would be devastating to coastal areas near or below sea level. The melting of the Greenland ice sheet would produce a twenty-foot rise in sea level, while that of the Antarctic ice sheet would produce a sixty-foot rise.[36] Most scientists believe that such effects will not be seen until into the next century, but are highly likely to occur if present trends continue.

Somehow, few think of a century as a comprehensible time span that has practical, concrete relevance. Even in relation to a three-hundred-year-old city. One might learn something from the ancient Hebrews, who posed the possibility that "the iniquity of the fathers" might be "visited on the children, to the third and the fourth generation."[37] Or from the Vedic Sages, who in the *Rig Veda* suggested that "the older shares the mistake of the younger."[38] Or from the Native Americans, who suggest that we consider the effects of our actions on the seventh generation. Or from the ancient Buddhist doctrine of karma, which, in literal terms, means taking responsibility for the way in which all the causes and conditions in which we are implicated have enduring consequences.

Kemp and others point out that if we can rebuild wetlands, the land will to a certain degree rise along with sea level rise. And it is indeed true that in many ways our coastal wetlands are more ecologically adaptable than other kinds of coastline. However, such restorative approaches can only offer long term hope if global climate change is addressed much more effectively than nation-states and corporations have done or are indeed structurally capable of doing. If the worst scenarios occur, as they are scheduled to, given business and statecraft as usual under the dominant global economic and political order, such projects will be no more than futile gestures in the long run.

Kemp concedes that "in a very large storm we are not going to be able to keep all the water out" but explains that after evacuation there will be "teams" that will "make sure that the property will be protected. The host, Tom Ashbrook, asks the incisive question: "Is New Orleans going to be around as we get higher sea levels?" But Kemp evades this question. In a conspicuously off-point response, he explains that the city's "original defenses" were vegetation and that "the marshes and swamps provided protection against surge and waves." He notes that "we have a big river to work with," implying that these traditional defenses will once again protect the city in the same manner that they once did, if we work diligently on coastal restoration.

But the current threats are of a different order from those faced when our "original defenses" did their job so well. In 2002, the *NOW with Bill Moyers* program did a piece that outlined starkly the dangers to New Orleans posed by what has long been called "The Big One."[39] In the segment, Emergency Manager Walter Maestri points out that a direct hit from a major hurricane that stalled over the city could fill up the natural bowl between the levees and leave twenty-two feet of water covering even the relatively high ground of the French Quarter. Maestri also remarks that when his office participated in a mock Hurricane emergency[40] and saw projections of the effects on the city caused by a major hurricane, model storm "Hurricane Delaney," "we changed the name of the storm from Delaney to K-Y-A-G-B . . . kiss your ass goodbye . . . because anybody who was here as that Category Five storm came across . . . was gone."

An exchange from the interview is instructive. Daniel Zwerdling asks, "Do you think that the President of the United States and Congress understand that people like you and the scientists studying this think the city of New Orleans could very possibly disappear?" This is basically the same question that Tom Ashbrook posed thirteen years later. But note the difference in the answer. Walter Maestri replies, "I think they know that, I think that they've been told that. I don't know that anybody, though, psychologically, you know, has come to grips with that as—as a—a potential real situation." They know, but they cannot *act* as if they know. In other words, they respond to the situation through disavowal.

This kind of brutal realism is refreshing, and quite necessary, since our response needs to be proportional to the true magnitude of the problem, and we have to cope with the fact that we are normally unable to respond in this manner. The documentary also included discussion of a proposal to build a large wall around the older parts of the city that are above sea level (more or less the quarter of the city nearest the river that didn't flood after Katrina), with huge gates that would be closed in times of heavy flooding, abandoning most of the city to destruction. This rather dramatic scenario may not be the correct approach, but it at least has the merit of taking the long-term hurricane threats seriously. Taking possibly catastrophic future sea level rise seriously would require an even more ruthless sense of reality.

There is a fundamental obstacle to clear recognition of our true ecological predicament. If one really grasps the problem, one is forced to admit that the only sane, rational, and humane response to such a problem is to take action that gets to its roots. This means becoming part of a local and global movement to destroy the system that is producing the catastrophe. Faced with this crisis of conscience and crisis of action, most who are not already lost in denial will succumb to the path of disavowal and try strategically to disremember what they have learned about the crisis. Fortunately for them, their path of bad faith will be supported by an entire world of systematically distorted discourse and practice.

## Resilencing: Dissident Voices and the Beloved Community

The final important thing that has been denied and disavowed, silenced and resilenced, is in fact the most positive thing that came out of the disaster. This is the story of the community self-determination, collective creativity, mutual aid, compassion, and solidarity that arose out of the devastated city. This story is perhaps told best in scott crow's book *Black Flags and Windmills* and in Francesco di Santis's *The Post-Katrina Portraits.*[41] It is a history that is obscured, minimized and even negated by the ideology of resilience.

Resilience is in itself merely an objective quality of a being, usually an organism or an ecosystem, and, by extension, a person or a community. It is not a moral virtue deserving of praise, though it is absurdly treated as one according to the resilientist ideology. The actual moral qualities related to resilience include diligence, perseverance, dedication, determination, and courage. Diligence or determination, which implies steadfastness and fortitude in the face of adversity, is in the Christian tradition one of the "Seven Heavenly Virtues" that are counterposed to the "Seven Deadly Sins." Similarly, both *adhiṭṭhāna* or resolute determination, and *vīrya* or diligence, are among the *pāramitās*, or "perfections" in Buddhist ethics. And courage has been one of the cardinal virtues since the time of the ancient Greek philosophers.

A community needs a measure of resilience merely to survive. However, it needs *resolute courage* in order to break the chains of illusion and domination so that it can become free and self-determining, so that it can flourish and realize itself. The Katrina catastrophe loosened those chains for a moment, and the spectacle of the abject failure of the dominant political and economic system, along with the flowering of grassroots mutual aid and solidarity, inspired the beginnings of a movement to shake them off entirely.

In the wake of the Katrina disaster, Common Ground Collective volunteers, echoing the language of the Zapatistas, talked about a "crack in history" or a "system crack" that had opened up, so that something new could emerge. A new world was emerging out of this fissure in the old, a new world based on values such as community and solidarity, care for one another, and care for the Earth. If one reflects on these basic values, it is apparent that this "new" world is in many ways a return to the very ancient idea of the Beloved Community. It is a return to the commons, a world in which all our ancestors once lived. Just as the People's Hurricane Relief Fund and others fought in the name of a "right of return" to New Orleans, we need to be inspired by a "right of return" to the freedom of the commons. It was this spirit of the commons and the common that inflamed tens of thousands of (primarily) young people who came to New Orleans as volunteers and sustained many thousands of local citizens who refused to leave or who returned quickly in order to serve and to save their own beloved communities.

The ideology of "resilience" is part of the process of paving over the crack, silencing the voice of insurgency. But not everyone looked to the Katrina anniversary as an opportunity to forget this history. In addition to the Tenth Annual Katrina March and Second Line,[42] there were the Common Ground Collective Ten Year Reunion[43] and the Fifth Annual

Southern Movement Assembly.[44] All of these dissident commemorations carried on the spirit of post-Katrina radicalism, looking back to a history of grassroots struggle and communal creativity and forward to a future that will not only remember but also continue that history.

Over ten years ago, reflecting on the scenes of post-Katrina destruction and on the recovery communities that were also emerging as communities of liberation and solidarity, I was able to make the following hopeful observation:

> At the same time that the state and corporate capitalism have shown their ineptitude in confronting our fundamental social and ecological problems, the grassroots recovery movement has continued to show its strength, its effectiveness, and its positive vision for the future. Most importantly, within this large and diverse movement, some have begun to lay the foundation for a participatory, democratically self-managed community based on mutual aid and solidarity.[45]

I took as the prime example of this communitarian creativity the work of the Common Ground Collective, which, I said,

> operates several distribution centers, two media centers, a women's center, a community kitchen, several clinics, and various sites for housing volunteers. Its current projects include house gutting, mold abatement, roof tarping, tree removal, temporary housing, safety and health training, a community newspaper, community radio, bioremediation, a biodiesel program, computer classes, childcare co-ops, worker co-ops, legal assistance, eviction defense, prisoner support, after-school and summer programs, anti-racism training, and wetlands restoration work.[46]

Fragments of this emerging community of liberation and solidarity have endured, and some have even grown and developed. True, this transformative vision has remained, as of today, largely unrealized in the face of the forces of normalization, co-optation, and resilencing. Yet many in New Orleans, indeed a growing number, still strive to realize this vision, and seek to learn from our traumatic history a way beyond the ideologies and institutions of domination to communal freedom.

Perhaps the solution to our impasse is simply a matter of recognizing the obvious and acting accordingly. We need to admit that the disaster is permanent and that it is of world-historical, indeed Earth-historical pro-portions. It seemed like a miracle that ten years ago, in the midst of dev-astation and abandonment, tens of thousands of volunteers could come together in post-Katrina New Orleans in a spirit of communal solidarity. Can there be a miracle today that is proportional to the magnitude of our challenge? The Earth itself, the *oikos*, is our Common Ground. Our Time in History, the *kairos*, is our Common Ground.

In a sense, I must ask today exactly the same question that I asked myself and others in the months after the Katrina disaster. In the spring of 2006, I wrote an article that probed the psychological and ontological depths of devastation, and posed the political, and ultimately existential, question, "Do You Know What It Means?"[47] This is still the question. Will we put the disaster behind us, even as it continues and indeed intensifies at its deepest levels, or will we finally learn its lessons? Will we finally learn how to think and act: for ourselves, for the community, and for the Earth?

The rest is resilence.

## NOTES

1   *Merriam-Webster's Collegiate Dictionary*, 11th ed. (Springfield, MA: Merriam-Webster, 2003).

2   See the website for his film *The Big Uneasy*, http://www.thebiguneasy.com/.

3   See the website for *Big Charity: The Death of America's Oldest Hospital*, http://www.bigcharityfilm.com/.

4   See the website for *My Louisiana Love*, http://www.mylouisianalove.com/.

5   Hurricane Betsy was a larger hurricane than Hurricane Katrina and hit New Orleans directly, with the eye passing slightly west (that is, on the "bad," or most destructive, side) of the city.

6   Cain Burdeau and Jeff Amy, "George W. Bush Visits Disaster Zone, 10 Years After Katrina," Associated Press, August 28, 2015, http://hosted.ap.org/dynamic/stories/U/US_KATRINA_BUSH?SITE=AP&SECTION=HOME&TEMPLATE=DEFAULT.

7   It is significant, and not widely known, that 28 percent of housing units in the city were not damaged, and 58 percent were not damaged seriously. See Rachel E. Luft with Shana Griffin, "A Status Report on Housing in New Orleans after Katrina: An Intersectional Analysis" in Beth Willinger, ed., *Katrina and the Women of New Orleans* (New Orleans: Newcomb College Center for Research on Women, December 2008), http://webcache.googleusercontent.com/search?q=cache:jd9AwzZZSWgJ:https://tulane.edu/newcomb/upload/NCCROWreport08-chapter5.pdf+&cd=8&hl=en&ct=clnk&gl=us.

8   Barack Obama, "important (don't delete)," email from Obama at dccc@dccc.org to author, Thursday, August 27, 2015.

9   "Transcript of President Obama's Katrina Speech," *NOLA.com*, August 28, 2015, http://www.nola.com/katrina/index.ssf/2015/08/transcript_of_president_obamas.html.

10  The phrase "jockamo fee nané" from the song "Iko, Iko" is a universal favorite, but it is not generally known that it was an invitation by Mardi Gras Indians to their rivals to engage in a certain submissive and humiliating act. See John Clark and Melissa San Roman, "If You Don't Like What the Big Chief Say . . . (An Interview with Mr. Donald Harrison, Sr., Big Chief of the Guardians of the Flame)," *Mesechabe: The Journal of Surregionalism*, no. 8 (Spring 1991), https://www.academia.edu/2948272.

11  "Lying Chiefs of State," which recalls the Chef Menteur Pass in New Orleans East, which, according to one story, was named by the Choctaw "Oulabe Mingo," or "Lying Chief," after the French colonial governor.

12  Polly Mosendz, "New Orleans Mayor Mitch Landrieu on the 10th Anniversary of Hurricane Katrina," *Newsweek*, August 29, 2015, http://www.newsweek.com/new-orleans-mayor-mitch-landrieu-10th-anniversary-hurricane-katrina-367046.

13  Mitchell J. Landrieu, "About the Project," Katrina 10: Resilient New Orleans website, 2015, http://katrina10.org/about-the-project/.

14  Jeff Adelson, "New Orleans Area Population Still Growing Post-Katrina, but Slowly: Post-Katrina Increase Slows to a Plateau," *New Orleans Advocate*, March 28, 2015, http://www.theneworleansadvocate.com/news/11941581-172/new-orleans-area-population-still.

15  This is according to a Bloomberg analysis, "Most Income Inequality, U.S. Cities," *Bloomberg Business*, updated April 15, 2014, http://www.bloomberg.com/visual-data/best-and-worst/most-income-inequality-us-cities.

16  Robert McClendon, "New Orleans Is 2nd Worst for Income Inequality in the U.S., Roughly on Par with Zambia, Report Says," *NOLA.com*, August 19, 2014, http://www.nola.com/politics/index.ssf/2014/08/new_orleans_is_2nd_worst_for_i.html.

17  Jesuit Social Research Institute, "Too Much for Too Many: What Does It Cost Families to Live in Louisiana?," *JustSouth Quarterly*, http://www.loyno.edu/jsri/too-much-too-many.

18  Alex Posorske, "The State of Transit Ten Years after Katrina," Ride New Orleans, August 17, 2015, http://rideneworleans.org/state-of-transit-ten-years-after-katrina/.

19  Legendary activist and cofounder of Common Ground Malik Rahim once replied to such sectarianism (expressed at a U.S. Federation of Worker Cooperatives national conference in New Orleans) that the goal must be the replacement of so-called public housing with democratic, resident-controlled *community housing*.

20  See Luft and Griffin, "A Status Report on Housing."

21  See the Save Charity Hospital website, http://www.savecharityhospital.com/ for extensive information on these issues. The film *Big Charity* is a good introduction to the entire story of deception, betrayal, and criminal opportunism. Spike Lee's *If God Is Willing and the Creek Don't Rise* also covers many of the Charity Hospital issues well. See the website for the documentary: http://www.hbo.com/documentaries/if-god-is-willing-and-da-creek-dont-rise.

22    Oscar Raymundo, "New Orleans Rebuilds as a Boutique City" *BBC Travel*, February 11, 2013, http://www.bbc.com/travel/story/20130207-new-orleans-rebuilds-as-a-boutique-city.

23    Andrea Gabor, "The Myth of the New Orleans School Makeover," *New York Times*, August, 22, 2015, http://www.nytimes.com/2015/08/23/opinion/sunday/the-myth-of-the-new-orleans-school-makeover.html?_r=2.

24    See the *NYRB*'s Diane Ravitch page at http://www.nybooks.com/contributors/diane-ravitch/ and her book *Reign of Error: The Hoax of the Privatization Movement and the Danger to America's Public Schools* (New York: Vintage Books, 2014).

25    Jessica Williams, "Tulane's Cowen Institute Retracts New Orleans Schools Report, Apologizes," *NOLA.com*, October 10, 2014, http://www.nola.com/education/index.ssf/2014/10/tulanes_cowen_institute_retracts_new_orleans_schools_report_apologizes.html.

26    New Orleans aspires to regain that image, as a recent editorial story in *New Orleans Magazine* recounts. See "Rebuilding the Gateway," June 2015, http://www.myneworleans.com/New-Orleans-Magazine/June-2015/Rebuilding-the-Gateway/

27    See Stephen Duplantier, ed. *The Banana Chronicles*, a special issue of *Neotropica* magazine devoted to the story of the United Fruit Company and the exploitation of Central America. http://www.neotropica.info/.

28    The other great bioregional reality is, of course, the Mississippi River, and this is what makes us also a geographically southern city.

29    Some of these themes are developed in chapter 19 of this volume.

30    An interview with representatives of the Congress of Day Laborers (Congreso de Jornaleros) from local radio station WHIV is an excellent introduction to the experience of migrant workers and their families in post-Katrina New Orleans. See "MarkAlain and Congress of Day Laborers," August 29, 2015, https://soundcloud.com/whivfm/sets. In this program, Dr. MarkAlain Dery interviews Brenda Castro and Santos Alvarado, representatives of the Congress of Day Laborers on the Katrina Tenth Anniversary. WHIV was founded by Dr. Dery, medical director for the Tulane T-Cell Clinic, and his coworkers. It is dedicated to "public health, human rights and social justice," and is New Orleans's only full-time grassroots community radio station. For information on the Congress of Day Laborers, a project of the New Orleans Workers' Center for Racial Justice, see http://nowcrj.org/about-2/congress-of-day-laborers/.

31    A clear recognition of the injustices done to migrants is so difficult for many because it necessarily leads to a questioning of the very foundations of nationalism and imperialism.

32    For the least privileged and least powerful, the state is less like the proverbial "nanny" of right-wing ideological fantasy and more like the babysitter of urban legend who puts the baby the microwave.

33    For an excellent survey of post-Katrina penal and legal issues, see Marina Sideris, "Illegal Imprisonment: Mass Incarceration and Judicial Debilitation in Post Katrina New Orleans," University of California–Berkeley, May 10, 2007, http://www.law.berkeley.edu/library/resources/disasters/Sideris.pdf.

34    "On Point," August 26, 2015, http://onpoint.wbur.org/2015/08/26/new-orleans-10-years-after-katrina.

35 James Hansen et al., "Ice Melt, Sea Level Rise and Superstorms: Evidence from Paleoclimate Data, Climate Modeling, and Modern Observations That 2°C Global Warming Is Highly Dangerous," *Atmospheric Chemistry and Physics* 15, 20059–20179, July 2015, abstract at http://www.atmos-chem-phys-discuss. net/15/20059/2015/acpd-15-20059-2015.html.

36 National Snow and Ice Data Center, "Quick Facts on Ice Sheets," https://nsidc. org/cryosphere/quickfacts/icesheets.html.

37 Numbers 14:18.

38 Thanks to Quincy Saul for this reference and many other helpful suggestions concerning this discussion.

39 "The City in a Bowl," November 20, 2002, transcript, http://www.pbs.org/now/ transcript/transcript_neworleans.html. Excerpts from the original documentary are included in NOVA scienceNOW, "Hurricanes," http://www.pbs.org/ wgbh/nova/education/earth/hurricanes-new-orleans-threat.html.

40 Louisiana Office of Emergency Preparedness exercise on June 18, 2002; see GlobalSecurity.org, "Hurricane Delaney," http://www.globalsecurity.org/ security/ops/hurricane-delaney.htm.

41 Scott crow, *Black Flags and Windmills: Hope, Anarchy, and the Common Ground Collective* 2nd ed. (Oakland: PM Press, 2014). The *Post-Katrina Portraits* collection (which will be discussed further in chapters 12 and 19) consists of images of survivors and volunteers sketched by artist Francesco di Santis and accounts of their experiences written by the subjects. A selection of several hundred images and stories was published as a large-format art book, *The Post-Katrina Portraits, Written and Narrated by Hundreds, Drawn by Francesco di Santis* (New Orleans: Francesco di Santis and Loulou Latta, 2007) and can also be found online at https://www.flickr.com/photos/postkatrinaportraits/show/. See also Part V, "New Orleans: Common Grounds and Killers," in Rebecca Solnit, *A Paradise Built in Hell: The Extraordinary Communities That Arise in Disaster* (New York: Penguin Books, 2009), 231–304.

42 "New Orleans Katrina Commemoration" Facebook page, https://www.facebook. com/thekatrinacommemoration.

43 "Common Ground Collective 10 Year Reunion" Facebook page, https://www. facebook.com/events/774116122702802/.

44 Anna Simonton, "Amid Katrina Commemoration Spectacle, a Southern Freedom Movement Takes Shape," *Truthout*, September 1, 2015, http://www. truth-out.org/news/item/32590-amid-katrina-commemoration-spectacle-a-southern-freedom-movement-takes-shape.

45 Originally published as "Postscript to 'A Letter from New Orleans,'" *Perspectives on Anarchist Theory*, no. 5 (Fall 2006): 33–41; reprinted in *Divergences: Revue Libertaire Internationale en Ligne*, no. 15 (June 2009), http://divergences.be/spip. php?article1485.

46 "Postscript to 'A Letter from New Orleans.'"

47 See chapter 12 in this volume.

**PART II**

# ANOTHER WORLD
# IS ACTUAL

6

# Homage to Lacandonia: The Politics
# of Heart and Spirit in Chiapas

For many years, I have been conducting an experiment to investigate the dominant ideology. I have asked people if there was any famous statement by Marx that they could quote from memory. I have found that there has been one almost universal response, namely that Marx said that "religion is the opiate of the masses." What is so striking about this reply is that it cites only part of Marx's famous saying and, rather suspiciously, leaves out what is quite possibly the most important part. The missing part states that "religion is the sigh of the oppressed creature, the heart of a heartless world, and the spirit of spiritless conditions."[1] Marx implies that religion has been and remains a powerful force in society because it is a source of "heart" and "spirit."[2]

If we think deeply about the implications of Marx's statement, we can learn something very important. It is something that has not been grasped well by radical and revolutionary movements (including, and perhaps even especially, by those movements called "Marxist"). If one wants to replace traditional religion with something else, the result will be a disaster if that "something else" does not contain at least as much *heart* and *spirit* as what is being replaced. The history of the Zapatista movement is the history of learning precisely that truth, as is revealed in *Autonomy Is in Our Hearts*, Dylan Fitzwater's eloquent and illuminating account of Zapatista politics and indigenous culture, which will be the major point of reference for this discussion.[3]

One of the most important lessons of the history of the Zapatista movement is the need to give up presuppositions of the dominant hierarchical, dualistic society and to learn from the wisdom of indigenous people. The EZLN, or Zapatista Army of National Liberation, grew out of the FLN, or Forces of National Liberation, which was a traditional Marxist vanguardist organization that focused on the seizure of state power and the reorganization of the economy under centralized control. The FLN militants inherited this patriarchal authoritarian model, which professes egalitarianism in theory but operates in practice as an ideological justification of the power of an elite that rules in the supposed interest of the masses. A small group of FLN militants were sent to Chiapas to organize the peasants according to the tenets of this ideology. Perhaps no one has summarized what followed with a more apt sense of irony than has Régis Debray. He says that

> it is in the nature of Indian communities . . . that power rises from below. This cult of consensus, this "all together or nothing" attitude has made its mark on the small band of hierarchical and self-confident Guevara supporters who, in the old manner, plunged into the unknown in 1984. These whites came to convert the Indians to the revolution, as their ancestors did in the old days, to the Gospel; and voilà, it is the Indians who have converted them to another conception of the world, horizontal and modest. Those who came from the city brought with them a sense of the individual, of the nation, and beyond, of the wider world; the natives a sense of harmony, of permanent referendum, of listening.[4]

Alex Khasnabish comments that "this encounter resulted not in the 'revolutionizing' of the indigenous communities but in the 'defeat' of Marxist dogma at the hands of these indigenous realities."[5] Perhaps we should say it was a triumph of their "hearts and hands," and perhaps the precise term for the deep change that the unsuspecting militants underwent is indeed, as Debray says, "conversion." Their social ontology was overturned. They were converted from a view of revolution as the imposition on the masses of a preconceived ideological paradigm under the tutelage of an enlightened vanguard, to a vision of revolution as a socially and ecologically regenerative activity that is deeply rooted in history, tradition, culture, and place, and is carried out through the cooperative activities of everyone in the community. The community took the place of the program. As the EZLN began to emerge from this process of transformation, its focus was no longer on seizure of state power and the leading role of the vanguard party, but rather on "local autonomy and self-determination" for the indigenous people themselves.[6]

Part of this transformation was expressed in social institutional and organizational form, in what is often described as a transition from a vertical, implicitly hierarchical model to a horizontal, explicitly egalitarian one. Perhaps the most striking expression of the latter is the invention of the Caracol. In many ways, this social form, as creative as it is, is less an invention than a reinvention of the Commune in the context of, and in continuity with, the history and culture of Chiapas and the larger history of communalism in Mexico and the Americas as a whole. Many examples can be given, including the famed Quilombo dos Palmares and diverse maroon communities scattered across South America, the Caribbean, and North America.[7] Even more to the point, John Womack states in *Zapata and the Mexican Revolution*, "In central and southern Mexico the utopia of a free association of rural clans was very ancient. In various forms it had moved villagers long before the Spanish came."[8]

The Caracol was established in 2003 as the successor to the five "Aguascalientes," or regional centers, that had previously existed. Khasnabish describes them as "political and cultural centers, gateways into and out of Zapatista territory in rebellion, and places of encounter between the Zapatistas and national and international civil society."[9] They are also much more than this. They are the sites for the Juntas de Buen Gobierno, or Good Government Councils, that have become, along with community assemblies, the most authentic expressions of base democracy. The Caracoles are also the administrative centers for the Zapatista Autonomous Rebel Municipal Zones (MAREZ) "with each of the Juntas including one or more representatives from each of the autonomous municipalities grouped together in each MAREZ."[10] In addition, the Zapatista Rebel Autonomous Education System has established elementary schools in every community, and these feed into secondary schools located in the Caracoles. Caracoles have also become communication centers for Zapatista independent media. Knoll and Reyes report that as of 2014 there were ten community radio stations, and at least one community had a media center for instruction in filmmaking and broadcasting.[11] Finally, there is a clinic in each Caracol and, in some cases, "high level clinics with ambulances, dormitories, dentists, doctors, laboratories."[12]

This is all impressive at the level of grassroots social organization. Yet we know that there is much more to the story than this. We know because none of it, in itself, explains why such a center is called a Caracol, which means "snail shell" or "conch shell." The more one looks into the art, music, poetry, and discourse of the Zapatistas, the more explanations are found for these connections.[13] Here is one. Pablo González Casanova explains the significance of the Caracol as follows:

> The conch is a large and cavernous seashell, pointed and spiral, which can amplify sounds—both what one hears and what one emits. The indigenous people of Chiapas, writes Subcomandante Marcos, "held the figure of the conch in great esteem." It was, for them, a symbol of knowledge and of life. They used it "to summon the community" and as "an aid to hear the most distant words."[14]

This short explanation already touches on many domains. Hearing, finding a voice, knowing, living, being communal, being in contact with important but distant realities. As impressive as the Caracol is as a communal social form, it is crucial that it be situated within its larger context, and to see the ways in which it is an integral expression of transformation both at the level of the person and at the level of social whole.[15] We can grasp this more clearly if we understand the manner in which the Zapatista conception of the political shifted from the traditional Western leftist privileging of social ideology and social institutional structure to a larger problematic that emphasizes very heavily the social ethos and the social imaginary as forms of communal self-expression.

## Making Connections

Central to this revolutionary ethos and radical imaginary are the concept of "heart" and the closely connected concepts of "soul" and "spirit." "Heart" appears almost two hundred times in Fitzwater's text, most often taken from indigenous Zapatista testimonies. The Zapatista movement brings to the center of radical political thought and practice these and related concepts that have generally remained on the margins of the Western Left, though they have been important in certain strands of communitarian anarchism and so-called utopian socialism and became familiar as the result of the forms of radical spirituality associated with liberation theology. Thus, in addition to offering invaluable lessons for a generally disoriented Left in what Vandana Shiva has called the "maldeveloped" world,[16] the Zapatista revolution can help that Left recover some of its own most important but largely neglected and submerged traditions.

These dissident currents have drawn upon all the sources of heart and spirit that were embodied in traditional religion, transforming them into a means for communal liberation and realization. For example, the concept of "heart" is quite central to Gustav Landauer's communitarian anarchism. He observed that "the more capitalism blossoms, the weaker the heart and spirit of the proletariat become."[17] This heart and spirit must be revived and the disintegrative effects of atomizing bourgeois society reversed, for the people to regain hope and creative energy. He states that "the community should not concern itself with efforts other than those that derive from its heart—a heart formed by the hearts of all of its members, united in a common will."[18] At least as important for Landauer was the concept of *Geist*, or spirit, which he describes as a "communal spirit," a "drive to the whole, to associate with others, to community, to justice" that "never rests."[19]

As was mentioned in the Preface, a similar radical spirituality is expressed powerfully in ecosocialist philosopher of liberation Joel Kovel's classic work *History and Spirit*. Kovel describes spirit as *"what happens to us as the boundaries of the self give way*. Or we could say that it is about the 'soul,' by which we shall mean *the form of 'being' taken by the spiritual self*."[20] It is this liberated spiritual self that is most capable of becoming the subject of revolution. It is significant that Kovel's work was profoundly influenced by his experience of radical spirituality in Central America, during the Sandinista Revolution in particular, and reflects the confluence of indigenous wisdom and liberation theology that also shaped the Zapatista revolution. For thinkers like Landauer and Kovel, as for the Zapatistas, revolution must be a movement of spiritual regeneration in which the greatest wealth of the community is found in the flourishing of its collective heart and spirit. These realities are the basis on which social and ecological regeneration can begin to emerge.

## The Language of Heart and Spirit

As Fitzwater explains, these crucial realities are expressed in the indigenous culture of Chiapas through the interconnected concepts of *o'on* and *ch'ulel*. In the course of his studies he learned that the former term means "collective heart," while the latter connotes both "soul" and "collective potentiality."[21] The collective heart is fundamental to the community because of its ability to "give rise to common thoughts and feelings."[22] Fitzwater explains that these two concepts should really be expressed through the single idea of "thoughts/feelings," since they "are understood as one and the same" and are interconnected as "realizations of the inherent potentialities of the heart,"[23] in which thinking and feeling are not separate. This account contrasts markedly with the reigning Western (and increasingly global) dualism exhibited classically in Hume's famous fact-value dichotomy, in which thought, which is supposed to be based on experience of an objective world, and feeling, which is supposed to be based on subjective, relativistic responses to that world, are relegated to entirely separate realms.

The dominant hierarchical and dualistic ideology of civilization, and especially its manifestation in Western modernity, expresses abstractly and fantastically the actual conditions of social alienation in a hierarchical and dualistic society. Under civilization, the society of separation and domination, the "what is," that is, the existing system of domination, cannot really be challenged by the "what ought to be," that is, by any alternative to that system. "What is," no matter how irrational it may be, is perceived as self-evident a priori truth that becomes a de facto categorical imperative. The discovery of nondualistic Tsotsil and Tzeltal cultural concepts, and the social practice based on them, has the power to destabilize this conventional wisdom. We might say that in a sense "all that is delusively solid melts into spirit." Alternatively, we might say that all that has been deadened and objectified is reanimated and reinspirited.

Another pivotal indigenous concept with deep ontological implications that is discussed by Fitzwater is *ch'ulel*. According to a study of Tzeltal usage carried out in the municipality of Cancuc, "a person is composed of a body (*bak'etal*), made up of flesh and blood, and a group of 'souls' (*ch'ulel*; plural *ch'uleltik*) residing within the heart of each individual."[24] This implies that selfhood is a multiplicity, a kind of unity in diversity, rather than the "simple substance" favored in Western egocentric metaphysics. Fitzwater suggests that references to this momentous reality as "soul" must be taken with a grain of salt, since the indigenous concept does not correspond to what we expect when we hear that Western term. It derives from the Tzeltal and Tsotsil root *ch'ul*, which means "holy" or "sacred," and "in a strict sense" it "denotes a thing's radical 'other.'"[25]

This explanation recalls Rudolf Otto's famous description of "the holy" or "the sacred" in *The Idea of the Holy* as a powerful and numinous reality that is "wholly other."[26] However, even more pertinent is what Kovel uncovers in diverse spiritual traditions in *History and Spirit*. Kovel says that "the self is not only its positive self; there is also its Otherness in relation to being, and the things we call spiritual take place in the zone of Otherness that links the self to being."[27] It is the discovery of this Otherness that leads us beyond the bounds of the ego to the community of humanity and nature. It also leads us to recognize the need for revolution against a system of domination and separation that tears that community apart.

## Attaining Greatness of Heart

It might not be immediately clear to those accustomed to the dominant Western models of politics (whether right or left) how the discourse of "heart" and "spirit" is a specifically political discourse. This is because the prevailing views focus heavily on social institutional structures, the ideologies that legitimate or challenge these structures, and the problematic of either defending or overturning them. The language of "heart" and "spirit" does not neglect these spheres, but it is also in a very strong sense a communitarian language that is grounded in a *communal ethos* and a *communal imaginary*. One of the weaknesses in mainstream radical thought is the weak connections that are made between ideology and institutions, on the one hand, and ethos and imaginary, on the other, so there is much to learn from indigenous cultures in which there is a stronger dialectical interrelation between all these spheres.

One of the most personally, communally, and politically significant indigenous concepts that illustrates how these dimensions intersect is *"ichbail ta muk'."* This Tsotsil phrase is defined by Fitzwater as "to bring (*ichil*) one another (*ba*) to largeness or greatness (*ta muk'*) and implies the coming together of a big collective heart." The reader may be surprised when Fitzwater reveals that the phrase can also be translated simply as "democracy."[28] Obviously, the Zapatistas impart a much fuller and deeper meaning to this term than that found in the impoverished conception of democracy inherited from the Western liberal tradition. The Zapatista concept is a profoundly social-ecological one, since it implies "respect" for and "recognition" of all beings in both the natural and social worlds, which are really seen as one continuous world.[29] It combines aspects of the ethics and politics of care with an ethics and politics of social and ecological flourishing. In this sense, it is one of the most radical and far-reaching conceptions of democracy yet to appear.

The process of *ichbail ta muk'ot*, or "carrying one another to greatness" through the creation of "a big collective heart" aims at the achievement of a nondominating unity in diversity. This process presupposes the existence of communal subjectivity, "the inclusive we (*ko'ontik*) that does not subsume the different exclusive 'our hearts' (*ko'onkutik*) that compose it."[30] Such an analysis refutes typical anti-communitarian arguments, which assume that communal institutions must entail a regression to reactionary and repressive, if not explicitly fascistic, concepts of homogeneity and identity.

The use of such repressive mechanisms is not, however, typical of indigenous communities and horizontalist organizations. Rather, they are usually the result of the contradictions that arise within highly atomized statist and capitalist societies or within evolving societies going through the traumatic process of integration into the statist and capitalist global order. In these societies, highly participatory traditional communities have either dissolved or are disintegrating under severe stress. The longing for the security that they once provided is co-opted for authoritarian and exploitative purposes. The increasingly atomized masses are offered a fantasized identity through mythic, ideological, and highly manipulative concepts of unity based on nationality, race, ethnicity, or religious background. What commodities in general inevitably fail to deliver is sold as part of the package called "your true identity," the powerful and alluring commodity of last resort.

The Zapatista "big collective heart" is diametrically opposed to such regressive tendencies. It is a creative, rather than reactive, response to the destructive and alienating tendencies of the corporate capitalist economy, the liberal political order, and the nihilistic culture of mass consumption. It responds to such threats through organic forms of solidarity, rather than mechanistic ones.[31]

## A Change of Heart

A final and extremely crucial aspect of the politics of heart concerns the nature of the transformative experience, the deep change of heart, or fullness of heart, that is necessary. Three passages from Fitzwater address this issue very pertinently. First, he says that heart (*o'on*) denotes "the space inhabited by a certain *ch'ulel*," or soul, including "a *ch'ulel* that traverses an entire community, and thus brings them together into the shared space of a single heart."[32] Thus, the politics of heart has a goal of communal wholeness and draws on an inherent potentiality within the community to "bring itself to greatness" collectively.

Second, Fitzwater explains that "in Tsotsil the wholeness or fragmentation of the heart describes the positive or negative emotional, physical and spiritual state of a collective or an individual."[33] Thus, there is a connection between the condition of the heart of the person and the condition of the heart of the community, the heart of the world. Depression, addiction, anxiety, alienation, aggression, and nihilism on the part of the person is a symptom of a deranged and diseased state of the world. Love, compassion, joy, enthusiasm, hope, and creative energy on the part of the person is a symptom of a sane and healthy state of the world or of a new world that is coming into being, in which one is taking part.

Third, Fitzwater points out the importance in the indigenous community of "the process of sadness overflowing the heart." He explains that "the spreading of shared sadness, and thus of shared *ch'ulel*" is "the first step in a process of self-organization, what might be called 'creating political consciousness' in English or Spanish."[34] This shows an awareness within the indigenous culture of the ways in which suffering and trauma can be the beginning of liberation. This point is particularly thought-provoking, since it addresses the question of what initial step could lead one to engage in personal and social transformation.

This analysis of transformative experience parallels the teaching in Buddhism (the "First Noble Truth") that the beginning of wisdom and compassion is awakening to the suffering in the world and its relation to one's own suffering. Buddhist philosophy concurs with Marx that most of religion is an opiate, rather than a curative treatment, but adds that almost everything else that conventional society offers is also an opiate, while usually lacking even the palliative effects that religion provides. Buddhism points out the need to move on to a cure. The truth of suffering only attains fulfillment when it becomes part of the comprehensive practice of a community of liberation and solidarity—the sangha, the revolutionary base community, the Beloved Community—that aims at getting to the causes of suffering and effecting a cure for it.

Such insights are not, of course, limited to Buddhism (except to the degree that Buddhism is taken simply as a generic term for the "awakened mind"). More generally and cross-culturally, there is an experience of a "Dark Night of the Soul," or transformative trauma, that signals the break with egocentric, patriarchal, hierarchical, dominating consciousness and leads toward personal and communal liberation. The function of a revolutionary movement is to assure that the transformed consciousness does not retreat into some comforting but illusory solution in the narrowly personal realm (the opiate of the person), but that it is expressed in effective social transformative practice of a flourishing community of liberation and solidarity.

## Celebrating the People and the Earth

One of the most revelatory aspects of Fitzwater's work is its account of the indigenous ontology of self and world. We are confronted with the implicitly revolutionary implications of the teaching of "no separate selfhood" and the indigenous practice of communal selfhood. Many passages are reminiscent of Dorothy Lee's analysis in her classic essay "The Conception of the Self Among the Wintu Indians."[35] Lee presents one of the most illuminating analyses of the contrast between the nondualistic, integral, yet differentiated Native American indigenous conception of the self and the civilized, domineering, egocentric conception. Her essays explore the ontological and epistemological aspects of selfhood and the ways in which they are related to a reciprocal and nondominating relationship to the world.

Its spirit is conveyed simply and concisely in the words of Lee's respondent Sadie Marsh, who informed Lee that the Wintu word for body was "*kot wintu*," meaning "the whole person." When Lee asked her for her autobiography, she recounted what she called "my story." Lee says that "the first three quarters of this, approximately, are occupied with the lives of her grandfather, her uncle and her mother before her birth; finally, she reaches the point where she was 'that which was in my mother's womb,' and from then on, she speaks of herself, also."[36]

This same spirit of relatedness and transpersonal selfhood is found in the worldview expressed in the testimonies cited by Fitzwater. The Zapatistas are a movement of storytelling par excellence, and when they tell their stories these are always told as "our stories." The members of every culture and subculture have a fundamental fantasy, and it is always a collective fantasy. Even when the fantasy is a fantasy of individualism it is still a collective fantasy. There is nothing so boringly monotonous as the self-justifying tales of "rugged individualists" telling how ruggedly individualist they are. The members of some cultures might well be embarrassed if they had to reveal in explicit terms the story of their deepest egocentric and avaricious longings. Others, such as the members of the indigenous cultures of Chiapas, can express their fundamental fantasies openly and joyfully through beautiful and poetic stories celebrating the people and the Earth.

And it is not only in words that they are celebrated. "The question of the party" is an inevitable one for radical politics. However, the Zapatista answer to the question might surprise many. When local people explained to Fitzwater that "the party" has been important in nurturing "a sense of collectivity," they were not referring to the vanguardist institution that the Zapatistas abandoned long ago. Rather, they had in mind the *fiestas* that the indigenous communities understand as central to building and strengthening the Zapatista movement. The celebration in question has subtleties of meaning that are perhaps conveyed better by the English term "festival," which connotes not only a time for collective jubilation but also harks back to ancient rites in which sacred beings, places, and objects are honored. As Fitzwater notes, the members of the community not only "have fun" at Zapatista parties, they also, as the Tsotsil phrase expresses it, make an offering to or have a festival for "the territory/earth/world."[37]

It is a "celebration," both in the sense of a shared experience of joy and in the sense of a tribute to that which is the source of joy. This is one of many important ways in which the Zapatista movement puts the social ethos and the social imaginary at the center of revolutionary transformation. Indigenous people have often understood what few laboring under the yoke of civilization have realized. To paraphrase slightly a famous maxim: "What's a revolution without general celebration?" The radical carnivalesque is one of the most effective catalysts of Landauer's "positive envy" or liberatory desire that will lead masses of people to the free community. Fitzwater notes that "there is a close relationship in Tsotsil between parties or festivals and the bringing of the heart to greatness."[38] Chiapas offers the often-missing link between "Carnival against Capitalism" and "Carnival for the Creation of the World." The Zapatista party is a form of deep play, in which the ludic intersects with the political and the ontological.[39]

## The Politics of Poesis

*Autonomy Is in Our Hearts* reveals that the Zapatista movement is based on a social ontology that poses fundamental questions about the nature of human social being. Many have looked rightly to the Zapatista revolution as perhaps the most instructive example in the contemporary world of the practice of horizontalist politics. It is important, however, to recognize the *horizonal* dimension of Zapatista *horizontalism*. The movement is deeply revolutionary in large part because it poses *the question of our horizons*. That is, it evokes critical reflection on and rethinking of the boundaries (and the unboundedness) of our social world. It calls on the members of the community (and ultimately calls on all of us) to recognize the natural and, indeed, sacred boundaries that have been transgressed at great cost to both human beings and to all other beings on Earth. But further, it urges us to question the artificial, destructive boundaries that have been imposed on the Earth's human and nonhuman inhabitants in the interest of the state, capitalism, and patriarchy. Zapatista horizonalism reminds us of lost and forgotten horizons, while at the same time opening up for us new and transfigurative ones.

The opening up of these horizons is called radical creativity. Fitzwater's account is invaluable for the degree to which it reveals Zapatista political practice to be a creative *politics of poesis*. He notes that the Tsotsil term for "political struggle and revolution" is *"pask'op,"* which is "a construction of *pasel*, the verb to do, to make, to create, to produce, and the word *k'op*, a noun meaning word, language, and speech."[40] This conceptualization focuses on the radically creative aspects of political praxis and revolution. Such activities are, above all, the creation of new or renewed, richer, and more compelling meanings. They involve the discovery or rediscovery of a new, or rather, renewed *logos* or expression of the nature of things. One of the great virtues of indigenous cultures is that they have so often preserved the transformative and regenerative powers of the word, of speech, and of all forms of non-alienated communal symbolization. This has often been exhibited in the poetic and mythic discourse of Subcomandante Marcos/Galeano, which draws deeply on communal traditions and narratives, and in the celebratory visual arts that are so integral to the Zapatista creation of communal space and place. Such expressions generate a communal social imaginary that pervades and conditions the Zapatista social ethos.

Fitzwater's analysis of how an indigenous language and the values it embodies have contributed to the Zapatista revolution shows how the interaction between traditional culture and institutions and emerging revolutionary and regenerative forces can play a crucial role in liberatory social transformation. He notes that the language he learned "is a particularly Zapatista Tsotsil that is being reflected on through the lens of the Zapatista movement."[41] This is an extremely significant point. Those who taught the language to him, explaining the subtleties of Tsotsil terms and concepts, are participants in a social dialectic between a rich cultural legacy and an ongoing process of creative, revolutionary praxis. Critics of radical indigenism (and other forms of radical communitarianism) reproach it unjustly as a misguided attempt to uncover some perfect, idealized past, or even dismiss it as an absurd quest for an impossible return to that mythical past. Yet the Zapatista experience illustrates strikingly that for self-conscious revolutionaries, it is in large part through the deepest and most intentional exploration of tradition that radical creativity, agency and autonomy can be unleashed. Like all forms of poesis, such a project is not an impossible effort to regain a lost past but a successful attempt to realize an impossible future.

## The Zapatista Critique of Domination

The question of the nature of power is a crucial one for revolutionary politics. If there are to be institutions such as an army, an administrative apparatus, a party, or even a quasi-state apparatus, these must all be subordinated to the self-organized autonomous (self-determining) community. The Zapatista revolution is notable for addressing this issue in relation to an army, just as the Democratic Autonomy Movement in Rojava is significant for broaching it in relation to a party. Both are important for confronting the issue of the quasi-state or proto-state dimensions of federative (or "confederative") organization and the ever-present tendencies toward the emergence of more explicitly statist and hierarchical structures.

Since its beginnings, under the influence of indigenous communal egalitarianism, the EZLN has made the critique of hierarchical power central to its revolutionary identity. This has involved an ongoing process of self-criticism. What is extraordinary is that an organization that has had, in effect, a territorial monopoly on the means of coercion could remain resolutely aware of the dangers of its own abuse of power and work actively to check that power. As Fitzwater notes, the EZLN addressed such dangers through the institution of revolutionary laws "creating an explicit separation between these civilian authorities and the armed forces of the EZLN."[42]

For once, the means of coercion were to be at the command of neither capital nor the state bureaucracy but would instead be subordinate to the community organized and mobilized democratically. The function of these means would not be to "command," in the sense of exercising "power over," but rather to "serve" by aiding the community in developing its collective power to flourish and achieve "greatness of heart." In the shift from vanguardist politics to communitarian democracy, a movement founded by a group of primarily male mestizo militants was transformed into a large, community-based movement of indigenous people, with membership and leadership that was both female and male, living in many communities and speaking six different languages.

Subcomandante Marcos/Galeano shows the depth of the Zapatista break with all forms of hierarchical power when he states with brutal and compassionate realism that "the military structure of the EZLN in some way 'contaminated' a tradition of democracy and self-government," and "was, so to speak, one of the 'antidemocratic' elements in a relationship of direct communitarian democracy."[43] The EZLN's coming to consciousness of the nature of domination and the corrupting effects of concentrated power can be compared to the primordial political process that we might call *archegenesis*, which Pierre Clastres describes in his classic work of anarchist anthropology, *Society against the State*.[44] Clastres argues that before conquest Amerindian cultures were haunted by the constant threat of the emergence of "the One," that is, the system of hierarchical power and social domination that we now call the state. He shows that these cultures engaged in an ongoing cultural war—an ethotic struggle—against this emergence. The Zapatistas recognize that now, as then, an ongoing battle is necessary to keep this development in check.

## The Leader as Servant

Another concept that Clastres shows to be central to the struggle of traditional Amerindian societies against hierarchy and domination is the idea of "the leader as servant." As shown here, this same idea has become fundamental to the Zapatista worldview through the movement's commitment to the guiding precept of *mandar obediciendo*, leading or commanding through obeying. This precept shapes the Zapatista vision of governing as a form of "good government." According to this outlook, almost all of what we ordinarily think of as "government" (undemocratic, hierarchical, statist, authoritarian, colonialist, technocratic, and bureaucratic government) is judged by the Zapatistas to be "bad government." Zapatista "good government" is reminiscent of Laozi's ancient Daoist concept of "ruling" as a form of *wuwei*, or "acting without acting," by which is meant nondominating action. Thus, Zapatista "good government" is a kind of "governing without governing."

Fitzwater explains that the Zapatistas see "governance as a particular form of work in service to the community, rather than as the exercise of power through administration or rule."[45] Such governance is nothing like the quest for power and influence and the imposition of a particularistic interest on the community that we see in politics as usual in capitalist and statist society. Fitzwater notes that those who serve the community through positions of responsibility "do not ask the people to elect them and certainly do not run election campaigns."[46] The fact that fines have been imposed for not carrying out official duties indicates that offices are more likely to be looked upon as a burden, albeit a necessary one, than as an opportunity to enjoy the exercise of power or to reap personal benefits.[47]

Positions of leadership are accepted as a *cargo* or charge on behalf of the community. They are a basic responsibility that is fundamental to the democratic functioning of the community and "those who are chosen as authorities by the communities must always obey the agreement of the communities."[48] This process of *mandar obediciendo* is a form of "obedience," not in the sense of a subordination to the community but in the form of careful listening to the community, attunement to its needs, and response to those needs. On the deepest level, it is not only a form of service but also a form of awakened or mindful care (close to the Buddhist concept of *appamāda*). In fact, Zapatista politics is perhaps the deepest expression of the politics of care in the world today, as this work reveals so eloquently, in the words of those who do the caring.

Despite their heavy emphasis on leadership as a mode of service and care, the Zapatistas remain aware of the danger that "even a group of people who do their work through the strength of their commitment rather than for money could transform into a new form of revolutionary governing elite with disproportionate influence and power."[49] Such a development would reverse all the gains that were made when the ELZN transformed itself from a centralist, hierarchical organization into a horizontalist, participatory movement in service to the community. So significant measures have been taken to avoid hierarchy and concentration of power.

While lengths of terms on decision-making bodies varies from community to community in accord with the principle of respect for diversity, terms are limited and periods of service are rotated, so that leadership functions are widely dispersed among the population, no class of permanent rulers or leaders emerges, and the concentration of power is avoided.

The Zapatistas deep understanding of the dangers inherent in the exercise of power, even in a formal system of grassroots democracy, is also exhibited through the institution of the *"comisión de vigilancia."* This is an oversight committee that supervises the councils and monitors all expenditures to prevent corruption and abuse of power from creeping in.

## The Zapatista Critique of Patriarchy

One of the most revolutionary aspects of the Zapatista struggle against all forms of domination is its rejection of patriarchal authoritarian conceptions of society and social change and its commitment to women's liberation, women's equality, and full participation by women at all levels of organization and decision-making. According to Khasnabish, "women make up approximately 45 percent of the Zapatista insurgents today" and "hold positions of political authority," including being some of the best-known comandantes.[50] This required a break with the movement's Eurocentric, hierarchical background and a radical transformation of existing practice within indigenous communities. Women have a long history not only of being silenced by social pressure but also of being subjected to systemic violence. A key element of the struggle for women's equality has been the demand for women to be not merely formal members of assemblies but also active, fully recognized, and respected participants in all democratic processes. Quotas for equality in leadership positions and council membership have gone a long way toward establishing equality, though as Fitzwater points out, progress is still thwarted in practice because of the persistence of "deeply ingrained gender hierarchies."[51]

As important as the formal political structures of assemblies and councils may be, equal participation at this level is not seen by the Zapatistas as the single magic key to the liberation of women. Rather it is only one element of a comprehensive struggle in all areas of society, and advances in this sphere are sometimes dependent on more deeply transformative progress in other spheres in which what is most "deeply ingrained" can be taken on more directly. Fitzwater reports that the great initial step in the process of liberation of women (by women) was their participation not in communal assemblies or councils, but rather in cooperatives. As one respondent remarks, it was there that "women first began to understand that we have rights," in the process of developing a means "to support each other" as they acted "to help the community."[52] This is not surprising, since, as long as the legacy of patriarchy persists, the assembly has certain inherently masculinist tendencies that are difficult to combat, while a cooperative, especially one that focuses on community subsistence and productive interaction with the Earth, has distinctively eco-feminist potentialities that can be developed.

Thus, Fitzwater points out both the far-reaching aspirations of the Zapatistas regarding the equality of women, and the failure to attain some goals. There is a rule that half of all council members must be women, but this has not yet been achieved in many, perhaps a majority, of communities.[53] A proposal to guarantee land rights, including the right of inheritance for women, is part of the Revolutionary Law of Women and has existed for two decades but still has not been ratified.[54] On the other hand, the *trabajos colectivos*, the Zapatista cooperative work projects, have made important advances toward equality by offering women practical control of land through their participation in communal labor. This offers empirical evidence that the movement toward gender equality and justice often proceeds unequally in different social spheres and that the sphere of formal decision-making, though always crucial, is not always the most advanced one in substantive terms.

## Beyond Hierarchical Dualism

The Zapatista political ideal is one that has long been dreamed of in radical political thought: the withering away of the division between society and the state, so that politics is no longer a mode of domination by any elite, class, sex, or ethnic group. The Fourth Declaration of the Lacandon Jungle calls for "a new political force" that is "based in the EZLN" and "which struggles against the State-Party System."[55] Fitzwater summarizes the goal of the Zapatistas as "a form of political existence in which there is no separation between the autonomous government and the communities, where everyone participates in governance and is prepared to take a turn in a governing body in the Caracol, the municipality, and the community."[56] This reflects an awareness that social alienation is only in part the result of a separation between the producers and their labor and the products of their labor. It is also the result of the separation between the community and all the products of its communal activity. This is what is addressed in the Zapatista program and the larger social ontological vision that it expresses.

The Zapatistas are undertaking a world-historical and Earth-historical project of overcoming the society of separation and domination that was instituted with the beginning of civilization and forms of systemic social domination. This is what Marcos/Galeano means when he refers to the importance of "opening up a crack in the wall of history" and to indigenous struggle as "a crack in the wall of the system."[57] It is perhaps only in Chiapas and Rojava today that there is a high degree of consciousness of the manner in which revolutionary political praxis relates to the great developments over geohistory and ethnohistory (the Earth Story and the Human Story), a widespread consciousness of the all-encompassing nature of the society of separation and domination and its underlying hierarchical, dualistic system of values (the History of Domination) and a pervasive consciousness of the need for a definitive break with that system not only in the sphere of social institutions but also on the level of social ideology, the social imaginary and, above all, the social ethos (the Story of Freedom).

In Rojava, this consciousness is nurtured by the pervasive influence of Abdullah Öcalan's critique of civilization's five-thousand-year history of domination and alienation and in aspects of traditional Kurdish culture that have resisted the system of domination. In Chiapas, it has even deeper roots in the actually existing communalism of indigenous society and in indigenous peoples' continuing struggle against conquest and imperial domination. Fitzwater cites Subcomandante Marcos/Galeano's recognition of the existence of "self-government" or autonomy in Chiapas long before the coming of the EZLN at "the level of each community."[58] One of the great achievements of the EZLN was to recognize and respect the traditional values and practices that constituted these indigenous roots of autonomy and make them the cultural-material basis for political organization, not only at the local level but throughout the regions and zones.

Communal assemblies have a long history in the traditions of indigenous people in Chiapas, as do practices of highly participatory discussion and consensus decision-making. This is a source of the ethical substantiality that makes revolutionary transformation a grounded possibility. To clarify this point, such "ethical substantiality" is "ethical" in the sense that it refers to the *ethos* or historical practice of the community, which is seen as having a deep normative significance. It is "substantial" in that it offers a material basis, and one might say "maternal basis," for the naissance and flourishing of communal autonomy. This process is radically opposed to the model of freedom as an abstract ideal that is imposed on a community as an object of transformation by some liberating agent that has a fundamentally external relation to that community. It is the definitive rejection of all forms of "forcing to be free," no matter how ideologically mystified and leftist these forms may become.

### Free Association

The Zapatista political ideal is a society based on voluntary cooperation, with the autonomy and individuality of each person and group protected and expanded through collective action that serves the good of the whole. Fitzwater finds such nondominating unity in diversity embodied in "the single most important commonality in Zapatista autonomous government," the fact that "every community, autonomous municipality, and Caracol does things differently and has the right to do things differently."[59] He illustrates this through examples of diversity in the manner in which the smaller communities organize themselves into municipalities, and municipalities organize themselves at higher levels.

An extremely important issue that is not often addressed is the functioning of democracy in "mixed communities." (This was a major area of contention in the anarchist collectives during the Spanish Revolution). Melissa Forbis explains that such communities "have Zapatistas, members of other peasant organizations, people who belong to political parties, people who might be Zapatista sympathizers, but not officially Zapatistas. The Zapatistas who are there would have their own meetings, make their own decisions, but wouldn't necessarily 'control' the whole community."[60] In her view, in these communities "there's a way of living side-by-side that works. There have been conflicts in some communities; there's been violence, not, by the way, started by the Zapatistas, but by people from other groups."[61] This history needs further examination. Javier Sethness Castro points out that there have been conflicts between Zapatistas and indigenous people who have internalized statist and authoritarian values, rather than traditional cooperative ones.[62]

Fitzwater says that "the heart of Zapatista governance is the 'agreement' that is reached between several communities or individuals and that only lasts as long as those communities or individuals remain in agreement."[63] Thus, voluntary agreement or consensus, as opposed to force and coercion, is at the core of all decision-making. The Zapatista goal is consensus at all levels, though they recognize that it cannot always be achieved. What is so striking is that this ideal is made obligatory, and it is achieved at the federative level, thus realizing in practice the anarchist nonhierarchical ideal. It should be understood that consensus agreement, another term for voluntary association, is the only purely anarchistic form of decision-making and that divergence from it, if necessary, must still be recognized as a departure from the noncoercive ideal.

The presupposition that either majority rule or consensus will be more effective in all places and at all times is a form of abstract idealism or dogmatism. Consensus processes will be more feasible to the degree that an ethos of voluntary cooperation, mutual aid, and solidarity prevails in a community. To the degree that such a cultural precondition does not exist, majority rule will seem more practical. Western leftists have tended to be skeptical of consensus and to have faith in majority rule, as is to be expected given their experience of living in cultures that do not have a strongly communitarian ethos. Nevertheless, one should not conclude that because consensus does not seem practical in some cultural climates, it is not an eminently practical possibility or, indeed, an extensively realized one in other cultural contexts.

Thus, the existence of a traditional libertarian and communitarian ethos in Chiapas makes possible a degree of consensus that seems utopian to those who take American or generic Western individualism as a cultural norm. Ironically, much of the contemporary (post-1960s) Left in the United States and some other countries has focused on organizing social strata that are more heavily conditioned to internalize such individualism (albeit in reactive, oppositional ways), while neglecting indigenous, immigrant, and marginalized groups that are more likely to have cultural traditions conducive to cooperative and communal modes of association. There are signs that this tendency is beginning to be reversed, especially as the result of the recognition of indigenous leadership in the water protector and pipeline resistance movements. This may help open the way for the American Left and even the global Eurocentric Left to learn from the experience of Chiapas and from other communitarian, indigenous-based movements.

## The Primacy of the Assembly

The question of the primacy of the communal assembly is an important one for contemporary left-libertarian thought, so Fitzwater addresses a key issue when he says that "the assembly is the heart of the Zapatista form of autonomous government."[64] And, indeed, his analysis presents a good case for the validity of this statement. However, he goes on to state that the assemblies and government "must always be aware of the multiple smaller collectives (ko'onkutik) that make up their collective heart (ko'ontik)."[65] So we discover that there is, in addition to the assemblies, another "heart" to the communal social organism. This might seem to be a contradiction, but it is not. Both the unifying processes of the assembly and the differences embodied in small groups and collectives are aspects of the communal "heart." Both must be given adequate recognition and must be allowed to function effectively if a true social unity in diversity is to be achieved.

Fitzwater explains that when the smaller collectives disagree, they are not forced to conform to a kind of artificial "general will" in which differences are submerged or denied. Instead, processes related to the "general heart" come into play. Specifically, the smaller collectives come together in the assembly and engage in a consensus process until an agreement is reached "through mutual recognition and respect (*ichbail ta muk'*)."[66] The previously mentioned voluntary agreement that is "reached between several communities or individuals" can also be looked upon as a third locus of the heart of the Zapatista body politic.[67] The quest for consensus as an expression of communal solidarity must also be associated with the communal heart. And finally (though we know that this account is not exhaustive), a fourth dimension of heart is pointed out. This is the "new form of work" that is understood as *a'mtel*, a form of mutual aid and caring labor.

The concept of *a'mtel* has revolutionary implications that are also found in the materialist ecofeminist concepts of caring labor and the subsistence perspective. Fitzwater shows how the political work of participating in assemblies, serving on councils, and accepting leadership positions are "a form of collective work in service to the collective survival of the community." Thus, "working in a cornfield so that the community can eat and participating in an assembly so that the community can reach an agreement are seen as two manifestations of the same form of 'collective labor for collective survival,'" and "the material work of governance is understood as identical and coequal to physical labor in the fields, emotional labor for rest and relaxation, celebratory labor in preparation for a fiesta, etc."[68] One finds in this concept of *a'mtel* the basis for a "caring labor theory of value" that challenges not only exploitative capitalist conceptions of exchange value but also instrumentalist patriarchal conceptions of use value that have continued to afflict the dominant Left. In the end, one discovers "the greatest wealth for the human being," the community's collective heart and spirit, in all the forms of caring labor through which its members shape communal freedom and solidarity into social realities.

Yet the assembly does, in fact, have a certain kind of qualified primacy in the political system. However, even here there is the important question of what level of assembly decision-making is primary, to the degree that it is primary. Fitzwater says at one point that "the assembly of all the communities of the zone should be the final authority for all decisions of the autonomous government," and that "all new agreements, projects, and governing structures that affect the entire zone must emerge from this assembly."[69] This might lead one to question how such "final authority" on the zonal level can be reconciled with the primacy of the local communities. But the larger point that Fitzwater is making is that officials at any level have no authority of their own and are bound by the directives of the local assemblies, which are, in fact, structurally primary. If there is a break in consensus at the Zone level, "all the local authorities in the assembly go back to their communities and discuss the problem and come back with proposals until all the communities can agree on how best to solve the problem."[70] Thus, any higher-level (federative) assembly of communities is merely an expression of the will and the solidarity of all the local communities, and its authority is identical with the authority of the social base in these communities.

One of the worst mistakes one could make in regard to Zapatista base democracy would be to transform this subtle and dialectical conception into a new base-superstructure model in which the communal assembly becomes the new material base and other institutions are reduced to mere superstructural expressions of what occurs at that level. In such a problematic, "the forces of decision-making" or, at best, "the forces and relations of decision-making" would occupy the place formerly held by the forces and relations of production. Programmatic politics, including programmatic forms of social ecology or libertarian municipalism, tends to lapse into such reductive base-superstructure thinking (B-S politics). This is precisely the kind of politics that the Zapatistas abandoned when they decided to open themselves up to the wisdom and experience of indigenous cultures. "In the last instance," social determination is deeply dialectical, and the social whole is shaped by the interaction between what goes on in assemblies and councils, in collective labor and cooperative projects, in the language that is spoken, in the rites and rituals that are celebrated, in the symbols and images through which the community imagines itself, and in many other aspects of communal *poesis*.

So, in the end, we must speak of both the primacy and the nonprimacy of the assembly.

## The Restoration of the Commons

Much of the attention that has been given to the Zapatistas focuses rightly on their major achievements in establishing a system of direct democracy and communal autonomy. What is often given less attention is how the Zapatista revolution has initiated forms of mutual aid and voluntary cooperation with deep and ancient roots in the commons and the gift economy. We might say that these forms contribute as much, or even more, to what we might call the deep structure of democracy. This dimension is manifested perhaps most distinctively through the practice of *a'mtel* described extensively in Fitzwater's text. As has been mentioned, this term refers to forms of work, or, more precisely, forms of caring labor, that are carried out voluntarily as a *cargo*, or responsibility, entrusted on behalf of the community or the collective.

In this case, as in so many others, Zapatista communitarian practice finds ethical substantiality through its roots in ancient communal traditions. Democracy in a large sense is much more than a decision-making process, even one as radical as assembly and council government. It arises as much, or perhaps even more, out of egalitarian, participatory practices that pervade social life. These are not created by any assembly or council but are at most reaffirmed through such bodies, because they have proven their rightness through their contribution over time to the community's mode of flourishing or "bringing itself to greatness." The restoration of the commons is part of this process of communal realization. It offers a means of overcoming barriers that seem intractable on the basis of the dominant statist and capitalist forms of decision-making (because these barriers are, in fact, impassable).

An important problem for the Zapatistas has been how to reconcile the autonomy of municipalities with what Fitzwater describes as "an unequal distribution of resources and ultimately an unequal process of development" of these municipalities. The problem of unequal distribution of resources is a classic one for decentralist and horizontalist systems, one that is often used by opponents to discredit these systems. The complexities of this problem are highlighted in relation to the issue of resources stemming from external aid to the Zapatista municipalities. In view of widespread need, the municipalities have looked to NGOs for such assistance. Though this support has benefited the communities, it has also created significant problems. First, the more advantaged municipalities have received proportionally more aid than the disadvantaged ones, thus exacerbating the existing inequalities. Second, the acceptance of aid, especially to the degree that it means deferring to the priorities of the NGOs, creates a form of dependency that tends to undermine the autonomy of the communities. In Fitzwater's words, the resulting system sometimes "looked more like charity and less like solidarity."[71]

The Zapatistas' response to these problems shows that as challenging as they may be, they are certainly not insoluble for a system that is both deeply libertarian and deeply communitarian. The Zapatista solution to the problem of external aid has been to require that NGOs negotiate aid with authorities at the level of the zone, rather than that of the individual municipalities. The distribution of such resources according to the needs of the individual communities can then be determined by the assemblies of the zones, based on their deliberations and the achievement of consensus among the communities. Through such processes of communal democracy, the Zapatistas are beginning to reestablish the commons and distribution according to need as a means of solving problems of resource inequality. The same principle is applied to the question of communities' unequal endowment with natural resources. If resources are appropriated merely on the basis of physical proximity, this will make the collective labor projects of some communities disproportionally more beneficial than those of other communities, thus creating inequalities. The solution has been to communalize such resources, treating them as a commons at the level of the zone:

> the Good Government Council of Morelia was given control over all the resources from these trabajos colectivos so that they could be distributed equally throughout the zone and create more trabajos colectivos, rather than just being spent on the individual sustenance or development of one community. The zone collectively decided that it was not fair to let a single community reap all the benefits of a very lucrative trabajo colectivo, because they are lucky enough to be located near a beautiful river, gravel mine, or source of salvaged wood.[72]

Another example of the reemergence of mutual aid and the commons comes from the organization of the system of cargos. The communities decided that, in order to honor and uphold the spirit of a'mtel, political service should always be a voluntary activity. However, the Zapatistas believe that just as those who serve the community were expected to give according to their abilities, they also deserve to be helped by the community according to their needs. Fitzwater observes that "some receive support from their community in work, in staple grains, different forms of support according to how the community comes to agreement."[73] Thus, we see a tendency to introduce the ancient communitarian practice of distribution according to need, a practice that has roots in the gift economy and that has always been typical of indigenous and other traditional communities.

## The Community against Empire

The Zapatista attitude toward governmental aid (that is, aid from the "bad government") illustrates the antistatist dimensions of the movement and its vigilance in regard to possible manipulation and co-optation. The movement is highly protective of the freedom and self-determination of local communities and recognizes that dependence on support from the centralized government and state bureaucracies inevitably undermines and destroys communal autonomy. The threat of withdrawal of aid and thus "the disappearance of its means of survival" can be used at any time to demand conformity to the alien will of the state and the dominant classes and interests that control it.[74]

Fitzwater shows how the experience of three communities with a major state-sponsored conservation program called ProÁrbol illustrates this danger. According to the glowing words of the program description, it is "a comprehensive program promoting actions for the conservation, restoration and sustainable use of Mexico's forests" that "works on the premise that sustainable forest management is best achieved by allocating the rights to exploit forest resources to forest owning *ejidos* and communities."[75] However, the reality of the program is like so many tragic stories known by local communities across the globe. In the end, the communities were prevented from cutting trees needed for firewood and construction, while the lumber companies gained control of their woodlands. Moreover, this expropriation of their resources forced the communities to resort to state aid, requiring them to divulge information that was then used to seize their land and displace the local inhabitants.[76]

The Zapatistas have discovered modes of communal self-organization that can resist such deceptions and abuses by the state and by private interests (collectively, the corporate-state apparatus). Fitzwater describes the local alternative that was developed to aid the communities. When citizens in one or more communities express the need for developmental programs, the Good Government Council meets with local councils and commissions to find out the nature of the need, as perceived by the community members themselves. A proposal for a project is then formulated by the local communities. The role of the Good Government Council is to try to find an NGO that will truly fulfill the needs of the communities, to the extent that solutions cannot be found in the community itself or among communities.[77]

Yet the goal is always to move toward finding all solutions at the level of the autonomous communities and their free associations through mutual aid and solidarity. Fitzwater concludes from his experience in Chiapas that "the center of Zapatista autonomous governance" is "in every Zapatista community."[78] This libertarian and communitarian ideal expresses the radically horizontalist nature of Zapatista politics that also poses the Zapatista challenge to the global political and economic order. Whether locally, regionally or globally, there will no longer be a powerful "core" and a powerless "periphery." The center is everywhere, in the sacred community and the sacred Earth. The Zapatista revolution announces the end of Empire.

## NOTES

1    In the German original of Marx's "A Contribution to the Critique of Hegel's Philosophy of Right: Introduction," the passage reads: "Die Religion ist der Seufzer der bedrängten Kreatur, das Gemüt einer herzlosen Welt, wie sie der Geist geistloser Zustände ist. Sie *ist das Opium des Volkes.*" (emphasis added). Karl Marx, "Zur Kritik der Hegelschen Rechtsphilosophie. Einleitung" in Karl Marx and Friedrich Engels, *Werke*, Band 1 (Berlin: Dietz Verlag, 1976), http://www.mlwerke.de/me/me01/me01_378.htm.

2    *Gemüt*, the word that is translated as "heart" also connotes "mind" or "soul," but here it clearly means "heart," in contrast to the "heartless" world. The word *Geist* means both "mind" and "spirit," and in this case connotes "spirit," in contrast to the "spiritless" conditions in that world.

3    Dylan Eldredge Fitzwater, *Autonomy Is in Our Hearts: Zapatista Autonomous Government through the Lens of the Tsotsil Language* (Oakland: PM Press, 2019).

4    Régis Debray, "A Guerrilla with a Difference," in Tom Hayden, ed. *The Zapatista Reader* (New York: Nation Books, 2002), 350.

5    Alex Khasnabish, *Zapatistas: Rebellion from the Grassroots to the Global* (London: Zed Books, 2010), 69.

6    Fitzwater, *Autonomy*, 11.

7    For an inspiring graphic introduction to maroon communities and the spirit of the maroon, see Quincy Saul, ed., *Maroon Comix: Origins and Destinies* (Oakland: PM Press, 2018).

8    John Womack, *Zapata and the Mexican Revolution* (New York: Vintage Books, 1970), 224.

9    Khasnabish, *Zapatistas*, 154.

10    Khasnabish, 155.

11  Andalusia Knoll and Itandehui Reyes, "From Fire to Autonomy: Zapatistas, 20 Years of Walking Slowly," *Truthout*, January 25, 2014, https://truthout.org/articles/from-fire-to-autonomy-zapatistas-20-years-of-walking-slowly/.

12  Melissa Forbis, "The Zapatistas at 20: Building Autonomous Community (Melissa Forbis Interviewed by Johanna Brenner)," *Solidarity*, March 23, 2014, https://solidarity-us.org/p4135/.

13  For a semiotic analysis of "Caracol" based on an ethnological interview of June 2007 with indigenous leaders in Oventik, Chiapas, see Thomas M. Urban, "Caracol de la Resistencia: Zapatista Symbol References Maya Past," *archaeolog: all things archaeological*, August 21, 2007, https://web.stanford.edu/dept/archaeology/cgi-bin/archaeolog/?p=141.

14  Pablo González Casanova, "The Zapatista 'Caracoles': Networks of Resistance and Autonomy," *Socialism and Democracy* 19, no. 3 (2005): 79.

15  This will help us avoid the errors of a programmatic approach to social change and the kind of abstract idealism and dogmatism that always goes along with such an approach.

16  This is a concept she developed at least as early as 1989 in *Staying Alive: Women, Ecology and Development* (London: Zed Books, 1989).

17  Gustav Landauer, *Revolution and Other Writings*, ed. and trans. Gabriel Kuhn (Oakland: PM Press, 2010), 263.

18  Landauer, *Revolution and Other Writings*, 132. Landauer invokes these words of the Medieval Council of Florence, borrowing a citation from Kropotkin's *Mutual Aid: A Factor in Evolution* (Boston: Porter Sargent Publishers, 1955), 106.

19  Gustav Landauer, *For Socialism* (St. Louis: Telos Press, 1978), 102.

20  Joel Kovel, *History and Spirit: An Inquiry into the Philosophy of Liberation* (Boston: Beacon Press, 1991), 1.

21  Fitzwater, *Autonomy*, 31–39.

22  Fitzwater, 30.

23  Fitzwater, 31–32.

24  Fitzwater, 32.

25  Fitzwater, 32.

26  Rudolf Otto, *The Idea of the Holy: An Inquiry into the Non-rational Factor in the Idea of the Divine and Its Relation to the Rational* (London: Oxford University Press, 1958), 25–30.

27  Kovel, *History and Spirit*, 46.

28  Fitzwater, *Autonomy*, 45. In my view, the implications of this sense of democracy for ecological thinking and sensibility are very strong ones. I am grateful to Javier Sethness Castro for pointing out that nevertheless, radical ecology has not been made explicitly central to the programs and activities of the movement (personal correspondence). Nor does it occupy the central theoretical place that it does in the Rojavan Revolution. On the other hand, the ecological dimension is implicit in the thinking and values of the Zapatista Movement, and has had important expressions, as discussed in John Ross, "The Zapatistas: An Ecological Revolution?," *Processed World*, no. 33, https://libcom.org/library/zapatistas-ecological-revolution-john-ross.

29  Fitzwater, *Autonomy*, 45.

30  Fitzwater, 56.

31  Using these terms in a more objective and empirical sense than in Durkheim's classic Eurocentric version.

32  Fitzwater, *Autonomy*, 34.

33  Fitzwater, 34.

34  Fitzwater, 39.

35  Dorothy Lee, *Freedom and Culture* (Upper Saddle River, NJ: Prentice Hall, 1963), 131–40. This essay and the complementary one, "Linguistic Reflection of Wintu Thought," are available online at https://www.scribd.com/document/50059829/Freedom-and-culture.

36  Lee, *Freedom and Culture*, 134.

37  Fitzwater, *Autonomy*, 170n32.

38  Fitzwater, 44.

39  On the concept of "deep play," see Max Cafard, "Deep Play in the City," in *Surregional Explorations* (Chicago: Charles H. Kerr, 2012), 13–45.

40  Fitzwater, *Autonomy*, 10.

41  Fitzwater, 9.

42  Fitzwater, 25.

43  Fitzwater, 57–58.

44  Pierre Clastres, *Society against the State* (New York: Urizen Books, 1977).

45  Fitzwater, *Autonomy*, 68–69.

46  Fitzwater, 127.

47  Fitzwater, 129.

48  Fitzwater, 69.

49  Fitzwater, 136.

50  Khasnabish, *Zapatistas*, 74.

51  Fitzwater, *Autonomy*, 148.

52  Fitzwater, 42.

53  Fitzwater, 146.

54  Fitzwater, 150.

55  "Fourth Declaration of the Lacandon Jungle. Today We Say: We Are Here, We Are Rebel Dignity, The Forgotten of the Homeland," http://woocommerce-180730-527864.cloudwaysapps.com/wp-content/uploads/2014/03/Fourth-Declaration-of-the-Lacandona-Jungle-.pdf. In this, the Zapatistas diverge from the Democratic Autonomy Movement in Rojava, which is more open to compromise with the state in the short to medium-term future, and which has embraced the form of the party. Javier Sethness Castro has pointed out the dangers and the apparent contradiction with their basic values in the Zapatistas' efforts to run María de Jesús Patricio Martínez in the last presidential election (personal correspondence). A critique of that candidacy can also be found in "The CNI's Presidential Run: Story of an Unforced Error," a translation of Erick Benítez Martínez's "Marichuy y el CNI: historia de una autozancadilla," *It's Going Down*, March 8, 2018, https://itsgoingdown.org/cni-presidential-run-error/. Such critique expresses valid concerns: however, Dylan Fitzwater and others have strongly defended the Marichuy candidacy as a tactic for promoting communal autonomy and defending the rights and asserting the power of indigenous people and women in particular. See Fitzwater, "Zapatistas and Indigenous Congress Seek to Revolutionize Mexico's 2018 Election," *Truthout*, https://truthout.org/

articles/zapatistas-and-indigenous-congress-seek-to-revolutionize-mexico-s-2018-election/. Fitzwater argues that the October 18 communique "May the Earth Tremble at Its Core" makes it clear that the Zapatista national electoral strategy is based on a continued "rejection of taking state power." See the text of the communique: https://enlacezapatista.ezln.org.mx/2016/10/18/may-the-earth-tremble-at-its-core/.

56    Fitzwater, *Autonomy*, 132.
57    This discourse has long been used by the Zapatistas, but it is perhaps expressed best in Subcomandante Insurgente Galeano's relatively recent text "The Crack in the Wall: First Note on Zapatista Method," *Enlace Zapatista*, May 10, 2015, http://enlacezapatista.ezln.org.mx/2015/05/10/the-crack-in-the-wall-first-note-on-zapatista-method/.
58    Fitzwater, *Autonomy*, 57.
59    Fitzwater, 51.
60    Forbis, "The Zapatistas at 20."
61    Forbis.
62    He raises the issue of the degree to which the result in Zapatista-dominated communities will be a kind of Rousseauian "forcing" of some "to be free" (personal correspondence). It is crucial to confront such issues in order to avoid lapsing into ideology. It is better to recognize the existence of constraints, and to debate the degree to which they are, or are not, a necessary evil, than to pretend that they do not exist (in the style of leftist ideological militants and apologists).
63    Fitzwater, *Autonomy*, 55.
64    Fitzwater, 68.
65    Fitzwater, 69.
66    Fitzwater, 69.
67    Fitzwater, 55.
68    Dylan Fitzwater (personal correspondence). There is a large body of ecofeminist literature on the ethics and politics of care and the radical implications of recognizing the importance of caring labor, especially by women and indigenous people across the globe. See Ariel Salleh's analysis of "regenerative labor" in "From Eco-Sufficiency to Global Justice," in Salleh, ed., *Eco-Sufficiency & Global Justice: Women Write Political Ecology* (London: Pluto Press, 2009), 291–312, and her discussion of caring and "meta-industrial" labor in her groundbreaking work *Ecofeminism as Politics* (London: Zed Books, 2017), throughout the work but especially chapter 10.
69    Fitzwater, *Autonomy*, 71.
70    Fitzwater, 70.
71    Fitzwater, 60.
72    Fitzwater, 117–18,
73    Fitzwater, 134.
74    Fitzwater, 95.
75    See "ProArbol," *REDD Desk*, 2016, at https://theredddesk.org/countries/initiatives/proarbol.
76    Fitzwater, *Autonomy*, 97.
77    Fitzwater, 102–3.
78    Fitzwater, 49.

# 7

# Lessons of the Rojavan Revolution

Rojava, like few other places in the world, poses in a radical manner the most crucial questions concerning the destiny of the person, the community, and nature. These are questions that for a long time seemed dormant in much of the contemporary world—an ideologically pacified world that has been at the same time seething with social and ecological contradictions. These burning questions concern the relationship between society and the state, between horizontal and vertical organization, between party and movement, between personal character structure and communal institutions, and between traditional culture and transformative vision. They demonstrate that in Rojava, history is moving toward certain answers, even if they remain at the moment less than definitive ones.

Given the explosive contradictions at the core of the dominant system, the idea popularized by Prime Minister Margaret Thatcher that "there is no alternative" is not only ideology but absurdity. The question has never been whether there is an alternative, but rather, which alternatives the system would blindly generate through the force of contradiction, and which would emerge in a more conscious, creative, and imaginative manner. As David Levi Strauss points out, both the Islamic State and the Rojavan Anti-State are "responses to capitalist modernity and neoliberal globalism" and thus represent the two poles of this opposition.[1] The system of domination long ago spawned its Malignant Other in the form of reactionary movements, extreme nationalism, and fanatical fundamentalism. For a certain period, the alternative response (the conscious, creative, and imaginative one) seemed lost in some virtual space of absent radical otherness. Revolutionary Rojava, along with the Zapatistas and various indigenous movements around the world, represent the resurgence of truly radical alterity, the return of the impossible real of revolutionary politics.

An understanding of the Rojavan Revolution requires an examination of the great diversity and complexity of social and political organizations that have emerged recently in Rojava. Such an understanding helps explain the still often ambiguous interrelationships between the forty-year-old Kurdistan Workers Party (PKK) in Turkey and the proliferation of new organizational forms in Rojava. The latter constitute an impressive spectrum: the Democratic Union Party (PYD), the Rojavan revolutionary party, allied with the PKK; the Movement for a Democratic Society (TEV-DEM), which is the governing coalition of the PYD and its allies in Rojava; the People's Protection Units (YPG), the Rojavan militia units; the Women's Protection Units (YPJ) and YJA Star militia, the all-woman militia units; the larger Kurdistan Communities Union; and the popular assemblies, councils, committees, and self-managed worker cooperatives that have been created at various levels of society. A Democratic Federation of Northern Syria was proclaimed in March 2016. It is significant that the area included in this initiative to create a larger sphere for democratic autonomy in Syria includes an Arab majority.

The questions of how these diverse social formations are interrelated and how effectively they function is not answered definitively in current reports on Rojava. This is the case, in part, because much more careful, detailed, and probing research is still needed, but also because these forms and their role in the larger society are still in the process of being worked out in practice. In some areas, progress is only rudimentary. Thomas Schmidinger has pointed out that while women's cooperatives have been an important part of the movement for gender liberation, "viewed from the economy at large, these cooperatives, founded with the support and under the influence of the new authorities, play a relatively unimportant role."[2] It is clear, however, that Rojava has already made extraordinary advances in the development of a radically libertarian, radically communitarian, and radically feminist revolutionary politics.

The Rojavan Revolution is extraordinary for the degree to which it has put its antiauthoritarian, antihierarchical ideals into practice in a very short period of time. It has made a concerted attempt to establish participatory, base democracy in the local communities, something that has so often been relegated to some postrevolutionary limbo or dismissed as unrealistic in view of the pressures of war, the strength of counterrevolutionary forces, or the dangers of "encirclement" (and Rojava is nothing if not "encircled"). As the concise handbook on the Rojavan Revolution, *A Small Key Can Open a Large Door*, sums up its process of radical political transformation:

> face-to-face assemblies soon became the backbone of their new government . . . neighborhood assemblies make up the largest number of councils. Every person (including teenagers) can participate in an assembly near where they live. In addition to these neighborhood assemblies, there are councils based on workplaces, civic organizations, religious organizations, political parties, and other affinity-based councils (e.g. Youth). People often are part of a number of local councils depending on their life circumstances. These councils can be as small as a couple dozen people or they can have hundreds of participants. But regardless of size, they operate similarly. The councils work on a direct democracy model, meaning that anyone at the council may speak, suggest topics to be decided upon, and vote on proposals (though many councils use consensus for their decision-making).[3]

Despite a legacy of ethnic cleansing and repression against the Kurds (and some evidence of ongoing retaliation that cannot be ignored) there has been an effort, as David Graeber explains, to achieve "careful ethnic balance" in decision-making bodies.[4] Even though Rojava is in the midst of a region noted for brutal ethnic and religious strife, and for patriarchal domination, it is mandated that "the top three officers" in these various deliberative bodies "have to include one Kurd, one Arab and one Assyrian or Armenian Christian, and at least one of the three has to be a woman."[5] There is an understanding that ethnic, religious, and gender realities cannot be ignored or bracketed for policy-making and organizational purposes, but rather must be recognized and respected within a context of nondomination and liberatory practice.

An enduring challenge to efforts at radical democratization has been the determination of a viable scale for truly participatory democratic units at the base. In Rojava, the local assemblies do not typically consist of the thousands or tens of thousands of nominal members that have been contemplated in some theories of base democracy,[6] but rather of a few hundred potential participants. Thus, they are closer the ideal established for general assemblies in the Mondragon cooperative system and are roughly comparable in size to the local assemblies in indigenous communities in Bolivia (in both of these cases, based on a long history of practical experience).[7] Active political participation is also manifested through local councils and committees. Paul Z. Simons, in his "Dispatches from Rojava," reports on a local council meeting at which he was told that "with the recent influx of immigrants into the city they were expecting the commune to expand, and that if it grows larger than 100 families it may be too unwieldy to be responsive" so "possible geographic divisions were discussed."[8] He explains that the local council must be of a scale that facilitates real engagement in the community, since it addresses everything from matters of everyday life, such as "dealing with marital issues" and "helping get gas and rides to and from clinics," to urgent life and death issues. Thus, in periods of open conflict it "kept the commune fed and clothed," "helped with YPG intelligence gathering," and "issued Kalashnikovs," so that the community could fight alongside the militia.[9]

A crucial question for Rojava as a radically libertarian experiment is the role of state power and the relationship between forms of popular self-organization and agencies of force and coercion. PKK Leader Abdullah Öcalan's position on the state is expressed at end of volume two of *Manifesto for a Democratic Civilization*, where he poses the question of whether "a compromise between the statist civilization and the democratic civilization" is possible.[10] The answer is "yes and no," or rather, "no and yes." Öcalan is clear about the fact that statist civilization must come to an end and that there can be no compromise on that ultimate goal. He attacks most modern reform and revolutionary movements for depicting the state as a historically progressive "problem-solving" institution and ignoring the reality that the modern nation-state is precisely "the structure that allowed for the absorption of society into the state and resulted in fascism."[11]

Yet he goes on to say that, for the present, compromise is not only possible but necessary. "It is possible for the state civilization and democratic civilization to coexist through compromise and without destroying each other. But for this to happen they first have to recognize and respect each other's identities."[12] He rejects "the tactics of the all-or-nothing approach" and concludes that "not losing the initiative in our struggle for freedom while making compromises with all the forces of the system at the right time and place" is "a more constructive method and will allow for making gains."[13]

He elaborates on this strategy in the texts included in the pamphlet *Democratic Confederalism*.[14] There he concedes that perhaps for a considerable period of time confederalism must coexist with the state, provided that the state allows it to continue its development (including developing larger confederations across the borders of nation-states). He argues for the need at present for "both vertical and horizontal formations," explaining that "democratic confederalism is open for compromises concerning state or governmental traditions," and accepts a modus vivendi of "equal coexistence."[15] He states that "democratic confederalism is not at war with any nation-state," but needs to defend itself against attacks by nation-states.[16] In many ways, policies in Rojava have followed Öcalan's position, both in relation to coexistence with existing nation-states and in regard to quasi-state developments within Rojava itself.[17]

Graeber alludes to the ways in which Rojava has undertaken the project of creating what some have called a "nonstate state," and Michael Taussig specifically points out "the paradox" that the Kurdish cantons "perform as if there is a state even if there is not and even though they are against the idea of state."[18] Graeber remarks on the extraordinary nature of "a dual power situation where the same political forces created both sides," which he identifies as a "democratic self-administration," that has "all the form and trappings of a state" and the TEV-DEM, which is "driven bottom up directly by democratic institutions."[19] If these two sides are actually in accord on the nature and exercise of power, then we do not, in fact, have a case of what has traditionally been labeled "dual power," but rather a kind of politically benign unity in duality. But the important issue remains of the degree to which the benignly *state-like* will become the dangerously *statist*.

There has been a concerted effort within the Democratic Autonomy Movement in Rojava to guard against this danger by destroying the monopoly on coercive power that has traditionally defined the state, a monopoly that inevitably undermines both democracy and autonomy. Graeber describes a visit to a police academy where he is told that "everyone had to take courses in non-violent conflict resolution and feminist theory before they were allowed to touch a gun."[20] The goal is to train all the citizens in community self-defense, so that the police as a force separate from the people can be eliminated completely. Graeber was struck by the extraordinary fact that the Rojava movement, "faced with dire war conditions" would "immediately abolish capital punishment, dissolve the secret police and democratize the army."[21] Indeed, Rojava has moved in a direction that is diametrically opposite to the typical leftist response to the attainment of power (the catastrophe of "actual existence"), which is to abandon democratization and communization of institutions under the pressure of internal and external threats, or even the illusion or pretext of such threats.

The process of radical democratization has also been applied to the military, the sphere in which hierarchical relations might seem most difficult to root out. Simons observes that in the People's Defense Units there are no traditional officers but rather "Team/Suite/Block/Company Leaders" who are chosen either by majority vote or by consensus. He reports that even this leadership is dissolved when there are no military operations, so that there remain only regional commanders, who are also chosen by vote or consensus and can serve only a single, six-month term.[22] Evren Kocabıçak notes that there is a recognition of some degree of hierarchical organization in these militias. She observes that there must of necessity be "a chain of command within a fighting guerrilla unit" because "its absence would simply cause the annihilation of the unit in a short span of time."[23] She explains that consequently the growth of hierarchy is kept in check by the existence of "really strong mechanisms to monitor and criticize the command structure," so that, for example, fighters "can even discharge their commander using their common will," and "every action, education or meeting is collectively evaluated."[24]

Such analysis is reminiscent of political anthropologist Pierre Clastres's classic study of the phenomenon of indigenous resistance to state formation. He points to the emergence of prophetic voices in Amerindian indigenous society that warned of the growing ascendency within the society of a "One" that is on the side of death and fragmentation and that would destroy the "Not-One" that is on the side of life and wholeness (as opposed to externally imposed unity). The indigenous prophets warned of something destructive that was evolving out of the previously benign power of the leader as the servant of the community. Öcalan expresses a similar idea when he says that in early societies the hierarchy based on "the authority of the wise elders" was a kind of "beneficial hierarchy" that might even be looked upon as "the prototype of democracy," and that this system was destroyed with the rise of "patriarchal hierarchical power" based on an alliance of "the organized force of proto-priest (shaman), experienced elder, and strong man."[25]

The antistatist message of the ancient Amerindian prophets is echoed in the conscious struggle of Rojava against authoritarian and domineering tendencies toward such a "One" (a struggle led, notably, by, in Luce Irigaray's classic formulation, "the sex that is not one."). To the extent that Rojava follows Öcalan's critique of domination, it recognizes the dangers of the hierarchical and state-like aspects of putatively anarchic formations and of the character-structures that inhabit those structures. This caution is necessary for two reasons: first, because these dangers really exist, and if they are ignored, this can only result in ideological bad faith; and second, because if they are denied or disavowed, they will tend to grow beyond any legitimate, containable levels, and this will ultimately signal the death of the free community.

One of the qualities that gives the Rojava movement world-historical significance is the unprecedented way in which it makes radical feminism and the critique of patriarchy central to the entire revolutionary process. The theoretical roots of this perspective are found in Öcalan's thought. Öcalan bases his outlook in a vast and sweeping understanding of the history of civilization and domination, in which women and the feminine are central. He sees what Engels famously called "the world-historical defeat of the female sex" as the pivotal event in world history—in effect, the historical Fall. In his discussion of Öcalan's thought, Peter Wilson commends the Kurdish leader for his insights into "the Mesopotamian Neolithic" as "a culture shaped by the feminine principle of life" and his recognition of the manner in which irrigation-based agriculture and bronze-based metallurgy generated surplus wealth that could be appropriated by a ruling class that imposed a patriarchal system of social domination.[26] Öcalan shows this to be the beginning of the historical epoch in which we are still living. In part through the influence of this analysis, there is a widespread conviction in Rojava that it must be the place, or one of the places, in which this epoch comes to an end.

Havin Güneşer also points out that one of Öcalan's major revisions of leftist thought is his view of capitalism as "a continuation of the five-thousand-year-old patriarchal society."[27] She explains that his vision of a thoroughly transformed, post-patriarchal "democratic civilization" is based on the recognition of women as "the first class nation and colony" (a concept developed by Maria Mies), the creation of an ecological mode of production, new participatory forms of self-defense, and a communal economy.[28] Bookchin, who influenced Öcalan regarding the need to overcome all forms of domination, held that an original "gerontocracy" preceded patriarchal domination, or what he called "patricentricity." Öcalan himself, however, takes an unequivocal stand in favor of the primordial nature of patriarchal domination. Furthermore, as Öcalan's own writings show, he is uncompromising in applying his critique of the legacy of patriarchy to all social realms. He says that "the male has become a state and turned this into the dominant culture," that "class and sexual oppression develop together," and that "masculinity has generated ruling gender, ruling class, and ruling state." He concludes—dramatically and, to some, perhaps shockingly—that "to kill the dominant man is the fundamental principle of socialism."[29] This analysis cuts to the social psychological core of domination and is equivalent to saying that the appropriating, domineering civilized ego that has been shaped by patriarchy must be annihilated, and with it all the personal and social institutional ego-extensions must disappear.

A commitment to such explicitly antipatriarchal values has become pervasive in the Rojava movement and there are suggestions that, as a result, a deeply transformed ethos is emerging. This is exemplified by Kocabıçak's comments on the growing number of Rojavan women fighters who are rejecting meat-eating. She attributes to these women an impressive grasp of the connections between history, culture, values, sensibilities and social practice. She says that as part of "the development of social ecological consciousness" they recognize that meat eating is "not a strict nutritional necessity for human kind," but rather something that has historically been "one of the factors that create war and violence." They realize that industrial meat production under capitalism "has created a horrid massacre" and is "harmful for human health." The Rojavan alternative is a new ecological sensibility in which animals are seen not "merely as food to be eaten" but "as part of the entirety of nature."[30] As these observations show, seldom has the concept of "the personal is the political" attained the kind of concrete universality as it has in the theoretically informed practice of these women fighters.[31]

Another key aspect of the emerging ethos is "the spirit of sacrifice" and even martyrdom that is pointed out by Dilar Dirik. This spirit contrasts sharply with the dominant values of Western political movements, including (and one might even say, particularly), those of the "postmodern" Left.[32] Taussig notes that the women fighters "spoke of collective suicide when ISIS surrounded them. They spoke of lying down to die on the body of a comrade dying on the battlefield, awaiting death with them; of apologizing on one's phone when dying while disposing of one's cell phone, codes, and weapons."[33] Taussig writes of the traumatic effect of such an attitude, which, he says, "struck me as strange and made me anxious, all the more so because the women were so calm and confident."[34] We see here a sensibility of nonheroic and even antiheroic being-toward-death that is a part of a larger affirmation of a creative and nurturing being-toward-life and being-toward-birth that is at the heart of the Rojavan Revolution. Notably, the chant of Kurdish revolutionary women is "Women, Life, Freedom!"

Such a sensibility is traumatically transformative in that it challenges the patriarchal logic of denial and domination on which civilization is based. Those living at the decaying core of nihilistic capitalist civilization have difficulty comprehending a logic of noneconomistic sacrifice and nonspeculative expenditure that is familiar to those who still live within a communal ethos. The primordial idea of sacrifice defies civilized, capitalist, and patriarchal definitions of reality based on a logic of accumulation. It teaches that one gains access to creative powers only through a rejection of the empire of power and that one gains deeper satisfaction through renunciation of the pursuit of self-defeating ego-centered satisfactions. Western leftists, when confronted with the idea of sacrifice, especially when associated with "the feminine" or "the maternal" are likely to associate it one-sidedly with backwardness and the oppression of women. There is seldom any recognition that it might have a core of truth that all human beings, and especially male human beings, might need to rediscover and learn to put into practice.

The word "sacrifice" comes from the root *sacer*, which denotes that which is sacred. The civilized mind is perplexed by the idea of sacrifice because it cannot comprehend the idea of realities that are more sacred than the ego and various extensions of the ego. Revolution is the intrusion of the sacred (or from a conventional perspective, the "accursed") real of communal and natural interbeing. It is a rejection of exchange value (along with instrumental use value) in favor of the intrinsic value that is at the basis of gift exchange between human beings and between all beings in the natural world. Thus, Taussig points to the significance in Rojava of "'precapitalist' ways of the gift," and of "Bataillian, Bakhtinian-Rabelaisian, and Maussian generosity" and suggests that the revolution "requires" and "promotes" such a "spirit of the gift."[35] Similarly, Dirik says that freedom "has a lot to do with love for the community."[36] Thus, we are taken back to the primordial realities of the gift, love, and the community. It is as if freedom took a five-thousand-year detour in southwest Asia (a detour called Empire and Patriarchy) and has finally returned home.

Although the Rojavan Revolution holds this vast promise, it is, as has been mentioned, not without certain ambiguities. The questions raised by its critics can certainly not be ignored and must be confronted honestly. For example, it is claimed that the PKK's antistatism is motivated less by principle than by a pragmatic recognition of the practical impossibility of establishing a Kurdish state. It is said that the PKK is opportunistic and will side with different interests and adopt different ideological positions based more on strategical goals than deep commitments. According to this criticism, the "nonstate" state apparatus is still responsible for the most significant decisions, leaving management of everyday life to the base, and when it can become even more state-like, this apparatus will seize the opportunity. Schmidinger claims that leaders of other militias "have always regarded the commanders of the YPG as their serious contact partners, not the representatives of the political structures," and that councils do not control all major decisions but "play an important role in the small daily administrative decisions and the supply of the population."[37] Critics point out that much of the economy is not cooperative but is rather based on wage labor, trade in smuggled goods, and the sale of petroleum, and that this material basis will exact its due. And finally, it is argued that the power and influence of global capitalism and surrounding nation-states will determine the future evolution of the Rojava system.

Some of these criticisms are clearly misguided and ideologically motivated. It is certainly implausible that the sweeping critique of civilization and the state developed by Öcalan is a mere rationalization, as is demonstrated by his extensive and eloquent defense of his position in diverse pamphlets and several major multivolume works. His influence on the Kurds is real and has struck a chord in the Kurdish psyche. Defenders of the revolution point out deeply rooted dimensions of Kurdish history and culture that both underlie and reinforce Öcalan's most revolutionary ideas. Some have noted the influence of radical concepts of freedom, justice, and equality within the Alevist Islamic tradition, and others have claimed that "throughout their whole history Kurds have favored clan systems and tribal confederations and struggled to resist centralized governments."[38] Furthermore, whatever the goals of some leaders may be, the widely functioning system of grassroots power becomes an increasingly effective material force to the extent that it continues to develop. It is clear that the test of the depth of popular power will come if and when autonomy can operate in peacetime, and emergency conditions and military necessity no longer take priority in decision-making.

There are some major ambiguities about the functioning of the economic system in Rojava. For example, Schmidinger contends that "Rojava's economy is based on a mixture of war economy, small capitalism, and subsistence production of food within which the cooperatives lead a niche existence instead of representing a new economic system."[39] On the other hand, defenders of the Revolution claim that "traditional 'private property' was abolished in late 2012, meaning all buildings, land, and infrastructure fell under control of the various city councils," and give as evidence the widely cited statement by economic co-minister Dr. Ahmad Yousef that "three-quarters of traditional private property is being used as commons" while only "one quarter is still being owned by use of individuals."[40] The degree to which actual democratic control prevails, whether through local councils or workers councils, is crucial, given the importance of the de facto mode of production within the dialectic of social determination.

Serious concerns have been expressed, including by those supportive of the Rojavan Revolution, about claims of human rights abuses by the YPG. There has been much discussion of the February 2014 report that pointed out unsolved murders and disappearances of YPG opponents, lack of due process, abuse of prisoners, and use of child soldiers. The latter claim was recognized, and the YPG pledged to end the practice.[41] In 2017, a highly critical article in *The Nation* by Roy Gutman, with a reply by Meredith Tax and colleagues and a rejoinder by Gutman, drew attention among the American Left to this debate, which continues, including among anarchists who are sympathetic.[42]

Furthermore, there are deep concerns about the co-optative power of regional and global systems of political and economic power. The specter of the emergence of Western and Russian spheres of influence in Syria and the prospect of manipulation of local actors is disturbing. The daunting challenges to the revolutionary problematic posed by the need for compromise and even collaboration with reactionary powers must be frankly recognized. The fact that survival is often at stake in assessing the need for such policies must also be faced. In short, the Rojavan Revolution is developing within real history, with all the complexities and contradictions of real history. Its achievements should be recognized as a struggle within these parameters and should be neither denied nor exaggerated.

It is impossible to know to what extent the Rojavan Revolution will succeed or fail. Its greatest predecessor, the Spanish Revolution, despite its ultimate defeat, still lives on as a great inspiration. The Rojavan Revolution itself, in the specific form that it has taken, has only been possible because the living legacy of that earlier revolution was passed on to it (as noted by Graeber). Yet that epoch-making revolution endured for less than three years and, indeed, less than even one before it was substantially undermined by the resurgence of the state, the power of the party, and the influence of reactionary forces. It is worth noting that these same factors are linked to some of the dangers that critics and critical supporters of Rojava point out today.

The Rojavan Revolution, whatever its ultimate fate may be, already constitutes an enormous achievement. It has given us a living example of a revolutionary movement with a spirit of courage, sacrifice, and hope. It has established an extensive system of participatory democracy. It consciously battles against all forms of domination and works to put an end to millennia of patriarchy, the most ancient of all forms of domination. It is an expression of a historic moment, a new opening up of creative possibilities for liberation and recommunization. For this, it has inestimable value.

## NOTES

1    David Levi Strauss, "Hope in Rojava," in Dilar Dirik, David Levi Strauss, Michael Taussig, and Peter Lamborn Wilson, eds., *To Dare Imagining: Rojava Revolution* (Brooklyn: Autonomedia, 2016), 12. The present discussion relies primarily on texts included in this collection.

2    Thomas Schmidinger, *Rojava: Revolution, War and the Future of Syria's Kurds* (London: Pluto Press, 2018), 121.

3    Strangers in a Tangled Wilderness, eds., *A Small Key Can Open a Large Door: The Rojava Revolution* (New York: Combustion Books, 2015), 26.

4    David Graeber, "Why Is the World Ignoring the Revolutionary Kurds in Syria?," in Dirik et al., *To Dare Imagining*, 21.

5    Graeber, "Why Is the World Ignoring the Revolutionary Kurds?"

6    For example, doctrinaire libertarian municipalism, which could not abide questioning of the possibility of authentic direct democracy on such a scale.

7    For a concise account of the neighborhood councils (assemblies) in El Alto, Bolivia, which are rooted in Aymara traditional practices, see Raúl Zibechi's extremely important work, *Dispersing Power: Social Movements as Anti-State Forces* (Oakland: AK Press, 2010), 24–37 and 65–72. Zibechi explains how proposals to expand the definition of a neighborhood and the scale of neighborhood organization to as many as ten thousand inhabitants were a calculated antidemocratic and counterrevolutionary tactic (35–37).

8    Paul Z. Simons, "Dispatches from Rojava," in Dirik et al., *To Dare Imagining*, 89.

9    Simons "Dispatches," 89.

10   Abdullah Öcalan, *Capitalism: The Age of Unmasked Gods and Naked Kings* (Porsgrunn, Norway: New Compass Press, 2017), 303.

11   Öcalan, *Capitalism*, 315.

12   Öcalan, *Capitalism*, 319. How to interpret such "respect" and the motivation for using such a term are intriguing issues that will be left for later exploration.

13   Öcalan, *Capitalism*, 321.

14   Abdullah Öcalan, *Democratic Confederalism* (London: Transmedia Publishing, 2011).

15   Öcalan, *Democratic Confederalism*, 22.

16   Öcalan, *Democratic Confederalism*, 32. Though it would seem to be in a certain sense necessarily at war with any nation-state that denies its right to exist and seeks to destroy it; that is, any nation-state that takes the modern theory of sovereignty seriously.

17   My own position on this issue, which differs from both Öcalan and most anarchists, was stated briefly in *The Impossible Community* (New York: Bloomberg Academic, 2013), 86. I note there that communitarian anarchist Gustav Landauer "considers the possible role for the state in the transition from the system of domination to a system of free community of communities, under certain historical conditions. He describes a socialist (meaning 'libertarian socialist') position that holds that after 'free and diverse forces of multiplicity' are achieved, 'the state is left with only one task: to prepare for its own abolition and to make way for the endless ordered multiplicity of federations, organizations, and societies that aspire to take its place and the place of economic individualism." [Gustav Landauer, *Revolution and Other Writings: A Political Reader* (Oakland: PM Press, 2010), 169.] I comment that this position "points to the need for an anarchist politics of the transitional state. . . . The possibility of such a transitional state would depend on socially transformative activity making the state in practice what it has been only in theory, as depicted in some forms of historical materialism: a purely superstructural phenomenon. It would, incidentally, realize precisely what Marx proposed in the 'Critique of the Gotha Program,' that is, 'converting the state from an organ superimposed upon society into one completely subordinate to it.'" [Karl Marx, "Critique of the Gotha Program," www.marxists.org/archive/marx/works/1875/gotha/ch04. htm] Whether such a transitional state is in any particular case a revolutionary or counterrevolutionary force is a historical and empirical question, and cannot be an article of faith.

18   Michael Taussig, "Kobane: The Mastery of Non-Mastery," in Dirik et al., *To Dare Imagining*, 116.

19   Graeber, in Dirik et al., 27.

20   Graeber, in Dirik et al., 27.

21   Graeber, in Dirik et al., 27.

22   Simons, in Dirik et al., 97.

23   Evren Kocabıçak, "The World's First Army of Women," in Dirik et al., 66.

24   Kocabıçak, "The World's First Army of Women," 66.

25   Abdullah Öcalan, *Liberating Life: Woman's Revolution* (Cologne: International Initiative, 2013), 16–17.

26   Peter Lamborn Wilson, "Abdullah Öcalan," in Dirik et al., 38–39.

27  Havin Güneşer, "No Miracles at Work," in Dirik et al., 49.

28  Güneşer, "No Miracles," 51.

29  Öcalan, *Liberating Life*, 51.

30  Kocabıçak, in Dirik et al., 69.

31  For extensive details on this topic, see the Arte documentary on Kurdish women's militias at https://www.youtube.com/watch?v=csLMrM0vUJw.

32  Dilar Dirik, "Rojava: To Dare Imagining," in Dirik et al., 104.

33  Taussig, in Dirik et al., 111.

34  Dirik et al., 112.

35  Dirik et al., 119.

36  Dirik, "Rojava," 105.

37  Schmidinger, *Rojava*, 202.

38  Strangers in a Tangled Wilderness, *A Small Key*, 83.

39  Schmidinger, 182.

40  Strangers in a Tangled Wilderness, 26.

41  Schmidinger, 197.

42  Roy Gutman, "Have the Syrian Kurds Committed War Crimes?," *The Nation*, February 7, 2017, https://www.thenation.com/article/have-the-syrian-kurds-committed-war-crimes/; Roy Gutman, "America's Favorite Syrian Militia Rules with an Iron Fist," *The Nation*, February 13, 2017, https://www.thenation.com/article/americas-favorite-syrian-militia-rules-with-an-iron-fist/; Meredith Tax, with Joey Lawrence and Flint Arthur, "The War of Disinformation," and Roy Gutman, "Gutman Responds," *The Nation*, February 21, 2017, https://www.thenation.com/article/the-syrian-kurds-and-allegations-of-war-crimes/.

# 8

# Papua Merdeka: The Indigenous Struggle against State and Corporate Domination

## Partners in Genocide

Around the turn of the millennium, major American and German corporations were embarrassed by ads placed in newspapers by former slave laborers in factories operated by these companies under the Nazi regime. The corporations were attacked for their "genocidal partnership" with the Nazis. Survivors are quoted as saying that they "were treated like animals" at the Ford Werke AG factory, while Bayer pharmaceutical corporation was cited for haggling over the price of women used in the testing of sleeping medications.[1] Today the public finds such corporate practices to be shocking and morally abhorrent, a relic of the barbarism of the Nazi era. But if we look carefully at corporate practices today, we find certain striking continuities. Today, major corporations are still willing to do business with dictatorships. They are still willing to profit from oppression and persecution. They are still willing enter into "genocidal partnerships."

The alliance between the Suharto dictatorship and the Freeport-McMoRan corporation in West Papua between 1965 and 1997 is a highly instructive case study of such a genocidal partnership. The present discussion will outline this case study. It will begin with some historical background on the Freeport-Suharto partnership, then comment on the clash between corporate and indigenous worldviews, continue with a summary of the social and environmental impact of Freeport on Papuan society, touch briefly on the larger global context of the Freeport case, and end with a few words about the continuing movement for freedom and justice for West Papua in the post-Suharto era.[2]

My interest in Freeport began in 1990, when the company's CEO, "Jim Bob" Moffett, bitterly attacked local environmentalists in Louisiana for opposing the company's proposal to dump radioactive gypsum waste into the Mississippi River. Regulatory agencies prevented the company from carrying out its plans and ordered it to contain its hazardous materials. It soon launched a public-relations campaign to convince the community of its deep concern for the Earth, as exemplified by its efforts to prevent radioactive gypsum from polluting the Mississippi River. It also began to endow professorships at area universities in environmental fields, hired the major environmental reporters away from the local media, so that they could do environmental PR for the company, and began advertising heavily its newfound environmental awareness. While such actions in Louisiana raised important ethical and political issues, I was unprepared for the shocking level of injustice and exploitation I discovered when I began to study Freeport's operations in West Papua.

## Neocolonialism in West Papua

Though Indonesia gained independence in 1949, the Dutch retained control of West Papua into the 1960s, promising independence by 1970. However, in response to pressure from Western powers and from pro-Indonesian factions in the Netherlands, it instead transferred control to Indonesia in 1963. To complete the legitimation process, manipulated elections were held in 1969, in which 1,025 handpicked representatives of the eight hundred thousand West Papuans were allowed to vote, under the pressure of Indonesian military occupation, in the so-called Act of Free Choice. Occupied West Papua was renamed "Irian Jaya."

From the outset, the independence movement, led by the OPM armed resistance, has been active. In turn, Indonesia quickly instituted and has continued for over four decades a program of military and police repression, including widespread torture, intimidation, destruction of property, and killing.[3] Estimates of the total number of Papuan casualties under Indonesian domination have ranged up to three hundred thousand, with one hundred thousand most frequently mentioned by human rights groups.[4]

Since 1969 Indonesia has sponsored a massive program of transmigration from Java and other densely populated islands in the archipelago. Its aims are to reduce population pressures in densely populated areas and to secure Indonesian political and social dominance in an economically crucial area. The result is the political and social marginalization of the Papuans within their own country, and, ultimately, a process of cultural genocide. In 1985 Indonesian Minister of Transmigration Martono said ominously that the goal is to "integrate all ethnic groups into one nation," so that "different ethnic groups will in the long run disappear" and "there will be one kind of man" in West Papua.[5]

## The Indonesia-Freeport Partnership in Exploitation of West Papua

Suharto's murderous coup in 1965 and the establishment of a repressive right-wing dictatorship were a turning point in Indonesian history and turned out to be a boon to Western corporations. Over the next three decades Suharto was to develop an oligarchical system in which the Suharto family, Indonesian political and military elites and foreign corporations were to play central roles. Freeport was the first foreign company to receive a permit to operate in Indonesia after the coup. For three decades the relationship between Freeport and Suharto was to be a close and mutually profitable one.

In 1984 Jim Bob Moffett took over as CEO of Freeport. It is reported that former secretary of state Henry Kissinger introduced Moffett to Suharto. Kissinger was to become a member of Freeport's Board of Directors for seven years, for which he would be paid $500,000 a year, and his law firm would receive an additional $200,000 a year (equivalent to over $1.2 million and almost $500,000, respectively, in current dollars). During the Suharto regime Moffett was to become a close friend and ally of the Indonesian leader, going so far as to call the genocidal dictator "a compassionate man."

Freeport has been rewarded with the right to exploit what developed into the second largest copper mine and the largest gold mine in the world. Freeport has in turn been Indonesia's largest corporate taxpayer and has provided the crucial expertise needed to exploit the mineral resources seized from the Papuans. Freeport contributed a total of $756 million to the Indonesian government in 2017.[6] In addition, Freeport's "community investment," which consists of various social, economic, and environmental programs in West Papua that are used for public relations and appeasement purposes, was $93 million in 2017.[7]

The Grasberg mine has become an increasingly valuable asset for both Freeport and the Indonesian government over nearly half a century. According to Freeport's annual report, copper production in 2017 was 981 million pounds, with a value of almost $3 billion and gold production was 1.5 million ounces, with a value of almost $1.9 billion. Copper production for 2018 is projected to be 1.2 billion pounds, which would have a value of $3.6 billion, and gold production is projected to be 2.4 million ounces, which would have a value of about $3 billion.[8]

## Cowboy Capitalism Confronts Indigenous Ethics and Spirituality

Moffett does not hide his fanatical dedication to his company's power and glory. He has said of his mining operation, "This is not a job for us, it's a religion." With more truth than he was capable of comprehending, Moffett once stated of Freeport's mining operations that it was "thrusting a spearhead of development into the heartland" of West Papua."[9] And he described Freeport's assault on a sacred mountain of the Amungme people in these terms: "We have a volcano that's been decapitated by nature, and we're mining the esophagus, if you will."[10] It is instructive to compare Moffett's religion of progress, power and profit with the spiritual values of the Amungme people, the traditional landholders dispossessed by Freeport.

In 1994 the Indonesian regime escalated its repression in West Papua. One of the victims was Mama Yosepha Alomang, the most prominent woman leader of the Amungme tribe, a tireless advocate for human rights, ecological integrity, and community development, and a recipient of the Goldman Environmental Prize. She was accused of giving aid to anti-government insurgents, and tortured and imprisoned for over a month, suffering a week of confinement in a small, dark, flooded closet reeking of human feces. Under interrogation by the military, she affirmed that she had given food and supplies to people in need who had come to her asking for help. She explained, "Our custom teaches us that if you have more than enough, you have to share. . . . I give it not to support them, but because if we live with other people, how can we not give if we have it, and people ask for it?"[11] Mama Yosepha acts out of a living tradition of the commons and of care that extends not only to other human beings but to the Earth itself.

Tom Beanal, head of the Amungme tribal council, recounts an Amungme origins story that tells of a primordial Mother (the personification of the island of Papua) who is the source of life. He notes that the narrative "tells us that if the mountains and nature are harmed, our Mother is hurt as well."[12] Each tribal group has a place of origin that has a symbolic location in relation to the body of the Mother. The Amungme "live on the land thought to reach from the Mother's neck to her navel. This is the place closest to her."[13]

This mountainous area is the site of Freeport's mining operations: what Moffett ironically calls "mining the esophagus" and which he compares to "thrusting a spear through the heart" of the land. While for the Amungme, "the mountain we see as our Mother is sacred," for Freeport it is a resource to be exploited in the most economically profitable manner possible. As Beanal states it:

> these companies have taken over and occupied our land. Even the sacred mountains we think of as our Mother have been arbitrarily torn up by them, and they have not felt the least bit guilty. . . . Gold and copper have been taken by Freeport for the past thirty years, but what have we gotten in return? Only insults, torture, arrests, killings, forced evictions from our land, impoverishment and alienation from our own culture. We have become strangers in our own land and this has been going on for the past thirty years![14]

## Social Injustices against the Papuan People

We might usefully look at some of the details of this tragic history. In April 1977 the OPM began a series of attacks on Indonesian military posts and later the Freeport mine itself, destroying the mine's slurry pipe. The Indonesian military responded by strafing and bombing Papuan villages using OV-10 Bronco counterinsurgency planes supplied by the United States.[15] This ruthless military operation, called "Operasi Tumpas" ("Operation Annihilation"), was supported by a Freeport contribution of $1 million.[16] BBC reporter George Monbiot reports of the rape, torture, and murder of girls from the villages and of Indonesian soldiers taking photographs of one another with their feet on the heads of murdered villagers. He claims that "American employees at the [Freeport] mine were well aware of what was happening and seemed to regard it as entertainment."[17] It is estimated that thousands of Papuans were killed in this one operation, and intermittent murder and state terror have continued up to the present.

After years of minimal scrutiny, except by a small group of dedicated critics, Freeport's role first came under widespread public scrutiny in 1995 after the appearance of shocking atrocity reports from the Australian Council for Overseas Aid, the Catholic Church of Jayapura and the National Human Rights Commission. The reports revealed numerous cases of murder, violence, and torture by the Indonesian military in and around the Freeport mining area, often with the use of Freeport equipment, facilities, and the cooperation of employees. In May 1998 three other

Papuan Church groups issued a report on human rights abuses in the area over the preceding two years, including "eyewitness accounts of the horrific brutality of the Indonesian army."[18]

In response to 1996 rioting directed against the company, Freeport set up a "1 percent plan," through which 1 percent of its gross revenues goes into social services and development programs for the local indigenous people (the "community investment" programs mentioned earlier). Although Freeport has lavishly congratulated itself in PR campaigns for these programs, the funds dedicated to the plan are minuscule in comparison to the mineral wealth that has been extracted and stolen from West Papua. The tragic irony of Freeport's PR slogan, "Giving Something Back," becomes evident when one considers that the year the program was set up, the Papuans were given $14 million in return for the expropriation and brutal exploitation of their land, while Jim Bob Moffett personally made over $41 million that year as CEO of Freeport. Such programs have remained on the level of a paternalistic tokenism that does nothing to fundamentally improve the lives of Papuans while providing useful content for Freeport's Giving Something Back–themed PR campaigns and reports to stockholders.

Beneath the ongoing human rights atrocities over the past decades are the structural conditions of oppression and immiseration that have been imposed on the Papuan people by Indonesian neocolonialism and global economic imperialism. It is these structural conditions that produce for the Papuan people continuing poverty, poor health conditions, poor housing, lack of education, political powerlessness, and cultural marginalization. In June 1980, for example, an epidemic killed 216 Papuan children in a resettlement area, due to poverty and inadequate medical care.[19] Two decades later, after several years of drought, mortality rates for Papuans soared because of a lack of fresh water in villages. It has also been reported that the rate of HIV/AIDS in West Papua is thirty times higher than the national rate, while prevention programs and medical treatment remain minimal.[20] It can truly be said that the misery and oppression of the Papuans is in direct proportion to the enormous wealth that is extracted from their land.

## Environmental Destruction Caused by the Freeport Mining Operation

Freeport's environmental record is as disturbing as is its history of human rights abuses, and the two often intersect in environmental injustice issues.

The Grasberg mine produces over two hundred thousand tons of tailings per day that are dumped into rivers, causing flooding that destroys surrounding forests and farmland. This has "turned a 230-square-kilometer lowland delta into a gray desert of dead trees."[21] Critics claim that tailings have introduced such pollutants as sulfuric acid, copper, mercury, and arsenic into the rivers. Sediments in the Ajkwa River have been found to contain copper concentrations thirty-eight times the minimum level for an area to be considered contaminated.[22] For many years Freeport has operated the mine according to procedures that would deposit three billion tons of overburden or waste rock over a period of forty years. Such enormous deposits pose serious threats, including landslides and leaching of acid.[23] The United Nations International Maritime Organization has warned that Freeport's operation may create "a massive environmental burden for future generations," and Indonesia has recently raised the target for tailings recovery from 50 to 95 percent of tailings. Freeport has, however, rejected this fundamental change as economically and technologically unfeasible.[24]

An instructive incident regarding Freeport's environmental record occurred in October of 1995. At that time Freeport faced a significant crisis when the Overseas Private Investment Corporation (OPIC), a federal agency that insures American companies doing business overseas, cancelled Freeport's $100 million political-risk insurance policy on the basis of environmental abuses. In New Orleans (site of the Freeport headquarters at the time) this resulted in a massive local PR campaign to control public opinion. Freeport called for support from organizations and individuals who had received its largesse. Heads of the area's major charities and the presidents of local universities took out a full-page newspaper ad lauding Freeport as a model "corporate citizen," while the New Orleans City Council unanimously passed a resolution citing Freeport's exemplary social and environmental record.

At the national level, Freeport and its political allies exerted heavy pressure on the Clinton administration to have the decision reversed. Influential politicians such as former Democratic senator John Breaux (later a lobbyist on behalf of health and energy corporations) rushed to the aid of Freeport, attacking OPIC for supposedly taking a dangerous antibusiness stance. In the end, OPIC temporarily reinstated Freeport's insurance, pending future investigations of supposed progress at the mine. These investigations never occurred, however, since Freeport later canceled its policy with both OPIC and MIGA, another insuring agency, to avoid such oversight.[25]

## Post-Suharto Developments

In 1998, the hated Suharto dictatorship fell after three decades of corruption, colonialism, oppression and genocide. This was followed by East Timor's successful referendum on independence in 1999. Later, former president Abdurrahman Wahid proposed changing the Indonesian name for West Papua (Irian Jaya) and granted the Papuans the right to fly their long-banned flag and to hold large meetings of Papuan organizations.

The movement for independence is supported by the overwhelming majority of indigenous West Papuans and remains strong. Papuans continue to reassert the case that the declaration of independence of 1961 should be recognized by Indonesia and the United Nations. Their case was given support when retired UN undersecretary-general Chakravarti Narasimhan, who was "the senior UN official who ran the ballot" in the so-called Act of Free Choice, said that the process was actually "a sham."[26] Freeport's actions came under closer scrutiny after the fall of Suharto. For example, there were calls for the U.S. Department of Justice to investigate under the Foreign Corrupt Practices Act illegalities committed during Freeport's collaboration with the regime.[27]

Relations between Freeport and the Papuans improve periodically when the company makes certain concessions and the level of repression declines. In August of 2000 Freeport and several Papuan organizations announced the signing of a "Memorandum of Understanding" in which Papuans would gain employment opportunities, new economic development projects would be set up, and buildings would be constructed for tribal organizations and elders. These organizations agreed to mediate disputes between indigenous people and Freeport.[28]

However, harsh repression and persecution have continued over the years as part of the Indonesian effort to contain dissent and maintain the basic structure of domination. A striking example occurred in September 2001, when Papuan Presidium Council chairman Theys Hiyo Eluay was kidnapped, tortured, and strangled. His death was followed by rioting and several large demonstrations, including a march of seven thousand to the provincial legislature. In the end, four Indonesian soldiers were convicted of the crime and given light prison terms, while those higher up in the chain of command who planned and ordered the murder retained their usual impunity. The deplorable record continues today. The *Guardian* recently reported that human rights violations have actually increased since current president Joko Widodo took office. Indonesia's Commission for the Disappeared and Victims of Violence reports "1,200 incidents of harassment, beatings, torture and killings of Papuans by Indonesian security forces since his election in 2014."[29]

### Freeport, Indonesia, and the World System

West Papua as a case study in global domination is instructive because of the contradictions that emerge as a result of its complex role as first, a neocolonial territory, and second, a partially integrated province in a semiperipheral state, and third, a peripheral (extractive industrial) region in the global system of economic imperialism.

Hopkins and Wallerstein note that "however much they may reinforce one another in certain times and in certain places," the two "broad organizing tendencies—that of integrating production on a world-scale and that of forming strong national states—are in principle deeply contradictory."[30] Under the Suharto dictatorship the two tendencies could coexist in relative harmony, since companies such as Freeport and its partner Rio Tinto/RTZ could bring to Indonesia experience, technical capabilities and capital that were needed in extractive industry, while at the same time offering avenues for increased wealth and power for the oligarchy (the crony capitalist regime) and pouring large amounts of tax money into the national treasury.

After Suharto, certain contradictions have emerged more clearly. Post-Suharto Indonesia imagines itself, however ideologically, as less an empire and more a mass-democratic nation-state. Yet overt militaristic repression of colonized areas remains in force and may indeed escalate dramatically because of increased separatist activity and the generalized militarization legitimated by alleged terrorist threats. The Indonesian state would ideally prefer a transition to less coercive, more normalized political means of control. Its goal of social integration of West Papua would seem to require greater concern for the attitudes, aspirations, and living conditions of Papuans, and there have indeed been some token concessions, but these do not threaten the basic structure of domination. Severe repression continues whenever needed, and the Papuans become progressively more powerless in their own land. It is likely that Indonesia sees West Papua as a dwindling threat that is unlikely to attract much attention globally. The

Indonesian policy of combining transmigration with social and economic oppression has been highly successful in its demographically genocidal mission. Some estimates indicated that Papuans were already a minority by 2010; however, more recent study has shown that this is not yet the case.[31] Nevertheless, demographic trends still point in this direction.

A final geopolitical factor that should be mentioned is that the balance of power between the nation-state and transnational corporations in Indonesia, as in some other powerful states, has tilted increasingly in a nationalistic direction. The renegotiation of the role of companies such as Freeport in the post-Suharto Indonesian power regime has resulted in greater power for the state, and to a certain degree, for regional and local communities. This trend culminated on July 12, 2018, with an agreement for the state-owned holding company Indonesia Asahan Aluminum (Inalum) to increase its stake in Freeport Indonesia's mining operations from 9.36 percent to 51 percent (including buying out Freeport's partner Rio Tinto). Thus, Freeport will no longer be the majority partner in the exploitation of West Papua's mineral wealth. The conditions under which Freeport will continue its participation in mining operations through 2041 are still being negotiated.

## Freeport and Its Critics

It might be useful to conclude with a few comments on the struggle between Freeport and its critics and the question of the efficacy of various strategies and tactics. Over the decade that I was heavily engaged in West Papua issues, I gradually came to the conclusion that the West Papua support movement was a case of asymmetric social struggle between strategic corporate management and tactical oppositional protest. Considering its vast resources, Freeport has often been tactically inept and has responded to attacks and criticism in a heavy-headed and self-defeating manner. On the other hand, it has promoted its interest in long-term, strategically effective ways: in Indonesia, through exploiting its crucial place in the national economy and through effective partnership with political and economic elites; and in the United States, through its regional economic importance, its political alliances and contributions to political campaigns, through its sponsorship of educational, charitable, and public service programs, and through its media campaigns and purchase of well-known media figures.

The magnitude of Freeport's strategic success has in some ways become a liability, for although its partnership with the Suharto dictatorship brought it enormous wealth and influence, the closeness of its ties to that discredited regime placed it in a precarious position. Nevertheless, it has attempted to adapt to changing power dynamics, and its pragmatic strategy of alliance with de facto powers has certainly been an economically rational approach. Furthermore, a crucial strength of a major transnational corporation such as Freeport is its ability to support a large corporate ideological infrastructure; that is, a staff of technical intelligentsia charged with the gathering and interpretation of information, with planning corporate communications strategy, and with shaping opinion among the media, the general public, and the relevant political and social elites.

Many of Freeport's critics tend to be loosely organized and focused on flagrant abuses that gain periodic media attention. There are notable exceptions, such as, for a number of years, Project Underground, which followed Freeport closely, published important analyses of corporate history and behavior, and worked with local activist groups. Highly capable and dedicated journalists such as Pratap Chatterjee and activist academicians such as anthropologist Steven Feld have also played a very important role. And several West Papuan support groups in Australia and elsewhere have continuously placed criticism of Freeport within the context of a deeper analysis of West Papuan and Indonesian issues.

Nevertheless, there is a need for more highly developed institutional structures for analysis, critique, policy formulation, and coordination of action. Successful struggle for justice in West Papua is tied to the general struggle for global organization capable of confronting the dominant world system, with its alliance between expansionist global capital and the global nation-state system. My own efforts and hopes in this struggle have been channeled through the global green and global justice movements. Yet, in comparison to the highly institutionalized and integrated nature of the nation-state and corporate systems, these movements remain in a nascent state.

It is clear that the struggle for ecology, peace, social justice, and grassroots democracy requires transnational organization and communication systems capable of mobilizing citizens and coordinating efforts much more effectively on a global scale. All efforts in this direction should be welcomed. However, the ultimate challenge is to create a growing, vibrant, engaged culture of liberation and solidarity, rooted in the everyday practice (ethos) of communities of liberation and solidarity everywhere. For it is only in the reality of such a culture and community that we can create the institutional, ideological, and imaginary preconditions for global justice and freedom.

## NOTES

1 Pauline Jelinek, "Holocaust Reckoning for Ford: Survivors Want Money from U.S. Firms Active in War," Associated Press, October 5, 1999. See also "Ford and the Führer: New Documents Reveal the Close Ties Between Dearborn and the Nazis," *The Nation*, January 24, 2000.

2 "Papua Merdeka" or "Free Papua" is the popular slogan for West Papuan independence. The Papuan freedom movement is called the Organisasi Papua Merdeka or OPM.

3 As Human Rights Watch reported, "For many years, the province was categorized as a military combat zone (Daerah Operasi Militer or DOM; literally, Military Operations Area)" and remained "under an effective state of martial law." Human Rights Watch, "Human Rights and Pro-Independence Actions in Papua, 1999–2000," vol. 12, no. 2(c), May 2000, https://www.hrw.org/reports/2000/papua/.

4 Julian Evans, in the *New Statesman*, suggested that "at least 45,000 have been killed, including 3,500 in 1967 alone." See Julian Evans, "Indonesia's Next East Timor?," *New Statesman*, July 10, 2000. The First International West Papua Solidarity Conference, and the Second Papua Congress (May–June, 2000) both asserted that "some 100,000 people have died due to Indonesian repression in West Papua since 1963" (*Australia West Papua Association* [AWPA] *Newsletter* 10 [October 2000], http://www.zulenet.com/awpa/pages/wp10.html). AWPA cites estimates of 200,000 or more. TAPOL, the Indonesian Human Rights Campaign, cites estimates of 100,000–150,000 as of the late 1980s. Carmel Budiardjo and Liem Soei Liong, *West Papua: The Obliteration of a People* (Surrey, UK: TAPOL, 1988), viii. See also the "West Papua Information Kit" at http://www.cs.utexas.edu/users/cline/papua/. International Aid for West Papua has claimed that almost 300,000 Papuans, which would constitute almost a third of the current total indigenous population, "have been killed or 'disappeared' so far in the hands of the Indonesian military." See "West Papua a Quagmire of Divergent Interests," August 10, 2000, IAWP website, http://www.koteka.net/quagmire.htm.

5 Quoted in Marcus Colchester, "Unity and Diversity: Indonesian Policy towards Tribal Peoples," *Ecologist* 16, no. 2–3 (1986): 89.

6 Viriya P. Singgih, "Indonesia Collects US$756m in State Revenue from Freeport in 2017," *Jakarta Post*, March 7, 2018, http://www.thejakartapost.com/news/2018/03/07/indonesia-collects-us756m-in-state-revenue-from-freeport-in-2017.html.

7 "Sustainability" section of Freeport-McMoRan 2017 Annual Report, https://www.fcx.com/sustainability/communities/community-investment/Indonesia.

8 Given the price for these metals at the time of the projection. Freeport-McMoRan 2017 Annual Report, http://www.annualreports.com/HostedData/AnnualReports/PDF/NYSE_FCX_2017.pdf.

9    *IWGA* (International Work Group for Indigenous Affairs) *Newsletter*, April–June 1992. He used the term "Irian Jaya," the name imposed on Papua by the Indonesian regime.

10   *IWGA Newsletter.*

11   Catholic Church of Jayapura, "Violations of Human Rights in the Timika Area of Irian Jaya, Indonesia," August 1995.

12   Tom Beanal speech at Loyola University, May 23, 1996, "Amungme Leader Tom Beanal Speaks at Loyola," *Freeport Watch Bulletin*, Summer 1996, 1.

13   Beanal speech.

14   Beanal speech.

15   Carmel Budiardjo and Liem Soei Liong, *West Papua: The Obliteration of a People* (Surrey, UK: TAPOL, 1988), 68.

16   *IWGIA* (International Work Group for Indigenous Affairs) *Newsletter*, April–June 1992.

17   Rainforest Action Network Action Alert, November 1990.

18   See Survival International, "Indonesia, New Human Rights Report," press release, May 25, 1998. The Church groups that issued reports were the Catholic Church of Jayapura, the Indonesian Evangelical Church of Mimika, the Three Kings Catholic Parish Church of Timika, and the Christian Evangelical Church of Mimika. Although the mining area is a continuing hot spot, atrocities abound throughout West Papua. Papuan groups claim that a "peaceful demonstration of the Papuan people in Biak during July 1st up to 6th [1998] was suppressed by the Indonesian army," which killed "hundreds of people." While the Indonesian government claimed that only one person died, Papuans contend that eyewitnesses saw "one hundred thirty-nine people" loaded onto boats and then "dropped into the sea," according to the Komite Solidaritas Rakyat Irian Kosorairi, in its fourth appeal to the Secretary General of the United Nations, August 7, 1998.

19   Budiardjo and Liem, *West Papua*, 36.

20   "Government Prepares New Strategy to Tackle HIV/AIDS in Irian Jaya," Fitri Wulandari, *Jakarta Post*, December 4, 2001.

21   Michael Shari with Sheri Prasso, "Freeport-McMoRan: A Pit of Trouble," *Business Week*, July 31, 2000. Tailings production is scheduled to reach 300,000 tons per day.

22   Danny Kennedy, Pratap Chatterjee, and Roger Moody, *Risky Business: The Grasberg Gold Mine* (Berkeley: Project Underground, 1998), 15; Julian Evans, "Indonesia's Next East Timor?," *New Statesman*, July 10, 2000.

23   Kennedy, Chatterjee, and Moody, *Risky Business*, 14.

24   Danielle Bochove and David Stringer, "Giant Waste-Spewing Mine Turns into a Battleground in Indonesia," *Bloomberg*, June 4, 2018, https://www.bloomberg.com/news/articles/2018-06-05/giant-waste-spewing-mine-turns-into-battleground-in-indonesia.

25   MIGA, the Multilateral Investment Guarantee Agency, is an agency of the World Bank Group. It was founded in 1988 to provide corporations with insurance covering risks related to currency transfer, expropriation, war, and civil disturbance, and breach of contract. MIGA underwrote Freeport's mining operation in West Papua for $50 million.

26   "Papua History Lesson," editorial in the *Sydney Morning Herald*, November 26, 2001.

27   It has been noted that according to Freeport's own disclosures it guaranteed $254 million in loans for a Suharto-controlled company to buy a 4.8 percent interest in the Freeport Indonesia from a third party and agreed lend the company funds. Suharto, his crony Bob Hasan, and Suharto's son were given "an asset worth a quarter-billion dollars," with Freeport taking all risks. Freeport has so far lent the company $43.7 million for loan payments. See Robert Bryce, "Inside Job," *Austin Chronicle*, August 18, 2000.

28   The "Memorandum" addressed "socioeconomic resources, human rights, land rights and environmental rights." The agreement established a company employing local Papuans in levee maintenance and related projects, an "integrated agriculture, aquaculture and animal husbandry project to be located in and around [Freeport's] tailings deposition area," sponsored by Freeport and including a "substantial share ownership" by Papuan organizations, and, finally, the construction of a LEMASA (the Amungme Tribal Council) office building. Papuan leaders had hoped to achieve some of these goals in their unsuccessful suits against Freeport. Freeport committed itself to "striving to uphold and improve human rights; providing expanded funding, technical assistance and other materials necessary to implement programs to be agreed upon in the future; and working to finalize an agreement for voluntary additional recognition for the Amungme and Kamoro peoples' land rights." The Papuan organizations agreed to cooperate in the programs, and to "mediate any disagreements between PT-FI and the local community." Freeport Press release (August 18, 2000).

29   Susan Schulman, "The $100bn Gold Mine and the West Papuans Who Say They Are Counting the Cost," *Guardian*, November 2, 2016, https://www.theguardian.com/global-development/2016/nov/02/100-bn-dollar-gold-mine-west-papuans-say-they-are-counting-the-cost-indonesia.

30   Terence K. Hopkins, Immanuel Wallerstein, and Associates, "Patterns of Development of the Modern World-State," in Terence K. Hopkins and Immanuel Wallerstein, *World-Systems Analysis: Theory and Methodology* (Beverly Hills: Sage, 1982), 43.

31   See "West Papuan Demographics Update Highlights Disparity," a Radio New Zealand interview with Jim Elmslie of Sydney University's West Papua Project, January 27, 2017, https://www.radionz.co.nz/international/programmes/datelinepacific/audio/201830960/west-papuan-demographics-update-highlights-disparity.

# 9

# Power to the Community:
# The Black Panthers' Living Legacy
# of Grassroots Organization

There was a historical moment in the late 1960s when the movement for "community control" seemed to promise hope for the creation a new direction for the Left in North America. The movement focused heavily on grassroots control of schools and the police yet hinted at a more all-encompassing vision of "power to the people" in the concrete, meaningful sense of effective power from below. What might have been was envisioned in David Morris and Karl Hess's almost-forgotten small classic *Neighborhood Power: The New Localism*, which was published just as the practical hopes of the movement for grassroots power were in the process of fading away.[1] Hess, who also wrote the complementary work *Community Technology*,[2] credited the Black Panthers very explicitly for their central role in inspiring these hopes. He praises the Panthers for being "neighborhood-oriented" and for demanding "freedom where they lived, freedom to have communities rather than colonies."[3] Yet today the Panthers are hardly known in the popular mind as pioneers of the idea of the neighborhood as the new liberatory *polis*.

If the Right and the political mainstream have dismissed the Panthers by branding them as violent extremists and criminals, much of the Left has highlighted the Black nationalist and vanguardist aspects of the party, while giving only glancing attention to its extensive grassroots initiatives. There has been a general neglect for the radically decentralist and anarchistic dimensions of the movement that are expressed in the call for community control. But these aspects were its vital core and remain an invaluable inspiration for the creation of a deeply transformative social movement with a broad base of support and participation. They reveal that the Panthers were an effective radical and revolutionary force to the extent that they were in touch with the radical and revolutionary *needs* of the community.

I know the importance of this tradition in part through the work of my friend scott crow, whose exposure to the Panthers began early in his life. In *Black Flags and Windmills*, scott's indispensable book on the Common Ground Collective, he explains some of this history and illustrates how the Panther heritage, combined with anarchist ideas, was at the core of the extensive relief work of Common Ground after Hurricane Katrina.[4] And I know the vitality of the tradition above all through the work of my friend and fellow local activist Malik Rahim, a Panther leader in New Orleans in the late 1960s and early 1970s who has been a tireless community organizer in the Bay Area and in New Orleans over the decades since and was the major inspiration of Common Ground.

While I was in the process of rereading the history of the Black Panther Party, I came across a video of a talk that Malik had done on the importance of the Panther legacy in the disaster recovery work of Common Ground. In it, he says that "the teachings that [he] learned in the party were carried out in Katrina." He points out that at the time that he was speaking nineteen thousand volunteers had worked with Common Ground and served two hundred thousand disaster survivors in southeast Louisiana and the Mississippi Gulf Coast. Referring to the decades-long movement to free the framed former Black Panthers known as the Angola 3, he says that Common Ground's work "wouldn't have happened if it hadn't been for the Angola 3. And there wouldn't have been an Angola 3 if there hadn't been a Black Panther Party."[5]

So what is the connection between the Black Panther Party of the 1960s and tens of thousands of volunteers devoting days, months, or even years of their lives to saving devastated local communities forty years later? Philip Foner, in the introduction to his collection *The Black Panthers Speak*, quotes Vice President Spiro Agnew as labeling the Black Panthers a "completely irresponsible, anarchist group of criminals."[6] If you look at the early Panther political program, you find much of it to be a radically decentralist, libertarian, and communitarian in nature.[7] It wouldn't be too much of a stretch to call this neglected dimension of the Panther legacy "a completely responsible anarchist plan to replace a criminal system." It is a part of American radical history that is usually ignored in mainstream and even many Left accounts, but which has already had an enduring influence and can still offer tremendous inspiration today.

The "October 1966 Black Panther Party Platform and Program," usually called the "Ten-Point Program,"[8] starts with an unambiguous communal libertarian statement. *"We want freedom. We want power to determine the destiny of our Black Community."*[9] Thus, "freedom" is not defined in the conventional individualist sense of the pursuit of narrow self-interest or personal inclination, but rather as the mutual self-determination of the members of a community. Much of the Program is an effort to spell out this concept of communal freedom, showing how it translates into the ability of the self-reliant community to provide for its own authentic needs.

The Program states that "if the white American business will not give full employment," which is something they knew would not happen, "then the means of production should be taken from the businessmen and placed in the community so that the people of the community can organize and employ all of its people and give a high standard of living." This is a proposal for worker self-management of workplaces that is at the same time community self-management of the local economy as a whole. The Program goes on to state further that "if the white landlords will not give decent housing to our black community," which is also something they knew would not happen, "then the housing and the land should be made into cooperatives so that our community, with government aid, can build and make decent housing for its people." This is a proposal for resident self-management of homes that is at the same time community self-management of local housing as a whole. The Panthers also aimed at creating a community-based system of medical care. Despite their limited resources, they were able to establish a People's Medical Care Center that had ten doctors, twelve nurses, two medical technicians, plus volunteer interns from local medical schools. The Center treated over one hundred patients per week.[10]

The Panthers also envisioned a revolutionized form of education that emphasized critical thinking that unmasked the nature of both the dominant ideology and the system of domination itself and that educated young people to become free and collectively self-determining beings. They demanded "education for our people that exposes the true nature of this decadent American society" and "that teaches us our true history and our role in the present-day society." Most strikingly, they called for "an educational system that will give to our people a knowledge of self." How many political movements have recognized that the basic problems of society are rooted in the kind of selfhood that has been imposed on people and that a basic political task is to carry a revolution at the level of self and subjectivity?[11]

An article on "Liberation Schools" sketches some of the details of a curriculum that pursues such goals. The well-known Panther programs of free breakfasts and lunches are included (in this, they were far ahead of most public school programs at that time). Schools were to have three days of formal classes each week, in addition to two days dedicated to films and field trips "throughout the community," so that the split between the educational process and the real life of the community could be eliminated. Finally, education was recognized as a lifelong process, so there would be adult political education classes in the evenings.[12]

One of the other core demands of the Program was direct democratic community control of not only the police but the legal system. Fifty years ago, the Panthers were already proclaiming, *"We want an immediate end to POLICE BRUTALITY and MURDER of black people."* One must wonder what would have happened if millions had followed the strategies they proposed rather than the path of slogans, street protests, and the lobbying of politicians that has prevailed. The immediate Panther response to police oppression and brutality was a combination of self-education and direct action. They thought it essential for all members of the community to "know their rights," but their position was that the whole community also had to *take direct action* to enforce those rights. Foner notes that "the Party established a system of armed patrol cars, completely legal, carrying both guns and lawbooks," so that "whenever black men or women were stopped by the police, armed Panthers would be on the scene, making sure that their constitutional rights were not violated."[13]

A longer-term goal involved carrying out a plan for community-based control of policing. This plan is outlined in a "Petition Statement for Community Control of Police.[14] It would involve "establishing police departments for the major communities of any city." This was to include all local communities, though the particular focus was on enabling major oppressed ethnic (or class) communities to control their own affairs. Control of the police would be in the hands of neighborhood councils that would be elected by the citizens of the neighborhoods to determine policies for the community police departments. Councils would have disciplinary power over the police and set policies for the commissions and departments to carry out. The council would have the power to recall the commissioners, and the community would have the power to recall the council members. The administration of these departments would be carried out by police commissions whose members would be selected by the councils. All police officers would come from the communities they serve. The result of this grassroots democratic structure would be effective power of the community over the police and policing.

The Program goes beyond the issue of law enforcement to that of community control of the legal system itself. It says, "We want all black people when brought to trial to be tried in court by a jury of their peer group or people from their black communities, as defined by the Constitution of the United States." The Panthers noted that a "peer" in a meaningful sense means "a person from a similar economic, social, religious, geographical, environmental, historical and racial background." They realized that the jury system is one of the most radically democratic aspects of the existing political system, one small remnant of a less bureaucratic and statist historical era. In a jury trial, ordinary citizens get to vote on questions that directly and often powerfully affect the members of their community—namely, the disposition of their lives, liberties, and possessions.

A radically democratic jury system provides a means for the community not only to avoid the injustices typical of the travesty of a jury system that we know today but also to fight against the injustices of a larger undemocratic political and legal system. I think we can assume that jury nullification is implied in the Panthers' proposal. A community-based jury can not only demand that the law be applied justly but can also in effect overrule unjust laws that are imposed on members of local community. The Panthers' demand for a jury of true peers is thus a very radical one. The Program states that "all black people should be released from the many jails and prisons because they have not received a fair and impartial trial." The Panthers were demanding that the whole system be reset—get out of jail and return to Go, we might say—so that the community can assure that all laws are applied justly and that unjust laws will not be applied at all.

The vision of community power in the original "Ten-Point Program" and the actual initiatives put into effect by the Panthers constitute an inspiring example that can help guide our practice today. Among those who have done most to put this legacy into practice is Lorenzo Kom'boa Ervin. Ervin is a former member of the Black Panthers and SNCC, and a founder of the Memphis Black Autonomy Federation. He is well known as the author of *Anarchism and the Black Revolution*.[15] In a very instructive interview about his ideas on organizing, he points out the weakness of tactics such as "lobbying politicians" and depending on "celebrity so-called leaders," which he sees as doing nothing "to build a grassroots movement from the bottom up."[16] Ervin believes that the crucial question as the radical communitarian one: "How do we turn neighborhoods and communities into self-governing communes?"

For Ervin, this implies very concrete creative efforts in which people can see before their eyes the growing power of community and feel this power through their participation in the communal creative process. So "on the local level people would start to build their own neighborhood institutions," which would include "some kind of economic base where people can be given jobs and can build housing and infrastructure for themselves." He sees urban farming as playing a key role in this process, as has recently occurred in many impoverished and marginalized urban areas, perhaps most notably in Detroit. But Ervin points out that even projects like community-based urban farms are of limited value unless they are part of what he calls "building a whole synthesis." He notes problems such as high rates of infant mortality, high cancer rates among women, economic segregation, and police terrorism, and stresses that all these issues have to be linked together, since underlying them all is "the problem of people being disempowered by institutions that exist now."

Consequently, the challenge is to take on all these institutions simultaneously at the local level. Paradoxically, it is by becoming more radically local that a movement is likely to spread far beyond its boundaries. Ervin argues that "when people see that you've got a sustainable movement wherever you started at, it can spread. People will emulate it. And that's essentially what happened with the Black Panther Party." He explains that he is "not saying that we won't help someone start up somewhere else, but our objective right now is to worry about Memphis." The point is that "worrying about Memphis" means at the same time worrying about the world. This is what "building a whole synthesis" means.

Ervin explains that even in the most local of actions "it has to be understood that we're trying to dismantle this entire society," including "this entire capitalist system and the whole system of white supremacy worldwide." This systemic focus is something that was always central to the Black Panther ethos. An area in which both Ervin and Rahim extend this outlook is in their awareness of the ecological dimensions of the necessary synthesis. They recognize that social revolution also means defying capitalism's and the state's definition of reality on behalf of a more bioregional, land-centered, and Earth-oriented approach. As Ervin says, we must move "to the question of a bioregional area as opposed to just a city: We cannot be limited to what the state says is the territorial limitation of an area."

So the "synthesis" means taking on capitalism, the state, racism, and the entire system of domination. The old slogan about thinking globally and acting locally never really made sense in a world that is radically local and global at the same time. The system of domination knows how to think and act both locally and globally simultaneously, and movements for liberation have to learn how to do this also. This is what the struggle between domination and liberation is all about.

And this is how the Panther legacy fits into the total picture. The struggle for an Oakland Commune as a commune of communes, or a Memphis Commune as a commune of communes, is inseparable from the struggle for Commune Earth, the commune of all communes.

## NOTES

1   Karl Hess and David Morris, *Neighborhood Power: The New Localism* (Boston: Beacon Press, 1975).

2   Karl Hess, *Community Technology* (New York: Harper & Row, 1979).

3   Karl Hess, *Dear America* (New York: William Morrow, 1975), 146.

4   Scott crow, *Black Flags and Windmills: Hope, Anarchy and the Common Ground Collective*, 2nd ed. (Oakland: PM Press, 2014).

5   Quoted in Bryan Shih and Yohuru Williams, *The Black Panthers: Portraits from an Unfinished Revolution* (New York: Nation Books, 2016), 217. On the Angola 3, see the powerful film *In the Land of the Free* (2010), written and directed by Vadim Jean.

6   Philip S. Foner, ed., *The Black Panthers Speak* (Philadelphia: J.B. Lippincott, 1970), x.

7   On the almost completely neglected communitarian dimension of the Black Panthers, see Robyn C. Spencer, "Communalism and the Black Panther Party in Oakland, California," in Iain Boal, Janferie Stone, Michael Watts, and Cal Winslow, eds., *West of Eden: Communes and Utopia in Northern California* (Oakland: PM Press, 2012), 92–121. The analysis there explores many of the deeper issues of values and personal life, including sexism and gender roles, that are not addressed extensively in the official statements of the party.

8   "October 1966 Black Panther Party Platform and Program: What We Want/ What We Believe" (October 1966) in Foner, *Black Panthers Speak*, 2–4.

9   Foner, 2.

10  Lincoln Webster Sheffield, "People's Medical Care Center," *Daily World*, May 16, 1970, reprinted in Foner, 173–75.

11  The radicalizing nature of the movement on the personal level can be gauged by the distance between certain notorious sexist and heterosexist statements

that are still cited by critics of the Panthers, and the appearance, within a short period of time, of statements such as Huey Newton's highly advanced and self-critical text, "A Letter from Huey Newton to the Revolutionary Brothers and Sisters about the Women's Liberation and Gay Liberation Movements," http://www.blogcitylights.com/2013/02/04/a-letter-from-huey-newton-to-the-revolutionary-brothers-and-sisters-about-the-womens-liberation-and-gay-liberation-movements/.

12    "Liberation Schools," *The Black Panther*, July 5, 1969, reprinted in Foner, *Black Panthers Speak*, 170–71.

13    Foner, xvii–xviii.

14    "Petition Statement for Community Control of Police. Summary of Police Control Amendment That Must Be Established in the Cities and Communities of America to End Fascism," *The Black Panther*, June 14, 1969, reprinted in Foner, 179.

15    Lorenzo Kom'boa Ervin, *Anarchism and the Black Revolution*, 2nd ed. (1993), http://theanarchistlibrary.org/library/lorenzo-kom-boa-ervin-anarchism-and-the-black-revolution.

16    J.G., "Racism Has to Be Challenged': An Interview with Lorenzo Kom'boa Ervin," *Deep Green Resistance News Service*, October 15, 2012, http://dgrnewsservice.org/2012/10/15/racism-has-to-be-challenged-an-interview-with-lorenzo-komboa-ervin/.

# 10

# From the Movement of Occupation to the Community of Liberation

Just over a week after Occupy New Orleans was founded, a message appeared on the local Occupy discussion list. Its gist: "the whole movement is stagnant," "no passion, just process"; "it is losing ground fast." Someone accused the writer of being an agent provocateur, but similar views were being expressed by other members of the movement. There was no need to look immediately for a conspiracy.

Disruptive agents are always lurking around, but they are far from being the greatest threat to our success. We suffer from certain tendencies that are widespread throughout contemporary culture, and which disrupt our work much more effectively than can any paid forces of disorder. We are often our own worst enemies and have the capacity to be the most effective agents of our own undoing. Fortunately, we have a great deal of control over whether we lapse into dissention and disillusionment or we become the vital, growing community of liberation and solidarity that we are capable of being.

We need to explore in some detail how we might do this. We might however consider first how Occupy would appear if our outlook were guided by such *communitarian virtues* as gratitude, patience, and dedication. At the very point at which some were making harsh, negative judgments on the movement, we had already worked miracles. There was so much to be grateful for! And there is even more to hope for, if we can be patient and if we are dedicated to the work of realizing the extraordinary possibilities that are emerging all around us.

What had Occupy New Orleans accomplished in just a few short days? We had established a General Assembly, in which two hundred people joined together to found the movement. We had a hugely successful initial march and rally, with four hundred exuberantly passionate people in the streets. We had initial General Assembly meetings five days in a row in which seventy-five to one hundred people devoted up to three hours each evening to getting our movement going, through their laborious efforts to work out participatory processes and planning organization and activities. We formed a variety of committees that were already doing good work and learning how to work together cooperatively. We planned another major march just nine days after the first large public event, and this one also ended up being highly successful. New groups were already forming around the city to support Occupy on a decentralized basis.

Not least of all, hundreds of people had, for the first time in their lives, participated in meetings organized according to principles of participatory direct democracy. Many small changes had begun to take place on the personal and group level, and the community was beginning slowly to grow and develop, as we learned, often with much difficulty and struggle, to practice solidarity and cooperation. All these large and small achievements occurred in just a little over a week. Yet, rather strangely from a certain perspective, some were already dropping out of the movement in frustration, and others were quickly losing much of their faith in it.

I once heard an interview with a Libyan activist who talked of the death of his father, who was a martyr for democracy over twenty years ago. He said that many times he wondered, as he saw little progress over those many years, if his father's life had been thrown away. But he always kept faith. Then, decades later, he saw masses of people revolting in the name of democracy, and his father's own words were quoted in mass demonstrations, as the dictatorship crumbled. Fortunately, he did not dismiss the value of his father's sacrifice after a week or two. Its ultimate effects have yet to be determined.

We should ponder what it means, on the deepest level, to be part of a movement. It has nothing to do with immediate gratification and egoistic satisfaction, which are the superficial and false promises of our pathological society of mass consumption. Fundamental social transformation and authentic liberation demand patience, dedication, compassion, and solidarity. The rewards are deep, not superficial. Some are long-term, but others come relatively quickly, if not instantaneously. The greatest of these is to be part of a community of solidarity and liberation, the Beloved Community, in the process of its own self-creation. Freud may have been misguided on many points (his patriarchal bias, his defense of what Marcuse called "surplus repression"), but one of his most incisive insights is the idea that what ultimately makes our lives worthwhile is the presence of love and good work. The Beloved Community is a community of people doing good work in the name of, and through the practice of, love and solidarity.

If this is true, then many of the most important goals of Occupy do not have to wait for the overthrow of the global economic order and the establishment of that "other world" that is possible in the future. It was once said of the early struggles of the working class that "the real fruit of their battles lies, not in the immediate result, but in the ever-expanding union of the workers." We might say that the real fruit of our struggle lies in both the immediate and long-term results, that is, in the ever-expanding self-realization of the free community. Our means are one with our ends.

Sometimes we get trapped in a world of false immediacy. Sometimes we put our own preoccupations above the community's occupation. We must strive against obsession with winning nonessential votes or getting our way in the short run, when the basic character and values of the movement are not at stake. We must learn to take satisfaction in the immediate good that we are achieving. We must learn to be able at times to disagree strongly with the majority and then take great satisfaction that in "standing aside" and refusing to block consensus, we are contributing to the needs of the community. We must learn to be able at times to experience the joy of sacrifice. When we achieve a consensus on some flawed, imperfect proposal that realizes some, but far from all of our hopes, this immediately fulfills what is perhaps our most important aspiration. It realizes our hope that we (flawed, imperfect beings) can practice direct democracy and build a cooperative community. We can do something extraordinary.

Everything we do in our meetings and organizing needs to be evaluated in the light of what it contributes to the full realization of our community. To the extent that our movement embodies, here and now, the community of liberation and solidarity, we will win over more and more others to our cause. In everything we do—in our participation in general assemblies, in our work in committees, in our messages to lists, and in our informal contacts—we need to ask if our mode of interaction will make others want to be part of our community. This seems obvious, yet we must remind ourselves of it constantly, since the obvious is often forgotten in the heat of controversy or lost in the minutiae of issues. If we practice love, solidarity, and respect for one another, those who come in contact with us will want to join us.

When a transformative movement is in the news and is growing, curious people often wander into meetings and events, or check out discussion lists and newsletters, mainly to see what the commotion is about. They may have only a vague and amorphous sympathy, but they will come under the spell of the transformative community, if it consistently practices its ideals of justice, love, and solidarity. This is what the great communitarian anarchist thinkers taught. As Elisée Reclus said, "It is step by step, through small, loving, and intelligent associations, that the great collegial society will be formed."[1] Gustav Landauer predicted that when free, cooperative communities begin to spread across the land, many will observe "their joy in life, in its inexpressible though quiet manner," and yearn to be part of such a community.[2]

Such experience was part of my own personal transformation. When I was in my late teens, a friend and I went to a civil rights meeting at Xavier University. Neither of us was sympathetic to the cause, but we wanted to see what was going on. We had been indoctrinated with conservative and racist ideas, and reactionary conditioning still had a great influence on us. However, we were curious, and, for some strange reason, open-minded in spite of ourselves. So we checked out the meeting. It turned out that we were both deeply impressed by the extraordinary spirit of the group, by the humanity, sensitivity, dedication, and enthusiasm of its members. When we left, my friend turned to me and said, "You know, these are really good people!" I knew at that moment that something had changed. We had encountered goodness! The event was a turning point and had a lasting effect on both of us.

In large part as the result of this experience, my friend decided to join an interracial youth exchange program. In the program, black youth from northern cities spent time with white families in the South, and white youth from the South stayed with black families in northern cities. My friend lived with a family in Detroit and had a teenager in the family as his roommate. This more or less completed the conversion process that had started at the meeting at Xavier.

The experience contributed equally to my own transformation. I was impressed not only by the *good points* the members of the group made but above all by what *good people* they were and how well they interacted with one another. They were joyful and hopeful, and cooperative and respectful to one another, in addition to being dedicated to the cause of justice and liberation. This encounter with charismatic community, a kind of positive trauma, quickly placed in question much the indoctrination to which I had been subjected and helped begin a longer-term process of confronting its effects. I had had a small taste of what the Beloved Community was all about and discovered that it could be a powerful antidote to the poison of racism and prejudice. Before long I was caught up in the quest for such a community, and I still am.

I have always taken this experience, and a number of similar ones (for example, work with inspiring and exemplary West Papuan freedom activists and Tibetans who are joyfully dedicated to serving their refugee community), as a standard by which to judge organizations and movements. Do they engender forms of community in which we can (in the famous phrase that Gandhi probably never uttered) "be the change we wish to see." In all the work we do together, we need to think about how each word and each action can help create the community that we yearn for. We need to train ourselves in the mindfulness, dedication, perseverance, and patience that this requires, because for most of us it doesn't come very easily. We need to learn how to reach out actively to those who might be ready to find fulfillment in a community of liberation and solidarity.

Of course, we need to communicate our ideas, to explain the meaning of consensus and other cooperative, communitarian processes. But above all, we need to learn how to practice communal solidarity among ourselves. We need to learn how to be more successful in the struggle against our own individualism, egocentrism, and narcissism. We are in many, sometimes obvious, but often subtle and devious ways, products of the system of domination we want to destroy. "It has put its poison in us." We should never be complaisant about the ways in which that system lives on within each of us. We must work from moment to moment to resist its manifestations. Resistance to domination, and overcoming resistance to liberation, is a continuous practice, both for the community and for the person.

Our greatest enemies in this struggle are the forces through which the system of domination occupies our own egos. We aspire to occupy and liberate public spaces, but we often neglect the occupied psychic spaces. These forces of occupation are particularly destructive of community, mutuality, and cooperation. They include egocentrism, self-indulgence, impatience, inattention, impetuousness, insensitivity, defensiveness, resentment, anger, and disrespect, to mention a few. We succumb to them quite naturally, because so much in our social environment has reinforced them throughout our lives. We can only avoid them successfully if we make a conscious and diligent effort to develop a cooperative, communitarian practice of solidarity, mutual aid, patience, mindfulness, sensitivity, openness, generosity, respect, and compassion. This means becoming part of a transfigurative community.

Such an all-encompassing communal practice is our deepest collective need. We need to work diligently on confronting the ways in which individualistic and narcissistic tendencies emerge in our meetings and events. There are some cases that are probably hopeless, such as the machistic persons who come to an assembly primarily to make a mockery its processes, whether consciously or unconsciously, and show off their own arrogance and sense of superiority. But there are difficulties with well-meaning people also. The topics of not silencing participants and the need for a more diverse movement often come up in the assembly. But ironically, some have spent more time talking about the problem of "silencing" than the majority of assembly members have spent talking about anything at all. The real need is not for more expression of concern about silencing, but for more dedicated, skillful efforts to broaden the active participation of members of the assembly. There is a real need not for a few to speak for and better represent the diverse members of the larger community, but rather for more dedicated, skillful efforts, inside and especially outside the assembly, to bring the movement into active dialogue and collaboration with diverse segments of the larger community.

Participation in the assembly sometimes takes a disruptively individualistic turn. Anger and resentment take over at times. Some seem to turn their interventions into attempts at personal performance, with greater or lesser success. Admittedly, all interventions are in a sense a kind of performance. But the crucial question is what kind of performance it is. The old cliché says that when we are angry we should "count to ten" before speaking or acting. It might not be a bad idea to count to ten whenever we are moved to intervene in an important collective deliberation. But instead of just counting, we might use some of those ten moments to ask ourselves how what we are about to say will contribute to the good of our community and the realization of its goals. We might ask ourselves not only whether we have a *good idea* but also whether our mode of presentation helps us reach a *good decision* and, even more importantly, helps us create the *good community*. This would be acting in the Daoist spirit of "not putting ourselves ahead of the world" and in the Zapatista spirit of "leading by obeying."

At one extreme, one's performance is the performance of a service to our community's common good (as in the Zapatista *cargo*). It constitutes a special effort to serve the community to the best of one's ability. At the other extreme, it is a form of self-indulgence that uses the community as a means toward ego gratification. Given the ways in which we are conditioned by the dominant society to be egocentric and self-indulgent (and militantly defensive of our egocentrism and self-indulgence), we can only expect the former tendency to win out over the latter if we undertake collectively a process of re-education and re-socialization in which we learn to be good community members. The overriding need is for a communal practice that we undertake diligently and collectively.

Our commitment to consensus is one of the strongest aspects of the movement, but it also poses daunting problems. We have done rather well in upholding our basic principles while recognizing the demands of practicality. The process of seeking consensus in good faith, allowing adequate time for dissenters to comment and then, if necessary, resorting to supermajorities of up to 90 percent, constitutes recognition of the importance of each person in the group and of the need to consider all points of view carefully.

At times, however, a few individuals have undermined our processes by taking up so much time in expressing dissent or pursuing perfectionism, usually on noncrucial matters, that little if any business could be completed. This is irrational and self-destructive. It shows a lack of respect for the needs and the good of the community. There is a point at which certain essential decisions must be made if the movement is to be actively engaged in the community, if it is to be not only a movement to "occupy" but a movement for "New Orleans" or for any other community. When this point is reached, and a decision is made, all can, whatever the decision, maintain their diverse convictions, discuss matters outside the assembly, and propose reconsideration of the issue in the future. It must be recognized that if a small minority destroys the possibility of action, when the vast majority is prepared to act, that small minority has imposed its authority on the vast majority.

Furthermore, continually ceding to single "hard blocks" (objections on basic principles that effectively veto collective action) is dangerous in a world in which there is a certain likelihood that government and corporate agents, sectarian dogmatists, and pathological narcissists may occasionally appear. And even if they are not present, the same dangers can be posed by well-meaning, quite sane people who get caught up in the immediate issues and fail to place those issues in the context of the larger interest of the community and movement. The early green movement in the United States (during the period of the Green Committees of Correspondence) at times adopted a decision-making process for large assembles in which a certain minimum number of blocks would result in the defeat of a proposal. This is a reasonable approach to balancing the need for consensus against the need for action. It is important to consider the difference between one person disagreeing in a small group of ten people (an affinity group or action group) and one or two disagreeing in a large assembly of fifty, a hundred, or many hundreds of participants (a general assembly).

This is not to deny that the slippery slope is sometimes a real threat. There are certainly dangers as a group moves step by step from unanimous consent, to allowing action when there are some blocks, to supermajority decisions by 90 percent, etc. The greater ease of decision-making in less consensual processes reinforces further steps toward less participatory and less democratic processes. With each step, it becomes easier to overlook the more subtle problems in the less consensual forms. Yet this danger can be recognized and balanced against the need to act quickly and decisively in some pressing situations and the need merely *to act* on some crucial issues of principles and organization. We could wait to act until we have achieved an ideally perfect consensus in an ideally perfect way on every matter. However, by that time the sixth great mass extinction of life on Earth might very well be over—and we will have achieved a consensus of silence.

Such debate over issues of consensus relates to an enduring and quite necessary tension between a recognition of the integrity of the person and a recognition of good of the larger community. Some have questioned the wisdom and practicality of making the creation and nurturing of community central to the goals of Occupy. Some have, indeed, been very harsh in their condemnation of this aspiration. However, I would argue that this decidedly communitarian impulse is not merely justified but is, in fact, the most essential aspect of our movement. We must face the fact that "We are the 99%" is a brilliant slogan but creates an ambiguous and in many ways contradictory and misleading self-identity. It encourages the strategy of seeking a minimalist and therefore innocuous coalition politics. Such a politics is in many ways a regression from economic class politics and in every way a barrier to the development of the more complex class politics and the radically communitarian politics that we need. On the other hand, creating a community of liberation and solidarity is the most important thing that we can possibly do, if we want to get beyond the folly of single-issue politics and move on to the creation of a new world of freedom and justice.

The bane of American oppositional politics has been its character as an incoherent collection of single issue and reactive protest movements. Whatever its multitude of failings, the great strength of the 1960s movement for change was its character as a many-sided community of liberation. This was true first of the civil rights movement of the first half of the decade and then of the countercultural and student movements ("the Movement") of the second half of the decade. What inspired the civil rights movement above all was its aspiration to create, and its quality of already in large part being, that "Beloved Community," that community of love and liberation that had not only a powerful collective political dimension but a profound personal, ethical, and spiritual one. What made "the Movement" of the late 1960s, albeit for a brief historical moment, a deeply transformative phenomenon, was its character as a realized liberatory community, with its own forms of organization, its own ways of living, its own means of communication, its own forms of art, music, and community design, its own language, its own ideas and theory, and its own communal rites and rituals.

It is tragic that such great developing movements for communal liberation could be displaced by an incoherent and largely conformist coalition of interest groups claiming to share the uninspiring quality of being vaguely "progressive." When we are marching resolutely toward the edge of a precipice, as we are now, the last thing we need is a movement that promises to help us progress more quickly and efficiently toward the looming abyss. We need, instead, a historic reversal of direction, a reversal to which Occupy has already contributed important elements.

James Joyce famously described history as "a nightmare from which I am trying to awake."[3] Awakening from that nightmare would mean reawakening to the object of the great dream of history, the dream that is both within history and against history. This age-old dream has been a vision of liberation from the nightmarish system of domination that has oppressed humanity and nature for millennia. It is the dream of a world of love and solidarity, a world in which the great community of humanity and nature will finally be free to live, to realize itself, and to flourish on this planet. This must be the long-term guiding vision of our movement, and must at the same time guide our personal practice from moment to moment.

## NOTES

1    Elisée Reclus, Letter to Clara Koettlitz, April 12, 1895, in *Correspondance* (Paris: Librairie Schleicher Frères, 1911), 3:187.
2    Gustav Landauer, *For Socialism* (St. Louis: Telos Press, 1978), 141.
3    James Joyce, *Ulysses* (New York: Everyman's Library, 1997), 52.

## PART III

# THE AWAKENING OF CONSCIOUSNESS

11

# Another Sun Is Possible:
# Thoughts for the Solstice

A few days before the annual Summer Solstice Gathering at Bayou La Terre, someone sent me a message. It included a question: "Why does the Solstice have so much power?"

I thought, "This is a really great question." I hesitate to say this, since in the current media culture today almost any question, no matter how obvious or trivial, always gets the response, "That's a really great question!" But this one really *was* a great question. I strongly suspect that the person who asked it probably knows the answer to it already, and possibly knows the answer much better than I do. Maybe this makes it an even better question. As I began struggling to answer it, it mutated into another question, "What do you think you're doing helping to organize a Solstice Gathering without having put a lot of thought into the question of why the Solstice has so much power?" As I began to think about this, some ideas came to me that I hope might at least begin to answer this really great question.

The Solstice is about the power of nature, and it focuses specifically on the power of the Sun, the great animating source of life on Earth (along with the Earth itself), and on the relationship between this great source and all the changes and cycles of life on the planet. Primal peoples had a tremendous sense of awe for these powers. They produced many powerful symbols, rites, rituals, and artifacts related to it. Stonehenge is the most emblematic expression of this creative impulse, but it was at work everywhere throughout human culture. There is on this very continent on which we stand, a little over a thousand miles from Bayou La Terre, a sacred site in New Mexico called Chaco Canyon. Long ago, or not so long ago, depending on your perspective, the stones there were arranged so that a dagger of light focuses on a point on a spiral petroglyph in a highly symbolic way at the precise moment of each Solstice or Equinox. This and other constructions in the canyon were an extraordinary expression of awareness of the great powers, and the great balance of powers, in the natural world. We have largely forgotten our connection to these forces and their dynamic balances, while thousands of years ago human beings were focused attentively on the very minute details of how they manifest themselves. As a result, they created, or discovered, sacred places where these connections were expressed most profoundly.

One of the greatest books ever written about nature is called *The Book of the Way and Its Power* or the *Daodejing*. Our first weekend program at La Terre Institute was a study of this text. I think that this was a good beginning point for our voyage of discovery here, for perhaps nothing deserves deeper reflection than the meaning of power and powers. One of the most important distinctions concerning power is the difference between "power over" and "power to." "Power over" is the dominating kind of power. It is the hierarchical or *archic* form that now rules over the world, devastates it, and drives it toward collapse. "Power to," on the other hand, is the liberating kind of power and concerns the unleashing of the energies and capabilities of a being that are elements of the flourishing of that being. The power of the Way relates to this kind of power and constitutes its larger context. To reflect on the Way is to reflect on both the powers within us, and the more encompassing source of the power that flows through all things (both the *de* and the *dao* of the *Daodejing*). We are reminded of these powers and their source when we reflect on the Solstices and Equinoxes, and, above all, the Summer Solstice. The Solstice reminds us that "our own power" and "our own powers" are not merely, and ultimately not really, "our own." They are forms and manifestations of "power through." They are ways in which we participate in greater powers that flow through all things, including ourselves.

What does this really mean? How are we to understand this, not as something vague and abstract that sounds appealing, or perhaps comforting, but rather as something that is practically meaningful and compelling? I often look to Rumi for guidance in answering important questions, and even not-so-important ones (though even the not-so-important ones usually get important answers).

So I opened Rumi. I selected a passage, hoping that objective chance would strike again, as it always does. I almost thought that Rumi had let me down this time. I had opened the book to the line:

If you throw dust at someone's head.[1]

This seemed like the craziest answer Rumi had ever given me. But sometimes a Rumi answer is only part of the answer, so I read few more lines.

If you throw dust at someone's head,
nothing will happen.
If you throw water, nothing.
But combine them into a lump.

Now, we were getting somewhere. As I should have known, Rumi never lets you down, though he sometimes requires more. So I continued, and it got even better:

If you throw dust at someone's head,
nothing will happen.
If you throw water, nothing.
But combine them into a lump.
That marriage of water and dirt cracks open the head,
and afterward there are other marriages.

Assuming that this passage is not a recipe for assault and battery, it offers us some quite illuminating guidance. The first part of it reminds me of Wordsworth's prescient judgment on the modern world: "We murder to dissect." It was prescient, though not quite as prescient as that of Rumi in the thirteenth century, or that of Laozi in the fifth century BCE. They all teach us that, increasingly, through human action, the elements of the world, and of everything in it, are torn apart and separated.

The Earth is separated from the Water.

The Water is separated from the Dust.

This is literally true. Billions of tons of rich earth turn to dust each year and blow away. It is literally true. Deserts continue to spread across the Earth. It is literally and metaphorically true. It becomes increasing difficult to (as Tristan Tzara phrased it) "cast anchor in rich earth." Nihilism, in its most material and nonideological form, spreads across the Earth. It is for this reason that we are being told today by the enemies of nihilism, by those who call themselves Water Protectors and Earth Protectors, that "Water Is Life."

It has long been taught that the marriage of water and earth, and indeed, of all the basic elements, is the origin of life. Many Native American creation stories are about the establishment of a proper balance between Earth and Water. Islam also says (in various passages in the Qur'an) that the Creator created the human being out of both earth (clay, dust) and water, and breathed into this being a soul. And the Hebrew Bible says that in primordial times "a mist used to rise from the earth and water the whole surface of the ground," and that the Creator then formed a Human from "dust from the ground" and "breathed into the nostrils" of this primordial Human "the breath of life" so that the Human could be "a living being."[2] In this story, as in many others, it is the union of water and earth, along with air, or breath, that opens up the human path of the Way and its Power.

The Solstice is about this Way of nature, and all the powers of nature that are expressions of this Great Way. The Solstice teaches us about the two worlds in which we live. The living world of nature (*natura naturans*, nature naturing) is the world of constant change, the world of dynamic balance of opposing forces, the world of discordant harmonies, the world of chaotic order. It is a world in which Chaos is also a god, along with Cosmos. In such a world, everything happens. The other world, the world of Civilization, the dominant world (dis)order, is a world that not only "murders to dissect" but also dissects to control and to dominate, to profit and to accumulate. In such a world, *Nothing* happens. Nothinging happens. Nihilism and annihilation happen. These two worlds with their opposing ways are described in the *Daodejing*:

> The Way of Heaven reduces whatever is excessive and supplements whatever in insufficient.
> The way of man is different.
> It reduces the insufficient to offer to the excessive.[3]

"The Way of Heaven" or Wild Nature is a world of dialectical unity in difference, of All Our Relations, of connection and solidarity. "The ten thousand things carry the yin and embrace the yang."[4] The great communitarian anarchist Gustav Landauer, a distant spiritual descendent of Laozi, described this Way as *Geist*, or Spirit, "a unity of separate things, concepts and persons."[5] From the beginning of Civilization, its project has been to destroy this unity in difference through the theory and practice of hierarchical dualism. Two and a half millennia ago, Laozi was already suggesting that we need to find our way back to the marriage, or remarriage, of what has been torn apart by the march of Civilization, the "Way of Man." It is, above all, the human community and the Earth community that have been torn apart.

It is this process of dissolution that we call the history of Civilization. It is a long history of decomposition. For a very long time, according to our sense of time, we have been condemned to suffer through this course of Civilization. This is the First Noble Truth of History. It is also what the historic Fall was all about, and what the mythical Fall symbolizes. The dominant institutions and the dominant ideology conspire to make the fallen state of Civilization identical with reality. History becomes a nightmare from which we work very hard not to awaken. So we need something that will crack our heads open. There must be "a crack in everything," including heads, because, as we know, "that's how the light gets in." That's how the light of the Sun gets in.

William Blake, another great follower of the Way, wrote about marriages, unities in difference, that are unimaginable to those who are blinded by murderous, dissecting "single-vision," as he called it, or "common sense," as we call it—rather ironically, since it is precisely what filters out our awareness of the common. Blake also wrote about what we become capable of seeing when our heads are cracked open. For example, we become capable of perceiving the Sun as the powerful expression of Spirit that it was clearly seen to be by so many primal peoples.

So it is appropriate to end with William Blake's striking account of what it means to perceive the Sun or, perhaps we should say, to see Another Sun beyond the shadow of the Sun that we have been taught to perceive:

> I ASSERT, for myself, that I do not behold the outward creation, and that to me it is hindrance and not action. "What!" it will be questioned, "when the sun rises, do you not see a round disc of fire somewhat like a guinea?" Oh! no, no! I see an innumerable company of the heavenly host crying "Holy, holy, holy is the Lord God Almighty!" I question not my corporeal eye any more than I would question a window concerning a sight. I look through it, and not with it.[6]

What Blake saw was perhaps "somewhat like" what the Ancients saw and celebrated at Chaco Canyon. It is perhaps something that we can glimpse as we celebrate the Solstice.

## NOTES

1    This and the following lines are from Rumi, "The Cat and the Meat," *The Essential Rumi*, trans. Coleman Barks, expanded edition (New York: HarperOne, 2004), 217. On Rumi's thoughts concerning "another Sun," see below, 207 and 215.

2    Genesis 2:6–7.

3    Laozi, *The Way of Lao Tzu* (Daodejing), trans. Wing-Tsit Chan (Upper Saddle River, NJ: Prentice Hall, 1963), 234.

4    Laozi, 176.

5    Gustav Landauer, *For Socialism* (St. Louis: Telos Press, 1978), 45.

6    From "A Vision of the Last Judgment," in William Blake, *The Complete Poetry and Prose of William Blake*, ed. David V. Erdman (Berkeley: University of California Press, 1982), 554–66.

12

# Do You Know What It Means?
# Reflections on Suffering,
# Disaster, and Awakening

## The Sound of Distant Thunder

The news reached Dharamsala that Hurricane Katrina had attained maximum strength and was heading across the Gulf of Mexico on a direct path toward New Orleans.[1] As Katrina approached the city, twenty Tibetan monks came together, here, on the other side of the world, to offer a *puja* for the threatened city and its people.

I was in India with the Louisiana Himalaya Association, a group from New Orleans that works with Tibetan refugees through its Tibetan sister organization, the Lha Charitable Trust. The monks, friends of the LHA, came to the group's center to express their compassion for and solidarity with those of us from New Orleans. We sat in a large circle, with the five of us from the city at the front of the room. A number of the students from the English class I was teaching were there. My monk friend Tsering Phuntsok led the chanting, which seemed to me the most beautiful I had ever heard: soothingly hypnotic and calming yet at the same time powerfully moving and uplifting. It continued for an hour. Whatever destruction through wind or tides the massive storm was to bring, our anxieties were soothed as we were immersed in waves of compassion and care.

By the evening we heard that the hurricane had turned slightly and was passing a little to the east of the city, saving it from the most dangerous winds. We breathed a collective sigh of relief. Apparently, the puja had worked! Once again, as for so many times over the past forty years, our city had been saved from disaster at the last moment.

Or so we thought, until the next day's news revealed what Katrina had actually brought to New Orleans. Over the next few days the horrifying tragedy unfolded. We watched the reports in disbelief, as did much of the world, astounded that the world's richest and most powerful empire could abandon one of its most historic cities to suffering, death, and desperation for days on end.

Four-fifths of the city was underwater. Bodies floated in filthy, toxic water. Thousands cried desperately for help, stranded on housetops without food, water, or medicine. At the city's hopelessly inadequate shelters tens of thousands suffered in sweltering misery as elderly people died in their wheelchairs, overcome by the heat, the stress, and perhaps the despair. Desperate citizens searched for food and water in the stores that had not been inundated. Some went on rampages of looting, carrying away the treasures of consumer society to a ravaged environment in which most of it would for the moment be useless. Huge quantities of drugs, alcohol, and firearms were plundered. Fights, shootings, arson, and vandalism broke out. The police responded with repression, violence, brutality, and occasional looting of their own. Mass arrests were made on the flimsiest of pretexts. Amid the breakdown of all institutions there was one civic initiative: a makeshift prison was set up at the bus and train station and its squalid wire cages with cement floors were quickly packed with prisoners. It came to be known as "Guantánamo on the Bayou."

We were later to discover that well over a thousand lives were lost in the New Orleans area that day. The equivalent of fifty years of destruction of the surrounding wetlands, the city's major protection from storm surges, had taken place in a few hours. Dozens of neighborhoods with many generations of rich history and cherished traditions were devastated and deserted. Several million people in the region were displaced refugees, to use the word that none wanted to hear. Hundreds of thousands from the city itself were fated to remain scattered for the next year, facing an uncertain future.

Fundamentalists gloated that God had finally destroyed a corrupt city of sin, home to a carnivalesque culture of licentious hedonism, to saint-worshiping Catholic idolaters and heathen voodoo practitioners, and to every form of sexual perversion, as epitomized by the city's annual "Southern Decadence" celebration. The irony that the devastation was greatest in quiet residential neighborhoods, while the notorious French Quarter survived almost entirely unscathed, was lost on these apostles of divine retribution.

In fact, whether or not an angry God fanned the furious winds of Hurricane Katrina, it was not these winds that brought catastrophe to

New Orleans. It has been demonstrated beyond any reasonable doubt that it was the failure of the unsafe, defective levees designed and built with abject incompetence by the United States Army Corps of Engineers that was the immediate cause this disaster.[2] It is also clear that the destruction of 1,800 square miles of the state's protective wetlands, most significantly by the ruinous practices of the oil industry, was its major long-term cause. Given the effects of human negligence, incompetence, injustice, and opportunism in creating the Katrina disaster in New Orleans, there was little room left for a vindictive God to take any credit.

## Touched by Devastation

An idea that recurs in all the great wisdom traditions is that the confrontation with death, dissolution, and mortality is often a path (perhaps even a necessary path) to spiritual awakening and metaphysical enlightenment. Western mysticism testifies to the existence of a Dark Night of the Soul in which, says St. John of the Cross, the spirit is purified and stripped of all attachments so that it can unite with God. According to the great German mystic Jacob Boehme, when one is lost in the depths of anguish, divine love wells up in its midst and leads one to Divinity itself, the groundless Abyss of Nothingness.

Similarly for Hegel, the great biographer of Spirit, we must to go through the "Night of the World" in order to develop spiritually. We must face death, whether literally or figuratively, fully experiencing the contingency of all things, including our own fragile existence. "The life of Spirit is not the life that shrinks from death and keeps itself untouched by devastation, but rather the life that endures it and maintains itself in it. It wins its truth only when, in utter dismemberment, it finds itself." "Spirit," he says, "is this power only by looking the negative in the face, and tarrying with it."[3]

All this is strikingly reminiscent of Buddhist practice, which also aims at an acute awareness of the emptiness of all things, including ones very self. It teaches that out of an apprehension of emptiness arises a profound appreciation of the world, a deep feeling of compassion, and dedicated compassionate action. In Dogen's famous formulation, "To study the Way is to study the self. To study the self is to forget the self. To forget the self is to be enlightened by all things. To be enlightened by all things is to remove the barriers between one's self and others."[4]

It is remarkable how this practice has been integrated into the daily lives of the Tibetan people. An endearing quality of many Tibetans is their calm and often lighthearted view of things; the manner in which they greet the small incidents of life with a smile and even laugh at aspects of life that others might find dismal and depressing. Also impressive is the extent to which kindness, consideration, concern for others, and a sense of gratitude pervades the everyday life of so many people. Buddhist compassion is expressed in an everyday ethics of care, and a pervasive spirit of generosity. And what is perhaps most astounding is how, in just a few decades, a small, once isolated people could have suddenly done so much to communicate this spirituality and ethics to a world in which such values as non-attachment, non-egoism, and compassion seem so alien.

There are, of course, causal factors. Tibetans have a thousand-year history of meditating on the emptiness of the self, the world, and the things that usually weigh us down with all their ponderous insubstantiality. Even Tibetan humor on the deepest level is a kind of ongoing everyday practice of non-attachment, coupled with a sense of generosity and sharing. In addition, Tibetan society is not so far from its roots in a traditional culture in which local ties, familial connections, and other intimate bonds are much more important than they are in the rationalized, economized, mediatized modern culture that we strangely think of as a normal environment for human beings.

But none of this seems to explain the Tibetan miracle adequately. It seems to me that it must also be understood in relation to the recent trauma of the Tibetan people. They have endured and are still enduring the dark night of their collective soul. They have faced destruction of their community on a terrifying scale—20 percent of the population killed, masses of people imprisoned and tortured, thousands of monasteries destroyed, much of their cultural heritage of art and artifacts sacked and ruined, and for many, perhaps unending exile. It is impossible not to ask to what extent the trauma of social catastrophe led to a rebirth, to the flowering of the Tibetan spirit. As the Dalai Lama has said, awareness of this connection should in no way lessen our sense of the injustice that has been done or reduce our resolution to help end the immense suffering that still continues. But miracles do come out of tragedy.

Reflecting on the fate of Tibet led me to pose another question: Might the catastrophe we are now suffering through in New Orleans lead us to a kind of awakening, to a new awakened practice, perhaps to finding a gift of great value that we can give to one another and to the world?

## One Stanza on Emptiness

"Everything is impermanent," said my friend Tsering as we walked along a road in Dharamsala the day after Katrina. "All things come to an end. Some just end a little more quickly than others. Some end sooner than we expect them to. But they are all impermanent."

"All things come to an end." It goes without saying, one might say. After all, in Buddhist teaching, impermanence is one of the Three Marks of all existence. I had heard the news. Why then would this compassionate monk mercilessly beat the dead horse of substantiality?

It was just a helpful, and quite necessary, reminder. For sometimes we forget the most obvious things. Ironically, we often forget them precisely when they become most obvious. I was soon to see New Orleans, the city I love deeply, the city in which my family has lived and died for twelve generations, illustrate this simple truth. And it would all seem quite unbelievable. It would be mentally and emotionally unacceptable, as predictable as it certainly was. The mind inevitably seeks escape from harsh realities.

## In the Land of Dreamy Scenes

As much as I loved Dharamsala and those around me, I yearned to return home as soon as possible. Almost two weeks after the hurricane I had finally ascertained that most of my family was scattered across several states, but one of my children, who was later found, was still missing. I yearned to be reunited with loved ones, to find out the fate of my home and neighborhood and those of my family and friends, and to get involved in the process of healing and recovery of my community. So I left India and looked for a way back. I flew from Delhi to Toronto, Toronto to Houston, Houston to Lake Charles, and finally from Lake Charles to Lafayette, the closest it was possible for nonmilitary aircraft to get to New Orleans. Thanks to the kindness of a friend, I got a ride into the city. A mandatory evacuation order was still in effect, but we managed to get by the roadblocks. I was finally home!

I never thought I could use the old Dickensian cliché "It was the best of times. It was the worst of times" in a nonironic sense, but this is precisely what I felt about New Orleans in the period after Katrina. On the one hand I was surrounded by almost unimaginable devastation. On the other, I saw an outpouring of love and generosity and a spirit of dedication and cooperation far beyond anything I'd ever experienced.

Devastation has many dimensions. One might be called the sublime horror of catastrophe. This was caught in some of the news photographs. Images of a vast urban landscape covered with water; of a huge area completely leveled, Hiroshima-like, in the Lower Ninth Ward; of large boats sitting in the middle of streets, cars sitting on top of houses, and houses on top of cars; of large crowds of battered and distraught victims clustered on overpasses and around shelters.

But as everyone who came to the city observed, no news photos or video footage quite captured the awful reality of the devastation. The feeling of overwhelming destruction really sets in when one travels through street after street, neighborhood after neighborhood, and sees many thousands of houses and other buildings ruined and deserted. Particularly at dusk or in the weird glare of headlights in the dark of night, one is overtaken by the nauseating and dispiriting feeling evoked by the decomposition, decay, and mortality that pervades the deserted neighborhoods.

Another dimension of devastation we might call the intimate world of catastrophe. Its truth is the subjectivity of disaster. Since my own home, though seriously damaged, was not destroyed, I first experienced it in its full force when I visited the ravaged home of my daughter's family. The experience is reminiscent of a certain kind of nightmare. I am in a place I know but it is horribly transformed into something radically different, something dead.

It didn't register immediately, but what I was seeing eventually sank in: it was the corpse of a place. There is rubble everywhere. Around the house everything is brown and gray, the grass, plants, shrubs, and trees. The floor is buckled, all the windowpanes shattered. Objects, scattered everywhere, are broken, twisted, covered with sediment, moldy. The refrigerator is turned on its side and sprawled across a doorway. The clothes dryer rests on top of the washing machine. The yellow-brown waterline cuts across the walls of each room, marking where five feet of water had stood in the house for weeks.

The most heart-wrenching experience of all is to see the most personal expressions of the family's life reduced to debris. For a family of artists this means sculptures, paintings, drawings, delicate handmade objects, photographs. On the floor lies sadly a mold-covered chart entitled "Brianne's Ancestors," a school project of my granddaughter. Personal history has enveloped personal history. Hundreds of thousands of our families have gone through this process of experiencing the death of their homes, the death of their neighborhoods, the death of the places that they loved.

If I spent too much time among these ruined homes and ravaged neighborhoods, it was difficult to resist the onset of severe, incapacitating melancholy. Meditating on a corpse is one of the most ancient and most useful meditative practices, but we are not meant to dwell in a community of corpses. Yet a confrontation with the reality of mortality can help us return to our living community with a new appreciation of its vitality and with a new spirit of engagement and compassion.

## A Street Named Desire

The day I returned to New Orleans I heard from my friend Leenie Halbert, who had opened up her home in an unflooded part of the city's Ninth Ward as a center for relief activities. A group of volunteers—a motley, high-spirited collection of anarchists, greens, activist students and neighborhood people—had materialized spontaneously, inspired in part by the Common Ground Collective that had organized a week before in the Algiers neighborhood. By that evening I had moved to Leenie's and began working with the group.

A reporter from the New York daily newspaper *Newsday* wrote an article about our work at Leenie's. He entitled it "On a Street Named Desire," for our little collective was indeed located on the street famed for its streetcar of bygone days. It is also known as the site of one of the city's largest and most historic, but also most blighted and crime-plagued housing developments. It is called, with inadvertent irony and pathos, "the Desire Project."

We were undertaking a kind of desire project ourselves. From a certain perspective, the cause of our problems today—the deep, underlying social and ecological crises of which the Katrina disaster is a cruel manifestation—is desire. And the solution is also desire.

There is a kind of desire that consists of hopeless craving for an impossible object. It rises up out of an emptiness of the spirit, a lack that may be imaginary but has a quite material basis far back in the history of our species and our civilization and a quite material, tangible effect on us today. It fuels a futile quest to fill up the illusory void. Strange as it seems, we're running on emptiness. What's more, we're running out of control, despite all our illusions of power. This emptiness has powered a long history of domination, despair, cynicism, and rage against reality.

But there is also another kind of desire, a desire that seeks to heal divisions, break the chains of illusion, and restore a certain contact with long-obscured or forgotten realities. Sometimes in the trauma of crisis it is reawakened. This was our desire project. It seemed to me that this project was very much in the spirit of the non-attached compassion that, according to Buddhism, arises out of the awareness of a kind of emptiness. In New Orleans this compassion became widely known as "Solidarity Not Charity," the motto of the Common Ground Collective. In fact, this is almost an exact synonym for "non-attached compassion"—for what is "charity" other than compassion distorted by condescension and ego-attachment?

The *Newsday* reporter said that for the first time in his life he had met a group of "communitarian anarchists, people who believe in do-it-yourself action within small groups" and who wanted to "feed the hungry and bring water to the thirsty, to fix the broken homes of [the] neighbors and to offer a sense of community in their deserted streets." He was willing to concede that "whatever Leenie and her friends called themselves and whatever they believed, though, they were doing a good thing." As Leenie herself explained it, "I just wanted to bring love back to my neighborhood."

What our little group tried to do on a very small scale for a short time was carried out on a large scale and for the long term by our original inspiration, the Common Ground Collective.[5]

## The Groundless Ground of Compassion

Common Ground began in the Algiers neighborhood of New Orleans one week after Hurricane Katrina, when, according to a now legendary account, a few friends sitting around a kitchen table, with nothing but a cell phone, fifty dollars, and their own energy and vision to work with, decided to take direct action to save the community.

During the crucial early months of Common Ground's existence, over eight thousand volunteers participated in its projects, and its aid programs helped eighty thousand people.[6] Volunteers ranged from students who came for a week at Thanksgiving or spring break to long-term relief workers who stayed for months or moved to the city more or less permanently to act as program coordinators.

The organization established projects in a number of neighborhoods, including a large center at St. Mary of the Angels School in the city's ravaged Ninth Ward. Every classroom in the school building was filled with cots, and up to five hundred volunteers have been housed there at one time. Common Ground established several distribution centers, a media center, a women's center, and several clinics, and instituted a vast spectrum of projects, including house gutting, roof tarping, tree removal, a newspaper, community radio, bioremediation, computer classes, childcare and worker cooperatives, educational and recreational programs, and wetlands restoration.

One of the volunteers I met immediately after returning to the city was Francesco di Santis. Francesco, who calls himself an "embedded artist" and "visual folklorist," arrived on September 11, less than two weeks after the hurricane. He immediately began talking to survivors, evacuees and volunteers and sketching their portraits. During his first eight months of work he created a collection of over a thousand powerful, stark, dramatic, expressive portraits, and on each of them its subject wrote his or her story or dictated it to a volunteer. Francisco's "Post-Katrina Portrait Project" became one of the official projects of Common Ground. Almost 350 pages of images and texts were put on a website, and anyone who wants a deeper insight into the experience of the grassroots recovery movement than these few words can begin to convey should explore this material.[7]

Gary Snyder has said that "the truly experienced person delights in the ordinary." To me, this is exactly what the portraits are about, the miracles in the everyday lives of ordinary people—though in extraordinary times. They are the story of how the shock of awakening can open us up to what the Surrealists called "the marvelous" that lies, usually hidden, all around us, in those we meet, within ourselves.

A few examples from this wealth of testimony to the miraculous:

One volunteer expressed a sentiment repeated by a great many others: that the confrontation with overwhelming disaster might have produced hopelessness and inability to act, but the precise opposite results when one acts as part of a caring community. "What could have become resignation instead sparked a desire, an awesome will to effect change. . . . Surrounded by those who care, I have realized a different future, a hope that can become a reality."

A survivor wrote of the mutuality that develops between residents and volunteers as this caring community emerges. "My eyes have been opened wide to those who come from afar to help us. I see your eyes open to us and our lives." She also described a new relation among local residents who endured the disaster together. "Once I met a fireman, who I helped in a very small way. Both of us with tears in our eyes promised to never forget, never forget, how much we needed each other. I see the hope and promise of a new day."

A volunteer expressed similar ideas. She writes of coming to work on the house of an elderly woman and seeing the tears in her eyes. "I sat and listened to her sing her heart song, and we cried together." The volunteer sees her caring efforts as part of a larger process of restoration and healing. "Louisiana sunshine rests cozily on a shoulder. Whole town sweats through universal pores. It beads and glistens as it slowly begins its descent down the crease of a back or the tip of a sunburnt nose. It's wiped away with a dusty finger as its creator labors away at the exhausting endeavor of making this body whole again, so that we all may breathe and laugh and dance and cry, as if New Orleans had never been severed before."

A persistent theme of survivors and volunteers is their new recognition of what is of real value. A survivor who had lost her home told the volunteers, "You know what? It's a relief. I feel free. . . . Sometimes it takes the complete stripping of your home or possessions to really see what life's about." This echoes the ancient ideal of the bhiksu, whose embarking on a spiritual journey is described as accepting a state of homelessness (pravraja). The idea is that the loss of exclusive attachment to one's home can lead to a larger sense of being at home in the world.

The portraits reveal a wide spectrum of experiences and emotions. One extreme is conveyed well by a volunteer who said of first seeing the city: "Emptiness . . . that's all my mind could comprehend." In almost all cases this experience of desolation was followed by one of powerful affirmation. "I see heaven in the eyes of every person I've met. . . . I'm going to do everything I can to better my own community, just like we're doing here. Heaven is everywhere sacrifice for humanity takes place."

Another volunteer spoke of "seeing flowers and birds coming back literally and figuratively." After coming briefly and finding in the relief effort "a lot of authenticity and a model of people being the power," he left for home. For the next three months he found himself all the while longing to return to a place where "out of deep hurt can come beautiful transformation personally and collectively." He came back for a longer stay.

One of the many reasons that the Post-Katrina Portraits are important is that they give an intimate human face to a profound truth. This truth is that out of an openness to the reality of suffering—both one's own and that of others—can come deep compassion; out of the encounter with the mortality and impermanence of all things can come a deeper love of other human beings, of the community, of the spirit of a place. This is certainly a pleasant thought, but as mere mental furniture it has no more than a faint reality. As the living truth of people's experience, it has overpowering, transformative force.

## The Killing Season
## (A Postscript from late May 2006)

Summer is near. The Blue Irises came to south Louisiana in March and April, spreading across the swamps in a magnificent blanket of brilliance. Then they faded away. Things come and go.

It is now nine months since Hurricane Katrina. Most of our fellow citizens remain in exile and there is no large-scale, official effort to bring them back. Some areas of the city remain in ruins, and there are no programs to rebuild them. Even if the repairs and reinforcement of the levees that are underway are completed, they are unlikely to prevent flooding if another storm at the level of Katrina should hit us in the coming months. Should a more powerful storm strike the city directly, the result would be much more catastrophic than anything we have ever seen in the city's history. The worst-case scenario foresees twenty feet of water covering even the highest ground and the city remaining inundated for months. At this time there is no plan to construct levees that would protect us from such a killer storm. Neither are effective plans being implemented to restore the wetlands that are our first line of defense against a powerful storm surge.

As the hurricane season begins this week, one must wonder, "Will this be the season of our disappearance?" Relatively few seem to take seriously such a possibility. In the city, most of the people who are back carry on, some immersed in the cares of everyday life, some busy trying to forget them. And once again we celebrate. The Mardi Gras Indians have marched. The second liners have second lined. The rhythm is back. And so are the blues.

Will the harsh light of everydayness blind us to the truths revealed in our dark night of the spirit, or are we at the dawn of a new awakening?

## NOTES

1    This text was written nine months after Hurricane Katrina. It has been updated slightly but has not been revised extensively, except for a few minor changes, so that the spirit of the moment and the sense of possibilities at that moment could be retained.

2   See, for example, Ivor van Heerden, *The Storm: What Went Wrong and Why During Hurricane Katrina: The Inside Story from One Louisiana Scientist* (New York: Viking, 2006), chaps. 9–10, 187–249.

3   G.W.F. Hegel, *Phenomenology of Spirit* (Oxford: Oxford University Press, 1977), 19.

4   This is the popular translation of the famous quote from the Genjo Koan. See Dogen, "Actualizing the Fundamental Point" [The Genjo Koan] in Kazuaki Tanahashi, *Enlightenment Unfolds: The Essential Teachings of Zen Master Dogen* (Boston: Shambhala, 1999), 35–39.

5   Information on all aspects of the work of Common Ground can be found online at http://www.commongroundrelief.org/.

6   According to the Common Ground website, over the years there have been sixty-five thousand volunteers and a half million recipients of services.

7   See http://portraitstoryproject.org for a collection of "Post-Katrina Portraits." Over the more than ten years since this text was written, Francesco has done five more portrait story projects, so that now, in addition to "Post-Katrina," the site includes "Appalachia," "Madtown," "Mariana," "India," and "Tampa."

# 13

# Buddhism, Radical Critique, and Revolutionary Praxis

What does it mean to inquire into the relationship between Buddhism, radical critique, and revolutionary praxis? It would never have occurred to me to juxtapose these three concepts in precisely this way. However, I was asked to be on a panel on Buddhism and left politics, and the organizer formulated our topic this way. So I welcomed the formulation as a kind of koan to meditate on and see what happened. "What is the sound of Buddhism, radical critique, and revolutionary praxis crashing into one another?"

One possible response, in fact the most obvious one, is that it implies that we might want to find out how Buddhism might help us engage in radical critique and revolutionary transformation. If we have this goal, we will then need to pose three obvious questions. First, what does "Buddhism" or perhaps more pertinently, "Buddha," mean? Second, what does "radical critique" mean?" And finally, what does "revolution" mean? Of course, there's also the perhaps less obvious question of what "mean" means. In the present context, it means that we need to consider the senses in which all three of these terms, taken together, can be significant to us, here and now, in practice.

## Awakened Mind

The term "Buddha" refers to one of the Three Jewels that are considered the core of Buddhist theory and practice. These are Buddha, Dharma, and Sangha and refer to the awakened mind, the teachings (truth, nature), and the compassionate community.

If "Buddha" refers to the "awakened mind," we must ask, obviously, what it is to which this mind becomes awakened. The paradigmatic narrative of the life of Shakyamuni Buddha tells us that awakening begins with a traumatic recognition of the real. This is the message of the story of "The Four Signs." According to the legend, the young Prince Gautama lived within a Palace of Delusion, a world of ideological fantasy in which the King, his Father (the Patriarch, the Big Other) shielded him from all knowledge of the apparent evils of human existence. The folly of the royal ideology was that it was designed to protect the Prince from the real. This myth depicts our ordinary civilized state of delusion, in which the real does not register. As long as we live in the ideological world of everydayness, we are condemned to a life of denial and disavowal.

In the story, Gautama finally looks beyond the confines of the Palace of Delusion and encounters a sick person, an old person, a dead person, and an ascetic. This means that he takes the risk of encountering the traumatic force of realties such as sickness, ageing, death, and the possibility of liberation. Gautama's confrontation with death is crucial since it means that he recognizes that he has not been truly alive. He has been dwelling among the Undead. His confrontation with the ascetic is crucial since it means that he recognizes a radical change in his mode of being as a real existential possibility. This shock of recognition is the beginning of his long struggle for full awakening.

The story continues, and we find that after six years of wandering and seeking, Gautama finally ends up in Bodh Gaya, where, mythologically, he sits under the Bodhi tree and experiences the fully awakened mind. He now assumes the name Shakyamuni Buddha, the Sage of the Shakya Clan who has an awakened mind. According to the story, after having further adventures, he touches the Earth to testify to the experience of awakening. This act, one of the most emblematic images in the entire Buddhist tradition, symbolizes that awakening is rooted in experience of the real: above all, the real of the Earth; the real of the natural world.

This theme is echoed much later in the Buddhist tradition in the story of the Flower Sermon, in which a large multitude assembles in order to hear some words of wisdom from the Buddha. Instead of giving them what they expected, he shocks them (that is, all but one of them) by merely holding up a flower before them and smiling. One of the core messages of this story is the primacy of the real, which cannot be replaced by our mental constructs, illusions, or fantasies, including the fantasy that we can somehow absorb enlightenment or liberation from some wise teacher or leader.

To get back to the earlier story, Shakyamuni Buddha's awakening is immediately followed by a trip to the holy city of Varanasi (Benares). On the outskirts of the city, at the Deer Park of Sarnath, he first teaches the Four Noble Truths, which demolish both the dominant values of civilization and the egoic self that is founded on them, and the Eightfold Path, in which the practice of personal and social transformation is outlined. As we will see, this sequence of events signifies that after "Buddhahood," the awakening of the mind, come radical critique and revolutionary praxis.

This account of the processes of awakening and liberation relates closely to the account of liberatory social transformation that I present in *The Impossible Community*.[1] There I argue that such transformation requires a radical break in both theory and practice with the dominant social institutional structure, the dominant social ideology, the dominant social imaginary, and the dominant social ethos, and that, further, the crucial step toward achieving this goal is the creation of communities of solidarity and liberation. I see Buddhism as offering the most valuable lessons about how such radical critique and transformative, revolutionary practice might be carried out.

## Radical Critique

Buddhist radical critique might be described in one sense as the movement from the ruthless critique of all things existing to a ruthlessly compassionate critique of all things existing. One can get a good idea of the radical nature of this critique from a brief look at three classic points of reference. The first is the Heart Sutra, which is sometimes called the best-known scripture in the history of Buddhism. It reads in part:

> Form does not differ from emptiness; emptiness does not differ from form. . . . Therefore in emptiness: no form, no feelings, no perceptions, no formations, no consciousness [a denial of the five aggregates or fundamental constituents of all things]; no eyes, no ears, no nose, no tongue, no body, no mind [a denial of the basic sources of knowledge]; no color, no sound, no smell, no taste, no touch, no object of mind [a denial of that which is known] . . . no suffering, no origination, no stopping, no path . . . no attainment [a denial of the Four Noble Truths, the Way, and its goal].[2]

In short, the Heart Sutra negates all the fundamental principles of Buddhism. We could in fact call it the Anarchy Sutra, since its basic message is the negation of every principle or *arche*. It warns that there are no ideas, beliefs, propositions, or supposed objects of knowledge that can be accepted dogmatically, ideologically, or as abstract universals having any reality beyond the limits of experience. The fundamental and anti-foundationalist Buddhist teaching of sunyata, that all things are empty of inherent existence, is a radical critique of all substantialism and essentialism and thus means death to all ideology.

Moreover, the Dharma, the Teaching, the "Law," the Way of Truth itself, is described as a "yana," which is translated as "vehicle." It is depicted specifically as a raft or boat that is used to take one to the "farther shore," or "other side of the river." It turns out that this farther shore is a destination that is a non-destination. One reaches it by merely continuing on the way, but now with a more fully awakened mind, open to the experience of the traumatic real. On such journey, only a fool would carry a heavy raft along. As a famous Zen saying states it: "Before enlightenment, chop wood, carry water. After enlightenment, chop wood, carry water."[3] Would you like to try chopping wood with a canoe strapped on your back? In fact, we do it all the time.

A second notable text that relates to radical critique is the most famous passage from Linji, the founder of the Rinzai tradition of Ch'an or Zen Buddhism. Linji says:

> Followers of the Way, if you want to understand the Dharma, do not be fooled by others. Whether you turn inward or outward, whatever you encounter, kill it! If you meet a Buddha, kill the Buddha; if you meet a Patriarch, kill the Patriarch; if you meet an enlightened being, kill the enlightened being; if you meet your parents, kill your parents; if you meet your relatives, kill your relatives. Only then will you find emancipation, and by not clinging to anything, you will be free wherever you go.[4]

Linji's renowned rant is another attack on sick attachments and abstract idealist views of reality. In fact, it is not unusual for Zen masters to attack mastery, master discourses, and master signifiers. Zen texts are tireless in heaping abuse on those who would substitute some concept or fantasy of "a Buddha" for the awakened mind that is the true Buddha Nature. For "Buddha" one might substitute "party," "vanguard," "movement," or "leader." It must be admitted that one could even substitute "community," or "affinity group." Delusion has no limits. The great obstacle to communism is communism. The great obstacle to democracy is democracy. And to mention the most notorious of all such travesties, the greatest obstacle to freedom is freedom.

A third notable point of reference for Buddhist radical critique is the negative dialectic of Nagarjuna and the Madhyamaka Prasanghika school of Buddhist philosophy.[5] Nagarjuna's tetralemma (A, not-A, both A and not-A, neither A nor not-A) challenges us to overcome all naively and dogmatically dualistic thinking. Thus, when we are tempted to affirm some proposition as true, we will consider the ways in which it is true, false, both true and false, and neither true nor false. When we are tempted to affirm the proposition that x is y, we will consider the ways in which x is not y, x both is and is not y, and x neither is nor is not y. The final, double-negation step of the tetralemma requires us to question our categorical scheme itself. And even beyond this, all affirmations or even negations of things in the phenomenal world (the objects of relative or conventional truth), including this one, will lead into further contradictions.

The result will be that in each case we will refrain from confusing conventional truth, which is an obvious necessity for its pragmatic value, with ultimate truth, which recognizes the dependent (or perhaps more accurately, interdependent) origination and the emptiness or non-substantiality of all things. A consideration of the meaning of the term "Madhyamaka" or "Middle Way" helps one understand the force of this critique. Buddhism was first called the Middle Way as an expression of the path that Shakyamuni Buddha took between the one extreme of destructive self-indulgence and the other extreme of debilitating self-denial. However, in the philosophical sense of Nagarjuna's school, it means the Middle Way between dogmatism (alias "eternalism") and nihilism. Dogmatism is the error of seeking absolute truth by imposing rigid, static, or reifying categories on a dynamic and non-objectifiable reality. Nihilism is the opposite error of falling into a relativistic or solipsistic collapse of meaning in which one loses faith in the world, that is, in reality itself.

These aspects of Buddhist radical critique may seem abstract (as they must until translated into concrete diagnosis and practice), but its core is expressed in something quite experiential: the analysis of suffering and craving presented by the Four Noble Truths. These state that there is suffering, a cause of suffering, a cure for suffering, and a way to effect this cure. Though its revolutionary implications are seldom drawn out, this analysis is an implicit critique of the civilized ego and of the entire history of civilization and its project of domination. According to the Buddhist analysis of *anatman*, or "no self," and *trishna*, or craving, this history has from the outset been the story of an insubstantial subject on an impossible quest for an unattainable object. As long as we remain trapped in this project we are perpetually haunted by two unanswerable questions: "Who am I?" and "What do I want?"

This means, in psychoanalytic terms, that as long as we live in world history (what in critical Marxian terms is called "prehistory"), we are plagued by obsession and hysteria. This is precisely what Buddhism pointed out 2,500 years ago: we are a civilization of obsessive hysterics and hysterical obsessives. The project of the ego is to give substance to its own inherent insubstantiality. It is, ironically, a ghost that is haunted by its own intrinsic lack, its own ghostliness. The project of the ego is to find an object that will fill up an ontological void, but its expedition is necessarily doomed from the start. It is trapped inside the Ontic Circle.

This ego, since the beginning of civilization, has been the primary imaginary object for the subject, so that even the most seemingly privileged objects of desire gain their power only as projections of that ego. Nevertheless, the ego has always appeared as an object that defies every project of definition and every attempt at objectification. Thus, the problem of civilization and of domination is not merely objectification but the *project* of objectification, the project of necessary failure that drives on the quest for domination.

In other words, under civilization, "there is suffering," and this suffering is inherent in the kind of ego that it generates and which in turn regenerates it. History is indeed a nightmare, a terrifying and suicidal fundamental fantasy, from which we are trying, if only unconsciously, and neurotically, to awaken. The problem, as Buddhism has always pointed out, is that we are trying to "awaken" by not awakening. This strategy of the Undead just doesn't work. You don't actually get brains by eating brains.

As Hegel shows, in part despite himself, the egoic project of self-recognition has been fundamental to civilization, and its origins are rooted in turn in its material basis, the historical processes of conquest and domination. Though his primary model for the dialectic of Lordship and Bondage is feudalism, he traces the roots of the phenomenon back to the beginning of conquest in the ancient world: the foundation of the imperial state and the system of patriarchal and class domination. The history of domination is founded on the social project of subjection, and on the dialectically identical spiritual project of egoistic subjectification. The latter reveals its impossibility almost immediately, at least on some level, while the former has required the entire tragedy of world history to do so. To say that these projects have spanned the history of civilization is not to underestimate the achievements of capitalism. Capitalism has continually perfected these world-historical processes, and late capitalism, the society of mass consumption, the society of the spectacle, has only brought them to a state of ultimate perfection.

These projects of domination are the processes that are questioned in the Buddhist analysis of anatman or no self, the denial of separate or egoic selfhood. What is the Buddhist non-self? It is the self that is not a self. It is the empty, indeterminate subject opening itself, or its non-self, to a determinate, or endlessly self-determining infinity of being. In other words, the Buddhist empty subject presupposes the idea of the transcendence (*Aufhebung*) of the ego. This is what Dogen meant when he said, "To study the buddha way is to study the self. To study the self is to forget the self. To forget the self is to be actualized by myriad things."[6]

As part of this critique, Buddhism, the quest for and practice of awakened mind, proposes a revolution in values. Awakened mind, which is mind open to the being and value of other beings, requires the absolute rejection of an abstract, objectified world based on exchange value, and the full recognition of the real, living world of intrinsic value. The leftist cliché that exchange value must be replaced by use value is at best a partial truth, and to remain fixated on this level of analysis is uncritical and counterrevolutionary. In fact, it's even counter-*evolutionary*. Use value is a form of instrumental value that necessarily implies the question: "use for what end?" The awakened mind recognizes the ontological and axiological primacy of the world of intrinsic value.[7]

This is what is implied in the Buddhist affirmation that all sentient beings have a Buddha nature and in the Boddhisattva vow to save all sentient beings. In a sense, the most important question that we can ask of any person and of any community is the question of what they hold sacred, what they hold to be of intrinsic value. The worlds of both exchange value and of use value as we have known them historically are based on the ultimate sacredness of the voracious, all-consuming ego. The Buddha world, the world of awakened mind, discovers a world full of wild, self-generating value (though the self-generation is systemic and "interdependently arising," and it takes place on a level that goes beyond what we ordinarily think of as selves). This world is the world of sacred places and of the sacred Earth. As Hakuin states in his famous "Song of Meditation," "This very place is the Lotus Land, this body is the body of Buddha."[8]

Hakuin is thinking here about what we call "the Earth and its inhabitants." He challenges us to think about our way of being and acting in such a world. How do we care for sacred ground? How do we care for the body of the Buddha? We might ask further: How do we respond to those who trample on sacred ground? How do we respond to those who trample on the body of the Buddha? These same ideas have been said in many different ways. The Dharma only states for the civilized mind what our indigenous ancestors knew before the beginning of historical time, the time of domination.

Paradoxically, it is also what we all always continue to know and continue to tell ourselves constantly, though we usually have limited awareness that we are doing so. As Buddhism recognizes, there is a powerful critical and transformative power of the personal and communal unconscious that has radically transformative power if brought to the surface. Buddhism is certainly not alone in affirming this, and it has been explored extensively by both radical psychoanalysis and Surrealism. But Buddhism, and especially Zen, carries further in many ways this inquiry into the dialectical truth of the body, the dialectical truth of the communal body, and the dialectical truth of the body of the Earth.

There is a recognition that the expressions of the unconscious are not only "the discourse of the other" but also the discourse of the whole (the whole that is never whole). This means also that these expressions are the discourse between the parts of that whole that have been cut off from one another. This is what is expressed in Zen koan practice and in the non-empty empty mind of meditation. As this practice teaches us, we need to allow ourselves to tell ourselves the truth at every moment. If we do not do this, we will either remain entirely oblivious to what we know, or when we do attain an insight we will certainly lose it quite quickly.

To return to what Buddhism takes as "Noble Truth," the "desire" that it sees at the root of suffering is obviously not simple desire, such as mere indeterminate hunger for mere indeterminate food (which in any case never appears in any such simple form). Rather it is "craving," that is, compulsive and ego-self-regarding desire that is deeply rooted in ethos, in ideology, and, above all, in the imaginary. Craving is aimed at satisfying an insatiable ego through a fundamentally unattainable object (what Lacan calls the *objet petit a*). Ironically, despite the egocentrism of the society and culture of domination, the ego, despite all its striving, does not itself do. Rather, "It," the Other, does, while its activity is misperceived as the self-activity of the ego. Rimbaud was right, "Je est un autre." "I" is indeed "an other." Buddhist liberation means deliverance from this self-affirming and ultimately self-defeating striving, this tragic charade.

The ultimate attainment of liberation, the annihilation (or, more precisely, the dialectical overcoming) of this domineering ego is called "nirvana." Nirvana is a state in which reality no longer appears in its egoic, reified, instrumentalized state. Put another way, nirvana means going beyond the symbolic order, the order of domination, the order of having and accumulating, and returning to the wild anarchic order, the order of being and flourishing. We are delivered not only *from* but also *to* the world. As in repeated often in Zen practice, "nirvana is samsara," Or, in Nagarjuna's formulation:

> There is not the slightest difference
> Between cyclic existence and nirvana.
> There is not the slightest difference
> Between nirvana and cyclic existence.[9]

The Buddhist critique of insatiable craving is not equivalent to the Stoic injunction to "be satisfied with what you can have." Rather, it is a recognition that satisfaction can never result from a quest for possession and having. It promises freedom from the fruitless quest for domination, and the suffering that results from it, as well as the positive freedom that comes from an openness to the wildness of the world:

> Just as the sea has one taste, which is salt, the Dharma has one taste, which is freedom.[10]

Buddhist radical critique must incorporate the truth inherent in the Marxist critique of capitalism, exploitation, and the fetishism of commodities, but it is identical in its overall implications to the larger anarchist critique of civilization and all forms of domination. The history of domination is larger than the history of capitalism and larger even than the history of class struggle, as usually conceptualized, though it encompasses all of that history. It is essential to understand the ways that economic domination continually takes a more central place in the dominant economistic society and the ways in which it pervades even the deepest levels of subjectivity. But there is a dialectic of domination beginning with the origin of patriarchy, the origin of the state, and the origin of economic class society, and the ego is a product of this entire history of domination. The idea of having "power over" and of "accumulating power" is rooted in patriarchal domination, statist conquest, and the accumulation of private property, in addition to other forms of domination.

A given phenomenon contains within itself the entire history of that phenomenon, though it incorporates that history, not simply and transparently, but in very complex and ordinarily opaque ways. All forms of domination are deeply conditioned by one another and their mutual conditioning is reflected in the elaborate and ever-transmuting structure of the ego. How it is reflected is a long and constantly changing story. The Buddhist analysis of the ego, suffering, craving, and liberation takes on much more critical force in today's economistic society as commodity fetishism develops, and as consumptionist institutions, the consumptionist ideology, the consumptionist imaginary, and a consumptionist ethos all take hold in an unprecedented manner.

## Re-evolution

They "take hold" to the degree that any alternative seems to be illusory. We hold on to the hope that "Another World Is Possible," but the conditions of life convince us that "There is No Alternative." Buddhism has an answer to this "taking hold." Another translation of the famous "one taste" passage goes as follows: "just as the ocean has a single taste—that of salt," the Dharma "has a single taste: that of release."[11] The answer is to transform the teaching into practice. Buddhism has a very radical idea of practice, though in a sense it is merely the most obvious concept imaginable: "Everything is practice." Every thought and every action either tightens the hold or helps release us from it.

Everything is practice. It exists at all times and in all places, including what are conventionally thought of as both "internal" and "external" times and places. Joshu (Zhao Zhou), the great Chinese Ch'an (Zen) master and inspiration for Rinzai Zen, was once asked, "Where is the practice hall?"

He replied, "Everything everywhere is the practice hall. There is no other place."[12]

So the place of practice is everywhere and the time for practice is the ever-present moment. But what is it that could possibly sustain such an all-encompassing practice? Just as I was thinking about this question, I happened quite by chance to see a quotation that shed light on it.

> Venerable Ānanda went up to the Buddha, bowed, sat down to one side, and said to him: "Sir, good friends, companions, and associates are half the spiritual life."
>
> "Not so, Ānanda! Not so, Ānanda! Good friends, companions, and associates are the whole of the spiritual life."[13]

It is very helpful to reflect on this crucial, if initially perplexing, quote. Buddhism emphasizes the importance of the Three Jewels of Buddha, Dharma, and Sangha. However, this passage seems to say that the last of these, the compassionate community, is *everything*. Why then are there three? Yet this makes perfect sense if we approach the matter dialectically. The whole, we then realize, is in each of the parts, which mutually determine one another. One cannot really have a fully awakened mind or appreciate deeply the meaning of the authentic teaching and truth without having the support of the compassionate community. As Western dialectic would state it, the three are "identical." The point is that though we must "work out our own salvation with diligence" or "mindful care," we must work it out together. Effective practice, that is, liberating practice is communal practice.

The compassionate community practices the Eightfold Path, which epitomizes the Buddhist practice of personal and social transformation. It is useful to consider the revolutionary implications of all eight aspects of the path, but we might note at this point that it includes not only wisdom and spiritual disciplines but also practical ethical practices such as right livelihood, which means engaging only in a wise and compassionate form and mode of production. It is significant that such a community also practices the six *pāramitās*, or perfections, one of which is dana, which means gift-giving or generosity. So great is the importance of dana that, in addition to being one of the six pāramitās, it is one of the five precepts of the *pañcasīla*, the core of Buddhist ethical practice.

I think that we should see this emphasis on dana as an affirmation that the compassionate community is a community of the gift. Shakamuni Buddha, like other Axial Sages, looked back to the gift economy as an inspiration for the future liberated society. He did so just as Laozi, the legendary Daoist sage, looked back to the mythical Dynasty of the Yellow Emperor, when communal ties and relations of generosity prevailed. This Daoist tradition, with its proto-ecofeminist ethics of care, passed into the heritage of

Zen. According to this perspective, the role of the sage, the awakened person, and ultimately, of every member of the community, is to defy the patriarchal order and to adopt a maternal model of care and responsiveness:

> To give birth and to nourish,
> to give birth without taking possession,
> to act without obligation,
> to lead without dominating[14]

The adoption of this model, which we might call dialectical maternalism, would mean the destruction of patriarchal authoritarian culture. It implies a revolution in sensibility and a revolution in social ontology. Buddhist ontology asks us to consider how beings appear to us. Do we experience them as resources, as instruments, as actual or potential property, as extensions of our own supposed ego, or as sources of power and domination? Or do we experience them, and especially the myriad forms of life on Earth, with a sense of wonder, with gratitude, and with a desire to see them flourish.

Zen Buddhism, in particular, expressing its Daoist heritage, encourages us to respect the way, the unfolding of potentiality, the striving for full flourishing, of each being and of the multitude of beings—"the Ten Thousand Things," as they were called traditionally. All these forms of being are manifestations of goodness that deserve to be respected. They are the elements of nature's great gift economy. Can we follow the anarcho-communist model of "Heaven and Earth"?

> Heaven and Earth combine to drip sweet dew. Without the command
> of men it drips evenly over all.[15]

The Buddhist ontology and axiology of the gift and of intrinsic value are dialectically identical with a Buddhist economics that is an economics of the gift and of intrinsic value. It is a vision of a world beyond exchange value and beyond use value. As Zen texts state it, when we free ourselves from delusion we find a reality that is "beyond profit and loss." We find that nothing is "owed" and nothing is "deserved." We find that nothing can be "possessed." We find that there can be no "accumulation." We realize that to pursue any of these delusions leads to ruin. In short, we recognize that property is the theft of being.

So, as Laozi might have phrased it, "What is to be done without doing it?" What is the meaning of awakened revolution? For an answer, we might contemplate the implications of the Bodhisattva Vow, which states that "sentient beings are numberless; I vow to save them all."[16]

In a world of material abundance in which over a billion sentient human beings live in absolute poverty, the practical implications of having an awakened and engaged mind become ever more obvious.

In the midst of the sixth great mass extinction of life on Earth, the ongoing holocaust of sentient beings, the practical implications of having an awakened and engaged mind become ever more obvious.

The Sword of Dharma cuts through delusion and cuts the world in one.

## NOTES

1    John P. Clark, *The Impossible Community: Realizing Communitarian Anarchism* (New York: Bloomberg Academic, 2013).

2    *The Heart Sutra*; online at many sites, including http://www.heartspace.org/writings/traditional/HeartSutra.html.

3    A popular Zen saying, thought to originate in dialogue 2 of *The Sayings of Layman P'ang*. See James Green, trans., *The Sayings of Layman P'ang: A Zen Classic of China* (Boston: Shambhala, 2009), 15.

4    Lin-chi, "Lin-chi Record," in Stephen Addiss, ed. *Zen Sourcebook: Traditional Documents from China, Korea, and Japan* (Indianapolis: Hackett, 2008), 49–50.

5    See Nagarjuna, *The Fundamental Wisdom of the Middle Way: Nagarjuna's Mulamadhyamakakarika*, translation and commentary by Jay L. Garfield (New York: Oxford University Press, 1995).

6    Dōgen, *Actualizing the Fundamental Point (Genjō Kōan)*, in Addiss, *Zen Sourcebook*, 152. Sometimes translated as "to find realization in the Ten Thousand Things."

7    Even this form of value is dialectically sublated (negated-preserved-transcended), since we must also recognize that intrinsic value is never intrinsic to individual things or separate beings, which are *sunya*, empty of inherent existence.

8    Hakuin, "Song of Meditation," in Addiss, 251.

9    Nagarjuna, *The Fundamental Wisdom of the Middle Way*, 331.

10    *The Uposatha Sutta.*

11    "Uposatha Sutta: Uposatha," trans. Thanissaro Bhikkhu, Access to Insight, last revised September 3, 2012, https://www.accesstoinsight.org/tipitaka/kn/ud/ud.5.05.than.html.

12    James Green, trans., *The Recorded Sayings of Zen Master Joshu* (Boston: Shambhala, 1998), 80.

13    From the *Avijjā Sutta*; online at https://suttacentral.net/sn45.2/en/sujato.

14    Sanderson Beck's translation of the *Daodejing*, 10:7; online at http://www.wayist.org/lindauer-daodejing-english-translation/94-scriptures/tao-teh-ching.

15    Wing-Tsit Chan's translation of *Daodejing* 32:3; online at https://terebess.hu/english/tao/chan.html#Kap32.

16    "The Bodhisattva Vow"; many translations online including at https://viewonbuddhism.org/zen/zen-bodhisattva-vow.html.

# 14

# Rumi and the Fall of the Spectacular Commodity Economy

Rumi's "Muhammad and the Huge Eater" is a story that tells us how obsessive desires devastate the soul and rob us of things of true value.[1] It also shows us how we can be saved from such destructive forces. In this story, Rumi epitomizes all the sick desires that plague human beings through the ridiculous and revolting image of a figure called the "Huge Eater." When I read Rumi's depiction of the Huge Eater, I imagine a character something like "Mr. Creosote," the extraordinarily large eater in Monty Python's film *The Meaning of Life*. The charming Mr. Creosote gorges himself to the point that he vomits periodically with the force of a fire hose yet continues stuffing himself until he literally explodes.[2]

In some ways, Monty Python's ludicrous exaggeration outdoes even Rumi in depicting a deeply disturbing image of obsession and excess. However, Rumi outdoes even himself in his skillful use of the image of the Huge Eater to convey crucial insights concerning the human condition. He begins by saying that he is not speaking "to materialists," the Huge Eaters themselves, but "only to those who know spiritual secrets." He assumes that his readers have some degree of moral and spiritual insight and that they seek things of true value and desire wisdom about life, including knowledge of how to relate to the Huge Eaters around them in the world. He observes that the things sought by those with spiritual insight might be described as "praiseworthy," but that in fact they have no need for our praise. According to Rumi, "What the sayer of praise is really praising is himself, by saying implicitly, 'My eyes are clear.' Likewise, someone who criticizes is criticizing himself, saying implicitly, 'I can't see very well with my eyes so inflamed.'" Rumi's question is not so much one of praise or blame but concerns, rather, whether we have insight and clarity concerning things that are good and valuable, and wisdom about how to pursue them.

Regarding this pursuit, Rumi states a bit cryptically, "Don't ever feel sorry for someone who wants to be the Sun, that other Sun, the One that makes rotten things fresh." He means by this the spiritual Sun that illuminates the truth, and whose light emanates through the lenses of the clear-eyed. One hears echoes of Plotinus's idea that "No eye has ever looked upon the Sun unless it has become like the Sun."[3] Rumi adds to this, "Don't ever envy someone who wants to be this world," warning against the desire to identify with a lusterless, unilluminated world. There is, for Rumi, a numinous reality that shines forth through the illuminated world. He implores, "If the nut of the mystery can't be held, at least let me touch the shell." True, the reality always goes beyond our perception and understanding, but we do have a kind of access to the numinous realm. Rumi depicts this mode of access as a form of both "seeing" and "touching," but he also introduces an auditory image. "Awe is the salve that will heal our eyes. And keen, constant listening." It seems strange to say that "listening" is a cure for the eyes, but Rumi's point concerns the importance of an all-encompassing awakened awareness, which goes beyond any particular sense. He is describing a kind of spiritual synesthesia in which many "doors of perception" are opened at once.

Another key idea that is introduced at this point is the pivotal nature of awe in the experience of deeper realities. Thus, while "praise" may not be the correct response to the numinous, awe is. Rumi is concerned with a reality that is deeply moving and awe-inspiring, and with our susceptibility or lack of susceptibility to it, our capacity to be moved and to be awed by it. We must open ourselves to such experience and what it reveals. As we will see in the narrative to come, we must not allow our biases and preconceptions to stand in its way. While Rumi says we should shun "the world," in another sense, he urges us very explicitly to venture out into the world and to embrace it, if we wish ever to encounter the object of our quest. "Stay out in the open like a date palm lifting its arms. Don't bore mouse-holes in the ground, arguing inside some doctrinal labyrinth." Here, he implores us not to get wrapped up in our own thoughts, ideas, and theories, and thereby to neglect the marvelous and miraculous world beyond our own preoccupations. In addition, he introduces a word that perhaps best describes our proper response to such a world. This takes us an important step closer to the story he is about to tell. The word that describes one's openness to the wonders of the world is "love."

Rumi tells us that if we are to manifest the openness and engagement with the world that we call love, we need to pay attention to certain evils that stand create obstacles to it. There are four specific vices of this kind, labeled by the Qur'an the "four birds." These birds are identified as "the rooster of lust, the peacock of wanting to be famous, the crow of ownership, and the duck of urgency." Three of these evils, the obsessive pursuit of "pleasure," "fame," and "wealth," are traditional objects of censure by many of the great philosophers. The one that Rumi labels "urgency" is a less familiar target, yet it also has a long history of denunciation within the wisdom traditions. Interestingly, Rumi does not say that these evils should be eliminated or repressed entirely. Rather, he recommends that we should "kill them and revive them in another form, changed and harmless." This approach is reminiscent of what Tibetan Buddhism did with all the demons of the old religion, changing them into Bodhisattvas, Deities, Dakinis, etc. William Blake, who abhorred the "braces" of repression and esteemed highly the "relaxes" of open expression, also followed this approach. There is a marriage of Heaven and Hell, not a war of annihilation between the two. Such a procedure recognizes that all these evils contain at their core something important to the human psyche that can be redirected toward beneficial ends.

It might seem strange that of the four metaphorical embodiments of evil, the most pernicious creature of all turns out to be, of all things, a duck. "Help, I'm possessed by a duck!" A different kind of moral and metaphysical imagination might have envisioned it as a ferocious dragon or some kind of "many-headed monster." But who really relates deeply to such dramatic images? Rumi is more realistic in suggesting that when you are afflicted with this evil, you find something like an annoying duck inside you, pestering you, driving you crazy. Buddhism goes in a similar direction when it describes one of the worst and most ubiquitous mental afflictions as "Monkey Mind." It is much easier for most of us to escape the monsters and dragons than to conquer the monkeys and ducks. The duck, Rumi says, frantically grabs at one thing after another "like the robber in an empty house cramming objects in his sack, pearls, chickpeas, anything." We are confronted with certain imperious urges that are obsessive, compulsive, insatiable, greedy, all-consuming, appropriating, predatory, and domineering. In a quest for satisfaction through dominion over the objects of desire, we also open ourselves up to domination in a multitude of forms.

This is another point at which Rumi's Sufism converges with the Buddhist diagnosis of the human condition. The underlying problem in both cases is seen as all-consuming obsessive desire, what Buddhism calls *trishna* or *taṇhā*, an unquenchable thirst for what cannot possibly be attained. This is also the theme of David Lynch's great film *Lost Highway*, which depicts the murderous nature of such desire and culminates in a scene in which "Alice Wakefield," the fantasized object of desire, says to her doomed, unawakened, and unawakenable pursuer, "You'll never have me!" According to Rumi, the victim of such obsession is "always thinking, 'There's no time! I won't get another chance!'" But it's really the same sick process, over and over again. Buddhism depicts those with the character structure of Rumi's "Huge Eater" as a "Hungry Ghost," a distorted being with a huge stomach, somewhat like Monty Python's Mr. Creosote, but with a narrow, tiny neck, so that it can't possibly stuff enough food down its throat to satisfy itself, but must spend all its time trying. It grows more and more desperate, more and more grotesque, as a result.

The next passage suggests that Rumi is not only revealing age-old truths about the human condition but that he has a message particularly well suited for our own age. Ours is the era in which the "Huge Eater" has reached an unprecedented level of enormity. Rumi describes this character as a kind of being that is "so afraid of missing out that it's lost all generosity," and one that has "frighteningly expanded its capacity to take in food." Especially if we take "food" and "eating" in the metaphorical sense that Rumi intends, this seems like an apt description of the ideal consumer in the age of mass consumption. It's not merely that the masses massify themselves through mass consumption. "Frighteningly," *each* consumer strives to turn him or herself into a mass. Perhaps the most frightening thing of all is how few are frightened today by this sad state of affairs.

Finally, in concluding this part of the text, Rumi introduces the alternative to the Huge Eater. Once again, we find commonalities between Rumi and Buddhism. The alternative to the Huge Eater is the mindful person who is diligent in seeking the good. As Rumi states it, "A True Person is more calm and deliberate. He or she doesn't worry about interruptions." We will hear more about this Person later. At this point, having explained the nature of the disease, and having briefly mentioned what a cure might look like, Rumi is ready to present the core of the text, the details of the story of the Huge Eater.

The story begins with a large group of Muhammad's guests arriving at his home. The guests are "unbelievers," that is, they are people who have no interest in the "spiritual secrets" mentioned by Rumi. Each of Muhammad's friends takes responsibility for one guest, desiring to help Muhammad in his role as host. However, they all avoid one guest, the Huge Eater, whom they find repellant, so Muhammad himself generously takes this guest in. It would seem, however, that the intuition of Muhammad's friends was correct, since this guest turns out to be an extraordinarily greedy and voracious character. He breaks all the rules of good guesthood, going so far as to devour everything in the house, including "the milk of seven goats and enough food for eighteen people!" Everyone is appalled, and when the Eater later goes to his room for the night, the resentful maid locks him in.

This is where the story gets extremely interesting, if also extremely gross. During the night, the Huge Eater feels "strong urges." He desperately tries to pry the door open, without success. He gives up, falls into delirious sleep, and then, while not literally exploding like Mr. Creosote, "squeezes out a huge amount, and another huge amount." He emerges slightly from his oblivion and realizes that he and the covers around him are all covered in excrement. He begins to become vaguely aware of certain connections. He remarks, "My sleep is worse than my being awake. The waking is just full of food. My sleep is all this." He begins to consider the possibility that being awake is better than being asleep. Maybe a life in which one is fully awake might be better than one consisting of various stages of oblivion. One might even sleep better when one is asleep if one is awake better when one is awake.

It is here that the link to the society of mass consumption becomes most evident. It is significant that the person who helps Muhammad teach the Huge Eater a lesson is a maid or housekeeper, someone responsible for the condition of the household or *oikos*. By locking the Eater in, she teaches him that there is a connection between his voluminous consumption and his inordinate production of waste. Even more important, the Eater learns a lesson about the connection between an unawakened waking life and a nightmarish sleeping life. Rumi describes the Eater's waking life as being awakened only in regard to the objects of obsessive desire, and the rest of his existence as a kind of sleep or oblivion. However, the oblivion is not a state of quietude. It is traumatically shaken by the return of the repressed or, we might even say, by the materially or spiritually undigested. The repressed returns materially through the torrent of excrement that is unleashed. And it returns mentally and spiritually as the Eater becomes "conscious enough" to perceive the filth all around him and to "shake with spasms of shame" as a result.

Here, Rumi describes a momentous spiritual phenomenon. He shows how the trauma of confronting the real can have a transformative effect. The confrontation with the real in this story emerges with the Huge Eater's traumatic awakening to the effects of his gluttony, but it describes equally the point at which the members of the society of mass consumption begin to experience traumatically the consequences of their devastation and degradation of the natural and social world. The problem so far, according to the story, has been that even as the disruptive effects have gotten worse and the household has become increasingly defiled and despoiled, the Huge Eater, the well-disciplined, out-of-control consumer, has not yet awakened fully to what is happening. The Eater is like the normalized person of today who has some awareness of the catastrophic direction in which we are headed but cannot become fully conscious of its implications or transform awareness into action. The Eater is like the liberal, progressive, or socially responsible person of today who does not deny reality, but rather recognizes it and then disavows it. The eventual result of the disavowal is the same as that of denial. Catastrophe.

But Rumi's story does not stop here. It continues, and there is a happy ending. The last part of the story is truly wonderful. It is a kind of warning that trauma may be salutary but not ultimately salvific. It often creates only a temporary awakening, and then the shaken and partially awakened person lapses back into obsession and oblivion. Rumi explains that we should not despair in the face of such failure, for more can be done to make the transformative experience a form of true and enduring liberation. In the end, the Huge Eater is saved! The manner in which this deliverance is carried out sounds like a miracle. Muhammad "becomes invisible so the man won't feel ashamed." Through this action, Muhammad gives us excellent advice. We just have to become invisible and then we can accomplish all kinds of wonderful things!

Unfortunately, we often find this rather difficult to do. We not only want to save, we want to be a Savior. But this is just the opposite of what we need to do. Rather than being conspicuous, we need to "become imperceptible" (as Gilles Deleuze says in a related context) and merely help the person in need do what is necessary. Muhammad says, in effect, we should be like Laozi's Anarchist Prince, the ruler who rules by not ruling. Laozi says that the best rulers are perhaps not even known by the people, and they are certainly not known as "rulers." Like Muhammad in Rumi's story, they quietly help create the necessary conditions, so that "all happens as it needs to happen." This is possible for someone who is in no way self-absorbed, but rather completely absorbed in what has been called by some the Divine, and by others the Dao.

This is the true meaning of what Aristotle called *phronesis* or "practical wisdom," and what in Buddhism is called *upaya* or "skillful means." It requires that we always be ready to expect the unexpected, including the unexpected things that each unique situation requires of us. Rumi points out that, unexpectedly, or counterintuitively, "many actions which seem cruel" in fact flow from "a deep Friendship." Nietzsche wisely said that to be a good friend you must know how to be a good enemy. But Rumi knew even more about friendship than Nietzsche did, as this story shows. Rumi also says that "many demolitions are actually renovations." This is reminiscent of Bakunin, who said that the urge to destroy is also a creative urge. But Rumi knew more about creative destruction than Bakunin did, as the story also shows. In his story, the adversarial acts, the cruelty, and the destructiveness are all at the service of deep love. This becomes clear as the story proceeds.

Muhammad takes on the task of washing the Huge Eater's filthy bed-clothes. All of his household and friends offer to help. This shows that Muhammad's compassionate example has already had a transforming effect on everyone, for earlier they had shunned the Huge Eater and would certainly not have touched his dirty linen. The centrality of this act to the story demonstrates that the most important work in the world is work that seems to many to be mundane, if not degrading. It has been called "women's work," "servants' work," and even "shit work." Rumi's point is similar to Dogen Zenji's message in his wonderful text, "Instructions to the Cook." In that little work, Dogen explains that to be a cook is the highest possible spiritual calling and the greatest possible honor. As the famous Zen saying goes, "Before enlightenment, chop wood, carry water. After enlightenment, chop wood, carry water." To which Dogen adds, "Do the cooking." And Rumi adds, "Wash the bedclothes." Muhammad rejects a follower's suggestion that he should not engage in the mundane, because

"Yours is the inner heart-work." However, Muhammad shows through his action that the inner heart-work can also be the outer hand-work. "There is great wisdom in washing these bedclothes," he says, "Wash them."

Finally, the Huge Eater returns to the scene. He has been profoundly transformed—though perhaps not yet deeply enough. He needs further instruction, a further traumatic experience through an encounter with the *mysterium tremendum,* and something more. We are told that the Eater "has left behind an amulet that he always carried." We might interpret this amulet as a kind of Lacanian *objet petit a,* in which the object of consumption is the object of obsessive and self-destructive desire, part of a failed fundamental fantasy that still needs to be overcome. In fact, the related Lacanian conception of the agalma as the alluring quality of the object is even more apt, since the term originally referred to a "cult object" or amulet. Rumi tells us that in his effort to regain this object, the Huge Eater "enters and sees the Hands of God washing his incredibly dirty linen."

This is the transformative experience. At this point, the Huge Eater comes into contact with something much vaster than his small egoic self (something symbolized as "the Hands of God"), and he comes to a realization of how his own well-being, indeed his own being, depends on this greater reality. So the Eater "forgets the amulet." His commodity fetishism goes down the drain with the filthy laundry water. Instead, "a great love suddenly enters him." The love that was directed toward his own egoic self, and toward the objects of his compulsive craving (which are only extensions and "inflations" of that very self), is redirected toward the world. He experiences a *great turning* within the depths of his being, a turning toward spirit. This is what Joel Kovel describes in his classic work *History and Spirit* as "what happens to us as the *boundaries* of the self give way."[4]

In case anyone might wonder how traumatic this ultimately transformative experience really is, Rumi gives us a few hints. The Eater tears his shirt open, beats his head against the wall, shrieks wildly, and then lapses into silent quivering. Rumi is here describing certain obvious withdrawal symptoms that relate not only to physiological and psychological withdrawal but also, and above all, to withdrawal on the most fundamental ontological level. The Eater is in the process of overcoming his addiction to the experience of obsessive consumption, and the objects of that obsession, something that can only be achieved through a break with his identification with his voracious ego as his "true self." Rumi points out that for this break to succeed an intermediate stage in the process of

213

liberation must be traversed. This is a reactive stage in which the break with egocentrism and excessive self-assertion leads to a process of excessive self-negation. The Eater shows that he is at this stage when he tells Muhammad, "You are the Whole. I am a despicable, tiny, meaningless piece. I can't look at You." The Eater has gone from being huge and constantly expanding to being less than nothing. He has gone from thinking of himself as the center of the universe to thinking of himself as an insignificant and worthless detail of that universe. At this point, further compassionate intervention is needed if the healing and transformation process is to continue.

There might seem to be enormous (huge!) obstacles in the way of such compassionate action. The Eater is the horrifying antithesis of everything in Muhammad's message. It is not surprising that initially all of the Prophet's followers were repulsed by him and shunned him contemptuously. Rumi shows that this is not the correct attitude toward those who are enslaved to destructive impulses and obsessions. In contrast to his friends, Mohammad responds to the Huge Eater with limitless love and compassion. True, it is tough love. But the toughness is entirely at the service of the love. The toughness is conditional, but the love is unconditional. So "Muhammad bends over and holds him and caresses him and opens his inner knowing." It is striking that it is ultimately this compassion that heals the Eater, not the original negative trauma or any formal, conceptual instruction concerning the good, as helpful and even necessary as these means certainly are. It is, in the end, an act of love that converts the Eater from his egocentric, alienated, destructive path.

At this point, Rumi concludes the narrative and begins to address the reader more directly. He introduces an image of the nature of things that is the dialectical opposite of his image of the Huge Eater. The Eater is a being who responds only to his own obsessive desire to consume. He always takes and never freely gives. He hoards all that he appropriates. He is in the grips of a kind of demonic possession, both in the sense of being possessed personally by his demons, and also in the sense of participating in a larger *system of possession*, or property system, that is at its roots demonic. In such systemic possession, what is consumed and accumulated is cut off from the normal psychological and ecological cycles and flows. It is cut off from the whole, the natural and social *oikos*. The distortion and alienation of the psyche or soul is the result of obsessively feeding the growth of the all-consuming ego.

This distortion and alienation is expressed in the grotesque physical image of the Huge Eater, but it is fundamentally about a grotesque spiritual distortion. It is just as likely (and today is perhaps more likely) that the Huge Eater will be fashionably thin and quite attractive physically. "You can never be too thin or too rich"—for spiritual death. Sometimes, the thinner and richer, the better. Similarly, the disruption of the ecological dimension is expressed through the disturbing image of Huge Eater's enormous retention of feces that ultimately pollutes everything around it. The Eater defiles even the household of the Prophet through his self-indulgence. Similarly, the inordinate processes of consumption and accumulation in the society of mass consumption pollute and ruin everything around it, including the sacred Earth household. In both cases, in the psychological or spiritual realm, and also in the ecological one, there is a disordered relationship between the "inner" and the "outer."

On this topic, Rumi reveals one of the "spiritual secrets" that are sought by his true readers. He depicts a quite different relationship between "inner" and "outer," a relation that is not only the correct spiritual path but that also follows the path of nature. He observes, "The cloud weeps, and then the garden sprouts. The baby cries, and the mother's milk flows. The Nurse of Creation has said, Let them cry a lot." This passage is reminiscent of Laozi's beautiful passage concerning the Way of Nature: "Heaven and Earth combine to drip sweet dew. Without the command of man, it drips evenly over all." Rumi explains that just as the sweet dew of vivifying rain falls equally on all (something that in our own era can no longer be taken for granted), so the sweet dew of compassion must fall equally on all. Even on the Huge Eater! Even on the consuming masses of the Spectacular Commodity Economy!

Rumi summarizes the message of the story as follows: "This rain-weeping and sun-burning twine together to make us grow." This is a dual image that refers to the realms of both *oikos* and *psyche*. It alludes to the literal rain that nourishes and cleanses the Earth and all living beings, and to the literal sun that illuminates the Earth and all living beings and gives them the power to grow. But it also refers to the spiritual rain of compassion and the spiritual sun of illuminating wisdom that bring the soul to the Truth. Rumi's Sufism here comes very close to the spiritual iconography of Tibetan Buddhism, in which the two great Bodhisattvas are Avalokiteśvara, the Bodhisattva of Compassion, and Mañjuśrī, the Bodhisattva of Wisdom. His injunction to "keep your intelligence

215

white-hot and your grief glistening, so your life will stay fresh" reiterates this emphasis on the central place of both wisdom and compassion in the liberated and realized spiritual life.

The delusive conventional wisdom of the world, ever since the beginning of patriarchy, has exalted a kind of "strength of character" (rigid character-armor) based on domination and accumulation that represses and denies deep love and empathy. Thus, Rumi says, "Listen to the Prophets, not to some adolescent boy." World history has been under the sway of patriarchal power-seeking, the social ideology of the adolescent boy, and egocentrism, the social ontology of the adolescent boy. Rumi challenges this dominant course of history when he exhorts us to "cry easily like a little child," that is, to live deeply responsive lives that are open to all the joys, suffering, and beauty of the world. "Diminish what you give your physical self," he says. Stop feeding the egocentric, accumulating, appropriating self—alias, the Huge Eater!

When this happens, "your spiritual eye will begin to open." As this eye opens, you begin see beyond the reductive hierarchical and dualistic vision of the system of domination, and to achieve a kind of Blakean manifold vision of a restored wholeness and reconciliation that affirms the value and sacredness of the multitude of beings in the world (Laozi's "Ten Thousand Things"). According to Rumi, "when the body empties and stays empty, God fills it with musk and mother-of pearl." Much as in the Buddhist concept of sunyata or emptiness, to be "empty" means, paradoxically, to be open the greatest possible fullness, for Rumi, by emptying oneself one opens oneself to the greatest richness of content. Renunciation of the illusory and impossible quest for a self-sufficient ego means reconnecting with the fullness of the whole, which is in reality an always-becoming-full of an always-becoming-whole. Seven centuries before Freud verified this through dream interpretation, Rumi knew that possessive individualism was nothing more than a futile attempt to accumulate excrement as part of an ego-building quest for power and control.

Rumi says that in the process of spiritual liberation a person "gives up dung" and "gets purity." This is not purity in some obsessive-compulsive perfectionist sense. It is the kind of purity that results from the cleansing powers of "rain and tears." It is the kind of purity that we find when we discover with Hakuin Zenji that "the very Earth on which we stand is the Pure Lotus Land." Rumi realizes, of course, that we cannot achieve such liberation alone, but only in community. The concluding lines of this text are an amazing and prophetic description of the kind of compassionate community that is needed to achieve personal and social transformation.

> Stay with friends who support you in [the necessary disciplines].
> Talk with them about sacred texts,
> and how you're doing, and how they're doing,
> and keep your practices together.

This is a depiction of the kind of sangha, base community, or affinity group that we so desperately need at this crucial point in the history of the Earth. This is the community of liberation and solidarity, the community of awakening and care, the Beloved Community. In our era, the Necrocene—the new era of death, in both spiritual and biological senses, the era of nihilism and annihilation—it must also be a community of revolutionary social transformation. It must be the era of a Great Turning of the kind that has only been seen twice before in world history, first in the agricultural revolution that gave rise to the state, patriarchy, and private property, and then in the industrial and technological revolution that led to global state capitalism, mass consumption, and the technological megamachine. In the end, it has produced what we might describe as one global "Huge Eater," the reigning monster called Empire that is intent on consuming the entire biosphere and turning it into a wasteland.

We are now at the end of the system of domination, once called "Civilization," that produced those great revolutions. The Huge Eater is not long for this world. The burning question is whether "this world," in the sense of humanity and most of life on Earth, can survive the death of Empire, and regenerate and renew itself. The process of renewing the Earth can only succeed, in Rumi's terms, if it is nourished by cleansing rain and cleansing tears. Thus, everything depends on our careful attention and dedication, as transformative communities, to the regeneration of both *oikos* and *psyche*.

## NOTES

1   "Muhammad and the Huge Eater," in Rumi, *The Essential Rumi*, trans. Coleman Barks, expanded ed. (New York: HarperOne, 2004), 64–69. For page numbers for the large number of passages that are quoted here, the reader is directed to any of the searchable online texts, for example, the ZBOHY Poetry Page version at https://zbohy.zatma.org/Dharma/zbohy/Poetry/huge-eater.html.

2   See https://www.youtube.com/watch?v=lhbHTjMLN5c for the culminating scene.

3    Plotinus, *Plotinus on the Beautiful: Being the Sixth Treatise of the First Ennead Literally Translated* (Stratford-Upon-Avon: Shakespeare Head Press, 1914), 29; online at https://archive.org/details/plotinusonbeauti00plotrich/page/n11. Slightly amended.

4    Joel Kovel, *History and Spirit: An Inquiry into the Philosophy of Liberation* (Boston: Beacon Press, 1991), 1.

15

# Regionalism and the
# Politics of Experience

Political ecologists have long lamented the destruction of bioregions, eco-systems, and communities by a rampant and rapacious system of mass consumption. As daunting as the task may have appeared, the general outlines of the oppositional project have often seemed relatively clear. We must "tread more lightly upon the Earth." We must "become more responsible global citizens." We must "live more sustainably." Et cetera. However, the nature of a truly ecological alternative to the dominant order has appeared much less clear. The art of creating a balance between flour-ishing human and natural communities is not something that emerges automatically out of the critique of capitalist predation and dedicated opposition to it. We know from the history of classic revolutionary strug-gles that the quest to seize the means of production can often turn into a process of *being seized by* the means of production. As Nietzsche suggested, when we fight against monsters, we might keep in mind the danger of turning into them.

So, in the search for socially and ecologically regenerative alterna-tives, some have looked to traditions that have preserved certain values and practices that might contribute to the creation of an ecological society. Many have turned wisely for inspiration to tribal communities that have maintained a balanced, caring relationship with the land, often across hundreds of generations.[1] We might also look for guidance from certain submerged traditions that have somehow survived within the developed (that is, the hyperdeveloped and maldeveloped) world. Among these are regionalist traditions. One such tradition that can make a very important contribution to the regenerative project within political ecology is French regionalist thought.

This might seem a rather surprising choice. The France that has been most familiar to the English-speaking world has been that of official French culture. It is the France of stylish Parisian philosophy and literary trends, of the Parisian press and the state bureaucracy, of the Cartesian mind and the French Academy, of the official Left and Right. In short, it is the France of political, economic and cultural centralization, and seems to have little to do with anything ecological.[2]

Much less familiar is *la France profonde* ("deep France," the French heartland). This is the France of the provinces, and, more deeply still, of the regions. French regional thinking is expressed in the concept of *le pays*, which means literally "the country" but also refers to the distinctive local region in which one lives. The term derives from the Latin *pāgus*, which referred to a country district. For some French people it still makes sense to speak of "my country" and to mean not the nation-state but one's own specific region—a usage that is rare, though not unheard of, in the English-speaking world.[3]

Even urbanized French people often cling to their regional attachments. They are drawn to the surrounding countryside, its natural particularities, and its local traditions of architecture, cuisine, viticulture, and artisanship. Radical regionalists are concerned that this attachment should not decline into mere localized tourism and commercialism, that the remaining social and ecological integrity of regions should be fiercely defended, that the regions should be restored and reinvigorated, and that they should finally gain wide political and cultural autonomy and ultimately pose a powerful challenge to the dominant industrialized and commercialized anti-culture.

Bernard Charbonneau is perhaps the most significant figure in French regionalist thought, though his almost twenty books have long remained untranslated into English, with only one recent exception.[4] Charbonneau (1910–1996) was a member of the personalist philosophical movement, a regionalist thinker and activist, and a critic of technology. Long before others began to speak of a "military-industrial complex," he described a looming social catastrophe produced by an alliance between capital, the state, and the technological system, and in which the militarization of society was a crucial element.

He looked upon the First World War as a crucial turning point in what he called "the Great Transformation" (*la Grande Mue*) of humanity. At the beginning of the last century William Graham Sumner wrote ironically of the Spanish-American War as "the conquest of the United States by Spain," pointing out that in the process of *defeating* an empire, the United States *succumbed* to Empire by transforming itself into an imperial power. Similarly, for Charbonneau the most far-reaching implication of the First World War was its profoundly pernicious effect on the societies involved, as new processes of social totalization engulfed them all, "winners" and "losers."

Charbonneau emphasizes the central role of an inherently authoritarian state in this process. Though he did not define himself strictly as an anarchist, his anti-statism is uncompromising. In 1949 he self-published an extensive work on the state, in which he compares the political totalitarianism of Stalinism to the developing technical and scientific totalization spreading throughout the world.[5] He also points to the horrifying incineration of Hiroshima as evidence of the major threat to our collective future in the limitless power of the military-industrial system. Furthermore, he proclaims, "The State is Power. To speak of 'the authoritarian State' is to commit a pleonasm. To speak of 'the liberal State' is speak paradoxically. Pluralism and freedom are not a part of its nature. The free play of creative activity is not its concern, but rather that of individuals and groups. A State might officially be a federal or democratic one, but left to its own devices, it does not waste any time becoming centralized and authoritarian."[6]

Despite the vehemence of Charbonneau's critique of the state and the megamachine, he did not neglect the ways in which the new totalitarian power was embodied no less in an all-encompassing economic system. As de Miller notes, Charbonneau "never ceased denouncing in turn the dictatorship of the economic that is hidden in a mist of the social, the lies of technoscience, veiled by the infantile fantasies of omnipotence in the minds of unconscious consumers; and the straying of political ecology when it merely coats our commodities with a layer of green."[7]

Charbonneau places in a more ecological and regionalist context the kind of radical critique of technological society for which his friend and colleague Jacques Ellul is so well known.[8] He describes the emergence of a process of social totalization in which tendencies in the direction of technological domination move forward and accelerate in a seemingly autonomous and inexorable manner.[9] He shows that these trends include the economic rationality of capitalism, the bureaucratic rationality of the modern state, and the technological rationality of both. As a result of these tendencies, human power is "raised to a planetary level," so that it takes on the task of "ruling an entire world, to its farthest reaches and to the depths of its complexity." In the end, "the network of laws must cover every single inch of the surface of the globe," and the world is subjected to "a totalitarian policing."[10] Charbonneau deserves recognition for his insight at an early date that eco-fascism is perhaps the most likely future for humanity, if these present trends continue. He predicted (in 1980) that "one fine day, power will be forced to begin practicing ecology," and "the despoilers of the earth will organize the salvaging of the little that remains." Consequently, despite all appearances, "the future belongs to eco-fascism." In order to secure enough oxygen for survival, it will be necessary "to sacrifice another vital fluid: freedom."[11]

Charbonneau was particularly interested in the devastating effects of agro-industrial production on the land and people. He points out that not only does it pollute the countryside and deface the landscape, but it also destroys the freedom of the local inhabitants. Moreover, it annihilates diversity of all kinds, ranging from that of agricultural products, landscapes and ecological realities on the one hand, to customs, tastes, cultures and communities on the other.[12] Charbonneau sees such devastation as part of a conflict between two conceptions of value and wealth. On one side is exchange value and the wealth associated with commodification, mass production, and manipulated needs. Somewhat in the spirit of the young Marx, he sees the most insidious evil of exchange value as its fundamental perversion of human experience. It dictates the dominion of the sign over "reality," in the sense of those personal and natural realities of experience and of the senses that are effaced, obscured, repressed. Under its reign we can neither love nor enjoy that which we "value," for we lack the contact with reality that both of these experiences require.[13]

On the other side is use value, and the wealth found in "the free goods provided by nature," and "the personal goods that are beyond price." "Use value" as usually conceptualized is also a form of instrumental rationality that necessarily conflicts with intrinsic value and the intrinsic goods on which the latter is based. However, in Charbonneau's sense of the term it does not, rather ironically, relate to "using" things, but rather to treating them as ends in themselves. They are "loved for what they are," rather than merely "valued for what they are worth." For Charbonneau, there is a mode of exchange between human beings and between humans and nature that is "a form of communion." In such exchange, "another law of supply and demand comes into play through love." With the reinstitution of such a system of values, "the market will retreat and once more reality will override the sign. Instead of trafficking in reality, we will learn how to enjoy it."[14]

The return to the region is thus in large part a return to experience, to the senses, and to living realities. For Charbonneau, much in the spirit of Elisée Reclus, we participate in nature by embodying nature: "Nature is my own sensing and active body, without which the mind would be only an abstract idea."[15] Our relationship to nature is neither, as mainstream Western thought would have it, an essentially intellectual one, nor, as mainstream Western practice would have it, an instrumental one in which we merely use of objects for our ends. It is rather a dialectical relationship of interrelated being and reciprocal experiencing. We are ourselves embodied nature. We reach out to the rest of nature through perception, and our experience is a form of intimate contact of nature with environing nature.[16]

The role of otherness in Charbonneau's regionalist ontology and ethics is a central one. He believes that human beings are fully natural beings and at the same time beings that are distinct and differentiated from the rest of nature. Quite dialectically, he contends that we experience our distinctiveness as our freedom to shape reality, but we can only exercise our freedom to the degree to which it is embodied (or "incarnated") through engagement with the world, including the natural world. Freedom thus depends on both an awareness of the otherness of nature and on a sensuous participation in nature.[17]

For Charbonneau, it is essential to recognize the otherness of nature and to refrain from projecting one's own values and concepts of reality onto it. It retains this otherness "when I no longer personify it, as the Ancients did, or, like the Christians, identify it with a Providence that is supposed to satisfy our needs and our reason. Or again, like some naturalists, [endow] it with specifically human rational and moral qualities: such naturalism too is only a form of anthropocentrism. In order to know nature, it has to be distinguished from oneself: one must love it for its own sake."[18] In a sense we not only recognize beings in nature as things-in-themselves, not reducible to our knowledge or use of them, but also as thing-for-themselves, having value independent of our valuing of them for our own purposes or interests.

This dimension of Charbonneau's thought might be compared to the ethics of Emmanuel Levinas, which is founded in a primordial perception of the other that precedes all instrumentalizing knowledge. But it has even stronger affinities with the feminist ethics of care, which emphasizes an openness and concern for a unique other that is valued for its own sake, and from which one is clearly differentiated. Ecologism sometimes proposes an ethical, spiritual, or even personal relationship with a nature that remains quite abstract and generic. But if we take a caring, engaged approach toward nature, we will dismiss any unqualified "unity" as a snare and a delusion. Just as a love of humanity, if it is lacking in an active, engaged concern for real human beings, risks becoming an empty abstraction, so a love of nature without an active engagement in one's encompassing region results in a vacuous idealism—an illusory attainment of "oneness" with what is, in reality, a mere projection of one's own ideas.

Charbonneau believes that the ecology movement has not generally grasped the nature of the present crisis and that it has fallen into a self-defeating dualistic view of society and nature. In *Le Feu vert*, he discusses the ways in which a sharp division between an idealized "ecological" realm of wild nature and a supposedly denatured and fallen human realm can legitimate ecological destruction. "Ecologism," he says, "is the ideology perfectly adapted for the few scientists and public servants in charge of managing the minute sector of 'chemically pure nature' from which human beings will be excluded—except for the certified naturalist" who is "acceptable in the industrial system for managing natural sanctuaries and national parks."[19] In other words, there is room today for a growing green technocracy that will work within the prevailing order. In doing so it splits humanity off dualistically from the rest of nature, while at best providing leisure-time opportunities to the masses along with an imagined harmony and oneness with a supposedly pristine nature.[20] Meanwhile, the ecology movement presents no radically transformative vision for reversing the social and ecological degradation of the world.

Regionalism is itself sometimes criticized for promoting an escapist retreat from this larger world into the exclusiveness of a narrow localism. But this is far from the goal of advocates like Charbonneau, whose ideas express a conception of universal particularity. They propose not only a more vivid experience of immediately surrounding realities, but also a more authentic reaching out to others beyond one's own region. Max Rouquette, another important French regionalist,[21] says that the regional (*Occitane*) consciousness of southern France expresses "a voice that is quite specific, like that of each and every people, and which has no meaning, no *raison d'être*, except to the degree that it aspires to join in the universal song, in the chorus of all peoples."[22] The regionalist is in accord with the most famous of the personalist thinkers, libertarian communitarian philosopher Martin Buber, who says that the larger human community, the "organic commonwealth," can only exist if it is "a community of communities."[23]

On a more practical level, Daniel Cérézuelle contends that a regionalist economics and agriculture will produce not only greater self-sufficiency and a renewal of local ecological diversity, but also a greater complementarity between regions and localities. They will lead not only to an increased respect of each region for the autonomy and distinctiveness of the others, but also to a greater and more meaningful interdependence, as the undifferentiated, anonymous quality of the universal, abstract market is replaced by an economy founded on an appreciation of the uniqueness of locales and the distinctiveness of their bounty.[24]

If one follows the paths opened by Charbonneau, one can find a regionalism that is even more radical, critical, and dialectical than the one he delineates and that has, indeed, revolutionary political, economic, and psychological implications. However, his own regionalism was already a great achievement for making two notable contributions to political ecology.

First, it points out very strikingly and concretely the horrifying destructiveness of an increasingly totalitarian system of economic, political, and technological domination. We are now seeing its fulfillment in what is usually called "globalization," but which should more accurately be seen as corporate-state totalization. Charbonneau warns us that human society is undergoing a qualitative transformation under the domination of capital, the state and the technological system. He challenges us to consider whether forms of domination and instrumental rationality have infected society so pervasively that even most critics of the dominant system ultimately seek no more than a better managed alienation from ourselves and nature.

Second, Charbonneau's regionalism contributes to the development of a non-dogmatic, experientially materialist, rather than abstractly naturalist, social and political ecology. It recognizes that the system of domination increasingly constitutes an all-encompassing ethos and can only be opposed through a politics of experience rooted in our relationships with persons, places, and other beings around us. It helps us comprehend that in opposing that system of domination we are fighting not only for survival, but also for a deeply rewarding and joyful life for all. This is a life in which our experience is liberated from the chains of domination, and we are able to rediscover "the greatest wealth for the human being," which is both "the other human being" and *also* the other beings in nature.

## NOTES

1   Ecofeminist thought has been particularly helpful in this area. See, for example, "A Barefoot Epistemology," in Ariel Salleh, *Ecofeminism as Politics: Nature, Marx and the Postmodern*, 2nd ed. (London: Zed Books, 2017), 196–220.

2   Kerry Whiteside's *Divided Natures: French Contributions to Political Ecology* (Cambridge, MA: MIT Press, 2002) makes a notable contribution by introducing Anglophone readers to a wide spectrum of French ecological social thought. It is one of the few works in English to devote any serious attention to French regionalism. See "Personalism and the State: Regionalist Ecologism," 153–63.

3   There are some notable exceptions, such as the Alaska that John McPhee describes in his classic *Coming into the Country* (New York: Farrar, Straus & Giroux, 1977), in which the "country" is the very particular one known by the indigenous people and other inhabitants.

4   *The Green Light: A Self-Critique of the Ecological Movement* (London: Bloomsbury Academic, 2018). Moreover, the secondary literature on Charbonneau has remained very sparse, even in French. Very welcome additions are Daniel Cérézuelle's *Écologie et liberté: Bernard Charbonneau, précurseur de l'écologie politique* (Lyon: Parangon/Vs, 2006) and *Bernard Charbonneau ou la critique du développement exponentiel* (Lyon: Le Passager Clandestin, 2018), a brief introduction to Charbonneau that includes a collection of short excerpts from his works.

5   Reprinted as *L'État* (Paris: Économica, 1987).

6   *L'État*, 54.

7   Roland de Miller, "Bernard Charbonneau (1910–1996): Biographie," http://www.globenet.org/demiller/charbon.html.

8   See Jacques Ellul, *The Technological Society* (New York: Knopf, 1967), and *The Technological System* (New York: Continuum, 1980). Certain parallels with Lewis Mumford's critique of the Megamachine from a perspective of ecological regionalism are striking. See Mark Lucarelli, *Lewis Mumford and the Ecological Region* (New York: Guilford, 1995).

9   These dangers accelerate even more rapidly in the age of artificial intelligence, biotechnologies, and digital technologies, as discussed above in chapter 1, 31–34.

10  Bernard Charbonneau, *Le Jardin de Babylone* (Paris: Gallimard, 1969), 32, quoted by Daniel Cérézuelle, "Wendell Berry et Bernard Charbonneau, critiques de l'industrialisation de l'agriculture," *Encyclopédie de l'Agora*, http://agora.qc.ca/Documents/Agriculture--Wendell_Berry_et_Bernard_Charbonneau_critiques_de_par_Daniel_Cerezuelle.

11  *Le Feu Vert*, 137, 100. Cited in Cérézuelle, *Bernard Charbonneau ou la critique du développement exponentiel*, 47.

12  Bernard Charbonneau, *Il court, il court le fric . . .* (Bordeaux: Opales, 1996), 156.

13  Charbonneau, *Il court*, 156.

14    Charbonneau, 156.

15    Bernard Charbonneau, *Le Feu vert: Auto-critique du mouvement écologique* (Paris: Éditions Karthala, 1980), 55, quoted in Whiteside, *Divided Natures*, 161.

16    The regionalist emphasis on life, the body, the senses, and sensuous experience is reminiscent of Merleau-Ponty's dialectical phenomenology, which began some time ago to receive well-deserved attention in ecological philosophy. See David Abram's landmark work, *The Spell of the Sensuous: Perception and Language in a More-Than-Human World* (New York: Random House, 1996).

17    For a highly enlightening analysis of the crucial distinction between non-dualistic differentiation and dualistic splitting in our relationship to ourselves and to nature, see Joel Kovel, *History and Spirit: An Inquiry into the Philosophy of Liberation* (Boston: Beacon Press, 1991).

18    Charbonneau, *Le Feu vert*, 65, quoted in Whiteside, 162.

19    *Le Feu vert*, 99, quoted in Daniel Cérézuelle, "Nature and Freedom: Introducing the Thought of Bernard Charbonneau," unpublished manuscript, 23.

20    See David Nicholson-Lord's article on the ironies of eco-tourism, "Green Tragedy," *Resurgence* 212 (May–June 2002), https://www.resurgence.org/magazine/article1311-green-tragedy.html.

21    Rouquette is the author of *Verd Paradis* (Toulouse: Institut d'Estudis Occitans/Institut d'Études Occitanes, 1961; 1974), a work written in Occitan, the traditional language of the Midi, and rooted deeply in the culture and landscape. It was translated into French as *Vert Paradis* (Paris: Le Chemin Vert, 1980) and into English as *Green Paradise* (Ann Arbor: University of Michigan Press, 1995).

22    Rouquette, *Vert Paradis*, 301.

23    Martin Buber, *Paths in Utopia* (Boston: Beacon Press, 1958), 136.

24    Daniel Cérézuelle, "Réflexions sur l'agriculture," http://agora.qc.ca/reftext.nsf/Documents/Agriculture-Reflexions_sur_lagriculture_par_Daniel_Cerezuelle.

**PART IV**

# POWER TO THE IMAGINATION (FIFTY YEARS LATER)

16

# In Search of the Radical Imagination: Two Concepts of the Social Imaginary

### I. The Radical Social Imaginary

In recent years, the corporate-state apparatus has vastly increased its domination over the social imagination. A half century ago, a similar acceleration of social domination was a subject of widespread discussion and widespread alarm, as witnessed by the attention given to radical critiques such as Debord's *The Society of the Spectacle* and Marcuse's *One-Dimensional Man*. Yet today, the expanding colonization of consciousness has been assimilated much more smoothly. We have seen the results of the further development of pervasive background conditions of late capitalist society, which include the saturation of the culture with consumptionist images, and state and corporate hegemony over mass communications media. The manipulation of consciousness in times of military crisis has evoked a certain degree of attention. Yet it must be conceded that thus far the state has been largely successful in vanquishing what was once called "the Vietnam Syndrome," which is another term for critical thinking about war and militarism.

While techniques for the manipulation and control by the corporate-state apparatus have advanced enormously, the battle for the social imagination by dissident forces—not only antiwar and antimilitarist movements but also movements for deep social and ecological transformation in general—has become more and more ineffectual. Much as Spanish exiles refought the Civil War from Toulouse for the four decades after it ended, the mainstream of the American left has been refighting the same imaginary war for over four decades and counting. At the same time, its strategy in the larger imaginary social war has focused primarily on modes of avoiding engagement. During the same period, the corporate-state apparatus has learned how to achieve not only "air supremacy" but also imaginary supremacy. Despite the plague of political fantasies that overwhelm the collective psyche today, such noteworthy realities as intensifying global social and ecological crisis are crowded out of the dominant imaginary universe.[1]

## Castoriadis and the Social Imaginary

The present moment is for all these reasons a good time to reassess the state of the social imagination and the political implications of its present state. In any such reassessment, it would be difficult to ignore the significance of Cornelius Castoriadis, for among recent social theorists, none has done more to inspire analysis and inquiry in this realm. Anyone interested in a comprehensive, dialectical theory of society, a liberatory, transformative politics, and above all, an adequate politics of the imagination needs to come to terms with both the crucial insights and also the limitations of his thought.

The central concept in Castoriadis's reformulation of social theory is the radical imaginary. He begins with the thesis that every society "institutes itself" through the creation of "social imaginary significations." The radical imagination institutes by "constituting new universal forms" that produce shared social meanings.[2] Its radicality comes from the fact that it is responsible for the appearance of "something new" in history that arises out of "unmotivated creation."[3] The nature of the creations of the social imagination cannot be predicted (even by the creators themselves) through any "series of logical operations."[4] Social imaginary activity results in "the emergence of radical otherness" and "nontrivial novelty."[5] This otherness is radical even in deep epistemological and ontological senses, because the most fundamental elements of social understanding depend on it, and the changing nature of social being arises out of it. Thus, even a society's conception of the "rational" and the "real" presuppose "the primary and unmotivated positing of areal and arational significations"[6] that emerge in the social imaginary.

For Castoriadis, the classic example of the revolutionary nature of the social imaginary is the instituting of capitalism by the bourgeoisie. That revolutionary class not only expanded the forces of production and replaced existing relations of production with new ones; it also created "a new definition of *reality*, of what *counts* and of what *does not count*—therefore, of what *does not exist* (or nearly so: what can be counted and what cannot enter into accounting books)."[7] Modern capitalism can be understood both as the further development of the traditional logic of domination that has been central to Western society and as a historical break in which this logic is developed in a qualitatively new manner.

Castoriadis sees the core of the traditional Western ontology in a mode of thought and valuation that he calls "*identitary* or *ensemblist* logic."[8] This logic conceives of all objects, whether in the natural world, the theoretical world, or the world of subjective experience, as distinct and well defined. Furthermore, it takes all realities as consisting of elements that can be assembled into wholes, disassembled, and reassembled into new wholes.[9] The paradigm for such thinking is mathematics. Castoriadis attributes the compelling quality of this logic in large part to the fact that it is an inescapable element of any society and is necessary for language, social practice, and indeed survival.[10]

However, beyond its social utility, this logic contains within itself the seeds of domination of humanity and nature. It is capable of becoming a kind of "madness of unification" that seeks to annihilate all difference and otherness and reduce all realities to its own terms.[11] The project of economic, political, and technological domination initiated by the bourgeoisie has over the past several centuries been inspired by this very madness, which has defined rationality and "the end of knowledge" in terms of "the mastery and possession of nature."[12]

## From Alienation to Autonomy

For Castoriadis, this modern project of domination is a specific instance of a generalized condition of social alienation that has spanned history. Social alienation in all its forms is a process in which "imaginary significations" become autonomous. Society loses awareness of the fact that its social institutions are the free creations of human beings, and these institutions take on an aura of sacredness and inherent authority. Yet social alienation and heteronomy cannot be traced entirely to disordered or restrictive social practices and forms of false consciousness. For Castoriadis, "an institution of society which institutes inequality corresponds much more 'naturally' . . . to the exigencies of the originary psychical core, of the psychical monad which we carry within us and which always dreams, whatever our age, of being all-powerful and at the center of the world."[13] Thus, social hierarchy builds in some ways on foundations within "the individual's psychical economy."[14]

Despite Castoriadis's break with classical Marxist analysis, his central political project is in an important sense the development Marx's concept of the End of Prehistory. For Marx, world history has thus far been the history of collective self-alienation in which the products of human creative activity have become alien forces that fetter humanity. The End of Prehistory will signal not only the reclaiming by humanity of the alienated products of its own activity but also the reclaiming of the creative activity itself. Castoriadis develops this theme by focusing on the necessity of reappropriating what he sees as the deepest dimension of this creative activity—the radical imaginary.

He contends that there are two imaginary poles that have structured the Western societies in recent centuries. First, there is "the capitalistic nucleus," which consists of "the imaginary signification of unlimited expansion of pseudo-rational mastery over nature and over humans," and, second, there is another nucleus centering around "the project of social and individual autonomy." This latter nucleus can also be called "the emancipatory project," "the democratic movement," or "the revolutionary movement."[15] Castoriadis claims that this later nucleus is part of an "autonomy project" that has its origins in ancient Athens, and "has dominated Western European history since the end of the Middle Ages."[16] Its modern history begins with the bourgeois revolt against feudalism, spans the period of the great revolutions and the workers movement, and continues into recent times in the social movements of women, gay people, students, and ecologists.

The goal of this project, according to Castoriadis, is a society in which the community realizes that the fundamental rules by which it organizes itself do not come ready-made from God, from Nature, or even from any historical necessity or inherent structure of rationality within history, but from the community's own creative choice. Postrevolutionary society, according to Castoriadis, "will be a society that self-institutes itself explicitly, not once and for all, but continuously."[17]

## The Roots of the Imaginary

Castoriadis is certainly one of the preeminent modern theorists of both the imagination and of social liberation. However, an examination of his analysis of the imaginary and his formulation of the "autonomy project" reveals certain deep problems. While his often-incisive analysis seeks to undercut the imperious Prometheanism of the "capitalist nucleus" with its "identitary logic" and the accompanying project of economic and technological domination, his formulation of the autonomy project seems to retain a certain residual element of "heroic will to power." Castoriadis seeks to avoid the decentering and loss of integrity of the self (and of the social collectivity as historical subject) that would come from tracing the roots of the imaginary in larger social realities. His solution is the theory of imaginative creation *ex nihilo* and the attribution of autonomous creation to individuals and to the collectivities they constitute. But there is a basic inconsistency between such a conception of autonomy, which locates agency within the subject, and radical creation, which always finds the sources of agency elsewhere. In reality, the radical imagination has always demolished the illusions of autonomy, and Castoriadis did not seem to be prepared to come to grips with this challenge.

One of the strengths of Castoriadis's theoretical project is his often-successful effort to avoid two errors. On the one hand, the imaginary has been looked upon reductively as a mere superstructural phenomenon, while on the other hand, it has been interpreted abstractly and idealistically as the spontaneous product of individual consciousness. For Castoriadis, the imaginary is something much greater than either of these views can conceive of. It is an instituted social reality that operates as a material force in history. However, while Castoriadis affirms this materiality of the imaginary and thus escapes some forms of idealism, his autonomy project nevertheless succumbs in certain ways to this snare. For example, he fails to offer an adequate mediating link between the reality of the imaginary as a form of collective social creation and the concrete historical project of creating an autonomous, self-managed society. One has no reason to believe that merely pointing out (and to whom—certain political theorists?) that humanity can autonomously create imaginary significations and that culture can be the free expression of human creativity will motivate large numbers of human beings to struggle concretely for communal autonomy or engage in revolutionary cultural creativity. Nor does it indicate why, indeed, they ought to.

Castoriadis implies that a realization that society makes its own rules according to its own free decision will somehow have revolutionary implications. But late capitalist, late modern "cynical reason" also has no illusions about the existence of preordained social rules, yet it has no authentic vision of liberation. The idea of autonomous value-creation was also at the core of a certain fascist conception of an elite of *Übermenschen* who are "beyond good and evil." And it is a well-known fact that Sartre thought that the existentialist conception of free self-creation might lead to Communism—or.perhaps Maoism—or perhaps more plausibly, anarchism, but the connection with any of them was never made quite clear. Something more was needed. It is difficult to find this something in the works of either Sartre or Castoriadis.

Castoriadis's conception of the radical imaginary is authentically radical in one sense but inadequately radical in another. It is radical in grasping the irreducible, creative dimension of the imaginary, but not radical enough in overlooking the rootedness of the imaginary. It is true, as Castoriadis notes, that there are cultures in the Pacific, for example, "whose technical ensembles are closely akin, but which differ among themselves and greatly as our culture differs from that of the European fourteenth century."[18] This refutes any technological or other reductionism. But how much of this difference can be attributed purely to the radical imaginary? A great deal can be correlated with the existence of either patriarchal or nonpatriarchal social structures, which have both material and imaginary determinants (patriarchy was not created *ex nihilo* and diverse patriarchal cultures show considerable institutional continuity). An adequate understanding of such cultures requires attention both to those elements that are irreducibly unique and seemingly "unmotivated," and to those that can be explained through an investigation of social determinants. And these determinants, including the imaginary ones, must be investigated in all their complexity. The imaginary does not merely *rest* on a material substratum but also interacts dialectically with that substratum, which is in turn not *merely* a substratum but a dimension of living nature.

## An Ecology of the Imagination

Despite Castoriadis's major contribution to theorizing the social imaginary, one does not find in his work a great deal of careful empirical investigation of the imaginary. We might compare his work with that of Gilbert Durand, who, in his magnum opus, *The Anthropological Structures of the Imaginary*,[19] investigates the rich content of the social imaginary over history in minute empirical detail. Though Durand was engaged in a structuralist theoretical project more than a politically liberatory and socially transformative one, any success in the latter undertaking will depend on a similar immersion in the phenomena.

Thus, we must ask, not only in regard to the vast expanse of history but also in relation to our own society, to what extent there is a social imaginary and to what extent there is an "imaginary of imaginaries." We must recognize that the imaginary is regional, not territorial, and devote careful attention to the various imaginary regions that are interrelated and mutually determine one another in very specific, and very complex, ways. An understanding of the contemporary imaginary requires a detailed inquiry into the dialectic of many imaginary regions. These include the productionist and consumptionist imaginaries, the statist and nationalist imaginaries, and the patriarchal imaginary, to mention some of the most important ones.

When Castoriadis approaches the phenomena most concretely, he focuses very heavily on the technical dimensions of the dominant imaginary—those elements that relate to the ensemblist-identitary logic and to productionist images of a powerful, rational, and effective technological system. These are very crucial aspects of the system of domination. But it is essential to realize that consumptionist ideology and the consumptionist imaginary also perform a powerful legitimating function and that this is carried out ever more insidiously in late capitalist society, since they are able do it through ideas and images such as "environmentalism," "good corporate citizenship," "green consumerism," and "caring for nature." In the consumptionist imaginary utopia, we can, in more senses than one, recycle ourselves into oblivion.

In Castoriadis's analysis, it is "the economy that exhibits most strikingly the domination of the imaginary at every level—precisely because it claims to be entirely and exhaustively rational."[20] Once again, Castoriadis points out an important truth about the system. But it is a truth about only (at most) half of the picture. In the productionist and technical realm, such "rationality" reigns supreme, in the form of instrumental, technical, and bureaucratic reason. But in the consumptionist sphere, it is a rationality of the irrational that rules. The realm of consumption is the realm of fetishism, of mysterious, quite irrational powers, of the harnessing of desires that are neither rational nor transparent, even to those who exercise the rational techniques of manipulation through all these means. Moreover, there is in the economic sphere as a whole (which increasingly means "in society") a perverse dialectic between this irrational rationality and this rational irrationality.[21] In late capitalism, the means sometimes appear sane while the object appears mad. At other times, the means appear mad while the object appears sane. Yet in all cases means and ends are all elements of a larger madness. And what of the motive? Whether mad or sane, it is indispensable for purposes of ideological mystification.

One last point cannot be ignored. Despite his movement in the direction of political ecology in his later work, Castoriadis never fully reformulated the central themes of his philosophy in the light of ecological thought. Had he done so in regard to his theory of the social imaginary, he might have undertaken a comprehensive ecology of the imagination. This would then have taken him back in the direction of the tradition of dialectical social thought that he largely abandoned in his formulation of the radical, unconditioned nature of the imaginary. We can, however, setting out from Castoriadis's illuminating insights and oversights, undertake exactly this project. In doing so, we will find it necessary to engage in a careful exploration of the various regions of the imaginary, to pay close attention to the phenomena of the imaginary, to investigate the material basis for imaginary transformations, to explore the politics of the imagination as a concrete social practice, and to analyze the dialectical interaction and mutual determination between the imaginary and other realms of social determination.

## II. The Liberal Ideological Imaginary

While the social imaginary has been a major theme in contemporary European and Latin American thought, it has been generally neglected in the Anglo-American intellectual world. In recent years, however, the concept has gained increasing attention from Anglophone political theorists, perhaps most notably as the result of Charles Taylor's influential work, *Modern Social Imaginaries*.[22] Taylor has become widely recognized as the leading figure on this topic in the Anglo-American world. In the inaugural issue of the new journal *Social Imaginaries*, the members of the Editorial Collective conclude that Taylor (along with, they concede, Cornelius Castoriadis and Paul Ricoeur) has "articulated the most important theoretical frameworks for understanding social imaginaries."[23] Many other philosophers and political theorists concur with this view. However, an examination of Taylor's analysis shows that it often tells us less about the social imaginary itself than about the role of ideology in the academic study of the social imaginary.

Any inquiry into the social imaginary presupposes both a certain rationale or problematic and also a conceptual framework on which investigation is to be based. In other words, embedded in all theoretical inquiry is a practical project. This project is always to varying degrees either a critical and emancipatory one, or a dogmatic and ideological one. Ronald Creagh, in *Utopies américaines*, delineates the principal aspects of an emancipatory theoretical project. He notes that "in the process of emancipation" a group manifests its "inimitable singularity" through its "mode of reflection," and in doing so, certain crucial questions arise: "Has it demarcated the limits of the dominant mode of thought, its unthinkable, its prohibitions, and its repressed aspirations? Is it capable of crossing the forbidden frontiers of 'unthinkability,' in order to create a radically new collective imaginary?"[24]

The present discussion will show that Taylor's analysis fails to pose such key questions, but instead remains within the limits of the dominant ideological discourse. On the one hand, it contains a highly confused and defective conception of the social imaginary itself. On the other, its investigation of particular "social imaginaries" performs an ideological and apologetic function, reinforcing conventional thinking about the course of modernity, and avoids critical consideration of the dominant moments in the history of the modern social imaginary. Needless to say, such an approach forecloses the possibility of uncovering, through the ruthless critique of the dominant imaginary, the grounds for "a radically new collective imaginary."

## Charles Taylor's Social Imaginary

In order to understand the complex dialectic between the social imaginary and other major social determinants, it is essential to establish clearly its nature as a form of consciousness and its relationship to other spheres of social determination. A fundamental problem with Taylor's concept of the social imaginary is that he does neither of these things.

At the beginning of his key chapter, "What Is a 'Social Imaginary?'" Taylor defines it as "the ways people imagine their social existence, how they fit together with others, how things go on between them and their fellows, the expectations that are normally met, and the deeper normative notions and images that underlay these expectations."[25] He is already in trouble in this initial formulation of his problematic. We might try to interpret this sentence as stipulating a series of objects of imagination ("social existence" "fitting together," "how things go on," etc.) that are imagined through the social imaginary. But this makes little sense, since by the end of the sentence we would be imagining things that cannot reasonably be considered objects of the imagination, social or otherwise ("deeper normative notions") and imagining "images" themselves, which is unhelpfully tautological. Based on Taylor's own explanation of what he thinks of as the "social imaginary," this realm ends up being a mishmash of social phenomena such as collective images, social relations, social norms, and social understandings.

The analysis that follows Taylor's efforts at definition confirms the eclectic and confused nature of his approach. He noncontroversially explains that the social imaginary encompasses "the way ordinary people 'imagine' their social surroundings," often through "images, stories, and legends."[26] He notes that it "is shared by large groups of people, if not the whole society."[27] This is a good point, for were it not true, we wouldn't call it the *social* imaginary. But he also holds that it consists of "that common understanding that makes possible common practices and a widely shared sense of legitimacy."[28] However, the social imaginary, if it is a distinctive social sphere, cannot consist of "understandings," since these are the elements of a theory, ideology, etc. Its contents must rather be shared *images, imaginary significations, fantasies*, etc. that are objects of the *imagination*. The social imaginary is the sphere of neither reason nor understanding.

Taylor often reiterates his intellectualistic interpretation of the imaginary, asserting, for example, that it "incorporates a sense of the normal expectations that we have of each other; the kind of common understanding which enables us to carry out the collective practices which make up our social life."[29] We will look in vain for any explanation of the difference between "an expectation" and "a sense of an expectation." However, the important point is that Taylor again confuses imagining and understanding. Indeed, he goes so far as to subsume under the imaginary an "understanding" that "supposes, if it is to make sense, a wider grasp of our whole predicament, how we stand to each other, how we got to where we are, how we relate to other groups, etc."[30]

As these formulations indicate, much of what Taylor includes in his analysis relates not to the social imaginary, but rather to forms of social ideology.[31] In fact, there is a curious tendency in his supposedly groundbreaking work on the social imaginary to avoid resolutely any attempt to take the social imaginary itself entirely seriously. Instead, Taylor consistently (and suspiciously) reverts to discussion of *theory, ideology*, and modes of *understanding* and *interpretation*. A fatal flaw in his approach is that, quite astoundingly, it does not occur to him to investigate in detail the nature of *the social imagination* itself or, indeed, the nature of *the imagination* itself, much less explore precisely how the diverse phenomena he analyses might or might not be products of such an imagination.

Taylor's approach can be compared to the very detailed analysis of the imaginary in Lacan and in the large body of social thought that has been inspired by that thinker's work. The social imaginary as I define it includes, in Lacanian terms, both the symbolic and the imaginary "registers," as expressed on the level of social practice and social institutions. Lacan's distinction could be maintained, but I find it more theoretically illuminating to trace the dialectical interaction between the social imaginary as symbolic-imaginary and three other large spheres of social determination. The study of the social imaginary must explore the social dimensions of both *demand*, which relates to the Lacanian symbolic order and the patriarchal "Big Other," and *desire*, which relates to the Lacanian imaginary order and the *"objet petit a,"* or projective imaginary object.

We have lived through a historical era during which cultural and psychical hegemony in the advanced industrial societies has moved from (in Lacan's terms) the symbolic to the imaginary. Žižek notes that accompanying this evolution has been a change in the primary superego injunction from the authoritarian "Thou Shalt Not!" to the pseudolibertarian "Thou Shalt—Enjoy!"[32] Superego mechanisms vary widely depending on one's location within the global capitalist system (so far are we from Taylor's fantasy of equidistance from the center) and thus there are many hybrid variations on the society of demand and the society of desire. The imaginary has triumphed most in the core while a patriarchal authoritarian symbolic is often much more in command at the periphery. This is the social imaginary world in which we live and which screams out at us at every moment through the "information," "communication," and "social" media, albeit in distorted and disfigured forms of expression. Empire in its death throes dictates that some merely demand death while others actually desire it.

While Taylor's vague and uncritical conception of the imaginary tends to collapse together theory, ideology, and the more properly imaginary, when he does distinguish them, he often attributes an exaggerated role to theory in shaping the imaginary. He explains, for example, that "when a theory penetrates and transforms the social imaginary ... for the most part, people take up, improvise, or are inducted into new practices," which "are made sense of by the new outlook, the one first articulated in the theory; this outlook is the context that gives sense to the practices."[33] The "new understanding" then "begins to define the contours of their world and can eventually come to count as the taken-for-granted shape of things, too obvious to mention"[34] In this account, theory transforms the social imaginary, while at the same time transforming the social ethos. This process allows theory to become even more hegemonic, and at the same time more meaningful, and in the end to become a kind of conventional wisdom. But it seems that the crucial variables in this account are ideology (theory) and ethos (practice) and that the imaginary is reduced to a mediating term between the two.

Why should we accept such a vague and reductive account, rather than the alternative of a dialectical view of ideology, imaginary, ethos, and institutions, in which determination is always mutual, and in which the relative weight of each determinant varies according to the historical context? The weakness of Taylor's analysis is shown in his attempt to apply his intellectualistic scheme to revolutions. In his account, the revolutionary process begins as "we set out to remake our political life according to agreed principles"[35] and is followed by the various steps leading to the principles becoming "taken-for-granted." However, such a view cannot account for the fact that prerevolutionary ideology often becomes more and more tenuously related to revolutionary and postrevolutionary practice and that rather than increasingly "giving sense to the practices,"[36] it requires increasingly higher levels of ideological blindness on the part of its adherents to believe in any congruity between revolutionary principles and obviously counterrevolutionary practice. There has been a similar fate for the ideology of "equality" under liberal capitalist revolutions and of "workers' power" under authoritarian "socialist" (or state capitalist) regimes. A parallel gap can be noted between imaginary significations and social practice, as in cases in which images of the heroic and powerful worker or the euphoric and fashionable consumer are used to legitimate an oligarchical or other disempowering system.

## Three "Social Imaginaries"

An aspect of Taylor's analysis that has received considerable comment is his discussion of three "forms" of the modern social imaginary. The first of these is the economy. Taylor contends that "coming to see the most important purpose and agenda of society as economic collaboration and exchange" is "a drift in our social imaginary that begins in [the eighteenth century] and continues to this day."[37] This formulation shows that it is precisely in the area of the social imaginary that Taylor's analysis is badly deficient. Certainly, in the ideology of capitalism, economic "cooperation" and "fair exchange" are quite central, but in the *capitalist imaginary*, especially in the *late* capitalist imaginary, it is the commodity and commodity consumption (not production and exchange) that reign supreme. This was shown presciently in Marx's chapter "The Fetishism of Commodities and the Secret Thereof," later in various Situationist texts, and recently in a wide spectrum of cultural criticism.

Taylor is correct in his view that an important development in the modern social imaginary was "our coming to see our society as an 'economy,' an interlocking set of activities of production, exchange and consumption, which form a system with its own laws and its own dynamic" and which "now defines a way we are linked together."[38] But he has little insight into the specifically *imaginary* dimensions that accompanied this historical development. He fails almost entirely to analyze the social and psychological processes by which the economic has gained its hegemonic imaginary power, and how the economistic imaginary evolves historically in relation to other spheres of social determination.

Instead, he once again falls into abstract idealism and overvaluation of theoretical concepts. Thus, he takes very seriously the idea (and, granted, the image) of "the invisible hand," which has been much more important as an ideological and theoretical concept than as an imaginary signification that has moved the masses. On the other hand, he has little to say about the utopian economistic image of the industrial megamachine as an awe-inspiring liberating force, or about the contradictory dystopian image of the industrial megamachine as an oppressive monster. Significantly, he misses the war that has taken place on the battlefield of the social imagination.

The second of Taylor's "forms" is "the public sphere," which he describes as "a metatopical, common space" that "knits together a plurality of [topical] spaces into one larger space of nonassembly."[39] Once again, the analysis is excessively abstract and idealist, in that it relies heavily for evidence on the history of political theory, rather than on social and cultural history, the relevant sources for determining the state of the social imaginary of any era. Taylor does not give adequate attention to the class nature of various dimensions of such social imaginary significations or to the ideological nature of an image of "the" public sphere, when much or most of society has been and still is excluded in various ways from active participation in such a sphere. He seems never to have encountered the critique of the spectacle.

In Taylor's liberal optimistic view (it is especially here we encounter his fatal meliorism), the "public sphere" is "a kind of common space . . . in which people who never meet understand themselves to be engaged in discussion and capable of reaching a common mind."[40] He clearly thinks that this is not an ideal model of what society might achieve, but rather a description of what really emerged with the modern social imaginary. But the idea of "a common mind" has functioned much more as an ideological concept used to legitimate systems and regimes, than as the object of the imagination of "ordinary people" in the society.

In real social history (the history of real social beings thinking, acting and imagining), ordinary people have often imagined society as the site of conflicts between social classes and between other contending social groups. However, one finds little discussion of this conflictual dimension of the social imaginary in Taylor's analysis. Moreover, the image of a "common mind" possessed by the whole of society has been most typical of authoritarian, pseudo-organicist regimes, and not of the liberal societies that Taylor takes as his model. A much deeper analysis than Taylor presents would be necessary to show the basis for the emergence of a liberatory "common mind" that could challenge the dominant repressive one. What we find in Taylor is the rather weak liberal concept of society as "one big debate."[41] This is no more than a projection upon the actual social imaginary of the Millian (and later Habermasian) liberal ideological concept of progress through the evolution of a purportedly unconstrained public opinion.

The third, and most theoretically important, of Taylor's "social imaginaries" is that of "society as a 'people.'" He claims that what is imagined under this rubric is "a metatopical agency that is thought to preexist and found the politically organized society."[42] But is this agency what "ordinary people" in modern societies have imagined as "the people" or is it a concept that political theorists and members of the intelligentsia have utilized in order to theorize or, indeed, *fantasize*, "the people"? Once again, Taylor confuses the ideological and the imaginary, in this case in a more ominous way than usual.

At various points, Taylor discusses the relation between "understanding a theory," "being able to put it into practice," and "making sense of the practices," concluding that "what makes sense of our practices is our social imaginary."[43] However, what ordinarily makes sense out of practices is the social ideology. The social imaginary often makes very little "sense" out of the specific practices that ideology defends, rationalizes, and justifies. Yet it plays a very large role in bestowing *legitimacy* on such practices, by evoking *an investment of libidinal energy.* It endows practices and institutions with charismatic authority and legitimacy. Far from *making sense* out of practices and institutions, it often performs the function of *defying sense* in order to justify certain social practices and institutions. This is the case, for example, when images of patriotic unity, heroic triumphs, and noble sacrifices are used to depict institutions as "the people's institutions" (the people's state, the people's representatives, the people's army, wars in defense of the people, etc.) when, in reality, these institutions have very little to do with authorization by the people, or representation of the people.

Nevertheless, Taylor thinks that the key to the modern social imaginary is its democratic and populist dimension. He contends that modern society is "thoroughly penetrated on all levels by the modern moral order," which impels us to "criticize and even transform" that which is "insufficiently 'democratic' or egalitarian."[44] He claims that earlier society had "a certain verticality," which "depended in a grounding in a higher time," and was a "society of mediated access" in which the place of all was mediated by a figure such as the king; whereas, modern society, he says, is, by contrast, characterized by "horizontal, direct access" in which each person is "equidistant from the center" and "immediate to the whole."[45]

It should be recognized that, with a certain deference to social reality, Taylor at times slips from his claim regarding "direct access" to more ambiguous formulations such as "the diffusion of images of direct access," people "conceiving of themselves as participating directly" in public discussions, and economic agents "seeming" to be "on an equal footing."[46] He even admits that the imagined "immediacy of access" involved in phenomena such as following fashion or worshiping media stars is illusory, to the extent that these practices "are in their own sense hierarchical."[47] Despite such moments of grudging insight, Taylor returns to his thesis that modern society is indeed a kind of society of "direct access," resorting to the flimsy grounds that such practices "offer all participants an access unmediated by any of their other allegiances or belongings."[48] His claim is not, in fact, true, since there is always a very complex network of interpenetrating mediations of social phenomena. But even if it were true, the fact that it would not be mediated by "other allegiances" would not prevent it from being highly mediated in its own sphere.

Finally, and perhaps most importantly, regarding Taylor's horizontality thesis, one must question his idea that previous societies have instituted a "higher time" that is "vertical" while present-day societies have not. In fact, the temporality of mass consumption, the temporality of the spectacle, the temporality of technobureaucratic institutions, the temporality of regimented work and leisure—indeed, all the variations on the temporality of Empire—are forms of "higher time" embodying the verticality of social hierarchy and domination, and are imposed on the authentic "horizonalist" temporality of the body, of life in place, of mindful experience, of nature and natural cycles, in short, the temporality of living with an awakened awareness of the horizons of the real.

At one point, Taylor admits that an imaginary can be "false" to the extent that it "distorts or covers over certain crucial realities."[49] But he claims that even if it does so, the imaginary is at the same time necessarily more than ideological, in that it "makes sense of" and "enables" practices, and is thus "an essential constituent of the real."[50] Unfortunately, however, such an admission, rather than strengthening Taylor's case, only adds to its incoherence. The social imaginary is often quite central to legitimating systems of social domination and plays a major role in systematically distorting reality. The mere fact that it always "gives meaning" to practices cannot, in itself, negate in any way its functioning as false consciousness within a system of social domination, and is, in fact, a necessary precondition for such functioning.

The one-sided and ultimately ideological nature of Taylor's analysis is betrayed when he notes "how much our outlook is dominated by modes of social imaginary" that are shaped by "the modern ideal of order as mutual benefit."[51] Granted, this is certainly one moment of the modern social imaginary, and it is understandable that an optimistic and apologetic liberal interpretation of history would stress it. But it is certainly not the *dominant* moment, if by "dominant" we mean that which dominates both consciousness and action in the world, that which most powerfully conditions modes of self-definition, ego gratification, and *jouissance*, and that which is at the core of the reigning fundamental fantasy of the age.

What, then, does Taylor miss in his strongly liberal and weakly communitarian analysis of the social imaginary? Only the most important dimensions: its fundamental role in the constitution of subjectivity, its place in the social whole, and the nature of its historical transformations.

## The Imaginary as a Sphere of Social Determination

The social imaginary is the sphere of a community's collective fantasy life. It includes images of the self, the community itself, the world, the cosmos, and the person's relationship to each of these. It includes the dominant myths and paradigmatic narratives of the society. Though the modern social imaginary reflects the entire history of social determination, it has been increasingly dominated by the dialectic between capital and the capitalist techno-bureaucratic megamachine, with an important role being played by the larger dialectic between these institutional structures and the modern nation-state and its own techno-bureaucratic megamachine. To this must be added the role of regressive institutions and identifications such as authoritarian patriarchy and religious fundamentalism, which gain new energy largely in reaction to the vicissitudes of capital, the state and the megamachine.

In the late modern period (the era of the end of Empire, the Necrocene), the elements of a productionist imaginary, a consumptionist imaginary, a patriarchal imaginary, a nationalist imaginary, a statist imaginary, and a technological imaginary all interact dialectically, and the nature of their interactions must be understood in specific detail. In order for this to occur, the social imaginary must itself be understood in dialectical relationship to the social institutional structure, the social ideology, and the social ethos (and all of these must be further understood in relation to the dialectic between "the natural" and the subset of the natural called "the social"). In the brief concluding remarks that follow, the focus will be limited to the interplay between the two most dominant moments of the economistic core of the actually existing system of domination.

Understanding the "modern social imaginary" requires a grasp of the increasing domination of economism in all forms of social determination and of the dialectic between the productionist and consumptionist moments of this economism. So-called advanced industrial societies have gone through a process of evolution from the productionist to the consumptionist era of economism. The typical productionist and disciplinary forms of social organization, such as the factory, the prison, the school, and the hospital were dominant in the earlier period and remain crucial in the later period. However, they are increasingly transformed and refashioned in a consumptionist direction. At the same time, strongly consumptionist institutions such as the shopping mall, the entertainment and recreation industries, and the highly commercialized "social" media, come to occupy an increasingly central place in society, and play a growing role in generating the social imaginary.

Ideologically, there is a shift from such productionist values as discipline, conformity, resignation, ambition, hard work, productivity, self-repression, self-control, obedience, scrupulousness, productivity, and accumulation to consumptionist values such as happiness, pleasure, gratification, enjoyment, fulfillment, stylishness, popularity, youthfulness, sex appeal, physical beauty, and conspicuous consumption. The transformation of the social imaginary, the fantasy life of society, accompanies this development. The system of consumptionist values focuses on the images presented in advertising and the mass media, images of personal gratification and power that come from the accumulation not merely of abstract wealth but of what we might call "subjective capital" that is, objects and experiences that are closely identified with images of successful selfhood (the aggrandizement of the ego).

The traditional hierarchical system of social domination, of power-over, generates a fundamental fantasy in which personal gratification comes from a sense of superiority, from real or supposed recognition by subordinates, from pleasure at the very idea of the subservience of others. Such a social formation is pervaded by psychical phenomena such as humiliation, frustration, self-doubt, self-contempt, resentment, repression, rage, and craving for revenge. All of this is transformed, and in many ways aggravated, in a stage of society in which human relations are more and more thoroughly mediated by things, or more precisely, by images of things. The society of mass consumption creates, even among the relatively powerless, a fundamental fantasy based on the exercise of power, and an increasing sense of actual power rooted in the immediate gratification provided through the consumption of commodities, ranging from fast food to pornographic images. But at the same moment that consumers come into possession of this vast technological and imaginary power, they feel increasingly less powerful, less satisfied, emptier. While verifiably having more of what the consumer culture promises, the consumers find themselves craving even more. There is a material abundance of the "stuff" of dreams (commodities) but an imaginary scarcity of the "stuff" of reality (the yearned for yet impossible substantiality of the subject). An awareness begins to emerge that on a deeper level, one needs, not more, but something more. The system thus generates dissatisfaction, aliena- tion, and potentially subversive impulses that are in contradiction to the fundamental fantasy.

A critical and dialectical analysis of the social imaginary will focus on such moments of negativity within the system of social determination (all of which are overlooked in Taylor's liberal account). The goals of such an analysis include, first, understanding how various spheres determine and reinforce the existing patterns of thought and action and, second, comprehending the nature of their current processes of evolution and transformation. However, another basic goal is to understand what must be done if patterns of thought and action are to emerge that truly chal- lenge and begin to overturn the system of social domination. Any effective movement for social transformation must consist of a growing community whose members are in the process of creating, for themselves, a liberatory institutional framework, a liberatory social ethos, a liberatory worldview, and a liberatory social imaginary founded on a new fundamental fantasy or image of nondominating personhood.

Ronald Creagh cites a pertinent example of how the utopian com- munal imaginary can generate such a powerful counterimaginary. He cites Kathleen Kinkade, one of the cofounders of the egalitarian and eco- logical community, Twin Oaks. Kinkade describes the community she first imagined, based on the book *Walden Two*, in this way: "I saw everything I wanted in that book. I imagined myself completely happy in this society. I imagined myself being able to find the mate of my dreams. I fell in love with *Walden Two*, and remained so for many years. It was the passion of my life."[52]

This passage gives us the key to the understanding and critique of the dominant social imaginary. Such a project must address the nature of the fundamental fantasy. We must first understand precisely how the dominant economistic imaginary colonizes our passion and desire, and how it creates the fatal illusion that it can supply "everything that we want." If we achieve such a critical understanding, accompanied by the appropriate liberatory, transformative desire, we can then move on to imagine, and begin to create, a world beyond the chains of illusion and domination. We can help give birth to a world that not only liberates our own deepest longings and hopes but also nurtures the flourishing of the human and Earth community.

## NOTES

1     For example, over the past several years American media have focused on the Trump administration's decision to withdraw from the Paris Climate Accord and the various criticisms of that decision. What has not been the focus of media attention includes: 1) the fact that the targets of the Paris Accord were an extremely inadequate response to looming global ecological disaster; 2) the fact that the parties to the agreement have not over the past three years come close to reaching these voluntary, unenforced, and inadequate targets; and 3) the nature of the coming global ecological disaster.

2     Cornelius Castoriadis, *Political and Social Writings*, vol. 3, trans. and ed. David Ames Curtis (Minneapolis: University of Minnesota Press, 1993), 131.

3     Cornelius Castoriadis, *Political and Social Writings*, vol. 1, trans. and ed. David Ames Curtis (Minneapolis: University of Minnesota Press, 1988), 30.

4     Castoriadis, *Political and Social Writings*, 3:180.

5     Cornelius Castoriadis, *The Imaginary Institution of Society* (Cambridge, MA: MIT Press, 1987), 184.

6     Castoriadis, *Political and Social Writings*, 1:30.

7     *Political and Social Writings*, 3:179.

8     Castoriadis, *Imaginary Institution*, 175.

9     Cornelius Castoriadis, *Crossroads in the Labyrinth* (Cambridge, MA: MIT Press, 1984), 209.

10    Castoriadis, *Crossroads in the Labyrinth*, 208.

11    Castoriadis, *Imaginary Institution*, 299–300.

12    Castoriadis, *Imaginary Institution*, 272.

13    Cornelius Castoriadis, *Philosophy, Politics, Autonomy* (New York: Oxford University Press, 1991), 135.

14    Castoriadis, *Philosophy, Politics, Autonomy*, 135.

15    *Philosophy, Politics, Autonomy*, 221; *Political and Social Writings*, 1:31.

16    *Political and Social Writings*, 1:31. Castoriadis's insights concerning the crucial contribution of Athenian society to the development of democracy and critical thought, and his neglect of the contributions of other premodern cultures, such as those discussed in the present work, are both worthy of attention.

17    *Political and Social Writings*, 1:31.

18    Castoriadis, *Crossroads in the Labyrinth*, 248.

19    Gilbert Durand, *The Anthropological Structures of the Imaginary* (trans. of 11th French edition; Brisbane: Boombana Publications, 1999). Much of the most important contemporary work on the social imaginary in France has not been done under the influence of Castoriadis, but rather in relation to the intellectual lineage Gaston Bachelard–Gilbert Durand–Michel Maffesoli or in political readings of the legacy of Jacques Lacan.

20    Castoriadis, *Imaginary Institution*, 156.

21    See Joel Kovel, *The Age of Desire: Reflections of a Radical Psychoanalyst* (New York: Pantheon, 1981) for what is still the best detailed analysis of the consumptionist, productionist and other fundamental institutional, ideological, and imaginary dimensions of society, as exhibited in contemporary subjectivities.

22    Charles Taylor, *Modern Social Imaginaries* (Durham, NC: Duke University Press, 2003).

23  The *Social Imaginaries* Editorial Collective, "Editorial," *Social Imaginaries* 1, no. 1 (2015): 7, https://books.google.ro/books?id=3EVwCQAAQBAJ&printsec=frontcover&source=gbs_ge_summary_r&cad=0#v=onepage&q&f=false. Žižek and Lacanian social theory, in which the imaginary plays a key role, are ignored.

24  Ronald Creagh, *Utopies américaines* (Marseilles: Agone, 2009), 306.

25  Taylor, *Modern Social Imaginaries*, 23.

26  Taylor, 23.

27  Taylor, 23.

28  Taylor, 23.

29  Taylor, 24.

30  Taylor, 25.

31  It would be false, of course, to deny that there is a relationship between "social understandings" (including social ideology) and the social imaginary. The error is to assume that the latter merely "incorporates" or includes the former. It would also be incorrect to assume that the social imaginary cannot be, to a greater or lesser degree, rational. This does not mean, however, that imagination can be reduced to a mode of reasoning or of understanding the world. A community tends to have a rational understanding of the world and a rational social imaginary to the degree that it has a rational relationship to the world, or, to use Heraclitus's ancient insight, to the degree that it embodies the common *logos*.

32  It is precisely because the superego "enjoins" most effectively when it enjoins without *explicitly saying* "Thou Shalt" or "Thou Shalt Now" that it functions in the social imaginary sphere (or Lacanian symbolic order) rather than in the sphere of social ideology.

33  Taylor, 29.

34  Taylor, 29.

35  Taylor, 29.

36  Taylor, 29.

37  Taylor, 76.

38  Taylor, 76.

39  Taylor, 86.

40  Taylor, 75.

41  Taylor, 84.

42  Taylor, 102.

43  Taylor, 114, 165.

44  Taylor, 146.

45  Taylor, 158.

46  Taylor, 160–61.

47  Taylor, 160.

48  Taylor, 160.

49  Taylor, 183.

50  Taylor, 183.

51  Taylor, 185.

52  Quoted in Erin Passehl, "Twin Oaks Community: Women's Liberation, Generational Divide, and the Evolution of Women's Culture," *Archive* (University of Wisconsin) 7 (May 2004): 38, https://uwarchive.files.wordpress.com/2017/04/twin-oaks-community.pdf. The fact that Kinkade could have found "everything

she wanted" in this awkwardly written, vulgarly reductionist, philosophically naive, and coldly dispassionate work is a great tribute to the power of the creative imagination. It shows Kinkade's ability to project a vast spectrum of personal and communally shared hopes, dreams, and imagined possibilities into Skinner's impoverished image of a behaviorist utopia, and then to create something magnificent and inspiring on this imaginary foundation.

# 17

# The Spectacle Looks Back into You: The Situationists and the Aporias of the Left

## A Brief Rupture in Time

Guy Debord's *The Society of the Spectacle*, the foremost work of the Situationist International, appeared almost half a century ago. Owing to a remarkable convergence of ideas and events, it quickly became a revolutionary force in real history, and it has since become a classic of modern radical thought. Whether or not it is, as its translator Ken Knabb claims, "arguably the most important radical book of the twentieth century,"[1] it is certainly one of the most important, and it cannot be ignored by anyone who wants to understand the world-historical transformations of the system of domination that took place in the latter half of the century. Debord showed more clearly than anyone else up to that point that critics of advanced capitalism ought to shift their focus from a preoccupation with the authoritarian state and repressive productionist ideology as the salient mechanisms of domination and instead focus more intently on the power of the commodity and of the consumptionist imaginary.

Debord was not alone in inspiring this shift in perspective. Foucault criticized the regressive nature of "the repressive hypothesis," in which power is always seen as being classically authoritarian and imposed from above, and Marcuse and the Frankfurt School introduced the ideas of the capture of desire through co-optative "repressive desublimation" and of the key role of the "culture industry" in late capitalism Yet, for better or worse, it was Debord's image of the spectacle that conveyed most compellingly the central role of commodity fetishism and the mass media in the contemporary system of domination.

Debord's tirade against the spectacle was very timely. The first generation that had been thoroughly socialized by electronic media was just coming of age, ready to break the disciplinary bonds of the obsolete paleo-technical industrial era and to usher in unwittingly the dawning age of domination by neotechnical digital media and drones. And just as the work appeared, the radical left in the U.S. was in the process of reaching a peak and then self-destructing, even as it chanted before the mass media, in a kind of trancelike invocation of the spectacle, "The Whole World Is Watching." The Situationists, and especially Debord, deserve recognition for their prophetic role at this turning point in world history, though history was not to turn in quite the direction they envisioned.

The Situationist International endured, despite numerous internal conflicts, splits, and expulsions, from 1957 to 1972. Though it had a cumulative total of only about seventy members, it had a vastly greater effect on history than these small numbers would suggest. Situationism[2] had its roots in artistic and cultural movements such as Dada, Surrealism, and Lettrism, and political movements such as Marxism, anarchism, council communism, and utopian socialism. Debord and Raoul Vaneigem were the best-known figures, and Debord's *Society of the Spectacle* and Vaneigem's *Revolution of Everyday Life* were by far the most famous and influential works produced by the movement.

After almost a decade of ruthless critique and scandalous provocations, the Situationists moved to the center of the political stage in 1966 when Situationist-influenced students at the University of Strasbourg published and distributed widely Mustapha Khayati's historic pamphlet *On the Poverty of Student Life*.[3] This document had a radicalizing influence on the French student movement and foreshadowed the major social convulsion that was about to arrive. Two years later, the Situationists, in alliance with the radical student group, the Enragés, emerged as a major instigating force in the May–June 1968 General Strike that mobilized over ten million people and nearly toppled the Gaullist regime. They achieved lasting fame through their role in street fighting, in the occupation of the Sorbonne, and even more for their slogans and posters, which seemed to cover every wall in Paris during the "events" and have illustrated a multitude of articles and books on the period over the years.

## A Ruthless Critique of All Things Spectacular

The Situationists introduced a number of concepts that were to revolutionize the Left's imaginary landscape. They took up Marx's idea of social alienation and developed it into what they called "the critique of separation."

Inspired by utopians like Fourier and by Surrealism, they focused on the need for the total destruction of repressive forces and for the liberation of desire. Most significantly, they updated Marx's idea of the fetishism of commodities, arguing that not only does the commodity become an alien force that dominates humanity, but the whole system of commodities fuses into an overwhelmingly powerful institutional, ideological, ethotic (practical), and, above all, *imaginary* reality that they labeled "the spectacle." They proclaimed that this spectacle must be recognized as the monstrous force behind all the separation and alienation that plagues everyday life under capitalism.

In defiance of such domination by the spectacle, the Situationists proposed the "creation of situations," which they defined as "the concrete construction of momentary ambiances of life and their transformation into a superior passional quality."[4] This might seem a bit on the abstract side, but they also developed certain concrete practices that revealed more clearly the kind of activity that flows from the critique of the spectacle, and the kind of situations that are worthy of creation. One such activity was *détournement*, which quickly became one of the most distinctive hallmarks of the movement. *Détournement* literally means "diversion" or, perhaps more pertinently, "embezzlement." For the Situationists, it came to mean the appropriation of a vast range of cultural artifacts in the most imaginatively subversive manner possible. Their particular target was popular culture, the culture of the spectacle par excellence, and their most notable success was the détournement of comics. They substituted revolutionary slogans or absurdist comments in the speech bubbles—and the rest is radical history. The mirror image of détournement is the process of *récuperation*, a term for the spectacle's seemingly infinite powers of co-optation. To be a Situationist is to be fully mobilized in the epic battle between the forces of détournement and those of récuperation.

Another major area of the Situationists' practice consisted of their investigations in psychogeography, which the first issue of *Internationale Situationiste* defined as "the study of the precise laws and specific effects of the geographical environment, whether consciously organized or not, on the emotions and behavior of individuals."[5] This field of study gave birth to a process of psychogeographical exploration of the city in what the Situationists called the *dérive*, or drift. They described the dérive as "a mode of experimental behavior linked to the conditions of urban society: a technique of rapid passage through varied ambiances."[6] This quest for the strange, the marvelous, and the liberating became one of the most famous Situationist concepts. It was to have a major influence on radical and avant-garde cultural trends, particularly after it and all things Situationist were swept along with the revolutionary tide of 1968.

The Situationists present their own interpretation of the world-historical significance of the May '68 events in their text "The Beginning of an Era." They call it "the largest general strike that ever stopped the economy of an advanced industrial country, and the first *wildcat general strike* in history."[7] They claim that it marked "the resounding verification of the revolutionary theory of our time," and constituted "the most important experience of the modern proletarian movement that is in the process of constituting itself in its *fully developed* form in all countries."[8] Finally, they assert that the movement was "a holistic critique of all alienations, of all ideologies and of the entire old organization of real life."[9]

Unfortunately, most of these claims turned out to be elements of a rather grandiose revolutionary fantasy. The theory, far from being definitively "verified" by the May '68 events, was shown by the subsequent course of history to be riddled with flaws and contradictions. The movement, far from being just on the verge of "full development," proved to be in a process of rapid decomposition. And ideology, far from being conclusively critiqued and sent on the road to oblivion, managed to come back in full force, not least of all among precisely the most engaged participants in the revolutionary movement itself.

As we look back at the role of the Situationists in this crucial historical moment, we find that they created an impasse in the area of socially transformative practice. This becomes clear if we examine their own ideas and activities and those of others who were influenced most by them over the past half century.[10] There have been two predominant directions of development. First, there has been a tendency toward detached aestheticization in the realm of cultural critique and *détournement*, focusing on image subversion, or what many would now call culture jamming. Second, there has been a tendency toward insurrectionary politics.

One-time Situationist Christopher Gray renders perhaps the most scathing judgment on the movement. He remarks that it had "a brilliant theoretical critique of society" but lacked "any grasp of the real problems of what to do about it." He concludes that consequently, "the Paris May days were the end for the S.I.," after which "it entered 'the heaven of the spectacle' by the scruff of its neck, and that was that."[11] Of course, in real history *that* is never quite *that*, so the Situationist legacy is a bit more ambiguous and worthy of reconsideration than Gray suggests.

## Power to the Popular Assemblies

One of the central preoccupations of the Situationists was the perennial question of the nature of the "revolutionary subject" and the possibility of the emergence of such a transformative agent in the foreseeable future. Readers of *The Society of the Spectacle* discover that the Situationists placed all their world-historical bets on something called "worker councils." They might be forgiven if they jump to the conclusion, first, that such entities are what we ordinarily think of as "councils," and second, that the councils would be elected by and composed of what we ordinarily think of as "workers." However, this would be misleading on both counts. An examination of the full range of Situationist texts,[12] reveals that the idea of workers' councils is more radical and also more realistic than it might initially appear. First, the Situationists define the "council" not as an elected representative body, but rather as a democratic, participatory *assembly*. And second, despite the term "worker," they recognized the crucial importance of assemblies in both the *workplace* and in the local *community*.

In developing these ideas, the Situationists were greatly indebted to Castoriadis, who influenced them profoundly with his analysis of direct political democracy and worker self-management.[13] Though he developed these themes in much greater detail and philosophical depth, the Situationists played a vital role in communicating them to a much wider audience. It should be recognized that well before the idea of local assembly government as a crucial political form began being promoted under the rubric of "libertarian municipalism," the Situationists had already presented a strong defense of the base-level assembly as the key popular institution. And while some contemporaries such as Castoriadis focused heavily on worker councils and assemblies, while others like Bookchin stressed the community assembly almost exclusively, the Situationists can claim to be farther-reaching in their vision, in that they recognized the importance to a radically democratic movement of both workplace and community assemblies.

Thus, in "The Beginning of an Era" they state that "the next revolution will recognize as councils only sovereign rank-and-file general assemblies, in the enterprises and the neighborhoods, whose delegates are answerable to those assemblies alone and always subject to recall by them."[14] In

"Preliminaries on Councils and Councilist Organization, " the council is described as the "permanent *basic unit*" of the political system, which is not a representative body, but rather "the assembly in which all the workers of an enterprise (workshop and factory councils) and all the inhabitants of an urban district who have rallied to the revolution (street councils, neighborhood councils) must participate."[15] Direct democracy would thus be decentralized even beyond the local neighborhood. Vaneigem proposes that in a revolutionary situation, workers' councils should expand to the surrounding neighborhoods and "rapidly take the form of local councils," which will then be "grouped together in 'Communes' of more or less equal size (perhaps 8,000 to 10,000 people?)."[16] Thus, the Situationists had already in the 1960s invented a version of "communalism" based on neighborhood assemblies and federations of assemblies.

In developing such ideas, the Situationists synthesize the most deeply democratic and participatory aspects of the radical democratic, anarcho-syndicalist, and anarcho-communist traditions. They present a vision of communal grassroots democracy that offered a constructive alternative to the forms of accommodation with corporate capitalism, the reaffirmations of bureaucratic statism, and the abstract idealist and voluntarist insurrectionism that have predominated on the left since that time. It might have actually become an effective alternative if these ideas had been situated within a historically grounded and theoretically incisive analysis of social determination and social transformation. Unfortunately, they were instead rendered largely inert by being incorporated into a fundamentally reactive framework that played into the hands of the very forces that the Situationists hoped to defeat.

## The Old World Catches Up

Some of the famous Situationist slogans hinted at how various dimensions of the May '68 revolt would ultimately fit into the logic of late capitalism. "What do we want—everything," proclaimed one graffito. The replacement of traditional revolutionary aspirations for freedom and justice by the expression of unlimited desire is revealing, for such a project of infinite desire is precisely the imaginary program adopted by the society of commodity consumption itself. When this is recognized, May '68 becomes the symbolic point in history at which the disciplined subject of classical capitalism is liberated to become the all-consuming ego of late capitalism. In this context, the Situationist slogan "Be realistic, demand the impossible" takes on a quite ominous meaning: "Accept new repressively sublimating Superego's injunction that you must demand the impossible." The ambiguity of the French verb *demander* should not be overlooked. Its most basic meaning is "to ask for." This raises a crucial question: "To whom precisely should one's request for the impossible be directed?" The answer is, of course, that after the authoritarian Father of the society of production has been deposed (at least in fantasy), it is the (fantasized) indulgent Mother of the society of mass consumption to whom one must look expectantly. However, there also exists a kind of consumptionist Big Brother superego that is always ready to shame us for our failure to realize the right kind of impossibility.

And this leads us to a final Situationist slogan, "Take your desires for reality." What is suppressed in this formulation is that while all desires are realities, they are also ideology, and if we do not *take them* for ideology, we will *leave them* as ideology—that is, they will simply retain their ideological character. It seems, to say the least, a bit paradoxical to tell us that the spectacle has created for us an entire world of manipulated desires and then to ask us to "take our desires for reality." The paradox dissolves however, if, like the Situationists, one adheres to a version of liberationist ideology, which holds that there are truly authentic desires lying just beneath the surface (much as Tahiti lies beneath the Parisian paving stones), waiting for the removal of restraints in order to express themselves. Unfortunately, the job of distinguishing true from false desires is not as easy as it might appear. If one takes a dialectical perspective one realizes that within the psyche, all desires interact mutually and condition one another, so that neither "true" nor "false" ones, "good" nor "evil" ones, "liberated" nor "bound" ones, will ever be found in some pure, uncontaminated state.

The most famous quote from Vaneigem illustrates well the nature of the problem. "Anyone who talks about revolution and class struggle without referring explicitly to everyday life—without grasping what is subversive about love and positive in the refusal of constraints—has a corpse in his mouth."[17] This passage illustrates both the power and limitations of the Situationists. They were expressing, on the eve of revolt, a desperately needed spirit of rebellion. However, critique in the name of liberation, if it is not to produce prisoners of liberation, must remain resolutely dialectical, asking critical questions about the ambiguous and contradictory nature of phenomena such as "love" and "constraints." It must ask, as the Situationists consistently failed to do, about the ways in which *love* can, in the name of subversion itself, subvert love, and the ways in which the *refusal of constraints* can, in the name of freedom itself, become constraining.

We find repeatedly in the Situationist texts instances of the naive liberationism that became a hallmark of 1960s and post-1960s radical politics. According to Vaneigem, "We only have to consider Stockholm or Watts to see that negative pleasure is forever on the point of tipping over into total pleasure—a little shove, and negative violence releases its positivity."[18] In short, we believe in magic. And though we should, most definitely, believe in magic, that does not mean that we should believe in *all* magic. Yet Vaneigem and the Situationists were willing to go all the way with this alchemy of revolution. They are capable of saying, with no hint of conscious hyperbole, not to mention irony, that "the complete unchaining of pleasure is the surest route to the revolution of everyday life, to the construction of the whole human being."[19] But the vanity of such a project is betrayed in the very mixed metaphor in which it is expressed. When has "construction" ever been carried out successfully through "unchaining"? The Situationists would have done well to go back to Hegel, where they would have discovered that even the "chained" can find a kind of liberation through "constructive" engagement in the world of creation, while "unchained" absolute freedom may well lead in the direction of new chains.

Vaneigem is capable of deducing from the correct premise that "the shock of freedom works miracles" the grandiosely absurd conclusion that "three thousand years of darkness cannot withstand ten days of revolutionary violence." To this he adds the naive rationale for his conclusion: that the "reconstruction of society" that results from such insurrection "will surely mean the simultaneous reconstruction of everyone's unconscious."[20] It is true that in revolutionary situations there is a moment of traumatic liberation in which a vast range of possibilities opens up. However, the concrete determination of which possibilities will be realized depends on the complex social context (institutional, ideological, imaginary, and ethotic) within which the possibilities unfold. To reduce these complexities of social determination to the single determinant of "revolutionary violence" opens the way to the abstract insurrectionism that is one of the most disturbing legacies of the Situationists.

## Cultural Revolution as a Market Development Strategy
A fundamental flaw of the Situationists was their failure to comprehend the ways in which the project of repressive desublimation was revolutionizing

late capitalism itself. Of course, they were hardly alone in overlooking what turned out to be the decisive moment of dialectical reversal in 1960s cultural history. However, as aficionados of radical critique they should have learned something from Marcuse's dissection of the process in *One-Dimensional Man* as early as 1964, and even before that in his brilliant new preface to *Eros and Civilization*, written in 1961, in both cases, well before the major Situationist works were published.[21] Marcuse described a late capitalist world in which "desublimated sexuality is rampant" and in which "what happens is surely wild and obscene, virile and tasty, quite immoral—and, precisely because of that, perfectly harmless."[22] Harmless, that is, to the hegemony of the system of domination, as addictively and devastatingly noxious as it might be to the personal and collective psyche.

According to the Situationists, the spectacle was creating a stupefying, deadening existence for the great majority. The world of commodity consumption was becoming increasingly alienating and, above all, boring. Consequently, the masses were always on the verge of awakening from their hypnotic trance. All they needed was to be clued in to how bad the old world was and that something much more exciting was possible—something like total cultural revolution. But, in fact, the system was in the midst of a transition into the era of acute hyperstimulation. It had no intention of allowing the masses to lapse entirely into socially dangerous and economically unprofitable boredom. It was mastering the trick of overstimulating consumers at the same time that it was depressing and boring them. It was also devising a system of mutual reinforcement, a positive feedback loop, between the two social-psychological processes. Moreover, it was at work on developing a vast spectrum of drugs with which to treat (interminably) the resulting diseases and disorders of consumption. It could look forward to the generation of unprecedented profits through such mining of the psyche. Any gratuitous help from radicals, revolutionaries, counterculturalists and Situationists in preparing the psychical terrain for exploitation was, of course, greatly appreciated, if not remunerated.

Failing to understand the imaginary competition, which was enlisting and mobilizing immense forces of liberation in the cause of domination, the Situationists also failed to understand how their own efforts would play a useful role in capitalism's processes of self-transformation, creative adaptation, and more successful colonization of all spheres of human existence. They would perform the function of creating momentarily radicalized *transitional subjects* who would play an important role in accelerating the lagging movement from productionist to consumptionist society. Had they paid attention to Marcuse's more dialectical account of the processes of liberation and pseudoliberation, they might have considered the possibility, or rather the inevitability, of dialectical reversals, and would have been able to see the necessity of carrying out a radical negation of the negation.[23] As Marcuse warns, "if there is any way in which the emergence of these possibilities [of liberation] could announce itself prior to the liberation, it would be an increase rather than decrease of repression: restraint of repressive de-sublimation."[24] In other words, there must be a conscious, critical practice of rejection of the forms of desublimation offered by the dominant system, which include many that masquerade as forms of rebellion and liberation. The system of domination already owned "freedom," was in the process of appropriating "liberation" in all its forms, and had more than enough spare change to buy up "libertarianism," if this could help promote the latest advances in ideological mystification.

Lacan said to the insurrectionists of May '68, "What you, as revolutionaries, aspire to is a Master. You will have one."[25] This might seem to be a rather perversely contrarian diagnosis of revolutionaries who were wholly captivated by the final arrival of the long-awaited assault against all gods and masters. But, in fact, Lacan's assessment was quite to the point on the issue of "mastery." As Žižek explains: "We did get one—in the guise of the post-modern 'permissive' master whose domination is all the stronger for being less visible."[26] To put it another way, after an initial moment of reactive revolt, there will either be a radical negation of the negation, or the process will degenerate into a form of regressive negation. There will be a *récuperation* of the negation. We have yet to see the radical negation of the negation. What we have seen instead is the most diabolical of bargains: the exchange of a Master whom we feared and resented for a Master whom we love and desire.[27]

## Whose Spectacle Is It?

As has been discussed, previous social theorists, including most social theorists of the Left, had badly neglected the role of the social imaginary, and Debord deserves recognition for correcting this deficiency through his analysis of the spectacle. But in his extreme spectaclocentrism, he falls into the opposite error of neglecting the role in that system of spheres of determination other than the social imaginary, and even of social imaginaries other than the most dominant one. In his account, the spectacle tends to become a relatively autonomous power over society. In reality, however, the dominant social imaginary is dialectically codetermined by increasingly spectacularized social institutions, social ideology and social ethos, by which is meant, fundamentally, *consumptionist* institutions, ideology, and ethos.[28]

The consumptionist universe is constituted in part by the institutional system of electronic media, including television, radio, film, and now, above all, the internet. It is constituted by the vast ideological system of advertising and marketing. It is constituted by a system of consumptionist spaces, including the mall, the department store, the boutique, the shopping center, and the "plaza."[29] And, we must not underestimate the extent to which it is constituted by the performances of the consumers themselves, through their consumptionist interactions, relationships, gestures, and acts. The late capitalist consuming subject is not a "passive consumer" but rather a highly active, indeed compulsively active, one. Furthermore, there is a constant dialectic between the consumptionist and productionist spheres of social determination, that is, a dialectic of consumptionist and productionist institutional, ideological, imaginary, and ethotic structures. The productionist spheres of determination are neglected in Debord's account, and in fact, do not fit well into his analysis of the highly consumptionist society of the spectacle.

Such complexities of social determination emerge to some degree when Debord distinguishes between the "concentrated," the "diffuse," and the "integrated" spectacle. The first, he says, is "primarily associated with bureaucratic capitalism" but may act as "a technique for reinforcing state power in more backward mixed economies or even adopted by advanced capitalism during certain moments of crisis."[30] The second is "associated with commodity abundance, with the undisturbed development of modern capitalism."[31] The third is a combination of the two but is based on "a general victory of the form which had showed itself stronger: the diffuse. This is the integrated spectacle, which has since tended to impose itself globally."[32] Debord uses the word "spectacle" here to refer to two divergent forms of the social imaginary: the statist/nationalist imaginary, which is largely a productionist phenomenon, and the consumptionist imaginary that he ordinarily associates most with the spectacle.

A fundamental weakness in Debord's analysis is his one-sided focus on the "diffuse spectacle" and its role as the strongly dominant moment of the "integrated" form. Though it is true that the consumptionist imaginary is increasingly dominant in "advanced" capitalist societies, the entire social sphere of consumption depends everywhere on the entire social sphere of production, so the productionist imaginary will always necessarily play an essential social role. Moreover, the statist and nationalist imaginaries in their most explicit forms are strongly resurgent in times of social crisis, above all as soon as war is declared (war being indeed "the health of the state" and also of that institution's legitimating ideology and imaginary). In his focus on the consumptionist imaginary, Debord underestimates the significance of quite powerful forces that constitute a counterspectacle based on nationalism, racism, patriarchy and religious fundamentalism.

These forces have over the last half century proven themselves to be much more tenacious than was predicted by Debord's analysis. This is not surprising, in view of the fact that the system has increasingly operated through policies of constant economic crisis on behalf of rational restructuring and constant low to medium-grade warfare on behalf on global hegemony. As Hegel points out, a healthy dose of traumatically violent shock reverses to a certain degree the tendencies of bourgeois society toward lethargy and complacency and increases the level of authoritarian awe. Such vicissitudes of the system indicate why an adequate social analysis requires a grasp of the complex dialectic between all the spheres and subspheres of social determination. Understanding this dialectic allows us to see how at the very moment at which "all that is solid turns into air," there will be a necessary dialectical countermovement on behalf of solidity, essentiality, and identity.

## The Elusive Community

This is not the only area in which the Situationists' spectaclocentrism leads them astray. One of the most unfortunate legacies of the movement is a reactively negative view of the existing society, which is depicted as hopelessly degraded and eviscerated by the overwhelming powers of the spectacle. In the end, there is nothing positive in the existing social world out of which the new world can grow organically. There must be an absolute break, followed by the creation of a new revolutionary order, which must emerge more or less ex nihilo. For example, Debord claims that "the lack of general historical life also means that individual life as yet has no history," and that consequently, the "individual experience of a disconnected everyday life remains without language, without concepts, and without critical access to its own past, which has nowhere been recorded.

Uncommunicated, misunderstood and forgotten, it is smothered by the spectacle's false memory of the unmemorable."[33] Over a decade later, he was still lamenting the spectacle's almost totalitarian dominance: "There is no place left where people can discuss the realities which concern them, because they can never lastingly free themselves from the crushing presence of media discourse and of the various forces organized to relay it."[34] In passages such as these, Debord seems to take much too literally the old revolutionary motto "We are nothing, we will be all." We are asked to believe that somehow, through the alchemy of revolution, the autonomy and agency of these deracinated, disinherited masses will miraculously expand to infinity.

What is missing in such an analysis is an appreciation not only of what things of great value are lost when society succumbs to forms of domination but, even more importantly, an awareness of what things of great value still endure. Those who are dedicated to the realization of the good society must be moved by a deep concern for both the preservation and the recovery of these realms of historically realized value. However, the Situationists, in their obsession with the devastating effects of the society of the spectacle, have suffered from a lack of attention to the ways in which the society of the nonspectacle always endures.[35] They have (like most of the contemporary Left) neglected the question of what it is that human beings care about most deeply, and aspire to most ardently. We know that it is neither some godlike ability to create ourselves out of nothing nor some Promethean power to master history or nature. Nor is it the late modern fantasy of satisfying infinite desires. What we care about most deeply are the persons, places, and communities that we love, and what we desire most strongly is the *good* of those persons, places and communities, their preservation and flourishing.

This has been the preoccupation of the communitarian anarchist tradition, especially as developed by theorists such as Elisée Reclus[36] and Gustav Landauer,[37] and it is the central focus of the ethics and politics of care that has been most fully developed in ecofeminist thought.[38] The most "directly lived truths" (as Debord sometimes expresses it) for beings who happen to inhabit the Earth are the living truths of being born, of growing and flourishing, of giving birth and nurturing life, of expressing themselves creatively, of sharing their gifts with one another, and of facing decline and death as members of a caring community. These are the truths that have been celebrated, albeit imperfectly and confusedly, across the history of human culture. Yet they do not seem to be at all central to the Situationist sensibility.

Perhaps even more surprisingly, there is little recognition by the Situationists of the subversive and emancipatory and utopian dimensions of historical and present-day popular culture. One would never guess from Debord's account of the "totally colonized world" that there is such a long and living history of subversive folk songs, labor songs and political music, radical poetry, subversive language and slang, people's history, radical and revolutionary stories and legends, dissident rituals, rites, and celebrations.[39] It is in such a culture (which is not merely "prefigurative" but "figurative") that we find that the hoped-for world already exists as (in Durruti's words) "a new world in our hearts." One might wonder whether, for all their radicality, the Situationists really had a new world in their hearts, or whether they could really inspire it in the hearts of others.

What is necessary in order to prepare the way for that world is, beyond all détournement, a radical *retournement*, a turning-around in all the fundamental spheres of social determination—institutional, ideological, imaginary, and ethotic. The ultimate challenge to the empire of illusion is the real of nature, life, and the human spirit as these are expressed in the unfolding powers of the free community. However, the Situationists present a quite different kind of challenge, one that goes in two different directions, both of which have been influential on the left, but neither of which has proven to be very promising.

## The Veritable Split

From the beginning, there were serious contradictions at the core of Situationist thought and practice. There quickly developed a fundamental theoretical and practical division within the movement. It consisted of an increasing polarization between a faction oriented toward the aesthetic, the creative arts, and radical architecture, and which was more continuous with the Surrealist and Lettrist heritage of the Situationists, and a more politically revolutionary and theoretically critical (Debordian) faction. In addition to this internal split, which led to the inevitable expulsion of the aesthetic faction, there was an implicit split between the Situationist elite and the external mass. Though most Situationists would vehemently reject such a formulation, Situationist practice clearly reflected the belief that an aesthetic and intellectual elite could focus on theory, critique, and subversive adventures in détournement, while the masses could somehow be counted on to revolt, sooner or later, catalyzed by revolutionary provocations and détournements, and inspired by the ideology and heroic history of worker councils and base democracy. This dichotomy at the core of the movement resulted in the development of the Situationist legacy in two radically divergent directions. On the one hand, there has been a depoliticizing aestheticization of the Situationist position that draws heavily on its ironic perspective toward the dominant culture. It presents itself as a form of elitist cultural vanguardism but, in reality, consists merely of the superficial trappings of Situationism, transformed by a sterile oppositional culture and by hip academia into a form of radical chic.

This tendency finds inspiration in the early Situationist accounts of the creation of situations. For example, the "Report on the Construction of Situations" describes "the Situationist game" as "taking a stand in favor of what will bring about the future reign of freedom and play,"[40] and "Preliminary Problems in Constructing Situations," explains that until "the collective takeover of the world" there will be "no real individuals," so meanwhile we can "promote the experimental game of revolution" by "raising at a few points the incendiary beacon heralding a greater game."[41] It is not surprising that for later readers who are immersed in the dominant consumer culture and cut off from living radical and revolutionary traditions, this ludic and harmlessly iconoclastic aspect will resonate, while the Situationist political project will fail to register. For these neo-Situationists, a detached aesthetic perspective seems eminently cool while active political engagement leaves them cold.

Neo-Situationist aestheticism goes as far as possible to turn the movement's (at least momentarily) engaged politics of social subversion into a permanent politics of the gesture. It reduces radical critique and détournement to forms of ridiculing the dominant culture. Yet the dominant culture already ridicules itself mercilessly, so this blends easily into late modernity's perpetual recurrence of the same. In the end, the Situationist game becomes a contest for the accumulation of countercultural capital. Along these lines, Critchley depicts a "mannerist Situationism" in which "*détournement* is replayed as obsessively planned re-enactment."[42] He imagines a neo-Situationist performance piece in which "one does not engage in a bank heist: one re-enacts Patty Hearst's adventures with the Symbionese Liberation Army in a warehouse in Brooklyn, or whatever."[43] This is the ultimate postmodern nightmare. Situationism is dissolved into the ubiquitous Whateverism.

But one does not have to resort to imaginary scenarios to depict the way in which Situationism lends itself to trendy co-optation. The paradigm case of assimilation of Situationists into a counterspectacle is Greil Marcus's *Lipstick Traces*, the work that also does the most to glamorize the movement. Marcus typifies the Situationist project as a quest for "absolute freedom," which he calls "the fire around which the dadaists and Debord's strangely fecund groups held their dances, and which consumed them."[44] Delving more deeply into the little-known history of strange fecundity, he explains that it was also "the prize seized by the Cathars, the Brethren of the Free Spirit, the Lollards, John of Leyden, the Ranters, and Adolf Hitler: the end of the world."[45] Finally, Marcus proclaims, in a formulation that is rather contorted even for him, that this prize "can be heard in the words [the Situationists] left behind because of the noise the Sex Pistols made."[46] Yes, it turns out that the fire of absolute freedom burned most intensely in the musical efforts of the Sex Pistols, and, indeed, "far more than it [did] in their precursors' writing."[47] So the Situationists, along with the Dadaists and Medieval millenarians, all become precursors of Sid Vicious and can in a certain sense bask retroactively in his reflected glory. In this way, Marcus dissolves the actual project of the Situationists into a vague essence whose secret history can be traced (at least by the right kind of journalistic cultural historian) from medieval mystical anarchists right down to Hitler and the Sex Pistols.[48]

## The Situationist Urge to Construct

What is most illuminating is not so much the way in which Marcus indiscriminately denatures the Situationist message, but rather the manner in which he quite specifically distorts certain aspects of it. In his view, Debord's claim to pop cultural fame lies above all in the fact that he "glimpsed the secret" of the "ephemeral." Marcus takes as his proof text on this matter the statement in "Report on the Construction of Situations" that "this is our entire program which is essentially transitory. Our situations will be ephemeral, without a future. Passageways."[49] He labels this "Debord's homily to the ephemeral," as it might well seem—assuming that one fails to read the rest of the article, which is largely about the Situationist plan for concerted, nonephemeral collective action.

This early text, which is much more programmatic than later Situationist works, opens with a call to actively challenge the dominant society. "First of all, we think the world must be changed. We want the most liberating change of the society and life in which we find ourselves confined. We know that such a change is possible through appropriate actions."[50] The very section from which Marcus takes his quote is an appeal for the creation of a Situationist International dedicated to long-term struggle for a future society in which all will be able to engage in "the construction of each particular moment in life."[51] Such activity will be "ephemeral" in the specific sense of having *immediate intrinsic value* rather than serving some *external end*. Further, Debord instructs the Situationists that their role is to influence the "critical development" of the program of the "international avant-garde" and to engage "the workers parties" through "effective ideological action in order to combat the emotional influence of advanced capitalist methods of propaganda."[52] As if these organizational demands were not enough, Debord adds that "we must everywhere present a revolutionary alternative to the ruling culture; coordinate all the researches which are currently taking place but which lack a comprehensive perspective; and incite, through critiques and propaganda, the most advanced artists and intellectuals of all countries to contact us in view of a collective action."[53] In short, Debord proposes, in terms that sound much more like a rallying cry than a homily, that the Situationists act as engaged militants with long-term strategic goals. One can hardly imagine the Sex Pistols signing up.

Marcus misses all of this. He claims to have insight into the esoteric secret of fire and ephemerality because of his own inflammatory experience in the Berkeley Free Speech Movement of the 1960s. As he remembers it, the participants "acted not for others but for themselves," and the movement then "completely disappeared, as if it had never been."[54] Based on this experience, he was drawn to Debord's vision of "situations without a future" that "leave nothing behind."[55] For Marcus, it's all about heroic burnout and ephemeral glory. When the fire dies out, "the end of the world" comes to the strangely fecund in many forms: slaughter by the forces of Church and State, blowing their brains out in a bunker, killing their girlfriend and then OD'ing on heroin. Marcus can put up with a lot in the name of ephemeral glory.

However, he ultimately contradicts himself and recognizes that all these movements and episodes that supposedly vanish, "leaving nothing behind," in fact leave quite a lot in their wake. He says that he was drawn to Debord and the Situationists as he "had been drawn to the noise in punk: to his frank and determined embrace of moments in which the world seems to change . . . moments that *leave nothing behind but dissatisfaction, disappointment, rage, sorrow, isolation and vanity."*[56] In other words, they leave behind a rich mother lode of *ressentiment* that can be mined for everything from postadolescent angst to postmodern irony.

In the end, this depiction expresses perfectly the reduction of Situationism to a form of reactive critique inspired by disillusionment with the world. As Gray asks pertinently of the Situationists at the opening of *Leaving the 20th Century*, "How could you feel such disgust with everything?"[57] Even more pertinently, what might you *do* if you feel such all-encompassing disgust? As Marcus's account suggests, you might form a nihilistic punk bank or join a neo-Nazi cult. Or, if you're literate and have a good sense of irony, you might become something like a Situationist.

## The Phantom of Insurrection

But the Situationist legacy lives on not only in the museum of cultural critique but also in the form of a neo-Situationist insurrectional tendency. In France, it has continued to shape radical politics through its influence on Tiqqun and the Invisible Committee. In the United States, the widely read student strike text "Communiqué from an Absent Future"[58] echoes the radical critique of Khayati's *On the Poverty of Student Life*. And CrimethInc., which has been a significant radicalizing force for young anarchists throughout the English-speaking world, would be unthIncable without the Situationists.[59]

*The Coming Insurrection* is the work that best represents this post-Situationist insurrectionist tendency.[60] It conveys more than anything that has appeared in many years the mood of excitement and expectation that was triggered by the early Situationist texts and is, in fact, a very hopeful sign in many ways. Arising out of a leftist culture in which denial and disavowal are endemic, it expresses a sense of possibility, the intimation that there is indeed still something *to come*. Furthermore, those who look to a resurgence of transformative affinity groups and base communities as a major step in the reemergence of radical and revolutionary politics can only be encouraged by the work's defense of such forms against all the worn-out and debilitating standard options of the mainstream Left. The text is noteworthy for expressing a certain energy of negation, in the name of which the Invisible Committee seems willing to tear apart, with the most noble savagery, all the fetishes of the Left. In reality, however, it is not quite willing to take on *all* of them, for it unfortunately perpetuates certain fetishisms of revolutionary action and organization that must be subjected to an equally ruthless critique. There is a need for an additional critical step that allows one to move from the invisibility of committees to the visibility of communities of liberation and solidarity.

Critchley offers some very astute insights into the achievements and failings of *The Coming Insurrection*. He observes that it is "a compelling, exhilarating and deeply lyrical text that sets off all sorts of historical echoes with movements like the Free Spirit: the emphases on secrecy, invisibility and itinerancy, on small-scale communal experiments in living, on the cultivation of poverty, radical mendicancy and the refusal of work."[61] But he warns that "the double programme of sabotage, on the one hand, and secession from civilization, on the other, risks remaining trapped within *the politics of abstraction*," and that "in this fascinatingly creative re-enactment of the Situationist gesture, what is missed is a thinking of political mediation where groups like the Invisible Committee would be able to link up and become concretized in relation to multiple and conflicting sites of struggle."[62] What needs to be added to this diagnosis is that in order to get fully beyond the Left's vicious cycle of struggle and reactivity, these "sites of struggle" must also be sites of social creativity, mutual aid, interdependence, and communal and ecological regeneration.

As Critchley intimates, one finds here, as for the Situationists, an absence of ethical substantiality, that is, a lack of situatedness in existing communities, institutions, and practices. For the Invisible Committee, "we have been completely torn from any belonging, we are no longer from anywhere," for "our history is one of colonizations, of migrations, of wars, of exiles, of the destruction of all roots."[63] What is most disturbing in this outlook is that it defies real history. In fact, social struggle today often arises out of a context not of *an absence of belonging*, but out of *a conflict of belongings*. One ignores at great peril the fact that masses of people around the world, and especially young people, are desperate to hold on to or to recover roots, whether real or imaginary, and they desire intensely to draw on those roots for sustenance in the face of severe social disruptions. Sometimes they find authentic roots (for contrary to the Invisible Committee, these have not in fact been entirely destroyed or torn away), but quite often they instead find manufactured and manipulated ones designed for more immediate and superficial consumption. In either case, it is overwhelmingly the right and regressive forces that benefit from roots and belongings that many on the left either simply deny or struggle to imagine away.

The Invisible Committee, rather than searching for a living history of liberatory and solidaristic practices and traditions, contends that "the decomposition of all social forms is a blessing," and is, indeed, "the ideal condition for a wild, massive experimentation with new arrangements, new fidelities."[64] As in the case of the Situationists, we find unrealistic expectations that, given the disintegration of the dominant institutions, sensational actions can be the catalyst for vast processes of liberatory social transformation. The Invisible Committee mentions strategies such as "knocking out" electrical stations, shutting down universities, blocking ports, and concludes that "with ten thousand people, the largest economic power in the world can be brought to its knees."[65] But what precisely does this dramatic turn of phrase mean?

We find that the actual result that the Invisible Committee imagines is the triggering of an economic recession. But we know that this cannot in itself bring down the capitalist system. That system has long been familiar with the business cycle and knows how to make use of it for its own purposes. Even severe recessions cannot be counted on to weaken it. In one historical context, a deep recession might be an opportunity for the system to undertake economic restructuring and to experiment with new methods of economic exploitation (such as those that came to be known as "disaster capitalism"). In another historical context, it might signal the opportunity for a transformative social movement to enact fundamental changes, given that it has gone through a long, painstaking process of critical self-formation. Certainly, without such preparation the results of crisis will ordinarily be reactionary, in one form or another. The point is that the kind of disruptive activities mentioned by the Invisible Committee are tactics to be assessed in very specific historical context, and to inflate them into universal strategies for social transformation is to lapse into abstract insurrectionary idealism.

## Communes Everywhere!

There is the hint of a real positive moment in the text when the Invisible Committee asks, "Why shouldn't communes proliferate everywhere? In every factory, every street, every village, every school. At long last, the reign of the base committees!"[66] But when the nature of the commune is described, it turns out to be something less communal and even less substantial than the workplace and neighborhood assemblies that the Situationists imagined. "A commune," they say, "forms every time a few people, freed of their individual straitjackets, decide to rely only on themselves and measure their strength against reality. Every wildcat strike is a commune; every building occupied collectively and on a clear basis is a commune, etc."[67] The commune is thus reduced to something like the temporary autonomous zone, an organizational form that can be of considerable value, just as the Situationist dérive can be an important liberatory experience. However, to be realistic, no such forms can in themselves go very far in creating the free society, unless they are part of a wide-ranging movement for social transformation that confronts all the basic spheres of social determination.[68]

Any movement for social transformation must consider carefully what forms of communal organization and activity are most likely to make possible significant liberatory change in a time of crisis. The insurrectionist tendency opts for tactics such as petty theft and illegality, marginal economic activity, and sabotage. According to the Invisible Committee, "all communes have their black markets" and that "aside from welfare, there are various benefits, disability money, accumulated student aid, subsidies drawn off fictitious childbirths, all kinds of trafficking, and so many other means that arise with every mutation of control."[69] It concludes that "the important thing is to cultivate and spread this necessary disposition towards fraud, and to share its innovations."[70]

It is essential for a community to ask itself constantly, "What is *the important thing?*" since the very definition of *the important thing* is "that which is systematically forgotten." However, it seems doubtful whether this is it. Perhaps the important thing for a community, or a commune, is to develop a moment-to-moment engaged consciousness of the nature of communal activity. Such consciousness might lead us to consider the dangers of dependence on either the statist-bureaucratic sphere of legality or the complementary sphere of illegality that the state creates as its malignant other. Even assuming that the liberation movement doesn't disappear into the black holes of narcotrafficking or slackerism, neither petty crime nor the dole is the royal road to the creation of the all-encompassing solidarity economy that both human and ecological communities need so desperately.

In the end, the Invisible Committee opts, not surprisingly, for a kind of invisibility. However, there are two ironic dialectical reversals entailed by this option. First, as the Invisible Committee states, this option is the result of "the conditions of the asymmetrical conflict which has been imposed on us."[71] Thus, it is a mode of activity that is to a great extent reactive, and is therefore, to a degree that the Invisible Committee refuses to admit, a form of nonactivity. It is true, as the Committee contends, that "the demonstration, the action with our faces unmasked, the indignant protest" results in reinforcing the system of domination by "feeding up-to-date information into the systems of control."[72] However, the reactive tactics that the Committee proposes, "anonymous sabotage, unclaimed actions, recourse to easily copied techniques, targeted counterattacks,"[73] also quite obviously reinforce the system of domination, given that system's hegemonic control of ideological and imaginary spheres of social determination.

This leads to a second dialectical reversal that the Invisible Committee fails to consider. Invisibility is only a certain mode of being visible. In reality, it opts not for absolute invisibility (which would mean literal or metaphorical suicide) but for an invisibility that is identical to visibility through sabotage, visibility through anonymous actions, visibility through whatever techniques, visibility through counterattacks, and, above all, visibility through controversial and widely discussed texts in which this manifest invisibility is explained and defended. The strategy of being visible primarily through texts and marginally subversive acts has often been tried and seems to have very limited transformative impact. A socially regenerative movement has a need for widely accessible visibility on the grassroots level in order to create the means for a broad-based solidarity. Indeed, it needs to be both strikingly visible and strikingly audible, if it is going to capture the imagination of a society in need of a transformative vision, and it needs to be intensely tactile in order to minister to the needs of the community. On the other hand, a movement that is largely invisible and generally imperceptible to the communities with which it seeks to establish bonds of solidarity, while at the same time remaining quite visible to an anonymous public via the dominant media, has become lost in the spectacle.[74]

## What Remains

The Situationist and Situationist-influenced texts offer certain indispensable lessons to those who hope either to understand the contemporary world or to change it. As resounding calls for radical negation and uncompromising critique, they possess an energy and imaginary force to which most of the contemporary left cannot even begin to aspire. They have inestimable value for their capacity to traumatize, to destabilize, to shake off the paralysis of the everyday, and to inspire. The Situationists and some of their successors have had the ability to inspire dissidents to break decisively with the dominant culture, to engage with that culture on the terrain of the imaginary, and to create in the process a distinctive oppositional milieu.

However, the greatest weaknesses of the Situationists have been related precisely to these strengths. In many ways, the movement became lost in its own negative moment of critical ironic distance. It opened itself up to marginalization, aestheticization, and self-absorbed adventurism: in short, to forms of false negativity. In the end, the desperately needed positive moment of engagement in processes of social and ecological regeneration was simply missing in any meaningful sense. In the place of such an authentic positive moment, one finds a false positivity, a fantasy of insurrectionary overturn that is ungrounded in historical materiality.

A community makes itself into a transformative subject through the deep evolutionary processes of organizing its own life, practicing communal solidarity, and fostering in each participant a communitarian personhood. In these processes, each moment is the decisive moment, the liberatory moment, the moment of communization. The vast majority of these moments can hardly be subsumed under the rubric of "revolutionary struggles," as the Western Left has imagined them. In both the beginning and in the end, our fidelity must be to the person and the community, not to the heroic event, and certainly not to heroic critique. If the most essential aspects of personal and communal transformation have not taken place before the revolutionary or insurrectionary moment, then the social transformation that takes place at that moment will be at best only superficial and fleeting.

## NOTES

1   Guy Debord, *The Society of the Spectacle*, trans. Ken Knabb (Berkeley: Bureau of Public Secrets, 2014). Citations of the work below refer to this translation and to the work's 221 numbered theses.
2   A term the Situationists rejected, claiming implausibly and clearly contrary to their practice, to be *ists* without an *ism*.
3   "On the Poverty of Student Life Considered in Its Economic, Political, Psychological, Sexual, and Especially Intellectual Aspects, with a Modest Proposal for Doing Away with It," in Ken Knabb, ed. *Situationist International Anthology* (Berkeley: Bureau of Public Secrets, 2007), 408–29. Knabb's anthology and his website Bureau of Public Secrets (http://www.bopsecrets.org/) are the most valuable sources for primary works of the Situationists.

4    "Report on the Construction of Situations," in Knabb, *Situationist International Anthology*, 38.
5    Guy Debord, "Introduction to a Critique of Urban Geography (1955)," in Knabb, *Situationist International Anthology*, 8.
6    *Internationale Situationniste* no. 1 (June 1958), in Knabb, 52.
7    "The Beginning of an Era," in Knabb, 288 (italics in original).
8    Knabb, 288 (italics in original).
9    Knabb, 289.
10   I was a member of a strongly post-Situationist group (the "Black Pearl Mutual Aid and Pleasure Club") in the 1970s, and I remain influenced by the movement in significant ways. Many of the points made in this analysis arise in part out of a process of self-critique, but also from the recognition of a moment of profound truth in the Situationist critique of late capitalist society.
11   Christopher Gray, *Leaving the 20th Century: The Incomplete Work of the Situationist International* (London: Free Fall Publications, 1964), 165.
12   Knabb, *Situationist International Anthology* should be consulted for the key texts.
13   Cornelius Castoriadis developed these ideas extensively over several decades, for example in "Workers' Councils and the Economics of a Self-Managed Society," originally published in the journal *Socialisme ou Barbarie* in 1957; translation online at https://www.marxists.org/archive/castoriadis/1972/workers-councils.htm#h24.
14   "The Beginning of an Era," in Knabb, *Situationist International Anthology*, 322–23.
15   "Preliminaries on Councils and Councilist Organization," in Knabb, 360.
16   "Notice to the Civilized Concerning Generalized Self-Management," in Knabb, 370.
17   Raoul Vaneigem, *The Revolution of Everyday Life*, revised ed. (Oakland: PM Press, 2012), 11.
18   Vaneigem, *Revolution of Everyday Life*, 105.
19   Vaneigem, 105.
20   Vaneigem, 242.
21   See "The Conquest of the Unhappy Consciousness: Repressive Desublimation," in *One-Dimensional Man: Studies in the Ideology of Advanced Industrial Society* (Boston: Beacon Press, 1964), 56–83, and "Preface to the Vintage Edition," in *Eros and Civilization: A Philosophical Inquiry into Freud* (New York: Vintage Books, 1962), vii–xi.
22   Marcuse, *One Dimensional Man*, 77.
23   This problematic always seems like news to much of the Left. Yet Marx explained it clearly over a century and a half ago in his discussion of "crude communism," a rudimentary form that bears all the marks of being a reaction to the system that it opposed, and which is therefore deeply conditioned by that system. The negation of the negation would be the negation of this reactive moment and would allow communism to unfold on its own terms.
24   Marcuse, *Eros and Civilization*, x.
25   Jacques Lacan, *Television* (Cambridge, MA: MIT Press, 1980), 126.
26   Slavoj Žižek, "The Ambiguous Legacy of '68," *In These Times*, June 20, 2008, http://inthesetimes.com/article/3751/the_ambiguous_legacy_of_68.

27  Fear and resentment are not dissolved but rather deferred and displaced. They succeed in finding suitable objects, resulting in a new mass psychology of fascism.

28  In the analysis of social phenomena, I make use of a theory of the dialectical interaction of these four major spheres of social determination. This framework is elaborated briefly in *The Impossible Community: Realizing Communitarian Anarchism* (New York: Bloomberg Academic, 2013), 32–37.

29  The term embodies the cultural evolution of capitalist society. Once designating a public square, it can now refer to the most squalid, run-down strip mall.

30  *Society of the Spectacle*, thesis 64.

31  *Society of the Spectacle*, thesis 65.

32  Guy Debord, *Comments on the Society of the Spectacle* (London: Verso, 1990), 8.

33  *Society of the Spectacle*, thesis 157.

34  Debord, *Comments*, 19.

35  This is one way in which Situationism has been a serious regression from Surrealism.

36  See John Clark and Camille Martin, eds. *Anarchy, Geography, Modernity: Essential Writings of Elisée Reclus* (Oakland: PM Press, 2013), in addition to chapters 2 and 3 in this volume.

37  Gustav Landauer, *Revolution and Other Writings: A Political Reader*, Gabriel Kuhn, ed. (Oakland: PM Press, 2010).

38  Once again, for a classic statement of the significance of the caring labor of women and indigenous peoples, see Ariel Salleh, *Ecofeminism as Politics* (London: Zed Books, 2017).

39  This is the theme of the final chapter of this book and its analysis of the interstitial and the antistitial.

40  "Report on the Construction of Situations," in *Situationist International Anthology*, 39.

41  "Report on the Construction of Situations," 50.

42  Simon Critchley, "Mystical Anarchism," *Critical Horizons: A Journal of Philosophy and Social Theory* 10, no. 2 (August 2009): 301.

43  Critchley, "Mystical Anarchism," 301.

44  Greil Marcus, *Lipstick Traces: A Secret History of the Twentieth Century* (Cambridge, MA: Harvard University Press), 443. A play on the references to fire and consumption in Debord's favorite palindrome, "In girum imus nocte et consumimur igni."

45  Marcus, *Lipstick Traces*, 443.

46  Marcus, 443.

47  Marcus, 443.

48  Sadly, they never had the chance to get together to form an actual group called "Hitler and the Sex Pistols."

49  "Report on the Construction of Situations," in Knabb, *Situationist International Anthology*, 41.

50  Knabb, 25.

51  Knabb, 42.

52  Knabb, 42.

53  Knabb, 43.

54   Marcus, *Lipstick Traces*, 445. The best-known figure in the movement was Mario Savio, who had worked as a civil rights volunteer in Mississippi, where he was beaten for "acting for others." He spoke the most famous and enduring words in the history of the Free Speech Movement: "There is a time when the operation of the machine becomes so odious, makes you so sick at heart, that you can't take part; you can't even passively take part, and you've got to put your bodies upon the gears and upon the wheels, upon the levers, upon all the apparatus, and you've got to make it stop" (http://www.lib.berkeley.edu/MRC/saviotranscript.html). This was hardly a call to put self-regarding actions above concern for others.

55   Marcus, 445.

56   Marcus, 446. Italics added to indicate dropping of jaw.

57   Gray, *Leaving the 20th Century*, 1.

58   Research and Destroy, "Communiqué from an Absent Future: On the Terminus of Student Life," 2009, http://wewanteverything.files.wordpress.com/2009/10/communique.pdf.

59   See the group's classic work, *Days of War, Nights of Love* (Atlanta: CrimethInc. Free Press, 2001).

60   Invisible Committee, *The Coming Insurrection* (Los Angeles: Semiotexte, 2009), http://tarnac9.files.wordpress.com/2009/04/thecominsur_booklet.pdf. Despite distinct theoretical influences of Foucault, Agamben, and others, the overall flavor of the work is unmistakably Situationist.

61   Critchley, "Mystical Anarchism," 303.

62   Critchley, 303.

63   The Invisible Committee, *The Coming Insurrection*, 22.

64   *The Coming Insurrection*, 26.

65   *The Coming Insurrection*, 40.

66   *The Coming Insurrection*, 67.

67   *The Coming Insurrection*, 68.

68   Note that the author of *T.A.Z.*, Peter Lamborn Wilson, has also written about "Permanent Autonomous Zones" and addresses the nature of such a transformative movement in Rojava, as cited in chapter 6 above.

69   *The Coming Insurrection*, 69.

70   *The Coming Insurrection*, 69.

71   The Invisible Committee, "The Call" (Chapel Hill, NC: Institute for Experimental Freedom, 2007), Scolium to Proposition V. The Invisible Committee shows signs of transcending its position through the development of what is implicit in that position. It is stated at the end of *The Coming Insurrection*: "What's essential is that action assume a certain form, that it give rise to a form instead of having one imposed on it. This presupposes a shared political and geographical position" (82). It needs to investigate the complex preconditions for "giving rise to a form," and the complex conditions of "geographical position."

72   "The Call."

73   "The Call."

74   This analysis refers only to the Invisible Committee of *The Coming Insurrection*. The Invisible Committee of *To Our Friends*, or more precisely, of the last two chapters of *To Our Friends* (South Pasadena, CA: Semiotexte, 2015) is a quite different matter. To co-opt a hackneyed term from contemporary media, the

Optics of Invisibility seem to have changed. Around the middle of chapter six it seems that either some kind of epiphany has occurred or else some more perceptive Committee members have taken over. In the last two chapters we discover a quite astute and visionary defense of the commune as the embodiment of universal particularity and of the radical dimensions of place. We find that "places are irreducibly loaded—with stories, impressions, emotions" and that "a commune engages the world from its own place" (201). The bioregional concept of reinhabitation is echoed by the view that "to inhabit is to write to each other, to tell one's stories from a grounded place" (203). We are told that the commune, to avoid the pitfalls of narrow localism, must "give some consistency to a territorial reality at odds with the 'general order,'" and "give rise to, establish links between local consistencies" (205). The Committee astutely warns that the solidarity economy and "cooperativist and mutualist ideologies" are a trap if they are devised as "an alternative to struggle, an alternative *to the commune*" (211). It cautions further that the object of the commune must not be "productions and needs" but rather "the desire for a shared life" (216). A more radical and dialectical conception of needs and production is possible, but the impulse here is correct. The Committee evokes the image of a shared power that is "invulnerable" because of "the joy that haloes each moment" and, echoing Landauer, of participation "in a spirit, a force, a richness shared in common" (218). And to cite only one more of many intriguing passages, it converges with ideas mentioned above such as "being-toward-birth" (134) and "dialectical maternalism" (204) in its affirmation that "*the commune is the organization of fertility,*" and that it "always gives rise to more than it lays claim to" (219). In these concluding chapters, the Committee achieves an admirable degree of translucence.

18

# Happy Birthday, Utopia!
# (You Deserve a Present)

We recently saw the five-hundredth anniversary of the appearance of *Utopia*, the classic work of English social philosopher, author, statesman, and Renaissance humanist Thomas More. It is just over five hundred years since Machiavelli's *The Prince*, the definitive *anti*-utopia, was published. We might say that the entire modern age has been a struggle between these two alternatives of utopia and anti-utopia. Even more, it is a struggle between utopia and the dystopia that is at the heart of the dominant utopia. This is perhaps an appropriate point, after half a millennium of utopian and anti-utopian speculation, to think about the fate of utopia.

The corporate-state apparatus and the dominant political culture that supports it have certainly been concerned with the idea of utopia.[1] In fact, they have been obsessed with it. This obsession has had both positive and negative dimensions. On the one hand, the corporate-state order has vigorously promoted its own vision of the technological utopia and the utopia of mass consumption. On the other hand, it has combated authentic, radical utopianism materially through surveillance, harassment, violence, and persecution and has fought it ideologically through a campaign to equate liberatory utopianism with the Gulag and totalitarian mass murder.

We have arrived at a point in history at which the quest for utopia has become a quasi-monopoly in the hands of corporations and the state, while liberatory utopianism has atrophied. This should not be a surprise. Whoever controls the imagination controls utopia, and the American Corporate State (that is, the U.S. government in alliance with U.S business) has been rather successful in creating the dominant social imaginary. Let's examine the positive side of the negative first, and then look at the negative side of the positive. On the macroutopian level, the Corporate

State has long promoted the idea of "America" as the utopian national community. On the microutopian level, it first idealized the small town as the human-scale utopia of nostalgia. Later, it increasingly relegated this ideal to the Wonderful World of Disney, while instead exalting Suburbia as the Überurbia, the ultimate utopian object of the fantasy called the "American Dream."

Suburban Utopia itself has been much more than a dream. It has been a massive social engineering project in the realm of material social reality. Government economic policies and tax laws after World War II promoted a suburban construction boom, the abandonment of the cities by the white middle class, and the building of a transcontinental superhighway system touted as "second to none" (though now deteriorating faster than most) to facilitate suburban sprawl. Since the 1950s, huge quantities of public money have been poured into support for the Suburban Utopia and the high-consumption suburbanite utopian lifestyle. At the same time, popular culture—through the mass media, and especially the long hegemonic television—socialized the public into the ideology of Suburban Utopianism.

Of course, we no longer live in the world of the 1950s and early '60s. The dominant utopia no longer seems quite as utopian as it once did. The golden image of Suburbia that compelled us to abandon great cities and traditional communities and consign them to rot and rust still retains some of its allure, but it has itself become badly tarnished over the last half century. The gated community has inherited much of the utopian mantle as real wages have stagnated for decades. The Gates of Heaven seem open to fewer than was once promised. China once had the Forbidden City. America now has the Forbidden Subdivision. The form of Ascension into Heaven called "Upward Mobility" seems increasingly mythological for most of the population.

This has been the ambiguous fate of the official American utopian vision in recent decades. But what of its dialectical opposite for much of the period in question? Russian imperial state capitalism created its own utopian community, the Stalinist collective farm. This workers' paradise within the larger paradise of the deified and deformed Workers' State was idealized in public speeches, in the press, in popular art, and in film epics. Just as American media depicted the happy suburban nuclear families of classic TV's *Father Knows Best, Ozzie and Harriet, The Brady Bunch,* etc., Stalinist media depicted ecstatic peasant families down on the collective farm. A major difference was that these Russian productionist utopians were more likely to be engaged in blissful utopian labor, while their American consumptionist counterparts concentrated on domestic euphoria, perhaps occasionally dabbling in hobbies.

The major commonality was that in both cases the ideological and imaginary apparatuses depicted the attainment of a utopian realm of freedom, and in both cases, the state helped create the material basis for this ideological and imaginary achievement. Both the so-called democratic state and the so-called Soviet state diverted massive resources into creating and sustaining their respective utopian communities and passed on huge costs to others. In the Western model, the Free World (that is, the dominating world) found it necessary to subject the rest of the world to brutal neocolonial conquest to sustain its high-consumption lifestyle grounded in the dream of Suburban Utopia, while in the Stalinist model, the Workers' State felt obliged to go so far as to consign those workers who resisted their Paradise to life in the Gulag, if not to mass starvation.

## The New Corporate Utopia

If the Stalinist Utopia is long dead and the Suburban Utopia moribund, there is one area in which radical utopianism is thriving today. This is the realm of the American Corporate Utopia. Check out popular journalism, and business news in particular, and you'll find usually wide-eyed (though occasionally cynical) depictions of the utopian creations of companies like Amazon, Apple, Google, and Zappos. Amazon's headquarters in Seattle have been labeled the "ultimate tech utopia." Google's new base of operations has been called a "glass utopia." Apple's headquarters have also been described in utopian terms, and Facebook's huge compound with vast gardens and open spaces has been depicted as a utopian "fantasyland."

Zappos is in some ways the most striking example. The company's CEO claims that he has been hooked on utopianism since the first time he went to a warehouse rave and got swallowed up in a kind of group mind. Apparently, the group mind instructed him to invest a huge amount of money, not only to build a utopian corporate headquarters in Las Vegas but also to create a business development zone around it that has been called a "startup utopia." In honor of this most extreme case, we might call the whole class of corporate utopian revolutionaries the "Zappo-tistas."

The monumental corporate headquarters created by the entrepreneurial utopian dreamers are the new billion-dollar incarnations of the American economistic utopia. In this case, the corporate-state apparatus acts primarily through its corporate dimension, in the form of prodigious sums invested in the headquarters itself and in the radical transformation of the surrounding neighborhoods, towns, and cities. But the statist dimension is always present in the form of tax rebates, subsidies, favorable zoning laws, planning collaboration, and of course the statist sine qua non of police protection locally and military protection globally.

The end product of this corporate-state symbiosis is the ultimate embodiment of the Capitalist Sublime, in which ethos and imaginary combine to overawe the spectator. The implicit message is that "Capital is great, you are small," and that if you identify with capital, some of its utopian greatness will rub off on you. Imperial CEOs have at their command architectural geniuses, armies of planners, limitless bank accounts, compliant host communities, and the best PR apparatuses their megabucks can buy. The result is an extraordinary achievement of the capitalist imagination in which beauty is reconciled with utility, work with play, and private life with public. As in the case of the small, intimate intentional communities of the past, these mega-utopias put the highest priority (at least in mission statements and press releases) on "personal growth" and "self-realization." And also like many traditional utopias, they try to create a self-contained sphere of life and work that is to a degree separate from and superior to the outside world.

## Fear of Utopia

The second side of corporate-state concern with utopian communities is a negative, and often malignantly negative, one. This concern has been directed toward communities that have broken with the prevailing system of domination and have challenged it overtly. While some radical utopian communities in the past benefited from a benign neglect, government officials and agencies have increasingly confronted them through infiltration, surveillance, and raids. They have been the focus of such attention because they have often been seen by the authorities as a threat to security, law and order, and, indeed, the entire "American Way of Life." This has been true especially when the general level of conflict in society has been high, and when there has been a marked clash between the values and practices of the communities and those of surrounding areas that are highly repressive and conservative.

Ronald Creagh's *Utopies américaines* (*American Utopias*) is the definitive work on libertarian (that is, anarchist) communities in the United

States.[2] In the original title of the book, he called these communities "Laboratories of Utopia" to stress the creative, experiential, and experimental nature of these projects. One of the striking things he shows about such communities in the nineteenth and early twentieth centuries is their ability to find places to carry out their experiments relatively free of persecution and intimidation by the state and by local reactionary and repressive cultures. One of the largest and most successful utopian communities (and which defined itself as socialist, not anarchist) started as the Llano del Rio community in California and later established itself as New Llano on thousands of acres in rural west-central Louisiana. This community, which had nearly a thousand members, and ten thousand people living there at some time during its history, not only escaped persecution but had excellent relations with the surrounding neighbors.[3] However, such a condition of relative immunity has been far from universal.

*West of Eden* is a diverse collection of essays on West Coast intentional communities.[4] It quotes FBI documents recounting its surveillance activities of these communities, which it considered to be, in its own words, "a menace to society," and a source of violent and revolutionary activities. FBI reports are often useful for ascertaining details of the history of communitarian projects, since agents often keep lists and describe things in detail that others may have neglected to note. However, one must be careful, since these reports may be wildly erroneous. In one of the more fascinating chapters of the book, the author cites an FBI report that observed with alarm that a radio transmitter and antenna had been installed at a certain commune, presumably to coordinate insurrectionary activities. But these suspicious apparatuses turned out to be nothing more than a washing machine and a clothesline, observed from afar with binoculars and an overheated imagination. The irony is delicious. Not only were the hippies not sending out conspiratorial messages, but they didn't even live up to their stereotype of being dirty.

This illuminating collection is unusual among histories of communities in that it includes the Black Panthers' grassroots organization in Oakland as an important example of communalism.[5] It documents the Panthers' efforts in collective housing, child care, and schooling, in addition to their work in food and medical programs. Needless to say, the state had a huge interest in the Panthers' utopian experiment. Agents went to great lengths to spy on it, infiltrate it, and attempt to destroy it. Claims of such activities are more than mere speculation. FBI documents that were long ago made public show that as part of the COINTELPRO dirty tricks program to disrupt radicalism and the New Left, radical political communes were specifically targeted, including those of the Panthers.

Perhaps the most infamous example of the state's assault on radical intentional communities was its murderous attack on the MOVE community. MOVE was a kind of anarcho-primitivist, black liberationist group in Philadelphia. Ongoing conflicts with the police resulted not only in attacks on individuals but in collective punishment and, indeed, lethal collective punishment, of the entire community. The police dropped a bomb on the commune, which was located in a row house in a crowded neighborhood, killing eleven MOVE members, including five children. The fire destroyed the MOVE house and over sixty other buildings in the neighborhood. In view of the state's treatment of the Panthers and MOVE, one can only conclude that it has had a particularly strong interest in meting out the severest penalties possible to those guilty of the crime of "being utopian while black."

## Primal Utopias

This kind of punitive and vindictive response to utopian communities goes back to the beginnings of the history of Empire on the continent. When the colonists first arrived, they assumed that they could conquer and appropriate everything, because the entire continent was considered "Terra Nullius," that is, effectually empty, because it was no one's legal, state-sanctioned property. We should think about the connection between the concept of Terra Nullius, the "land of no one," and Utopia, the "land of nowhere." Indigenous land was thought to contain nobody and be nowhere, until Empire could conquer it and bring it within the dominant imperial imaginary. Indigenous communities were the original Impossible Communities on the continent, because they escaped the categories of the dominant imaginary, the categories that defined the parameters of possibility. They were epistemic impossibilities, part of the irrational, incoherent, unknowable realm of wildness.

This concept was expressed in William Bradford's famous description of America as "a hideous and desolate wilderness" that was "full of wild beasts and wild men." It allowed Hobbes to say in *Leviathan*, the great apology for subjection to the State, that if anyone wanted to know where they could find a life that existed outside the social contract and remained "solitary, poor, nasty, brutish, and short," it was among the supposedly "solitary" and asocial savages of America. This is what led Bradford's people to build what they and every patriotic demagogue since has called "A City on the Hill." They have had in mind the image of such a City as the utopian paradigm for all of civilized humanity. However, we can instead read into this imperialist image the idea of a fortress, a Citadel on the Hill, that looks down on conquered territory, a vantage point of superiority from which the conquerors can survey their domain.

The irony is that not only was this wild land a land of someone (a communal *topos*), but it was also a *eutopia*—a "good place" in the only meaningful sense of this term, that is, a place in which both human beings and other beings can flourish. The Empire has always had a strong interest in such eutopian utopias. Its immediate interest has been in preventing its subjects from learning about and defecting to these dangerously practical utopias or using them as a model for what is possible. Its ultimate interest has been in annihilating them. In short, the state's special interest in the original utopian eco-communities that predated Empire can be summarized in one word: utopicide.

## The Utopia of Oblivion

Fifty years ago, the American visionary designer and futurist Buckminster Fuller posed the alternative of "Utopia or Oblivion." Today, more than ever, we are capable of understanding the full meaning of this dilemma. Only utopia can prevent oblivion. But a certain kind of utopia is also the cause of oblivion. Unfortunately, the utopia of oblivion is the dominant one today. Mussolini said that the twentieth century was the century of the state. In fact, it turned out to be the century of the corporate state and the corporate state utopia. Its corporate moment spawned the post–World War II Suburban Utopia that mutated into the end of the century gated community. Its statist side had already come to rotten fruition in the Workers' Paradise of the Stalinist collective farm that now lives on only in certain vodka-fueled bouts of Cold War nostalgia.

Today, we're faced with the dominance of late capitalist pseudo-topias and pseudo-utopias, spaces that fake place and fake goodness. They are the spaces of economistic, bureaucratic, and technocratic domination. They are the spaces in which the imitation of life replaces life, and a simulacrum of society devours community. They are the spaces in which nihilism, the loss of faith in life and community, is internalized so completely that those who rebel against the ruling version of utopia can only do so through a reactive nihilism.

One must wonder where the liberatory utopian communitarian impulse is today. Where is the creative spirit of community? Our problem is that the spirit of *Nowhere* seems to be nowhere (if one follows the dominant means of communication of seeming). Even worse, the spirit of *Where* seems to be nowhere. The dominant system has an almost absolute monopoly on materialist, real-world utopia, while the Left, at least since the dissolution of the Stalinist Workers' Paradise, specializes in idealist utopia. One side constructs actually existing pseudo-utopias and inundates the masses with hyperutopian propaganda, while the other propagates the edifying thought that "another topos is possible." To paraphrase the White Queen, "Utopia tomorrow, utopia yesterday, but never utopia today." Utopia deserves a present.

### What Are We Waiting For?

Marx posed an excellent question: "Who will educate the educators?" But he never found an excellent answer. He is not alone. Communitarian anarchists haven't found convincing answers to questions like "Who will anarchize the anarchists," and "Who will communize the communists? ("Answers" mean "doing it.") Charisma (what makes us love what we love) is still with capitalism. How can we co-opt charisma? How can we create the charismatic community, that is, the free community as the object of collective utopian desire, the community that lies at the heart of each person's fundamental fantasy?

We might reflect on the fact that after a century and a half of anarchist communalism, there is not a single anarchist intentional community of ten thousand people, or five thousand, or even a thousand, in which mutual aid and voluntary federation are embodied in everyday life. We claim that people can organize themselves into free and cooperative communities of communities, yet we do not have functioning examples.

It would be a lie to claim that the state or capitalism forbids us to establish them, whatever obstacles they may create. We forbid ourselves. Maybe we should just concede utopia to the corporations and openly declare ourselves the utopian Zappotistas. We've been Zapped. It's no accident that "Just do it!" is a corporate slogan, symbolizing corporate victory in the realm of action. For the most part, we "just do it" for them, and we just think about doing it for ourselves.

What we urgently need are realized communities of liberation and solidarity that are also communities of awakening and care. Such utopian communities are "impossible communities" because they are outside the bounds of the dominant institutional structures, the dominant social ideology, the dominant social imaginary, and the dominant social ethos. They become possible when they become actual. They find inspiration in the many impossible communities that are or have been actual. There are many encouraging examples throughout the history of indigenous communities, maroon communities, and intentional communities. They become possible through the process of creating, *here and now*, a new social institutional structure, a new counter-ideology or worldview, a new social imaginary, and a new social ethos.

We realize utopia by becoming citizens of utopia.

## A Topian Utopia

The true citizens of utopia are awakened beings. ("Where y'at?" is the most revolutionary question in history). They are awakened to their own experience, to the living reality of all beings around them, to the life of the human community, to the life of community of nature. They are *topian* utopians. They renounce the abstract, alienated and totally insane world we call normal everyday life, and dwell instead in the rich, dense, exquisite and astounding life-world, the world of Where We Are. This is a world that is, as Surrealists have always proclaimed, a world of wonder, infused with the marvelous. The topian utopian is the "truly experienced person," who, in Gary Snyder's apt depiction, "delights in the ordinary." Such a down-to-earth utopian knows that the extraordinary (the eutopian) is at the very heart of the everyday (the topian).

This is why a thinker like Gustav Landauer, the great libertarian communitarian philosopher, is so important to the anarchist tradition. Landauer proclaimed the need for the creation of both liberated base communities and a larger community of communities, a rich and thriving communitarian culture. Landauer pointed out that we will never have a free communal society unless what we aspire to in the larger society is already present within the person and small group. Everything depends on the material and spiritual base, where we find the greatest intensity of experience, of life, and of relatedness to other beings, to the world, and to the chaosmos of nature.

Landauer realized that the communitarian impulse can only spread throughout society (we might say "like an epidemic of healing") through the powerful force of example offered by the existence of realized practice. He understood that social revolution is not possible if the system of domination has an iron grip on the social ethos. It is time to move from *prefiguration* to *figuration* and *transfiguration*. We must actually see the new Face of the Real. There must be living examples of the new way of life embodied in thriving communities of liberation—preferably within walking distance from our own town, village, or urban neighborhood. We should all be able to walk to utopia. When this becomes possible, masses of people will then abandon a corrupt and moribund society. Motivated by a kind of "positive envy" (as Landauer describes it) or communitarian desire, they will flock to the new communities in which human and natural potentialities freely flourish.

It is only when utopian aspirations are embodied in the actual practice of communities in all fundamental spheres of social determination that utopia can finally become more than a noble fantasy or a noble lie. Only then can it become a topian and eutopian reality. Utopia will finally receive its well-deserved present.

## NOTES

1    Elsewhere I refer more generally to the functioning of "the system of domination" and the "spheres of social determination." Here I focus on the "corporate-state apparatus" as the major institutional structure within that system that is directly concerned with both coercive and ideological control. This apparatus encompasses all the mechanisms of both corporate and state power, ranging from the coercive force of the police and military to the ideological force of the advertising and communications industries. One goal of this analysis is to point out the interdependence and mutual determination of the two dimensions of the apparatus and to subvert the ideological disjoining of its two moments, in which either the corporate realm is abstracted from the system of domination and idealized as a realm of individual freedom (as in right-wing "libertarianism" or "anarcho-capitalism") or the statist realm is abstracted from the system of domination and idealized as a realm of social justice (as in contemporary welfare-state liberalism, "progressivism," or social democracy, alias "democratic socialism").

2    Ronald Creagh, *Utopies américaines: Expériences libertaires du XIX<sup>e</sup> siècle à nos jours* (Marseilles: Agone, 2009).

3    John Clark, "New Llano Community," in *Encyclopedia of the American Left*, 2nd ed. (New York: Oxford University Press, 1998), 453.

4    Iain Boal, Janferie Stone, Michael Watts, and Cal Winslow, eds., *West of Eden: Communes and Utopia in Northern California* (Oakland: PM Press, 2012).

5    This is discussed in some detail in chapter 9 of this book.

# 19

# Carnival at the Edge of the Abyss: New Orleans and the Apocalyptic Imagination

## The Mysterious Crescent

New Orleans is known as the Crescent City. According to conventional wisdom, the name refers to its position within a curve of the Mississippi River. But over 160 years ago, the geographer Elisée Reclus could already note that on such a basis it should already have been known as the "double-crescent city."[1] And now all the crescents have disappeared, yet the idea is alive and well in the local imagination.

So one might, forsaking all literalistic explanations, ask, "What is the secret meaning of the crescent?" Of course, there are as many secrets of the crescent as there are devotees of the city. But what is the relevant meaning for our purposes (which we will soon discover to be interstitial, antistitial and apocalyptic ones)? Perhaps it is the crescent itself that can best pose, and best answer, this question.

The crescent is the figure that results when a circle has a segment of another circle removed from its edge. It thus consists of an area enclosed by two circular arcs that intersect at two points. Thus, there is a question, or *mystery*, implicit in the crescent itself: "What lies within the missing circle?" The crescent defines a relationship between two realities: the explicit one "within" the crescent and the implicit one inscribed in the crescent through the striking presence of its own absence. In a sense, it is the implicit that is most explicitly designated or *pointed to*.

Isn't the crescent a kind of monstrance, holding out to us and revealing some numinous reality that ordinarily escapes our attention? That reality, we will see, is the other side, the dialectical other, of the city, of the civic, and of civilization. It is the suppressed complementary or contradictory reality. It is the reality of forgotten nature, forgotten life, forgotten history, forgotten colonies, forgotten peoples, and forgotten depths of being.

This sacred realm of oblivion is the matrix out of which emerges the utopian promise of apocalyptic transformation. We should remember that the word "crescendo" comes from the same root, *crescere*, as does "crescent." "Crescendo" connotes both a continual increase in intensity, and also the peak or fulfillment toward which that growth in intensity aims. Loci of intensity and a qualitative leap in intensity may be taken as our guides into the quest to uncover the secret of the crescent, the secret of interstitiality and antistitiality.

## Interstitial New Orleans

When filling out forms online, I have often been required to choose from a menu specifying what "state" my city is in. Fortunately, I have sometimes been able to choose the option "Minor Outlying U.S. Island Possessions." This seemed to say more about our local condition than any of the other choices. New Orleans is one of those edgy, borderline, indeed *interstitial* places that are hard to pin down, which confound conventional notions of place, position, and location. They defy standardized conceptions of core and periphery, Global North and Global South, First World and Third World, Empire and Colony. While "edges" and "borders" are quite familiar concepts, "interstial" is far less so. So it may be useful to reflect a bit on the meaning of this key concept. It may, indeed, offer the key to the city.

The term "interstitial" derives from the Latin *inter*, "between," and *stare*, "to stand."[2] Thus, interstices consist of what lies in the gaps between the "stitial," that which stands. What "stands" is conventional reality, and particularly those elements of the dominant reality that are raised up highest above all else. "What stands" includes hierarchies, structures of domination, social and ontological barriers, social statuses, sacred ideologies, and, not least of all, the state. Both "status" and "state," like "interstice," derive from the Latin *stare* "to stand." The interstitial is thus not "in a state," but rather "between states."

The word "state" came to us via the Anglo-French term *l'estat*, which perhaps not entirely coincidentally evokes the famous fictional vampire from New Orleans. Nietzsche, in one of his most politically incisive moments, called the state "the coldest of all cold monsters." Andrei Codrescu has argued that the first nation-state was Romania and that it was founded by Vlad the Impaler. This would make Dracula the Father of the modern state, which is certainly true symbolically, if not entirely literally.

"Interstice" is also related to "static," which means "characterized by a lack of movement, animation, or progression" and "exerting force by reason of weight alone without motion."[3] The "stitial" is a realm in which Nietzsche's spirit of gravity prevails and weighs down not only the lightness of being but also all lightness of spirit. It is the domain of the object-like, the reified, and the ossified. The interstitial, in escaping this gravitational force, is a realm in which life, motion, and radical transformation find promising possibilities. The most crucial of questions about the interstitial and about New Orleans as an interstitial city is the degree to which *interstices* can and will become *antistices*. If the interstitial is that which lies between the "stitial," that which stands, the *antistitial* challenges that which stands and has the potential to overturn it.

Then there is the question of what we might call "glycolocality." What is the relation between the interstice and "the spot," and, more specifically, the "sweet spot?"[4] Interstices might be described loosely as 'spots,' in the sense that they are locations. But we might ask whether they are necessarily sweet or might often be experienced as sour, bitter, salty, savory, pungent, or metallic. To help answer this question, we might consider the fact that the term "sweet spot" has at least three meanings. First, in acoustics, the "sweet spot" is the point at which something is heard "as intended." Interstices are in some ways the opposite of sweet spots in this sense. Interstices defy what is "intended." They are the locus of the unintended, the misintended, and the anti-intended. Second, in athletics, the "sweet spot" is the point at which there is maximum effect for effort. But this also has relatively little to do with interstices, much less antistices. The interstitial overturns accepted ideas of cause and effect, of instrumental rationality, of utilitarian calculation. It is the realm of shocks and surprises, where effect has an unexpected relationship to effort, and to effortlessness. Fortunately, there is a third realm of glycolocality that offers some promise of revealing a degree of overlap with interstitiality.

In phonetics, the sweet spot is the point of maximum vibration. This brings us back to the crucial question of levels of intensity. If the stitial is the realm of stability and stasis, or the quest for these, or the illusion of these, the interstitial is the sphere in which there is such intensity of motion and vibration that the possibility arises of destitializing the stitial, or of shaking the stitial off its foundations. In other words, there is the possibility of the emergence of the antistitial. Such antistitiality can be sweet music to the ears of some, but it is at the same time a bitter pill for others to swallow. Indeed, the interstice, when it rises to the level of antistitiality, takes on some of the qualities of the famous Hitchcockian anamorphic "blot" or "stain" explicated in Lacanian film analysis. The spot remains innocuously in the background until, at the decisive moment, it intrudes into the foreground, perhaps subtly and discreetly at first, but ultimately with tremendous ontological force. For all its revelatory virtues, it is the bitterest spot of all from the standpoint of everyday, ordinary reality, since it disrupts and radically destabilizes that reality. Thus, to be as faithful as possible to the range of relevant phenomena, we might want to describe interstices as bittersweet spots.

## The Social Ontology of Yat

New Orleans itself specializes in a kind of unruly disruptiveness, a quality that arises to a certain degree from its interstitiality. The city tends to overturn many preconceptions—for example, those concerning North and South. This does not refer primarily to the preconceptions of outsiders who come to New Orleans expecting to hear a melodic, lilting accent exuding honeysuckle and molasses, and who are then shocked when they encounter Yat, the brash and rough-edged local working-class quasi-Brooklynese dialect. Yat's classic self-referential query, "Where y'at?" can in fact initiate an investigation of the ambiguities of our psychogeographical and socio-ontological coordinates.

It is a cliché that New Orleans is "a southern city." In fact, it has been nicknamed "the Queen City of the South." Nevertheless, it is also a northern city in a very strong sense, and perhaps most significantly, it is a city on the boundary between North and South. It is located on the southern edge of North America, of the American nation-state, and of "America" as a cultural territory. The most momentous Earth-historical and geographical reality for it is that it is at the southern end, the delta, of one of the world's great rivers, the Mississippi, the Gaealogical force that gave birth to it. But it is also at the northern edge of its bioregion, the littoral region that runs from the Florida Keys to the northern coast of the Yucatan Peninsula. It is also at the northern edge of the great basin of the American Mediterranean Sea, which encompasses the Gulf of Mexico and the Caribbean. And finally, with its Mediterranean cultural heritage, including almost a century as a French and Spanish colony, it is at the shifting northern edge of Latin America. "Where y'at?" can be a very challenging question.

To take another example, we might ask which "world" New Orleans inhabits. Is it located in the First World? The Third World? The nonexistent Second World? None of the above? At one time, there was a popular bumper sticker in New Orleans that proclaimed, "New Orleans: Third World and Proud of It!" It was appealing because it evoked the Latin and African roots of the city, and its affinities with the global South. It expressed a defiance of the Northern, Anglo-Saxon, Calvinistic work ethic and an appreciation of values like play, enjoyment, sensuality, desire, fantasy, celebration, wildness, and creativity. It represented the New Orleanian Dream as opposed to the American Dream.

That bumper sticker was never seen again after the Katrina Disaster. We learned something that we had not fully understood about what it means to be a bit too "Third World" on the fringes of Empire in a time of extreme crisis and desperate need. Through our interstitial position between worlds we (or at least those of us who didn't quickly retreat into the high, dry, elitist "bubble," as it was called) gained a unique insight into what it means today to be "Third World," and a part of "the South," in a First-World, northern-dominated global imperial order.

However, the more meaningful theoretical question is not whether we are Third World or First World but whether we are "core" or "periphery." In world-systems theory, the core is the center of wealth, power, privilege, and prestige. Though the land area of the planet that this core occupies is proportionally a bit larger than the apple core that might come immediately to mind, and although it is geographically dispersed over several continents, it can still be looked upon as the "center" of the global system of domination. The periphery, on the other hand, has relatively little wealth, power, privilege, and prestige, though it covers most of the surface of the Earth. We can also speak of a global semiperiphery. This is an interstitial geopolitical space that has some characteristics of the core and some qualities of the periphery, yet it is not predominantly one or the other.

A nation-state may be a core country but nevertheless contain within itself semiperipheral and even peripheral areas. In the United States, many Indian reservations and the most devastated urban zones qualify as periphery, however much the banner of the core may fly over them. New Orleans occupies a complex geopolitical space, in that it is a part of the semiperiphery that lies at the edge of the core and not very far from the periphery, while at the same time having islands of core and periphery within it. It is strongly interstitial to the extent that it lies between parts of the core that "stand" rather high (the Houstons and Atlantas), and in as much as it lies between the core ("America") and the periphery (the other "Americas"). Its interstitial significance has increased markedly as its connection with Central America, and especially Honduras and El Salvador, two peripheral countries that are among those most devastated by Empire, has grown significantly.

To live mindfully in New Orleans is to dwell dialectically on the edge, to border borders ambiguously, and to inhabit interstices precariously. This puts one in a privileged position to understand what lies either inside or over the edge, what exists on each side of the border, and what stands outside the interstices. It allows one to be both inside and outside at the same time. It allows one to take the inside outsider perspective: to be "in" yet not "of."[5] To be a New Orleanian who is fully awakened to our perspective of place gives one a certain "double vision," a certain privilege of parallax.[6] It makes possible the move from an interstitial topianism to the antistitial utopianism that is at the heart of New Orleans' apocalyptic nature.

## Apocalyptic New Orleans

The term "Apocalypse" originates, we are told, in certain Jewish and Christian writings from the period between 200 BCE and 150 CE that are "marked by pseudonymity, symbolic imagery, and the expectation of an imminent cosmic cataclysm in which God destroys the ruling powers of evil and raises the righteous to life in a messianic kingdom."[7] The term derives from the Greek word "apokalyptein," which means "to uncover." In the messianic Apocalypse, that which has been covered up, obscured, or occluded by layers of social domination and social ideology (that is, by the stitial) is "uncovered," in the sense of both "being revealed" and "being released into being."

"Apocalypse" implies cataclysmic change, but a kind of change that does not result in mere destruction and loss. Rather, the change opens up new utopian, antistitial possibilities that emerge out of what has existed all along within the interstitial gaps of civilization. The apocalyptic imagination envisions a return to a Paradise beyond the bounds and bonds of domination. A Land of Dreamy Scenes. A Garden of Eden. A Heaven Right Here on Earth. This seemingly impossible return to the place where we have never been is indeed possible, but only because the roots of Paradise lie all around us, in the interstices.

As the invocation of certain familiar phrases hints, the thesis here is that New Orleans is the apocalyptic city par excellence. If one looks into the history of New Orleans and the city's social imaginary, one finds that in both its fantasies and its reality, it is not only an apocalyptic city, in both the destructive and utopian senses, but also an *edge city*, poised at the brink of an abyss; an *interstitial* city, lying in the gaps between "that which stands"; and an *antistitial* city, always threatening, sometimes with the help of nature but always with the help of culture, to overturn "that which stands."

An essential element of the apocalyptic nature of New Orleans is its position at the edge of the abyss. One might well ask what precisely it means to say that a city is situated in this manner, "at the edge" and "of an abyss?" Presumably, we are not interested in an exercise in vague dramatics or local colorist exaggeration. Any decline into the kind of mindless puffery that might be labeled "Big Easyism," is a betrayal of the city and its momentous destiny. In fact, the abyss above which the city is perched exists in two quite specific and clearly defined senses, both of them apocalyptic. There is the *abyss of non-being*, and there is the *abyss of becoming*.

The abyss of non-being is the frightening apocalyptic nothingness of collapse, catastrophe, and fall. It is the loss of that fragile being that assumes an illusory substantiality and concreteness when it is part of the structure of everydayness. I have heard the phrase "the unbearable lightness of being" misremembered as "the incredible lightness of being." The concept is misremembered, if not entirely forgotten, for very good reason. The lightness of being is *incredible* precisely because it is so obviously *credible*. The expression designates a quality that in ancient Sanskrit was called *anitya*, or impermanence. It is, according to the ancient philosophy of awakening, one of the Three Marks of Existence on which human beings always have so much trouble focusing consciously.

New Orleans is an apocalyptic city because it exemplifies in such a striking manner the reality of impermanence. It *announces* impermanence to the world. Though, admittedly, more than a few New Orleanians seem to require a state of permanent oblivion to avoid thinking about what they unconsciously realize to be true, many are aware, either with full consciousness or with a certain degree of recognition, of the lightness of the city's being. The sometimes unbearable truth is that city could disappear at any time and is indeed likely to disappear in the not-too-distant future. Any given hurricane season, it could be devastated by "the Big One" that has yet to arrive. And beyond this looming disaster lies the Big One to End All Big Ones, the chain of social and ecological events that will almost certainly end the city's history entirely through inundation. It is highly unlikely that this three-hundred-year-old city will be around to celebrate its four-hundredth anniversary. In fact, the odds are not so great for it to see three hundred and fifty candles on its cake, if the present course of global climate change and sea level rise merely progresses as expected. As a result, the city is left with an apocalyptic fate and a correspond- ingly apocalyptic social imaginary. The probability of vast devastation increasingly shapes its conscious imaginary. The inevitability of complete destruction slumbers uncomfortably in its unconscious imaginary.

Beyond this abyss of non-being lies another abyss. This is the abyss of becoming, the apocalyptic abyss of possibility. Nietzsche famously warned us to beware of looking into the abyss, because the abyss looks back into us. He might have warned us more explicitly against the problem of not looking deeply enough into certain abysses, and against preventing them from looking back into us. We should never settle for Abyss Lite. Those who look most profoundly into the abyss of non-being and allow it to look back into their own nothingness are able to do so because they recognize that there is a second moment of Apocalypse, the abyss of becoming. This second face of Apocalypse is the moment of possibility, of creativity, and of hope.

New Orleans, in expressing these two faces of Apocalypse, takes its place as a prophetic city at the forefront of world history, which increas- ingly reveals itself as apocalyptic history, the story of the end of civiliza- tion. The city's prophetic message in this connection is: "What we are, you shall be." We are the *mauvaise conscience*, the bad conscience, and we might even say the *mauvais inconscient*, the bad unconscious, of civilization. Yet we are perhaps also the liberatory unconscious of what comes beyond civilization. Both these qualities are keys to the city's apocalyptic nature. We (in this case, all of humanity) are in the midst of an apocalyptic age, though awareness of its apocalyptic nature is just beginning to emerge. It is for precisely this reason that New Orleans as the harbinger of this age is such a prophetically apocalyptic city. It is a city built on a foundation of impossibility, yet its impossible history and impossible destiny offer us indispensable messages regarding both possibility and inevitability.

## The Other Face of Apocalypse

The Apocalypse will not be televised, though attempts will certainly be made to capture it on the small screen. Its untelevisability means that it is inherently wild and can never be domesticated or tamed. New Orleans is fertile ground for apocalyptic utopianism in large part because of its unconquerable wildness (one of the great books about it is, in fact, called *A Walk on the Wild Side*).[8] It is a wild place in several senses. Abandon your house for a few months or years and see what's there when you get back. Vines will have woven the back yard into a thick mat, interspersed with rainforest vegetation. Dozens of species of trees and bushes will have sprung up in what was formerly lawn, garden, or even cracks in the sidewalk. Vines will have invaded every wall and colonized the roof, which will have turned into a bright green meadow interspersed with vivid yellow flowers. As New Orleans art critic, photographer, and psychogeographer Eric Bookhardt has said astutely of the city, "The Jungle Is Near."[9] This undeniable truth is meant in both a natural and a cultural sense. Abandon your narrow little prosaic mind for a while, let your wider mind walk on the wild side of the spirit, and the mythopoetic mental jungle will reappear. In New Orleans, the wild cultural rainforest vegetation seems always to be striving to take root and to spread across the landscape. In New Orleans, *interstitiality is destiny.*

Given its insistent interstial and antistitial impulses, New Orleans has inevitably become the site of a neverending war between the wild and the domesticated, the free and the dominated. It is the battleground in the Splace Wars. Splace, a fundamental psychogeographical concept, is the battlefield on which space and place clash. Space is abstract, geometrical, analytical location. Space has Pythagorean mathematical, Cartesian philosophical, Newtonian scientific, statist techno-bureaucratic, and capitalist economistic forms. In urbanist terms, space is the terrain for the designs and devices of developers. It is the privileged domain of development. In all its overlapping and mutually reinforcing forms, space reduces a location to its abstract parameters for instrumental ends and for purposes of political, economic and technological domination. The dominant system has been obsessed with a space race, a compulsion to reduce everything to *instrumental spatiality* as rapidly as possible.

Place, on the other hand, is concrete dialectical location. It is the field on which physis, psyche, eros, pneuma, poesis, ethos, and mythos all unfold and manifest themselves. It is the plane on which the lives of persons and communities are lived. Ancient metaphysicians were right when they said that things have a natural place, but they were wrong to think they could define that place or impose any general principle or *arché* upon it. All beings have their own way of being, and they do it in their own time and place. If you want to know the details, ask the persons and things themselves. "Where y'at, Ding-an-Sich?" Where things are at is where they are going, in their own way. Though everything must always be in its place, that place itself is always out of place. The Thing-in-Itself is always outside itself and beside itself.

Since the beginning of civilization, every location has been the site of the dialectic of space and place, the scene of Splace Wars. Today, antistitial New Orleans wages war against space on behalf of place. If Wordsworth warned astutely regarding the modern scientific spirit, "We murder to dissect," radical localists warn regarding postmodern gentri- fiers, "We murder to develop." They fear that living New Orleans culture will be murdered, embalmed, and carried away in a Kabacoffin,[10] all to the accompaniment of a traditional brass band. They fear that Carnival will be cannibalized.

New Orleans is known above all for being the carnivalesque city, the city of the Mardi Gras. Carnival is the dialectical festival par excellence. It is the temporary emergence of a world in which, quite manifestly, every- thing is what it is not, and everything is not what it is. It is a particularly dialectical phenomenon in its New Orleanian incarnation. It radicalizes the fundamental cultural contradiction of New Orleans. It is an American city, yet it incarnates what America is not. The city was founded as a Latin, carnivalesque city, yet for two centuries it has been increasingly assimi- lated into a dominant Anglo-Saxon, decidedly anti-carnivalesque, capital- accumulation-obsessed culture.

The city's enduring Saturnalian spirit therefore has a subversive, oppo- sitional quality that is central to its antistitiality and its utopian apocalyp- ticism. It flaunts the subversive idea that contrary to Napoleon's dictum that "power is never ridiculous," it is, in fact, *always* ridiculous. It confronts *le pouvoir* with its own sublimely ridiculous *puissances*. As a result of these antagonistic contradictions between power and powers, several carnivals have emerged. At times, a War of the Carnivals even breaks out. On the one hand, there is domesticated carnival, the official carnival, a contrived spectacle, a festival of wealth and power, a mechanism for controlling the masses through repressive desublimation, a means of attracting tourists through the image of an ersatz Bacchanalia, and thereby contributing mightily to the grossly domesticated product. This is the Fat Tuesday of the Fat Cats. On the other hand (the left hand, of course), there is wild carnival, the popular carnival, dissident carnival, carnival with an edge, the festival of joy, creative self-expression, and defiance of convention. This is the Fat Tuesday of the Fat of the Land, the overflowing abundance of natural richness and of wild becoming.

The connections between the concept of the anarchic carnivalesque developed here and Mikhail Bakhtin's analysis of carnival are obvious.[11] In Bakhtin's classic work, *Rabelais and His World,* he develops a number of themes that are echoed in the present discussion. Thus, he describes carnival as "the second life of the people, who for a time entered the utopian realm of community, freedom, equality, and abundance."[12] Carnival, he says, allowed people to be "reborn for new, purely human relation" that "were not only a fruit of abstract thought" but were actually experienced, so that "the utopian ideal and the realistic merged."[13] Furthermore, he sees carnival as a fundamental challenge to the "old authority and truth" that are "gloomily serious." Carnival, with is immersion in the moment and in bodily materiality, exposes "the comic nature of their pretentions to eternity and immutability."[14]

However, despite these commonalities, there is a fundamental difference between Bakhtin's concept of carnival and the one with which we are most concerned here. For Bakhtin, "the feast was a temporary suspension of the entire official system with all its prohibitions and hierarchic barriers. For a short time life came out of its usual, legalized and consecrated furrows and entered the sphere of utopian freedom," and thus "the atmosphere of ephemeral freedom reigned."[15] Bakhtin's carnival was thus in many ways similar to what Hakim Bey describes as the "temporary autonomous zone."[16] While the present analysis recognizes this dimension of carnival as the realm in which such ephemeral freedom is realized, it relates this particular carnivalesque moment to the larger carnivalesque reality of a culture that has a dialectically ironic relationship to the dominant order, a relationship that is ongoing and, we might say, "structural" in its very urge toward destructurization.

Wild carnival functions as an ecstatically destabilizing force. It is the temporary collapse of normality and a temporary unleashing of unruly aesthetic and erotic forces. Carnival is antistitial in that it mocks all that stands. It pulls the rug out from under what stands. The roots of the city's unique expression of the carnivalesque lie in its original Latin heritage, and the African and Afro-Caribbean one that was later superimposed, or, we might say, super-subversively "subimposed." Its specific historical origins are in the Mediaeval Feast of Fools, in which the dominant order is ridiculed and relativized, if only for a day. But what happens in a day has imaginary implications that can be very far-reaching. If the day is good enough, it might even lead to a *Grand Soir*. The African heritage takes this insurgent antistitiality one step further with the Mardi Gras Indians' defiant affirmation of wildness and their spirit of "won't bow down" to the dominant culture. Thus, one finds implicit in the carnivalesque the seeds of social transformation, the dream of a permanent carnivalesque community in which hierarchical power is definitively relativized and thus defanged. Power descends to the streets. Antistitial antistructures walk the streets.

Thus, Carnival produces the dream-image of a community founded on wild beauty and mad love that can become a powerful imaginary counterforce to the dominant dream-image of the commodity. Note that such a "permanent" carnivalesque community is anything but permanent. In Carnival, nothing is ever merely *what it is*. It is a community that is constantly changing. It changes its costumes, of course, but it also changes its identities and imaginings. It is also constantly exchanging. It exchanges such things as gifts, experiences, and acts of creation. Carnival is the experience of finding enduring value in the free exchange of that which constantly changes hands, hearts, minds, and souls. Carnival is the ultimate evidence that samsara is nirvana, that the profane is profoundly sacred, that your own home is the promised land. In Carnival, your feet won't fail to walk on sacred ground. In Carnival, the very gumbo ground on which you walk is the Pure Lotus Land.

## On Mystery Street

At the outset, it was said that the secret of the crescent lies in the revelation of mysteries. Nowhere have these mysteries been explored more intriguingly than in the novel *Mysteries of New Orleans*. This work, which might well have been called *The Manifesto of Apocalyptic New Orleans*, was written in the 1850s by the Bavarian immigrant nobleman Baron Ludwig von Reizenstein.[17] The German title, *Die Geheimnisse Von New-Orleans*, means literally "Secrets of New Orleans," but it was part of the "mysteries" genre that was the rage in the mid-nineteenth century. However, this extraordinary work explosively burst the limits of that genre and initiated the world into what might be called the literature of apocalyptic mysteries. In it, Reizenstein investigates strange, mysterious, subterranean, and surrealist elements of the city's culture and geography. This epic tale remains one of history's greatest examples not only of apocalyptic fiction but of literary surregionalism and psychogeography.

Reizenstein explores an interstitial New Orleans that encompasses a multitude of regions and locations that defy the prevailing order of domination in the era. Each embodies a "mystery" or "secret" that escapes the boundaries of conventional wisdom, challenges the dominant view of what can be recognized as real, and prefigures a new reality beyond the limits of all forms of domination. The "mysteries" exhibited by Reizenstein's characters and settings are *radical breaks* vis-à-vis the state, capitalism, patriarchy, heterosexism, racism, repressive morality, authoritarian religion, technological rationality, and the domination of nature. Thus, these subversive sites are both deeply interstitial and radically antistitial.

In the central plot theme, the mysterious two-hundred-year-old Hiram the Freemason contrives to bring together, magically, a mixed-race couple who will produce an offspring who will liberate the enslaved people, and thereby make possible the regeneration of a corrupt and accursed social order. As Steven Rowan, the translator and editor, summarizes: "Reizenstein's tale foretells the descent of a bloody retributive justice upon the American South. Slavery is a massive sin that would soon be made right by a bloodbath, heralded by the birth of a black messiah, a deliverer of his people.... Without sentimentality or hopeful liberalism, Reizenstein portrayed the coming revolution in frankly apocalyptic terms."[18] In fact, he did it in terms that express precisely the conception of Apocalypse developed here.

For Reizenstein, it was the deeply contradictory, indeed dialectical, nature of New Orleans that gave it a unique apocalyptic destiny. On the one hand, the city exhibited starkly the evils of brutality, exploitation, slavery and domination. But on the other hand, it also constituted an oasis of freedom that had certain redeeming qualities that made it unique in American society."[19] It is the very intensity of the expression of evil that conditions the intensity of utopian possibility. Reizenstein describes the city as the scene of all forms of misery and degradation, but nevertheless as an exception to the repressiveness of the dominant American culture: *"Much is forbidden, but much is also tolerated.* This makes New Orleans the freest city in the United States."[20] He notes further that "New Orleans has always been the leader in the United States in everything that heightens enjoyment of life and makes the dullest people into Epicureans."[21] New Orleans as a hotbed of corruption and oppression was particularly well suited to be the scene of an apocalyptic fall. New Orleans as a haven of freedom was uniquely ordained to be the scene of the ultimate redemption of society. So it is in New Orleans that Reizenstein imagines the emergence, out of the interstitial oases of freedom, of a new world released from the chains of domination. In his apocalyptic imagination, New Orleans holds the promise of being a *passionate utopia* whose subtropical wildness and earthiness would eclipse anything imagined by Fourier.

But Reizenstein was aware that many barriers would have to be broken before this utopia could emerge. Thus, his attack on slavery and racism is only the beginning of an assault on the manifold abuses of a vicious and brutal civilization. He condemns not only the South with its regressive, neofeudal slave system but the entire corrupt American society, which by the mid-nineteenth century had already shown itself to be deeply perverted by the forces of economic exploitation, racism, social repression, and imperial conquest. Reizenstein presents a remarkable litany in which the evils of that society are enumerated and the cataclysmic revolt against all of them is envisioned. Despite its length, it is worth quoting this entire passage for the sake of its extensive enumeration of forms of domination (forces of *stitiality*) to be abolished and forms of liberation (forces of *antistitiality*) to be nurtured and protected:

> Wherever the law claps love in permanent manacles, where the Church proclaims sensual denial, where false modesty and inherited morality keeps us from giving nature its rights, then we lie down at the warm breasts of Mother Nature, listening to her secrets and surveying with burning eyes the great mechanism in which every gear moans the word *Love*.
>
> There is rejoicing in all the spheres, the fanfares of the universe resound, wherever love celebrates its triumph. But lightning bolts flash from dark clouds whenever tyrannical law and usurped morality seek to compel the children of earth to smother their vitality and entomb their feelings.
>
> How small and pitiful the nattering of parties seems, how petty the drama even of our own revolution, against the titanic struggle of sensuality against law and morality.

"Revolution!" the nun cries out in her sleep, throwing her rosary in the face of the Madonna.

"Revolution!" the priest of the sole-salvific Church mutters as he rips his scapular into shreds.

"Revolution!" thunders the proletarian when he beholds the fair daughter of Pharaoh.

"Revolution!" the slave rattles, when he sees the white child of the planter walking through the dark passageway of cypresses.

"Revolution!" the horse whinnies, mutilated by greed.

"Revolution!" the steer roars, cursing its tormentors under the yoke on its shoulders.

"Revolution!" the women of Lesbos would storm, if we were to rebuke their love.[22]

Thus, Reizenstein defends love, life, nature, sensuality, feeling, equality, and justice, against capitalism, slavery, the state, authoritarian religion, repressive morality, sexism, heterosexism, racism, and even speciesism and the devastation of the natural world. In 1853, a specter was haunting the Mississippi Delta. It was the specter of total liberation! While many specters have died since then, this one, as we shall see, still finds interstices in which to dwell, and still has some serious antistitial haunting to carry out.

## Apocalyptic Urban Nightmare

Though Reizenstein's *tour de force imaginaire* has never been equaled by any single literary work about the city, the Katrina disaster signaled the high point in the overall flowering of the New Orleanian apocalyptic imaginary. This is true regarding both sides of Apocalypse, the negative imagery of cataclysmic destruction, and the positive imagery of rebirth and transfiguration. We might call the one-sidedly negative expression of this imaginary that was so common in the post-Katrina period "the Official Apocalypse" or "the apocalyptic urban nightmare."

President George W. Bush's notorious comments immediately after the disaster are very instructive. His words were part of a project of instrumentalizing Apocalypse, and more specifically, part of the strategy of the militarization of Apocalypse. Bush describes a post-Katrina wasteland in which it was "as if" the region had been "obliterated by a—the worst kind of weapon you can imagine."[23] The worst kind of weapon one could imagine, at least if one happens to live on Planet Earth, is quite obviously a multi-megaton nuclear warhead. Thus, his message, if clearly spelled out, is an injunction to think "New Orleans was nuked." Certain useful conclusions follow from this apocalyptic thought experiment. First, a disaster of the imagined magnitude would certainly create a "state of exception" in which the legitimacy of extreme measures such as the displacement and disempowerment of masses of people, and the extensive militarization of the community would be beyond question. Second, the image of the city as a post-nuclear-holocaust tabula rasa plays into the larger long-term agenda of reengineering it into a more gentrified "boutique city," according to the demands of capital and with the help of the ideology of the New Urbanism. Thus, the myth of a postapocalyptic social tabula rasa would be used to *obliterate consciousness* of the interstices and antistices, and, to whatever degree possible, to *annihilate* them.

Bush concludes by saying that "now, we're going to try to comfort people in that part of the world." He (and his speechwriters) obviously realized that the idea that a few more bumbling words on his part would comfort anyone was ludicrous, so the question is what the actual message of such an assertion might be. The implicit message of his statement was, first, that the overriding "recovery" strategy that the masses of local citizens should expect would be to fight fire with rhetoric (though in this case the "fire" to be fought was primarily water). Second, it was that the people of New Orleans were to be imagined as distant, alien others and treated accordingly. Almost any chief of state in the world would refer to disaster victims from the same country as "fellow citizens," as fellow nationals ("Americans," "Mexicans," "Russians," etc.) or as "brothers and sisters." So the objectification of New Orleanians as strangers and foreigners ("people in that part of the world"), albeit in a patronizingly sympathetic mode, is particularly telling. Finally, a pertinent subtext in Bush's comments is his message that if people in New Orleans are in *that part* of the world, they are by definition not in *our part* of the world but rather in *another part* of it. This makes sense if we realize that Bush was speaking from a position that was unambiguously from within and on behalf of the core, while the position of New Orleans in the world system was within the semiperiphery, and its position according to the dominant social imaginary at that precise moment was decidedly at the periphery.

The mainstream media worked diligently to propagate a complementary Apocalyptic Urban Nightmare scenario. The very real problems that emerged in New Orleans (as described in chapter 12) were ludicrously exaggerated, distorted, and misrepresented. Several days after the flooding, Maureen Dowd in the *New York Times* lamented the supposed fact that "America is once more plunged into a snake pit of anarchy, death, looting, raping, marauding thugs, suffering infrastructure, a gutted police force, insufficient troop levels, and criminally negligent government planning."[24] The same image was expressed in Allen G. Breed's Associated Press report, "New Orleans in the Throes of Katrina, and Apocalypse."[25] Breed arrived two days before Katrina and shortly after the disaster concluded that "a walk through New Orleans is a walk through hell," albeit "punctuated by moments of grace." He reports: "There is nothing to correct wild reports that armed gangs have taken over the convention center. That two babies had their throats slit in the night. That a 7-year-old girl was raped and killed at the Superdome." There was nothing to correct this entirely false account other than the accurate information that only surfaced after the indelible image of New Orleans as "Urban Hell" had deeply penetrated the American social imagination.

Government officials reinforced the image presented by mainstream media. FEMA Director Michael Brown spoke of the difficulties of working in New Orleans in "conditions of urban warfare."[26] Local officials also contributed powerfully to creating this scenario. In an interview with Oprah Winfrey, a weeping Chief of Police Eddie Compass lamented, referring to conditions at the Superdome, "We had babies in there. Little babies getting raped." Mayor Ray Nagin elaborated, informing Oprah that people "were trapped" and as a result "got to this almost animalistic state. . . . We have people standing out there, that have been in that frickin' Superdome for five days watching dead bodies, watching hooligans killing people, raping people. That's the tragedy. People are trying to give us babies that were dying."[27] So goes the story of the terrifying outbreak of asymmetrical warfare in the remote Third World Banana Republic of Bigeasya.

Yet while there certainly was tragic violence in the city, it was minimal in comparison to what was imagined in the Urban Apocalypse scenario. This became strikingly evident with the debunking of claims about violence in the Superdome and Convention Center, which became shelters for tens of thousands of citizens seeking refuge. Isak Winkel Holm notes that in order to justify a "large military operation, unprecedented on American soil," it was necessary to transform the citizens of New Orleans from "disaster victims" into "urban insurgents," so that Katrina was turned into "a natural disaster *and* a cultural disaster at the same time." It was "an example of cultural framing of a disaster with disastrous consequences."[28]

## Apocalyptic Utopia

While mainstream media and government officials (in effect, the representatives of Capital, the State, and White Patriarchy) were presenting their image of Apocalypse, a quite different one was emerging on the grassroots level. It was an image that accords with the deeper spiritual and political dimensions of Apocalypse that go back to ancient times. Hurricane Katrina (or, more accurately, the floodwaters that followed) leveled "that which stands," including social hierarchy, the State, and Capital. What resulted included the emergence of a "state of exception" in a very liberatory sense, perhaps we might say an "antistate of exception," a gap in history in which many of the citizens who remained found themselves in the extraordinary position of being a community of equals faced with the task of determining the destiny of their community (including defending it from a range of threats such as demolition, ethnic cleansing, capitalist plunder, and state repression).

Francesco di Santis, the "embedded artist," "visual folklorist," and anarchist activist mentioned in earlier chapters,[29] came to New Orleans less than two weeks after the hurricane, to work in the recovery and to participate in processes of liberatory social transformation. When I met him a week later, he was already talking to survivors and volunteers and sketching their portraits. Over the next several years he created "the Post-Katrina Portrait Project," a collection of several thousand of these works.[30] These portraits recount, in the words of the survivors and volunteers, the real-world apocalyptic history of dystopian destruction and devastation on the one hand and of utopian creation and communal liberation on the other.

One of the volunteers describes the apocalyptic "Dark Night of the Soul" that is the traditional path to a breakthrough in both European and Asian spiritual practice. "Last night, I woke to the shaking of my room. The walls were rattling and the whole house moved. I clung to my bed. The earth was quaking and I thought, 'this is it.' Pieces of the world were coming apart and I tried to grasp onto the remaining fragments of reality—before it was all gone. I woke again." This is the classic apocalyptic experience of the world coming apart and collapsing. A survivor who went through many terrifying experiences says, "You can never know what it was like for me and my child to see everything disappear right in front of our faces." This is the apocalyptic experience of the collapse of the everyday world. Many of the post-Katrina stories recount feelings of absolute abandonment, abject despair, and devastating fear of death and apocalyptic destruction.

This part of the post-Katrina story is well known, though not so often through the direct testimony of those who experienced it, or with the depth that such witnesses convey. What is amazing and inspiring is how so many of the Portrait Stories tell of the other face of Apocalypse: of ultimate redemption, of the restoration of hope, and of the surging up of a sense of utopian possibilities. As mentioned earlier, one survivor comments that "sometimes it takes the complete stripping of your home or possessions to really see what life's about," while a volunteer observes that "out of deep hurt can come beautiful transformation personally and collectively."

It is striking that so many described what was occurring in terms of a "crack" in the structure of history and in everyday reality. One volunteer says that "what matters most" in the Katrina experience is that there was a "system crack" in which new realities had become possible and "we now have the chance to help enact a transformation." The community becomes a kind of focal point of larger social transformation, so that through "all points radiating outward from our swampy heaven" we can know that "a paradigm shift is possible." The crack symbolizes the brokenness of the system, the community, and the lives of people, but it also signifies an opening through which germinating forces of creativity, imagination, love, and radical possibility are liberated. The crack thus signifies *the becoming-antistitial of the interstitial.*[31]

Common Ground Collective cofounder scott crow summarized the work of the organization using precisely this imagery. His account clearly points out the interstitial and antistitial nature of the "crack." We see that it is a space that first opens up in the midst of "that which stands" and then goes on to threaten the standing of "that which stands in the way." In scott's own words, "We had created a crack in history. We had revealed the lies, corruption, and failures of the state, and, without hesitating, we had done something about it. I had seen a transition from hopelessness to hope as thousands of people answered the call to come to the Gulf."[32] One might even say that the radically antistitial project of the Common Ground Collective was to expand that small systemic crack into a great "Gulf" in which freedom surges forth and sweeps away the forces of domination. We were involved in a Gulf War of the Spirit, a war at the heart of the Abyss.

As di Santis expresses it, "Since Katrina, New Orleans has only become more of itself, relentlessly perpetuating its own follies and glories so profoundly endemic to it since French imperialists first settled a port city among the swamps of the Mississippi Delta."[33] These follies are the strategies of domination, of the state and stases, that Reizenstein had already delineated as early as the 1850s, and which have become "more of themselves" most horrifically by policies of exclusion, ethnic cleansing, and the effective denial of the "right of return." The glories are expressed above all in the flowering of cultural and communal creativity in which the community of liberation and solidarity, the Beloved Community, has continually become "more of itself" in pursuing its destiny.

## Beasts of the Apocalypse

The film *Beasts of the Southern Wild* is not set in New Orleans, but it is very much about the predicament of the city and the region in which it is embedded. As the director, Benh Zeitlin, explains in a revealing interview, its story is not specifically about the Isle Jean Charles (its location), but rather about "the current moment of living in south Louisiana" in a world that is "under threat constantly."[34] In fact, it is about an apocalyptic world that is also both an interstitial and an antistitial one. It is a world that is an exception to American exceptionalism. America has attempted to step outside the order of nature and of primordial human nature (something that is an impossible impossibility). *Beasts* depicts an ongoing communal act of radical interstitiality in which the community steps back into that chaosmic order. The film is inspired not only by the city's southeast Louisiana region but in large part by the history and historical fate of the city of New Orleans itself. Its sources, according to Zeitlin, are "New Orleans culture," "south Louisiana culture," and an "aesthetic" that is "taken from the Bayou."

While the most striking and heroic character by far is the six-year-old Hushpuppy, the true protagonist of the film is the community itself, called "the Bathtub." The Bathtub reflects faithfully the two faces of Apocalypse. On the one hand, it is constantly threatened with apocalyptic destruction, both by a natural world that is distorted by a disordered society, and also by the direct intervention of that corrupt society itself. The very being of the community is at stake. On the other hand, the community expresses a mythic and apocalyptic utopian response to these threats. As Zeitlin puts it, "The whole idea of the Bathtub is that it's a society where all the things that divide people have been removed. So there's no religion, no politics, no money, no one sees race, there's no rich and poor because there is no currency." The Bathtub is the mythic image of a community beyond the bounds of all forms of domination.

*Beasts* is a defense of the wild and the wild community. Critics who attack the film for glorifying *poverty* and *ignorance* entirely miss the antistitial and apocalyptic point. First, some read the mythic plot in a stupidly literalistic manner. Second, some fail to notice the most significant qualities of the community: it is both *rich* and *wise* (even if not every single member of it is quite so brilliant). Zeitlin says that his hope is that the viewer will conclude that "if these things [stitial forces] didn't divide me from everyone around me, I would have this incredible freedom and I would fight for this place." This is an excellent expression of the core concept of apocalyptic New Orleans, with its promise of liberation and redemption, as the interstitial becomes radically and transformatively antistitial.[35]

Zeitlin makes it clear that the film expresses a certain conception of reality, a metaphysics of beasts. Indeed, we might say that it espouses a particular conception of the real, in the disruptive, subversive, traumatic sense of that term. Its central theme is that a corrupt and misguided dominant social order, the realm of the state and the stitial, has released powerful and ferocious, indeed apocalyptic, forces of nature with which it must ultimately reckon. These forces are embodied symbolically in fierce primal beasts called "aurochs" that awaken from their millennial slumber and stampede across the landscape. We might describe these forces as the return of the repressed, the answer of the Wild to the question we forgot to ask.

Zeitlin's interviewer raises the issue of whether these menacing forces should be seen as real or merely as a child's fantasy. Zeitlin replies with striking subtlety that Hushpuppy "thinks that the aurochs are coming out of the ice caps and charging toward the Bathtub, and they are." They are the real of the fantasy! In other words, however literally or symbolically we might choose interpret the aurochs, the central point is that the real of global ecological crisis is not a mere fantasy, as it appears from the perspective of the dominant order. The impossible real is more intensely and insistently real than is a seemingly inescapable and untranscendable, yet finally unsustainable, "reality." As the film faithfully conveys, this real reveals itself as emphatically real for the Earth itself and for those who have not lost contact with the Earth.

At one point, the interviewer comments to Zeitlin, "Your movies have a very redemptive feel, but they have a unique vision of redemption, in which it seems like redemption is only possible through complete destruction or annihilation—as though destruction and redemption are synonymous in a certain way." His question is, in other words, whether this work is about what we have been analyzing here as the two faces of Apocalypse. Zeitlin responds that this is, indeed, precisely his theme:

> Redemption, or enlightenment, or some sort of truth is found very close to destruction. It's in the most extreme situations where you find this, where you get this abandon that allows you to understand yourself or understand other people. It's part of what fascinates me about Louisiana. There's just some sort of internal and external freedom that exists there that I don't feel anywhere else in America.

It is the kind of freedom that is inconceivable from "within" America and is only conceivable (and capable of realization) from the "inside/outside" of America, the Interstitial States, or Non-States, of America, or Un-America, or Ur-America (Native America and Nature's America).

Zeitlin expresses this wild, antistitial spirit of freedom in the utopian image of the community. It is noteworthy that this *utopian* community (which is at the same time a *topian* community—a community deeply rooted in place) rejects both the state and capitalism. Statist (prostitial) leftist and "progressive" critics have attacked the film because it presents agencies of the state as a destructive force that crushes local community and local liberty. In other words, they criticize the film because it presents the state as doing precisely what the state has always done historically and what it certainly did in the Katrina disaster (that is, act *stitially*). What these critics overlook is that the film presents a consistent, liberatory image of radical freedom that rejects not only the paternalistic, bureaucratic state but also the late capitalist society of mass consumption and commodity fetishism.

As Zeitlin formulates the community's message, it proclaims, "We have the most freedom, we don't need money, we don't need all these things that are thought of as necessary. We don't need that because we have this place that feeds us both literally and spiritually." *Beasts* thereby expresses the millennia-long human dream of defending and fully realizing communal freedom in the face of all the destructive and devastating forces of Empire and social domination that threaten it. This is the perennial Dream of Apocalypse.

## The Coming Apocalypse

Will New Orleans fulfill its apocalyptic promise? The answer is "probably," "inevitably," and "possibly," depending on which moment of Apocalypse we have in mind.

First, it is *highly probable* that an apocalyptic disaster, "The Big One," will arrive during the brief remaining period of human habitation. Measures to improve levees and drainage will be of some limited assistance; nevertheless, continued coastal erosion will aggravate the catastrophic effects when the fateful time comes.

Second, it is *inevitable*, barring a global social revolution that fundamentally changes the ecocidal course of world history, that New Orleans will meet its final apocalyptic fate before long. It will, probably at some time within the next century, become a New Atlantis, as it sinks beneath the rising seas, along with much of Florida, most of Bangladesh, and many other of the world's coastal regions. In the ultimate irony, the sea will occupy Wall Street.

And finally, it is *possible* that New Orleans will realize its apocalyptic utopian dream. It is possible that what is entirely impossible according to the dominant ideology, imaginary and ethos, will occur: that New Orleans will fulfill its world-historical and Earth-historical revolutionary and regenerative destiny and that its transformative apocalyptic message of creative destruction will spread to the larger world.

Over a decade after Hurricane Katrina, New Orleans is at a critical cultural moment. The significantly depopulated city[36] has remained the site of an extraordinary heritage of highly particularized and communally rooted, yet radically creative and imaginatively diverse, culture. To this milieu has been added an influx of young activist volunteers, artists, musicians, poets, urban homesteaders, political radicals, spiritual seekers, and visionaries. As a result, it is the locus of one of the greatest concentrations of interstitial, and more significantly, incipiently antistitial culture. It is at such a moment of ethotic intensity that apocalyptic possibility appears, that the missing Circle of the Real begins to emerge out of the Mysterious Crescent.

Faith in this possibility, the one expressed over a century and half ago in Reizenstein's vision of cataclysmic liberation, lives on. This passion of creative destruction, the antistitial quest to liberate humanity and nature from the nihilistic and egoistic forces that are destroying everything of value, is expressed in a recent issue of the local publication *Uncontrollable*:

Here we must and may only forge a liberation that is grounded in New Orleans' glorious, incomparable, horrifying and boundlessly rich history and particularities. As we eat New Orleans food, as we sing New Orleans songs, we build a New Orleans destruction of the state and capitalism. In all we do and all we attempt, we honor her. We live for her, we fight for her, we sacrifice everything for her—our mother—our city—our goddess—our home—New Orleans.[37]

As we gaze out across the gaping Abyss of late modernity, not with our merely corporeal eye but with the eye of the apocalyptic imagination, we envision the Mysteries of New Orleans, as they can never be, but nevertheless must be, fully revealed and perfectly realized.

**NOTES**
1   Elisée Reclus, *A Voyage to New Orleans*, eds. John Clark and Camille Martin (Thetford, VT: Glad Day Books, 2003), 35.
2   Online Etymology Dictionary, http://www.etymonline.com/index.php?term=interstice.
3   *Merriam-Webster's Collegiate Dictionary*, 11th ed. (Springfield, MA: Merriam-Webster, 2003).
4   A version of this text was originally published in a collection entitled *Sweet Spots: In-Between Spaces in New Orleans*, eds. Teresa Toulouse and Barbara C. Ewell (Oxford: University Press of Mississippi, 2018), 249–72.
5   On the importance of "the outside" and the outsider within, see Andrei Codrescu, *The Disappearance of the Outside: A Manifesto for Escape* (St. Paul, MN: Ruminator Books, 2001).
6   This is, not so incidentally, the Heraclitean dialectical position: between land and sea, in the subtropics, on the fringes of Empire, in a period of world historical transformation. See Max Cafard, *Lightning Storm Mind: Pre-Ancientist Meditations* (New York: Autonomedia, 2017).
7   *Merriam-Webster's Collegiate Dictionary*.
8   Nelson Algren, *A Walk on the Wild Side* (New York: Farrar, Straus and Giroux, 1956).
9   Eric Bookhardt, "The Jungle Is Near: Culture and Nature in a Subtropical Clime," *Mesechabe*, no. 2 (1988–1989): 1–5.
10  In reference to HRI Properties, the leading local real estate development corporation, and its CEO, Mr. Maurice Pres *Kabacoff*.
11  This relationship has been pointed out by Max Cafard. See "Laughing Matters, or, In Praise of Folly," in *Surregional Explorations* (Chicago: Charles H. Kerr, 2012), 162–73.
12  Mikhail Bakhtin, *Rabelais and His World* (Bloomington: Indiana University Press, 1984), 9.
13  Bakhtin, *Rabelais and His World*, 10.
14  Bakhtin, 213.

15   Bakhtin, 89.

16   See Hakim Bey, *T.A.Z.: The Temporary Autonomous Zone, Ontological Anarchy, Poetic Terrorism* (Brooklyn: Autonomedia, 1991).

17   Baron Ludwig von Reizenstein, *The Mysteries of New Orleans* (Baltimore: Johns Hopkins University Press, 2002).

18   Reizenstein, *The Mysteries of New Orleans*, xxviii–xxix.

19   Reizenstein, 130.

20   Reizenstein, 130 (italics in original).

21   Reizenstein, 189.

22   Reizenstein, 150–51.

23   "President Arrives in Alabama, Briefed on Hurricane Katrina," *White House Press Release*, September 2, 2005, http://georgewbush-whitehouse.archives.gov/news/releases/2005/09/20050902-2.html.

24   Maureen Dowd, "United States of Shame," *New York Times*, September 3, 2005, http://www.nytimes.com/2005/09/03/opinion/03dowd.html?_r=0.

25   Allen G. Breed, "New Orleans in the Throes of Katrina, and Apocalypse," *USA Today*, September 2, 2005, http://usatoday30.usatoday.com/news/nation/2005-09-02-katrinawalkthroughhell_x.htm.

26   "Relief Workers Confront 'Urban Warfare'" *CNN*, September 1, 2005, http://www.cnn.com/2005/WEATHER/09/01/katrina.impact/.

27   CNN transcript from Anderson Cooper report, September 28, 2005, http://transcripts.cnn.com/TRANSCRIPTS/0509/28/asb.02.html.

28   Isak Winkel Holm "The Cultural Analysis of Disaster," in Karsten Mainer and Kristin Veel, eds., *The Cultural Life of Catastrophes and Crises* (Berlin: Walter De Gruyter, 2012), http://curis.ku.dk/ws/files/46389505/Cultural_Analysis_of_Disaster.pdf.

29   See chapters 5 and 12 in this volume.

30   See Francesco di Santis, *The Post-Katrina Portraits* (New Orleans: Di Santis and Latta, 2007) in which about 350 of the portraits are reproduced. Thousands were put on the walls of Common Ground sites. Some were collected and put in the Historic New Orleans Collection, but a large number were lost when the sites were closed. See the online collection at https://www.flickr.com/photos/postkatrinaportraits/show/.

31   I have attempted to tell part of this story in a series of articles related to Post-Katrina New Orleans. See "New Orleans: Do You Know What It Means?" in *New: Translating Cultures/Cultures Traduites* 2 (2006), revised as chapter 12 of this volume; "A Letter from New Orleans: Reclusian Reflections on an Unnatural Disaster," *Capitalism Nature Socialism* 17, no. 1 (March 2006): 7–18, https://www.academia.edu/2540532/_A_Letter_from_New_Orleans_Reclusian_Reflections_on_an_Unnatural_Disaster_; and "Postscript to a Letter from New Orleans," *Perspectives on Anarchist Theory*, no. 5 (Fall 2006), http://divergences.be/spip.php?article1485. The latter two articles were incorporated in "Disaster Anarchism: Hurricane Katrina and the Shock of Recognition," in John P. Clark, *The Impossible Community: Realizing Communitarian Anarchism* (New York: Bloomberg Academic, 2013), 193–215.

32   Scott crow, *Black Flags and Windmills: Hope, Anarchy, and the Common Ground Collective*, 2nd ed. (Oakland: PM Press, 2014), 165. Scott explicitly traces his

own use of the idea of a "system crack" back to the Zapatistas (personal correspondence).

33  Francesco di Santis, afterword to *The Post-Katrina Portraits*.

34  All quoted material is from Jeremy Butmanjun, "'Beasts of the Southern Wild' Director: Louisiana Is a Dangerous Utopia," http://www.theatlantic.com/entertainment/archive/2012/06/beasts-of-the-southern-wild-director-louisiana-is-a-dangerous-utopia/259009/. The brief discussion here merely points out some of the most important aspects of the film. A very detailed analysis and defense of the film (based can be found in John P. Clark, "The Political Imagination of Beasts: Domination and Liberation in 'Beasts of the Southern Wild'"; https://www.academia.edu/3264979/_The_Political_Imagination_of_Beasts_Domination_and_Liberation_in_Beasts_of_the_Southern_Wild_.

35  For the real-world apocalyptic story of southeast coastal Louisiana, see the documentary film, *My Louisiana Love*, directed by Sharon Linezo Hong. It is the story of Monique Verdin, her family and its Native American roots, and the struggle to save her threatened coastal community and culture.

36  In 2017 New Orleans had a population of 393,000, as compared to 485,000 in 2005 before Hurricane Katrina, and a high of 627,000 in the 1960 census.

37  *Uncontrollable*, no. 2 (Winter 2013–2014): 1.

# Oikos and Poesis: On Earth and Rebirth

Thoreau famously proclaimed that "in wildness is the preservation of the world." And, as Gary Snyder explains, the poetic mind, the mind of the creative artist, is a realm of wildness. Thus, the eco-syllogism: Preservation of the world depends on the wild. The poetic mind is wild. Therefore, the preservation of the world depends on the poetic mind.

What we call "art" is, in reality, technopoesis—the convergence of skillful technique and the creative act. The techne in question may be the use (or creative nonuse) of words, paint, pen and ink, stone or marble, clay, film, the human body and voice, musical notes, or building materials. However, the crucial factor is always that the techne becomes an expression of poesis.

The problem of our age is that techne and poesis have split. Techne, under the control of Capital, has become the great destructive force, devastating mind, spirit, and nature. We have been under the sway of the global death drive, as expressed in the classic self-replicating formula "Money–Capital–Money." It has been said that our hope lies in *l'imagination au pouvoir* (power to the imagination). This is true to the extent that this means the power of poesis, life, and creativity.

Both nature and artistic creativity act through what Daoist thought calls *wuwei*, that is, doing without "doing," in the sense of manipulating or dominating. This is what the creative artist does through negative capability and what creative nature has been doing throughout the history of life on Earth. As Bashō described the process: "Sitting quietly, doing nothing, spring comes, and the grass grows, by itself." The system of domination annihilates this perpetual greening of the Earth, this perpetual greening of the mind.

The combat for the soul of art is thus one with the combat for the soul of nature. It is about *arché* versus *anarché*. It is about the defense of vitality, creative growth, and emergence against the forces of power and profit. Artistic and ecological struggles are one in defending the wild against their common enemy, the ethos and psychology of domination that has been shaped by the Megamachine, Capital, the State, and Patriarchy.

As has been discussed, a burning question recently has been what we should call our current geological era. It has been argued here that although "Anthropocene" has been winning, we might want to be a little less self-centered and much more planet-centered. We might then choose to call it the "Thanatocene," the era in which the planetary death drive has become dominant.

However, the most precisely accurate term is "Necrocene," the "new era of death" that follows the Cenozoic, which was a "new era of life." The current era is the era of the reversal of the creative activity, the poesis, of the Earth.

But what should we call the next era, if there is one, in which we put an end to this period of *Death on Earth*? We should perhaps call it the Poeticene, since it would be the era in which the creative powers of both the Earth and the creatures of the Earth would be allowed to reassert themselves.

It would be an era in which all would be allowed to be artists, or poets, in the sense of radically creative beings. In such a poetic democracy, poets would become the acknowledged legislators of the world. And the Earth would be acknowledged again as the Great Poet, the Artist of all artists.

# Emergency Heart Sutra

For the Emergency Heart,
The Practice of Perfect Wisdom
Is Nothing but the Practice of Perfect Compassion
For all Suffering Beings.

All things are Nothing to it,
Except as they alleviate
The needless Ills and Misfortunes
Of all Suffering Beings.

Nothing it can do, say, or think
Matters, apart from this.
Nothing it can gain or lose
Matters, apart from this.

The Emergency Heart is distracted by Nothing,
Even its own distractions.
The Emergency Heart fears Nothing,
Even its own fears.

---

The Emergency Heart Sutra is inspired by the Common Ground Collective and its slogan "Solidarity Not Charity!" and by the "emergency heart" writings of my friend scott crow, a cofounder of Common Ground. It is modeled after the Heart Sutra.

It goes beyond Everything
To practice the Perfect Wisdom
That is Nothing
But the Practice of Perfect Compassion.

Gone, gone, gone fully beyond!
Beyond Poor Charity
To Perfect Solidarity!
Emergency Heart Sutra!

# Acknowledgments

I would like to give special recognition to two friends and comrades whom we lost recently and who influenced profoundly what is written here.

Joel Kovel was one of the most brilliant and visionary social theorists of the last generation, a prophetic voice for love, justice, and the rebirth of spirit, and one of my most treasured friends for the past thirty-five years. For years I have been buying used copies of his out-of-print masterpieces *The Age of Desire* and *History and Spirit* and passing them on to those who show promise of being inspired by them to reflect deeply and to act boldly. I cannot begin to express how grateful I am to Joel and how much I miss him.

Mama D (Dyan French Cole) was a legendary civil rights and social justice activist, gadfly of the establishment, enemy of nonsense and hypocrisy, tireless advocate for the people, and tough and benevolent matriarch of her neighborhood community in the Seventh Ward of New Orleans. I learned much from her in the post-Katrina period that changed my life so profoundly. In the image below, I am at the center with Mama D on the left, surrounded by (from the bottom left) Merc from the Soul Patrol and members of the Family Farm Defenders.

There are others to whom I am grateful for encouragement, inspiration, suggestions, criticisms, practical assistance, and being the change I want to see in the world. These include Randall Amster, Stanley Aronowitz, Simon Berz, Jacqueline Bishop, Laura Borealis, Pat Bryant, Todd Burst, Sean Burns, Max Cafard, Ethan Clark, Nathan Clark, Andrei Codrescu, Ronald Creagh, scott crow, Laurence Davis, MarkAlain Dery, Rossella Di Leo, Francesco di Santis, Brian Drolet, Claire Duplantier, Steven Duplantier, Francis Dupuy-Déri, Jeanie Egan, Tom Egan, Salvatore Engel-Di Mauro, Scott Eustis, Barbara Ewell, Dylan Fitzwater, Jeremias Frogg, Andrej

Grubačić, Neil Guidry, Leenie Halbert, DeeDee Halleck, David Hensley, Renate Heurich, Christopher Holmes, Nathan Jun, Paul Kahn, Ramsey Kanaan, Cynthia Kaufman, Mat Keel, Megan Kelley, Chris Kortright, Monica Lark, Erin Lierl, Peter Linebaugh, Lucci, Gaetano Manfredonia, Peter Marshall, Kent Mathewson, Steven Miles, Gregory Nipper, Shuji Ozeki, Joey Paxman, Michael Pelias, Tsering Phuntsok, Danny Postel, Malik Rahim, Lala Rascic, Anne Rolfes, Penelope Rosemont, Ariel Salleh, Ed Sanders, Alyce Santoro, Quincy Saul, Christopher Schaberg, Javier Sethness-Castro, Kalan Sherrard, Gary Snyder, Amos Soma, Simon Springer, Harvey Stern, Karsten Struhl, Robert Desmarais Sullivan, Michael J. Thompson, Teresa Toulouse, Nat Turner, Michel Varisco, Christophe Washer, David Watson, Peter Werbe, Susan Williams, Peter Wilson, and many others.

I would also like to acknowledge publications in which earlier versions of parts of this work appeared and thank the editors of these publications for permission to use this material.

"Lessons from the School of Radical Change (Notes of a Slow Learner)" is based on a presentation at a PM Press authors' session on "Ideas for Action: Relevant Theory for Radical Change" at the Left Forum on June 3, 2017. An expanded version appeared on my PM Press blog.

"Ecological Thinking and the Crisis of the Earth" originally appeared in the tenth anniversary issue of the *Journal of Environmental Thought and Education* (Tokyo: Society for the Study of Environmental Thought and Education, 2017), 17–24. A revised version appeared on my PM Press and Changing Suns Press blogs.

"How an Anarchist Discovered the Earth" and "Education for the Earth or Education for Empire?" are revised versions of texts presented at the American Association of Geographers' Annual Meeting, April 10, 2018, in New Orleans.

"The Summit of Ambition: The Paris Climate Spectacle and the Politics of the Gesture" appeared on "It Is What It Isn't," my Changing Suns Press blog, December 18, 2015.

"Against Resilence: Hurricane Katrina and the Politics of Disavowal" appeared on the site *New Clear Vision*, September 21, 2015.

"Homage to Lacandonia: The Politics of Heart and Spirit in Chiapas" is a revised and expanded version of "A Politics of Heart and Spirit," the foreword to Dylan Eldridge Fitzwater's *Autonomy Is in Our Hearts: Zapatista Autonomous Government through the Lens of the Tsotsil Language* (Oakland: PM Press, 2019).

"Lessons of the Rojavan Revolution" is a revised and expanded version of "Imaginare Aude! Lessons of the Rojava Revolution," from *Capitalism Nature Socialism* 27, no. 3 (September 2016): 103–10.

"Papua Merdeka: The Indigenous Struggle against State and Corporate Domination" is a revised version of "Between Earth and Empire: West Papua's Struggle against State and Corporate Domination," a paper presented at "Réflexions sur l'impact des entreprises multinationales américaines sur la société" ("Reflections on the Social Impact of American Multinational Corporations"), Université Pierre Mendès France, Grenoble, France, January 11, 2002.

"Power to the Community: The Black Panthers' Living Legacy of

Grassroots Organization" appeared on my Changing Suns Press blog, November 25, 2015.

"From the Movement of Occupation to the Community of Liberation" appeared in *The Raging Pelican*, November 5, 2011.

"Another Sun Is Possible: Thoughts for the Solstice" is based on a talk given at the Summer Solstice Gathering at La Terre Institute for Community and Ecology," Bayou La Terre, Dedeaux, MS, June 24, 2017. An expanded version appeared on my Changing Suns Press blog.

"Do You Know What It Means? Reflections on Suffering, Disaster, and Awakening" was published as "New Orleans: Do You Know What It Means?" in *New: Translating Cultures/Cultures Traduites* 2 (2006): 61–74.

"Buddhism, Radical Critique and Revolutionary Praxis" was presented at a panel with that title at the Left Forum, John Jay College of Criminal Justice, New York City, May 31, 2014.

"Rumi and the Fall of the Spectacular Commodity Economy" originated in a series of emails to Megan Kelley. I am grateful to Megan for posing questions to me about the meaning and power of this story. An earlier version appeared on my PM Press blog.

"Regionalism and the Politics of Experience" appeared as "Bernard Charbonneau: Regionalism and the Politics of Experience" in *Capitalism Nature Socialism*, no. 51 (2002): 41–48.

"In Search of the Radical Imagination: Two Concepts of the Social Imaginary" includes material from "Cornelius Castoriadis: Thinking About Political Theory," in *Capitalism Nature Socialism*, no. 49 (2002): 67–74, and "The Modern Social Imaginary: Toward a Critical-Dialectical Approach," in *Rêves et passions d'un chercheur militant: Mélanges offerts à Ronald Creagh* (Lyon: Atelier de Création Libertaire, 2016), 29–39.

"The Spectacle Looks Back into You: The Situationists and the Aporias of the Left" appeared in *Radical Intellectuals and the Subversion of Progressive Politics: The Betrayal of Politics*, edited by Gregory R. Smulewicz-Zucker and Michael J. Thompson (New York: Palgrave Macmillan, 2015).

"Happy Birthday, Utopia! (You Deserve A Present)" appeared in *Fifth Estate*, no. 396 (Summer 2016).

"Carnival at the Edge of the Abyss: New Orleans and the Apocalyptic Imagination" first appeared in *Sweet Spots: In-Between Spaces in New Orleans*, edited by Barbara Ewell and Teresa Toulouse (Oxford: University Press of Mississippi, 2018), and is reprinted with the permission of the Press. The present version also contains material from "The Political Imagination of Beasts: Domination and Liberation in 'Beasts of the Southern Wild,'" a presentation at the Heartland-Delta Conference on "Eloquentia Perfecta," Loyola University, New Orleans, February 23, 2013.

"Oikos and Poesis: On Earth and Rebirth" appeared as "Oikos and Poesis: Art and Our Planetary Future" in the *Brooklyn Rail* (November 5, 2015), as part of a collection of twenty-seven short articles on the theme "Social Ecologies."

"Emergency Heart Sutra" appeared in scott crow, *Emergency Hearts, Molotov Dreams: A scott crow Reader* (Cleveland: GTK Press, 2015), 193.

# Index

"Passim" (literally "scattered") indicates intermittent discussion of a topic over a cluster of pages.

# About the Authors

**John P. Clark** is an eco-communitarian anarchist writer, activist, and educator. He lives and works in New Orleans, where his family has lived for twelve generations. He is director of La Terre Institute for Community and Ecology, which is located on Bayou La Terre in the forest of the Mississippi Gulf Coast. His most recent books (several as Max Cafard) include *Surregional Explorations*, *The Impossible Community*, *The Tragedy of Common Sense*, and *Lightning Storm Mind*. An archive of over three hundred of his texts can be found at http://loyno.academia.edu/JohnClark. He is professor emeritus of philosophy at Loyola University and a member of the Education Workers' Union of the Industrial Workers of the World.

**Peter Marshall** is the author of seventeen books, including *Riding the Wind: Liberation Ecology for a New Era* (2002). PM Press has republished his *Demanding the Impossible: A History of Anarchism* (2010) and *William Godwin: Philosopher, Novelist, Revolutionary* (2017). His most recent works are *Poseidon's Realm: A Voyage around the Aegean* (2017) and his early memoir *Bognor Boy: How I Became an Anarchist* (2018).

# ABOUT PM PRESS

PM Press was founded at the end of 2007 by a small collection of folks with decades of publishing, media, and organizing experience. PM Press co-conspirators have published and distributed hundreds of books, pamphlets, CDs, and DVDs. Members of PM have founded enduring book fairs, spearheaded victorious tenant organizing campaigns, and worked closely with bookstores, academic conferences, and even rock bands to deliver political and challenging ideas to all walks of life. We're old enough to know what we're doing and young enough to know what's at stake.

We seek to create radical and stimulating fiction and nonfiction books, pamphlets, T-shirts, visual and audio materials to entertain, educate, and inspire you. We aim to distribute these through every available channel with every available technology—whether that means you are seeing anarchist classics at our bookfair stalls, reading our latest vegan cookbook at the café, downloading geeky fiction e-books, or digging new music and timely videos from our website.

PM Press is always on the lookout for talented and skilled volunteers, artists, activists, and writers to work with. If you have a great idea for a project or can contribute in some way, please get in touch.

**PM Press**
**PO Box 23912**
**Oakland, CA 94623**
**www.pmpress.org**

**PM Press in Europe**
**europe@pmpress.org**
**www.pmpress.org.uk**

# FRIENDS OF PM PRESS

These are indisputably momentous times—the financial system is melting down globally and the Empire is stumbling. Now more than ever there is a vital need for radical ideas.

In the years since its founding—and on a mere shoestring—PM Press has risen to the formidable challenge of publishing and distributing knowledge and entertainment for the struggles ahead. With over 300 releases to date, we have published an impressive and stimulating array of literature, art, music, politics, and culture. Using every available medium, we've succeeded in connecting those hungry for ideas and information to those putting them into practice.

*Friends of PM* allows you to directly help impact, amplify, and revitalize the discourse and actions of radical writers, filmmakers, and artists. It provides us with a stable foundation from which we can build upon our early successes and provides a much-needed subsidy for the materials that can't necessarily pay their own way. You can help make that happen—and receive every new title automatically delivered to your door once a month—by joining as a Friend of PM Press. And, we'll throw in a free T-shirt when you sign up.

Here are your options:

- **$30 a month** Get all books and pamphlets plus 50% discount on all webstore purchases

- **$40 a month** Get all PM Press releases (including CDs and DVDs) plus 50% discount on all webstore purchases

- **$100 a month** Superstar—Everything plus PM merchandise, free downloads, and 50% discount on all webstore purchases

For those who can't afford $30 or more a month, we have **Sustainer Rates** at $15, $10 and $5. Sustainers get a free PM Press T-shirt and a 50% discount on all purchases from our website.

Your Visa or Mastercard will be billed once a month, until you tell us to stop. Or until our efforts succeed in bringing the revolution around. Or the financial meltdown of Capital makes plastic redundant. Whichever comes first.

## Anarchy, Geography, Modernity: Selected Writings of Elisée Reclus

Edited and translated by John P. Clark and Camille Martin

ISBN: 978-1-60486-429-8
$22.95   304 pages

*Anarchy, Geography, Modernity* is the first comprehensive introduction to the thought of Elisée Reclus, the great anarchist geographer and political theorist. It shows him to be an extraordinary figure for his age. Not only an anarchist but also a radical feminist, anti-racist, ecologist, animal rights advocate, cultural radical, nudist, and vegetarian. Not only a major social thinker but also a dedicated revolutionary.

The work analyzes Reclus' greatest achievement, a sweeping historical and theoretical synthesis recounting the story of the earth and humanity as an epochal struggle between freedom and domination. It presents his groundbreaking critique of all forms of domination: not only capitalism, the state, and authoritarian religion, but also patriarchy, racism, technological domination, and the domination of nature. His crucial insights on the interrelation between personal and small-group transformation, broader cultural change, and large-scale social organization are explored. Reclus' ideas are presented both through detailed exposition and analysis, and in extensive translations of key texts, most appearing in English for the first time.

*"For far too long Elisée Reclus has stood in the shadow of Godwin, Proudhon, Bakunin, Kropotkin, and Emma Goldman. Now John Clark has pulled Reclus forward to stand shoulder to shoulder with Anarchism's cynosures. Reclus' light brought into anarchism's compass not only a focus on ecology, but a struggle against both patriarchy and racism, contributions which can now be fully appreciated thanks to John Clark's exegesis and [his and Camille Martin's] translations of works previously unavailable in English. No serious reader can afford to neglect this book."*
—Dana Ward, Pitzer College

*"Finally! A century after his death, the great French geographer and anarchist Elisée Reclus has been honored by a vibrant selection of his writings expertly translated into English."*
—Kent Mathewson, Louisiana State University

*"Maintaining an appropriately scholarly style, marked by deep background knowledge, nuanced argument, and careful qualifications, Clark and Martin nevertheless reveal a passionate love for their subject and adopt a stance of political engagement that they hope does justice to Reclus' own commitments."*
—Historical Geography

# The Impossible Community: Realizing Communitarian Anarchism

John P. Clark

ISBN: 978-1-62963-714-3
$24.95    352 pages

*The Impossible Community* confronts a critical moment
when social and ecological catastrophes loom, the Left
seems unable to articulate a response, and the Right
controls public debates. This book offers a fresh and highly readable reformulation
of anarchist social and political theory to develop a communitarian anarchist
solution.

In this stunningly original work, John P. Clark, author, lifelong activist, and one of
the most fascinating anarchist luminaries of our time, skillfully argues that a free
and just social order requires a radical transformation of the modes of domination
exercised through social ideology, the social imaginary, the social ethos, and social
institutional structures. Communitarian anarchism unites a universalist concern
for social and ecological justice while recognizing the integrity and individuality of
the person. *The Impossible Community* is a renewed examination of the anarchist
principles of mutual aid and voluntary cooperation and provides convincingly lucid
examples in various contexts, from the rebuilding of New Orleans after Katrina to
social movements in South Asia.

Ambitious in scope and compelling in its strength and imagination, *The Impossible
Community* offers readers an accessible theoretical framework along with concrete
case studies to show how contemporary anarchist practice continues a long
tradition of successfully synthesizing personal and communal liberation. This
provocatively innovative work will appeal not only to students of anarchism and
political theory but also to activists and anyone interested in making the world a
better place.

*"In this often insightful and illuminating book John P. Clark sets out his vision for a
radically democratic 'communitarian anarchism.' . . . Clark's deep commitment to the
anarchist ethics that he advocates, and his work in putting them into effect, lend weight
to the distinction between ethics as working ideals and the kind of 'abstract moralism'
he criticizes. . . . This book is valuable for several important reasons. . . . Clark adeptly
deploys Marx, Hegel, Aristotle, Enlightenment philosophers, Žižek, and a host of other
modern and ancient thinkers, making this work erudite and rich."*
—Chris Tomlinson, *Red Pepper*

# William Godwin: Philosopher, Novelist, Revolutionary

Peter Marshall
with a Foreword by John P. Clark

**ISBN: 978-1-62963-386-2**
**$29.95    544 pages**

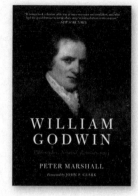

William Godwin has long been known for his literary connections as the husband of Mary Wollstonecraft, the father of Mary Shelley, the friend of Coleridge, Lamb, and Hazlitt, the mentor of the young Wordsworth, Southey, and Shelley, and the opponent of Malthus. Godwin has been recently recognized, however, as the most capable exponent of philosophical anarchism, an original moral thinker, a pioneer in socialist economics and progressive education, and a novelist of great skill.

His long life straddled two centuries. Not only did he live at the center of radical and intellectual London during the French Revolution, he also commented on some of the most significant changes in British history. Shaped by the Enlightenment, he became a key figure in English Romanticism.

Basing his work on extensive published and unpublished materials, Peter Marshall has written a comprehensive study of this flamboyant and fascinating figure. Marshall places Godwin firmly in his social, political, and historical context; he traces chronologically the origin and development of Godwin's ideas and themes; and he offers a critical estimate of his works, recognizing the equal value of his philosophy and literature and their mutual illumination.

The picture of Godwin that emerges is one of a complex man and a subtle and revolutionary thinker, one whose influence was far greater than is usually assumed. In the final analysis, Godwin stands forth not only as a rare example of a man who excelled in both philosophy and literature but as one of the great humanists in the Western tradition.

*"The most comprehensive and richly detailed work yet to appear on Godwin as thinker, writer, and person."*
—John P. Clark, *The Tragedy of Common Sense*

*"An ambitious study that offers a thorough exploration of Godwin's life and complex times."*
—*Library Journal*

# Demanding the Impossible:
# A History of Anarchism

Peter Marshall

**ISBN: 978-1-60486-064-1**
**$28.95    840 pages**

Navigating the broad "river of anarchy," from Taoism
to Situationism, from Ranters to Punk rockers, from
individualists to communists, from anarcho-syndicalists
to anarcha-feminists, *Demanding the Impossible* is an
authoritative and lively study of a widely misunderstood
subject. It explores the key anarchist concepts of society and the state, freedom
and equality, authority and power, and investigates the successes and failure of
the anarchist movements throughout the world. While remaining sympathetic
to anarchism, it presents a balanced and critical account. It covers not only the
classic anarchist thinkers, such as Godwin, Proudhon, Bakunin, Kropotkin, Reclus
and Emma Goldman, but also other libertarian figures, such as Nietzsche, Camus,
Gandhi, Foucault and Chomsky. No other book on anarchism covers so much so
incisively.

In this updated edition, a new epilogue examines the most recent developments,
including "post-anarchism" and "anarcho-primitivism" as well as the anarchist
contribution to the peace, green and Global Justice movements.

*Demanding the Impossible* is essential reading for anyone wishing to understand
what anarchists stand for and what they have achieved. It will also appeal to those
who want to discover how anarchism offers an inspiring and original body of ideas
and practices which is more relevant than ever in the twenty-first century.

"**Demanding the Impossible** *is the book I always recommend when asked—as I often
am—for something on the history and ideas of anarchism.*"
—Noam Chomsky

"*Attractively written and fully referenced… bound to be the standard history.*"
—Colin Ward, *Times Educational Supplement*

"*Large, labyrinthine, tentative: for me these are all adjectives of praise when applied to
works of history, and* **Demanding the Impossible** *meets all of them.*"
—George Woodcock, *Independent*

## Romantic Rationalist: A William Godwin Reader

Edited by Peter Marshall
with a Foreword by John P. Clark

ISBN: 978-1-62963-228-5
$17.95   192 pages

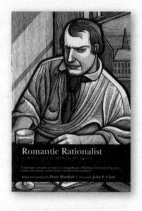

William Godwin (1756–1836) was one of the first
exponents of utilitarianism and the first modern
proponent of anarchism. He was not only a radical
philosopher but a pioneer in libertarian education, a
founder of communist economics, and an acute and powerful novelist whose
literary family included his partner, pioneering feminist writer Mary Wollstonecraft,
and his daughter Mary Godwin (later Mary Shelley), who would go on to write
*Frankenstein* and marry the poet Percy Bysshe Shelley.

His long life straddled two centuries. Not only did he live at the center of radical
and intellectual London during the French Revolution, he also commented on some
of the most significant changes in modern history. Shaped by the Enlightenment,
he became a key figure in English Romanticism.

This work offers for the first time a handy collection of Godwin's key writings
in a clear and concise form, together with an assessment of his influence, a
biographical sketch, and an analysis of his contribution to anarchist theory and
practice. The selections are taken from all of Godwin's writings including his
groundbreaking work during the French Revolution, *An Enquiry Concerning Political
Justice*, and arranged by editor Peter Marshall to give a coherent account of his
thought for the general reader.

Godwin's work will be of interest to all those who believe that rationality, truth,
happiness, individuality, equality, and freedom are central concerns of human
enquiry and endeavor.

*"Peter Marshall has produced the most useful modern account of Godwin's life and now
the most useful modern anthology of his writings. Marshall's selection is sensible and
valuable, bringing out the important points. . . . His introduction is a good summary of
Godwin's life and work. . . . Marshall is right to see him as 'the most profound exponent
of philosophical anarchism.'"*
—Nicolas Walter, *New Statesman*

*"A handsome and handy little book, excavating nuggets of Godwinian wisdom from the
whole range of his writings."*
—Colin Ward, *Times Educational Supplement*

## Autonomy Is in Our Hearts: Zapatista Autonomous Government through the Lens of the Tsotsil Language

Dylan Eldredge Fitzwater
with a Foreword by John P. Clark

**ISBN: 978-1-62963-580-4**
**$19.95    224 pages**

Following the Zapatista uprising on New Year's Day 1994, the EZLN communities of Chiapas began the slow process of creating a system of autonomous government that would bring their call for freedom, justice, and democracy from word to reality. *Autonomy Is in Our Hearts* analyzes this long and arduous process on its own terms, using the conceptual language of Tsotsil, a Mayan language indigenous to the highland Zapatista communities of Chiapas.

The words "Freedom," "Justice," and "Democracy" emblazoned on the Zapatista flags are only approximations of the aspirations articulated in the six indigenous languages spoken by the Zapatista communities. They are rough translations of concepts such as *ichbail ta muk'* or "mutual recognition and respect among equal persons or peoples," *a'mtel* or "collective work done for the good of a community" and *lekil kuxlejal* or "the life that is good for everyone." *Autonomy Is in Our Hearts* provides a fresh perspective on the Zapatistas and a deep engagement with the daily realities of Zapatista autonomous government. Simultaneously an exposition of Tsotsil philosophy and a detailed account of Zapatista governance structures, this book is an indispensable commentary on the Zapatista movement of today.

*"This is a refreshing book. Written with the humility of the learner, or the absence of the arrogant knower, the Zapatista dictum to 'command obeying' becomes to 'know learning.'"*
—Marisol de la Cadena, author of *Earth Beings: Ecologies of Practice across Andean Worlds*

*"Autonomy Is in Our Hearts is perhaps the most important book you can read on the Zapatista movement in Chiapas today. It stands out from the rest of the Anglophone literature in that it demonstrates, with great sensitivity, how a dialectic between traditional culture and institutions and emerging revolutionary and regenerative forces can play a crucial role in liberatory social transformation. It shows us what we can learn from the indigenous people of Chiapas about a politics of community, care, and mutual aid, and—to use a word that they themselves use so much—about a politics of heart. A great strength of the work is that the author is a very good listener. He allows the people of Chiapas to tell their own story largely in their own words, and with their own distinctive voice."*
—John P. Clark, from the Foreword

# Revolution and Other Writings: A Political Reader

Gustav Landauer

Edited and translated by Gabriel Kuhn

ISBN: 978-1-60486-054-2
$26.95    360 pages

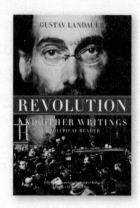

"*Landauer is the most important agitator of the radical and revolutionary movement in the entire country.*" This is how Gustav Landauer is described in a German police file from 1893. Twenty-six years later, Landauer would die at the hands of reactionary soldiers who overthrew the Bavarian Council Republic, a three-week attempt to realize libertarian socialism amidst the turmoil of post-World War I Germany. It was the last chapter in the life of an activist, writer, and mystic who Paul Avrich calls "the most influential German anarchist intellectual of the twentieth century."

This is the first comprehensive collection of Landauer writings in English. It includes one of his major works, *Revolution*, thirty additional essays and articles, and a selection of correspondence. The texts cover Landauer's entire political biography, from his early anarchism of the 1890s to his philosophical reflections at the turn of the century, the subsequent establishment of the Socialist Bund, his tireless agitation against the war, and the final days among the revolutionaries in Munich. Additional chapters collect Landauer's articles on radical politics in the US and Mexico, and illustrate the scope of his writing with texts on corporate capital, language, education, and Judaism. The book includes an extensive introduction, commentary, and bibliographical information, compiled by the editor and translator Gabriel Kuhn as well as a preface by Richard Day.

"*If there were any justice in this world—at least as far as historical memory goes—then Gustav Landauer would be remembered, right along with Bakunin and Kropotkin, as one of anarchism's most brilliant and original theorists. Instead, history has abetted the crime of his murderers, burying his work in silence. With this anthology, Gabriel Kuhn has single-handedly redressed one of the cruelest gaps in Anglo-American anarchist literature: the absence of almost any English translations of Landauer.*"
—Jesse Cohn, author of *Anarchism and the Crisis of Representation: Hermeneutics, Aesthetics, Politics*

"*Gustav Landauer was, without doubt, one of the brightest intellectual lights within the revolutionary circles of fin de siècle Europe. In this remarkable anthology, Gabriel Kuhn brings together an extensive and splendidly chosen collection of Landauer's most important writings, presenting them for the first time in English translation. With Landauer's ideas coming of age today perhaps more than ever before, Kuhn's work is a valuable and timely piece of scholarship, and one which should be required reading for anyone with an interest in radical social change.*"
—James Horrox, author of *A Living Revolution: Anarchism in the Kibbutz Movement*

## Liberating Society from the State and Other Writings: A Political Reader

Erich Mühsam
Edited by Gabriel Kuhn

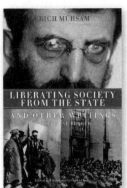

**ISBN: 978-1-60486-055-9**
**$26.95    320 pages**

Erich Mühsam (1878–1934), poet, bohemian, revolutionary, is one of Germany's most renowned and influential anarchists. Born into a middle-class Jewish family, he challenged the conventions of bourgeois society at the turn of the century, engaged in heated debates on the rights of women and homosexuals, and traveled Europe in search of radical communes and artist colonies. He was a primary instigator of the ill-fated Bavarian Council Republic in 1919 and held the libertarian banner high during a Weimar Republic that came under increasing threat by right-wing forces. In 1933, four weeks after Hitler's ascension to power, Mühsam was arrested in his Berlin home. He spent the last sixteen months of his life in detention and died in the Oranienburg Concentration Camp in July 1934.

Mühsam wrote poetry, plays, essays, articles, and diaries. His work unites a burning desire for individual liberation with anarcho-communist convictions, and bohemian strains with syndicalist tendencies. The body of his writings is immense, yet hardly any English translations have been available before now. This collection presents not only *Liberating Society from the State: What Is Communist Anarchism?*, Mühsam's main political pamphlet and one of the key texts in the history of German anarchism, but also some of his best-known poems, unbending defenses of political prisoners, passionate calls for solidarity with the lumpenproletariat, recollections of the utopian community of Monte Verità, debates on the rights of homosexuals and women, excerpts from his journals, and essays contemplating German politics and anarchist theory as much as Jewish identity and the role of intellectuals in the class struggle.

An appendix documents the fate of Zenzl Mühsam, who, after her husband's death, escaped to the Soviet Union where she spent twenty years in Gulag camps.

*"We need new ideas. How about studying the ideal for which Erich Mühsam lived, worked, and died?"*
—Augustin Souchy, author of *Beware! Anarchist! A Life for Freedom*

## Re-enchanting the World: Feminism and the Politics of the Commons

Silvia Federici
with a Foreword by Peter Linebaugh

ISBN: 978-1-62963-569-9
$19.95    240 pages

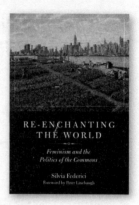

Silvia Federici is one of the most important contemporary theorists of capitalism and feminist movements. In this collection of her work spanning over twenty years, she provides a detailed history and critique of the politics of the commons from a feminist perspective. In her clear and combative voice, Federici provides readers with an analysis of some of the key issues and debates in contemporary thinking on this subject.

Drawing on rich historical research, she maps the connections between the previous forms of enclosure that occurred with the birth of capitalism and the destruction of the commons and the "new enclosures" at the heart of the present phase of global capitalist accumulation. Considering the commons from a feminist perspective, this collection centers on women and reproductive work as crucial to both our economic survival and the construction of a world free from the hierarchies and divisions capital has planted in the body of the world proletariat. Federici is clear that the commons should not be understood as happy islands in a sea of exploitative relations but rather autonomous spaces from which to challenge the existing capitalist organization of life and labor.

*"Silvia Federici's theoretical capacity to articulate the plurality that fuels the contemporary movement of women in struggle provides a true toolbox for building bridges between different features and different people."*
—Massimo De Angelis, professor of political economy, University of East London

*"Silvia Federici's work embodies an energy that urges us to rejuvenate struggles against all types of exploitation and, precisely for that reason, her work produces a common: a common sense of the dissidence that creates a community in struggle."*
—Maria Mies, coauthor of *Ecofeminism*

# Maroon Comix: Origins and Destinies

Edited by Quincy Saul with illlustrations by Seth Tobocman, Mac McGill, Songe Riddle, and more

**ISBN: 978-1-62963-571-2**
**$15.95    72 pages**

Escaping slavery in the Americas, maroons made miracles in the mountains, summoned new societies in the swamps, and forged new freedoms in the forests. They didn't just escape and steal from plantations—they also planted and harvested polycultures. They not only fought slavery but proved its opposite, and for generations they defended it with blood and brilliance.

*Maroon Comix* is a fire on the mountain where maroon words and images meet to tell stories together. Stories of escape and homecoming, exile and belonging. Stories that converge on the summits of the human spirit, where the most dreadful degradation is overcome by the most daring dignity. Stories of the damned who consecrate their own salvation.

With selections and citations from the writings of Russell Maroon Shoatz, Herbert Aptheker, C.L.R. James, and many more, accompanied by comics and illustrations from Songe Riddle, Mac McGill, Seth Tobocman, and others, *Maroon Comix* is an invitation to never go back, to join hands and hearts across space and time with the maroons and the mountains that await their return.

*"The activist artists of* **Maroon Comix** *have combined and presented struggles past and present in a vivid, creative, graphic form, pointing a way toward an emancipated future."*
—Marcus Rediker, coauthor of *The Many-Headed Hydra: Sailors, Slaves, Commoners, and the Hidden History of the Revolutionary Atlantic*

*"With bold graphics and urgent prose,* **Maroon Comix** *provides a powerful antidote to toxic historical narratives. By showing us what was, Quincy Saul and his talented team allow us to see what's possible."*
—James Sturm, author of *The Golem's Mighty Swing*

*"The history and stories that the Maroons personified should inspire a whole new generation of abolitionists. This comic illustration can motivate all those looking to resist modern capitalism's twenty-first-century slavery and the neofascism we are facing today."*
—Dhoruba Bin Wahad, Black Panther Party, New York Chapter, executive director of Community Change Africa

# Black Flags and Windmills: Hope, Anarchy, and the Common Ground Collective

scott crow with forewords
by Kathleen Cleaver and John P. Clark

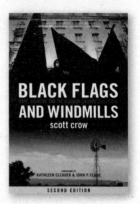

ISBN: 978-1-60486-453-3
$20.00    288 pages

When both levees and governments failed in New Orleans after Hurricane Katrina, the anarchist-inspired Common Ground Collective was created to fill the void. With the motto of "Solidarity Not Charity," they worked to create power from below—building autonomous projects, programs, and spaces of self-sufficiency like health clinics and neighborhood assemblies, while also supporting communities defending themselves from white militias and police brutality, illegal home demolitions, and evictions.

*Black Flags and Windmills*—equal parts memoir, history, and organizing philosophy—vividly intertwines Common Ground cofounder scott crow's experiences and ideas with Katrina's reality, illustrating how people can build local grassroots power for collective liberation. It is a story of resisting indifference, rebuilding hope amid collapse, and struggling against the grain to create better worlds.

The expanded second edition includes up-to-date interviews and discussions between crow and some of today's most articulate and influential activists and organizers on topics ranging from grassroots disaster relief efforts (both economic and environmental); dealing with infiltration, interrogation, and surveillance from the State; and a new photo section that vividly portrays scott's experiences as an anarchist, activist, and movement organizer in today's world.

*"scott crow's trenchant memoir of grassroots organizing is an important contribution to a history of movements that far too often goes untold."*
—Amy Goodman, host and executive producer of *Democracy Now!*

*"This revised and expanded edition weaves scott crow's frontline experiences with a resilient, honest discussion of grassroots political movement-building."*
—Will Potter, author of *Green Is the New Red: An Insider's Account of a Social Movement Under Siege*

*"It is a brilliant, detailed, and humble book written with total frankness and at the same time a revolutionary poet's passion. It makes the reader feel that we too, with our emergency heart as our guide, can do anything; we only need to begin."*
—Marina Sitrin, author of *Horizontalism: Voices of Popular Power in Argentina*

# *Wobblies and Zapatistas: Conversations on Anarchism, Marxism and Radical History*

Staughton Lynd and Andrej Grubačić

**ISBN: 978-1-60486-041-2**
**$20.00    300 pages**

*Wobblies and Zapatistas* offers the reader an encounter between two generations and two traditions. Andrej Grubačić is an anarchist from the Balkans. Staughton Lynd is a lifelong pacifist, influenced by Marxism. They meet in dialogue in an effort to bring together the anarchist and Marxist traditions, to discuss the writing of history by those who make it, and to remind us of the idea that "my country is the world." Encompassing a Left libertarian perspective and an emphatically activist standpoint, these conversations are meant to be read in the clubs and affinity groups of the new Movement.

The authors accompany us on a journey through modern revolutions, direct actions, anti-globalist counter summits, Freedom Schools, Zapatista cooperatives, Haymarket and Petrograd, Hanoi and Belgrade, 'intentional' communities, wildcat strikes, early Protestant communities, Native American democratic practices, the Workers' Solidarity Club of Youngstown, occupied factories, self-organized councils and soviets, the lives of forgotten revolutionaries, Quaker meetings, antiwar movements, and prison rebellions. Neglected and forgotten moments of interracial self-activity are brought to light. The book invites the attention of readers who believe that a better world, on the other side of capitalism and state bureaucracy, may indeed be possible.

*"There's no doubt that we've lost much of our history. It's also very clear that those in power in this country like it that way. Here's a book that shows us why. It demonstrates not only that another world is possible, but that it already exists, has existed, and shows an endless potential to burst through the artificial walls and divisions that currently imprison us. An exquisite contribution to the literature of human freedom, and coming not a moment too soon."*
—David Graeber, author of *Fragments of an Anarchist Anthropology* and *Direct Action: An Ethnography*

*"I have been in regular contact with Andrej Grubačić for many years, and have been most impressed by his searching intelligence, broad knowledge, lucid judgment, and penetrating commentary on contemporary affairs and their historical roots. He is an original thinker and dedicated activist, who brings deep understanding and outstanding personal qualities to everything he does."*
—Noam Chomsky

## *Journey through Utopia: A Critical Examination of Imagined Worlds in Western Literature*

Marie Louise Berneri with a Foreword by George Woodcock, Introduction by Matthew S. Adams, Afterword by Rhiannon Firth, and Postscript by Kim Stanley Robinson

ISBN: 978-1-62963-646-7
$28.95    464 pages

*Journey through Utopia* is a richly detailed and critically compelling examination of utopian literature, beginning with Plato's *Republic* and continuing through to Huxley's *Brave New World*. Utopias have been penned with diverse intentions: some as pictures of an ideal society, some as blueprints for action, yet others, especially in times of severe censorship, as covert criticisms of existing conditions.

Marie Louise Berneri exposes the dark shadow that lingers above most utopian works by emphasising the intolerant and authoritarian nature of these visions, and she warns of the doom that awaits those foolish enough to put their trust in an ordered and regimented world.

This new edition is framed with an Introduction from Matthew S. Adams that situates Berneri's work in the context of her life, and concludes with an Afterword from Rhiannon Firth that extends Berneri's analysis into contemporary utopias. *Journey through Utopia* is a necessary companion, and in many cases an antidote, to imagined fictions from antiquity to the present.

*"Berneri's comments, explicit and implicit, are for the most part acutely discerning . . . . This is a fascinating work."*
—*Times Literary Supplement*

*"As an old student of utopias, I have a special regard for Marie Louise Berneri's Journey through Utopia; for it is the most comprehensive and the most perceptive study of that ideal land that I have come across in any language."*
—Lewis Mumford

*"A demolishment of dream worlds (not ones that have been put into practice) in this historical survey and analysis of utopian thought from antiquity to modern times underscores the regimentation, authoritarian and narrow concepts of freedom that such prospectuses embodied."*
—*Kirkus Reviews*

# Stop, Thief!
# The Commons, Enclosures, and Resistance

Peter Linebaugh

**ISBN: 978-1-60486-747-3**
**$21.95    304 pages**

In this majestic tour de force, celebrated historian Peter Linebaugh takes aim at the thieves of land, the polluters of the seas, the ravagers of the forests, the despoilers of rivers, and the removers of mountaintops. Scarcely a society has existed on the face of the earth that has not had commoning at its heart. "Neither the state nor the market," say the planetary commoners. These essays kindle the embers of memory to ignite our future commons.

From Thomas Paine to the Luddites, from Karl Marx—who concluded his great study of capitalism with the enclosure of commons—to the practical dreamer William Morris—who made communism into a verb and advocated communizing industry and agriculture—to the 20th-century communist historian E.P. Thompson, Linebaugh brings to life the vital commonist tradition. He traces the red thread from the great revolt of commoners in 1381 to the enclosures of Ireland, and the American commons, where European immigrants who had been expelled from their commons met the immense commons of the native peoples and the underground African-American urban commons. Illuminating these struggles in this indispensable collection, Linebaugh reignites the ancient cry, "STOP, THIEF!"

*"There is not a more important historian living today. Period."*
—Robin D.G. Kelley, author of *Freedom Dreams: The Black Radical Imagination*

*"E.P. Thompson, you may rest now. Linebaugh restores the dignity of the despised luddites with a poetic grace worthy of the master . . . [A] commonist manifesto for the 21st century."*
—Mike Davis, author of *Planet of Slums*

*"Peter Linebaugh's great act of historical imagination . . . takes the cliché of 'globalization' and makes it live. The local and the global are once again shown to be inseparable—as they are, at present, for the machine-breakers of the new world crisis."*
—T.J. Clark, author of *Farewell to an Idea*

# Look for Me in the Whirlwind: From the Panther 21 to 21st-Century Revolutions

Sekou Odinga, Dhoruba Bin Wahad,
Jamal Joseph
Edited by Matt Meyer & déqui kioni-sadiki
with a Foreword by Imam Jamil Al-Amin,
and an Afterword by Mumia Abu-Jamal

ISBN: 978-1-62963-389-3
$26.95   648 pages

Amid music festivals and moon landings, the tumultuous year of 1969 included an infamous case in the annals of criminal justice and Black liberation: the New York City Black Panther 21. Though some among the group had hardly even met one another, the 21 were rounded up by the FBI and New York Police Department in an attempt to disrupt and destroy the organization that was attracting young people around the world. Involving charges of conspiracy to commit violent acts, the Panther 21 trial—the longest and most expensive in New York history—revealed the illegal government activities which led to exile, imprisonment on false charges, and assassination of Black liberation leaders. Solidarity for the 21 also extended well beyond "movement" circles and included mainstream publication of their collective autobiography, *Look for Me in the Whirlwind*, which is reprinted here for the first time.

*Look for Me in the Whirlwind: From the Panther 21 to 21st-Century Revolutions* contains the entire original manuscript, and includes new commentary from surviving members of the 21: Sekou Odinga, Dhoruba Bin Wahad, Jamal Joseph, and Shaba Om. Still-imprisoned Sundiata Acoli, Imam Jamil Al-Amin, and Mumia Abu-Jamal contribute new essays. Never or rarely seen poetry and prose from Afeni Shakur, Kuwasi Balagoon, Ali Bey Hassan, and Michael "Cetewayo" Tabor is included. Early Panther leader and jazz master Bilal Sunni-Ali adds a historical essay and lyrics from his composition "Look for Me in the Whirlwind," and coeditors kioni-sadiki, Meyer, and Panther rank-and-file member Cyril "Bullwhip" Innis Jr. help bring the story up to date.

At a moment when the Movement for Black Lives recites the affirmation that "it is our duty to win," penned by Black Liberation Army (BLA) militant Assata Shakur, those who made up the BLA and worked alongside of Assata are largely unknown. This book—with archival photos from David Fenton, Stephen Shames, and the private collections of the authors— provides essential parts of a hidden and missing-in-action history. Going well beyond the familiar and mythologized nostalgic Panther narrative, *From the Panther 21 to 21st-Century Revolutions* explains how and why the Panther legacy is still relevant and vital today.